International Environmental Law Compliance in Context

This book explores how compliance with   .cal law has
changed over time, offering a critical analysı.   .ıg patterns.

Beginning with an overview of compliance   .ıonal environmental law, the book goes on to explore the follown.   .tail: compliance in the
different legal regimes instituted by Multilateral ∟nvironmental Agreements
(MEAs), the addition of new subjects of international law, the legal relationship between developed and developing countries, and the emergence of new
compliance mechanisms in global environmental law. The analysis takes two key
developments into consideration: the evolution in forms of compliance and non-
state involvement in compliance with international environmental law. In the
final section, three case studies are provided to demonstrate how these changes
have occurred in selected areas: climate change, biodiversity and water resources.
Throughout the book, topics are illustrated with extracts from specific international environmental law jurisprudence and relevant international environmental
law instruments. The book hereby offers a comprehensive analysis of compliance
with international environmental law, providing original insights and following
a clear and systematic structure supported by reference to the sources.

This book will be of interest to professionals, academics and students working
in the field of compliance with international environmental law.

Belen Olmos Giupponi is an Associate Professor of Law at Kingston University
London.

Routledge Research in International Environmental Law

International Environmental Law and Distributive Justice
The Equitable Distribution of CDM Projects under the Kyoto Protocol
Tomilola Akanle Eni-Ibukun

Environmental Governance in Europe and Asia
A Comparative Study of Institutional and Legislative Frameworks
Jona Razzaque

Climate Change, Forests and REDD
Lessons for Institutional Design
Edited by Joyeeta Gupta, Nicolien van der Grijp and Onno Kuik

International Environmental Law and the Conservation of Coral Reefs
Edward J. Goodwin

International Environmental Law and the International Court of Justice
Aleksandra Cavoski

Enforcement of International Environmental Law
Challenges and Responses at the International Level
Martin Hedemann-Robinson

Marine Pollution, Shipping Waste and International Law
Gabriela Argüello

Compensation for Environmental Damage Under International Law
Jason Rudall

International Environmental Law Compliance in Context
Mechanisms and Case Studies
Belen Olmos Giupponi

www.routledge.com/Routledge-Research-in-International-Environmental-Law/book-series/INTENVLAW

International Environmental Law Compliance in Context

Mechanisms and Case Studies

Belen Olmos Giupponi

Routledge
Taylor & Francis Group

LONDON AND NEW YORK

First published 2021
by Routledge
2 Park Square, Milton Park, Abingdon, Oxon OX14 4RN

and by Routledge
52 Vanderbilt Avenue, New York, NY 10017

Routledge is an imprint of the Taylor & Francis Group, an informa business

British Library Cataloguing-in-Publication Data
A catalogue record for this book is available from the British Library

Library of Congress Cataloging-in-Publication Data
A catalog record has been requested for this book

ISBN: 978-1-138-49184-7 (hbk)
ISBN: 978-0-367-75628-4 (pbk)
ISBN: 978-1-351-03194-3 (ebk)

Typeset in Galliard
by codeMantra

To my children

Contents

Table of cases

Table of treaties, legislation, and other instruments

Acknowledgements

I first came up with the idea for this book when I was a Lecturer at the University of Stirling in Scotland in 2016. I took a long journey to get here and the list of persons I am thankful for is quite lengthy. I am most grateful to my colleagues from the University of Stirling. I am indebted to Professor Gavin Little, who generously welcomed me to the team in 2013; his academic rigour and guidance have proved extremely valuable over the years. A special thanks to the former Director of Research, Dr Kay Goodall, for her good advice while at the University of Stirling (and afterwards). Huge thanks also to Dr Hong-LinYu, Professor Fraser Davidson, Dr Rebecca Zahn, Dr Raphael Heffron and Professor Douglas Brodie for fostering an excellent research environment and for their inspiring conversations.

During the writing process, I had the good fortune to meet with practitioners from the INECE and UNECLAC; a special thanks to Georgina Nunez and the colleagues from the Principle 10 process. This book has benefited from the Organisation of American States award prize on the Environmental Rule of Law Seminar organized in September 2017 in Santiago (Chile) and in November 2017 at the University of Salamanca. Since this is a book structured around the case-analysis methodology, I ought to thank Andres Rossetti for introducing me to this amazing world some years ago. Fruitful conversations with Professor Donald Mc Gillivray about environmental law while finishing the writing of the book kept me going to finish it amidst a global pandemic.

Parts of this book have been presented at international conferences, such as the Latin American Society of International Law (SLADI), European Society of International Law (ESIL) and World Agrarian Law Conference. Some of the research for this book was done while I was a fellow of the Von Humboldt Foundation at the Free University in Berlin, hosted by Professor Sergio Costa and Professor Barbara Göbel, Director of the Ibero-Amerikanische Institut (IAI). I shall always be grateful for the opportunity to further develop my career as a senior researcher. In addition to that, the CONICET Argentina Raices programme from the Argentine Government awarded the necessary funding to conduct fieldwork in August 2019.

Working with the editorial team was great. I am thankful to them for their patience and support. Writing this book required periods of solitary retreat, taking time away from my family, so a big thanks to my daughter Kirsten for her understanding and to Lars for his unconditional support. Special thanks to the rest of my family for being a source of strength.

Abbreviations

BAT/BEP	Best Available Techniques/Best Environmental Practices
BATEP	Best Available Technologies which are Economically Feasible
CBDR	Common But Differentiated Responsibilities
BCRC	Basel Convention Regional and Coordinating Centers for Training and Technology Transfer
BREFs	EU Best Available Techniques reference documents
CDM	Clean Development Mechanism
CEC	Commission for Environmental Cooperation
CITES	Convention on International Trade in Endangered Species and Wild Fauna and Flora
CO_2	carbon dioxide
COP	Conference of the Parties
CPE	Core Performance Element
EMAS	European Eco-Management and Audit Scheme
EMS	Environmental Management System
EPA	Environmental Protection Agency
EPR	Extended Producer Responsibility
ESM	Environmentally Sound Management
EU	European Union
FAO	Food and Agricultural Organisation
GHGs	greenhouse gases
ICJ	International Court of Justice
IEA	International Energy Agency
IEL	International Environmental Law
IMPEL EU	Network for the Implementation and Enforcement of Environmental Law
INECE	International Network for Environmental Compliance and Enforcement
IPCC	Intergovernmental Panel on Climate Change
IWC	International Whaling Commission
INTERPOL	International Criminal Police Organization
IPPC	Integrated Pollution Prevention and Control
ISO	International Organisation for Standardisation

IUCN	World Conservation Union
IWC	International Whaling Commission
LRTAP	Convention on Long-Range Transboundary Pollution
MEAs	Multilateral Environmental Agreements
NCP	non-compliance procedure
NGOs	non-governmental organisation
OECD	Organisation for Economic Cooperation and Development
OH&S	Occupational Health and Safety
OHSAS	Occupational Health and Safety Assessment Series
PACE	Basel Convention Partnership for Action on Computing Equipment
PIC	Prior Informed Consent
POPs	Persistent Organic Pollutants
SD	sustainable development
SDGs	Sustainable Development Goals
SME	small and medium-sized enterprise
SR	state responsibility
UNCLOS	United Nations Conference on the Law of the Sea
UNECE	United Nations Economic Commission for Europe
UNEP	United Nations Environment Programme
UNFCCC	United Nations Framework Convention on Climate Change
WHO	World Health Organization
WSSD	World Summit on Sustainable Development
WTO	World Trade Organization
WWF	World Wildlife Fund

Foreword

The world stands at a point that will be remembered historically for action or inaction. The effects of the way society lives are visible as they have never been before. For example, through technology we can all see the reports of destruction from Asia to Africa to the Americas. Technology is bringing into our own houses images of climate change and environmental degradation. In addition, in today's world, a COVID-19 has affected our daily existence, and we are all suffering from the economic consequences. Ensuring economic recovery is an imperative, but there are many other questions to answer, the environment and climate change being two central issues of focus and conflict.

In this context the question of 'how' the world achieves an economic recovery is of central importance. The nexus of energy, environmental and climate change issues has to be addressed. Too often this nexus is seen as contributing to increased costs, and therefore it is thought that it impacts negatively on economic growth. There needs to be a change in mind-set however, and the opportunity for transformation to a green economy needs to be presented and realised. For example, new data demonstrates that more jobs are being created at a national level in the green economy than in the traditional energy sources.

With its goal to accelerate this thinking and the faster development of low-carbon economies this book on compliance with international environmental law is timely. There has been great progress in international environmental law scholarship and practice over the last decades; however, one major criticism has always been around compliance. As stated already, the modern world cannot afford to wait anymore; action on environmental issues (and equally on energy and climate change issues) has to be more than just about what is written in international law. This book deals with these issues directly, focussing on how countries should comply and are complying, with additional evidence in the form of three novel case studies: on climate change, biodiversity and water resources, respectively.

In this book that is clearly of excellent research quality, there is a section which details the latest developments in terms of compliance in international environmental law. This section will be of keen interest for policymakers and members of the academic research community who are interested in current forward-looking policy initiatives that are already beginning to affect and change the current business-as-usual approach. The focus here is on the energy sector specifically, which is so important, given how it is responsible for the majority of greenhouse gas emissions. Other focusses here are on dispute resolution and participation, both of which are issues on the rise and have the potential to be extremely important in ensuring more compliance happens and is not just a researched 'construct' in international environmental law.

Finally, given the aforementioned trajectory the world is on at this time, this book by Professor Belen Olmos Giupponi is a timely reflection on the state of international environmental law. 'Compliance' is the central issue of whether the discussions around the value of environmental law move beyond that and into legal practice at international, national and local levels. It is an enlightening examination of how effective in reality international environmental law is. It marks one of the first forays into this subject area, and Professor Giupponi has more than accomplished her objectives in this project.

Raphael J Heffron
BA, MA, MLitt, MPhil, MSc, PhD, Barrister-at-Law
Professor in Global Energy Law & Sustainability &
Jean Monnet Professor in the Just Transition to a Low-Carbon Economy
Centre for Energy, Petroleum and Mineral Law and Policy, University of
Dundee, UK
*Senior Fellow of the UK Higher Education Academy – Fellow of the Royal
Society of Arts – Fellow of the Royal Society of Edinburgh's
Young Academy of Scotland*
Visiting Lecturer at the ESCP Business School (London and Paris) –
Visiting Professor Université Paris-Dauphine (France),
Queen Mary University of London, Eduardo Mondlane University
(Mozambique) and Associate Researcher, Energy Policy Research Group,
University of Cambridge (UK)
October 2020

Introduction

This book makes an effort to explain how genuinely compliance with International Environmental Law (hereinafter referred to as 'IEL') plays out in contemporary international society. Analysing compliance with IEL entails scrutinizing the main functions of the international environmental legal system. This analysis is intended to take place 'in context' – in other words with reference to case law and state practice – contributing to the current IEL scholarship on compliance.

Ideas of progress and development in compliance with IEL are understood differently depending on the angle from which they are observed. In terms of numbers, by merely looking at the volume of multilateral environmental treaties (MEAs) and treaties embodying environmental protection clauses (TEPs), one can conclude that, in fact, this growing body of conventional IEL represents progress. Reflecting on the nature of the mechanisms adopted and the effectiveness of the measures taken to secure compliance, however, it may be revealed that development is moving at a slower pace. This is because mechanisms impeccably set out on paper often fail to come to fruition for a number of reasons. It might be that the wording of the treaty does not account for the environmental problem it aims to resolve. It may be a question of the choice of the appropriate mechanism. It might happen that the targets or goals set are less ambitious than the environmental problem requires.

Equally, the adoption of innovative mechanisms of compliance should be put into context. Innovative compliance can develop over time into a model to be followed. It is useful to note the lack of a centralized system to monitor compliance, i.e. an international environmental court or compliance body which interprets, implements and enforces IEL. Therefore, compliance is scattered, fragmented and takes place in diverse realms. Compliance is related to institutional effectiveness. Legal norms and institutions impact on behaviour in different manners, with various degrees of effectiveness.

Compliance with IEL evokes a number of different practices and various meanings. Enquiring about this compliance involves posing such fundamental questions as: What is the specific content of the obligations under IEL? Who are the actors involved in these processes? What other informal methods with which to assess compliance are available? A similar difficulty arises when it comes to implementation. A classification of IEL terms for the purpose of this book discerns between compliance, non-compliance, implementation and enforcement.

Compliance, understood as conformity to International Environmental Agreements (IEAs), may be induced by various factors not strictly related to the treaty itself. This distinction is relevant when analysing non-compliance as a form of conduct that does not correspond to that which is expected or mandated in the treaty. IEAs may prescribe or proscribe actions ordering States and other international law actors to take action or refrain from acting in a certain manner. Absence of the expected action denotes non-compliance. Lack of compliance or conformity may be observed as a whole or only partially. Partial compliance with IEL can turn out to be as problematic as an absolute lack of compliance. Implementation refers to the series of measures adopted in States' internal jurisdiction in order to ensure the performance of the IEAs. The rhetoric of compliance with IEL, rather than the effectiveness of norms, has prevailed in many scholarly studies of compliance.

Effectiveness is critical in IEL. While methods monitoring compliance may be available they will not necessarily have an impact on the problem and may not lead to behavioural changes. Compliance lies at the heart of the effectiveness of the IEL architecture. Success or failure in IEL is determined by the degree of state compliance with the international commitments. In defining what an acceptable level of compliance is, several factors should be considered, such as the clarity of the treaty wording, the mechanism designed to ensure compliance and the possibilities of enforcing the norms in the absence of compliance. While acknowledging the predominant significance of compliance as a category of analysis, the book critically questions compliance in light of the developments (and shortcomings) observed in IEL.

Demystification of compliance and questioning of new alternative methods are thus common elements in the analysis put forward in this book. An increasing and wide range of phenomena with harmful effects on the environment poses significant challenges to IEL. In turn, technological revolutions and science-sound decisions related to compliance with IEL have also shaped compliance. There is no one-size-fits-all approach as different legal systems offer various perspectives. Regional approaches to IEL may determine distinctive features observed under the specific treaties. Hence, these disparities between legal systems may lead to diverse mechanisms to implement, comply with and enforce IEL. Bearing in mind the various sub-areas of IEL, what is applicable to one particular area might not be of relevance to another area. Ultimately, compliance is a matter for behavioural change and effectiveness, in terms of behavioural or environmental changes induced by IEL.

This book focusses on international mechanisms and sanction systems built into MEAs, not on the national implementation of treaty obligations; thus, domestic measures are not included in its scope. IEAs should be interpreted in light of IEL principles. The book's chapters tackle the question of compliance 'in context', illustrating the topics examined in reference to cases, reports and guidelines issued by international bodies. Most of the cases are international law cases, but, because of the overall relevance for the building of IEL, some cases originating in the domestic jurisdictions are included. We have put a considerable effort into keeping footnotes to a minimum, refraining from including long citations.

Innovation is defined in terms of the introduction of novel forms for monitoring the implementation of IEL norms, such as global market-based mechanisms or technology-driven solutions. New mechanisms and novel approaches or norms can inspire a wave of change, as already seen with the Montreal Protocol and its cascading effect on other MEAs, which embodied similar non-compliance mechanisms.

The main objective of this book is to present an evolving view of compliance with IEL, illustrated by reference to legal text and reports including evidence from law-making. It is addressed to students, practitioners, teachers, decision-makers and policymakers who are interested in the subject from both a theoretical and a more pragmatic approach to the matter.

In keeping with this spirit, the emergence of transnational environmental law and environmental regulation should be underlined. Transnational environmental law encompasses a series of recently developed processes and norms. The transnational character of conflict resolution stems from the nature of the various actors involved in environmental conflicts (with a focus on non-state actors) and processes which transcend the boundaries of a single state.

IEL compliance in context remains the focal point of this book. Thus, the scope of this study is to address compliance with IEL in various sectors, including biodiversity, international climate change and international water law. IEL regulations has expanded to cover further areas of environmental protection. One may argue that the ever-growing body of IEL offers more possibilities to enhance compliance. Yet compliance may slip out of reach of the goals of specific IEL norms.

The nature of these norms, particularly those regulating various aspects of environmental protection, may vary and alternate between soft and hard law. Soft-law instruments have paved the way for the adoption of binding norms regulating sectoral environmental problems. For example, the 1972 United Nations Conference on the Human Environment ('the Stockholm Conference'), the Report of the World Commission on Environment and Development, *Our Common Future 1987* ('the Brundtland Report') and the United Nations Conference in Environment and Development 1992 ('the Rio Conference'), despite being soft-law instruments, heralded a new era in IEL. As result of the Rio Declaration, other binding international instruments were adopted, such as the Convention on Biological Diversity and the Framework Convention on Climate Change. Environmental governance and policy approaches draw attention to other elements related to political ecology and environmental policy. In the protection of global commons (territories and resources beyond state sovereignty that are under the sovereignty of no State), innovative mechanisms were mandatory to facilitate a solution aligned with the nature and relevance of interests to be protected.

A substantial body of literature has been devoted to studying the effectiveness of IEL underlying the several aspects involved in compliance. This literature usually speaks about compliance and effectiveness. It is estimated that there are more than 200 international environmental treaties currently in existence. Despite the exponential growth of IEL and its expanding force, in terms of implementation, there is no central or global environmental institution with the function of interpreting, applying or enforcing IEL. Different types of IEL norms, including self-executing norms, give rise to different patterns of compliance.

COMPLIANCE WITH INTERNATIONAL ENVIRONMENTAL LAW IN CONTEXT

Parameters of effectiveness

Which treaties would score high on achieving effectiveness?

1 How does the MEA define itself and its goal?
2 What is the nature of the specific agreement's commitments?
3 What are the treaty assumptions?
4 What are the suggested measures?
5 How does the international norm affect behaviour?
6 How do these changes in behaviour lead to better environmental outcomes?

Source: Author's own elaboration

---

1 The book's structure

The book's analysis of compliance with IEL is divided into ten chapters. The opening part, or introduction, addresses its general purposes alongside the analysis of the topic in contemporary international law.

Following the introductory part, Chapter 1 deals with the definition of compliance with MEAs. At least three different terms are associated with the idea of 'observing the international environmental law rule': compliance, implementation and enforcement. Other related expected effects of environmental legislation are impact on the behaviour of the relevant stakeholders (not only the States and traditional addressees of international environmental norms) and effectiveness of the rules in fostering a behavioural change. While there have been areas of significant improvement for compliance, several obstacles remain.

Chapter 1 defines 'compliance' in terms of the purpose of the book. It touches on the question of compliance from different angles, referring to relevant scholarship in the field. It deals with issues such as negotiations; assessment of domestic capabilities for implementation; a review of the impact and effectiveness of

IEL instruments, and the availability of compliance mechanisms after an MEA comes into effect; and the enforcement of IEL provisions, including dispute settlement provisions. In examining compliance, the chapter looks into the legal divide between the global North and the global South, and the differential approaches taken by their legal approaches to IEL. This chapter also addresses questions relating to implementation, including an indication of the variety of possible national measures.

Chapter 2 deals with the theoretical framework for IEL compliance. This chapter dissects the essential features and specific characteristics of compliance with IEL. It looks at the differences between compliance and enforcement, providing a general framework for international responsibility and liability under various regimes. In an extensive examination of these regimes, the chapter indicates the main trends in terms of mechanisms and approaches to compliance in IEL.

Chapter 3 addresses compliance with IEL in context, focussing on the tools and mechanisms geared to obtaining compliance from the main IEL actors. In this chapter, a variety of hard- and soft-law mechanisms are analysed, including market-based mechanisms and guidelines on IEL compliance issued by different bodies.

Continuing with the topic of IEL compliance in context, Chapter 4 focusses on actors, identifying 'traditional actors' and 'strategic players', alongside a number of new and emerging actors. A substantial part of this chapter is devoted to the study of regional organisations and the role they play in securing, promoting and monitoring IEL compliance. Transnational regulations and networks tasked with compliance functions are also examined.

Part 2 of the book is entitled 'New features of compliance with International Environmental Law'. It scrutinizes new processes and mechanisms available in IEL compliance. In contrast to the classical command-control approach in environmental compliance and to overcome the rigidity of regulatory requirements, recent trends have led to an emphasis on private-public partnerships and to the use of market-based mechanisms.

Chapter 5 unveils the intricacies of intersections, interactions and conflicts between IEL and other branches of international law. Overcoming the dichotomy between unity and fragmentation, the chapter proposes new and different synergies between the various branches, fostering a new model of interrelations which leads to the furtherance of IEL. There is a considerable overlap between the various fields, such as in the case of the protection of biological diversity and intellectual property rights. This includes the protection of indigenous communities' rights and conservation considerations.

In turn, Chapter 6 explores the question of non-compliance and dispute resolution. Amicable dispute settlement of conflicts has become a catch-all phrase in international law for legal disputes involving other aspects of other means of settlement. There is a growing recognition of non-formal means of dealing with international or transboundary environmental conflicts or disputes, such as the resort to Peoples' Tribunals or specific ad-hoc commissions instituted outside formal government or state channels.

Taking stock of a growing trend in IEL literature, Chapter 7 refers to private sector involvement and civil society participation in IEL compliance, identifying its crucial elements. The chapter deals with their role in counteracting the behaviour that harms the environment.

Part 3 of the book features case studies. These are intended to provide examples of regimes in order to illustrate the main theories underpinning compliance with IEL. Selected case studies demonstrate the foremost means of complying with IEL in the contemporary landscape, stressing the flaws observed in practice.

Chapter 8 deals with the climate change regime, underscoring the advances and pinpointing the innovative aspects of compliance. The regime represents a significant example of compliance, comprising the UNFCCC (including the decisions adopted at the COPs), the Kyoto Protocol and the Paris Agreement as well as the subsequently adopted instruments.

Chapter 9 is devoted to examining compliance within the biodiversity regime, established with the aim of avoiding the loss of biodiversity. The analysis is based around the main legal instruments adopted under the regime: the Convention on Biological Diversity (CBD) and the Cartagena and the Nagoya Protocols.

Finally, Chapter 10 addresses compliance with IEL on the protection of water resources, dealing with matters such as water availability, pollution and scarcity, and overall management of water resources.

Part 1

General aspects of compliance with international environmental law

1 Introduction to compliance

1 Introduction

International environmental law (IEL) scholars and international lawyers have traditionally assessed the effect of norms by referring to the level of compliance of states with their commitments. Significant changes have occurred in sub-areas of IEL due to various driving forces that have shaped the way compliance operates. While most studies have focussed on the extent to which States adjust their behaviour to what is required under international environmental agreements (IEAs) less attention has been devoted to non-state actors and compliance with customary IEL. Compliance is a matter of state behaviour, which involves different motivations to abide by IEL and state capacity to carry out implementation measures on a domestic level.[1]

Compliance has several different meanings: It often refers to the implementation of a treaty by individual States, sometimes being equated with the range of measures adopted in domestic law to bring a particular treaty to life. The corpus of IEL offers multi-layered systems of implementation and compliance. Different kinds of treaties encompass diverse compliance mechanisms and enforcement methods, and include different problem-solving institutions. This diversity of treaty provisions observed in practice leads, in turn, to uneven levels of compliance with IEL.[2] This disparity helps us understand why some IEAs perform better than others and why the practice is fragmented.

Compliance mechanisms under MEAs can take a wide variety of forms, comprising not only monitoring mechanisms but also education, technical assistance, voluntary compliance programmes, and subsidies as well as other forms, such as incentives or financial assistance at the international level. They also include mechanisms developed to ensure compliance and enforcement through

---

1 Lee Paddock (ed), *Compliance and Enforcement in Environmental Law. Toward More Effective Implementation* (Edward Elgar- The IUCN Academy of Environmental Law series 2018).
2 Carl Bruch, 'Is International Environmental Law Really "Law"?: An Analysis of Application in Domestic Courts', (2006) 23 *Pace Environmental Law Review*, p. 423. Anthony D'Amato, 'Is International Law Really "Law"?' (2010) Faculty Working Papers, p. 103, available at https://scholarlycommons.law.northwestern.edu/facultyworkingpapers/10 accessed 1 April 2020.

the adoption of non-mandatory guidelines, such as the UNEP's Compliance and Enforcement Guidelines.[3] Under these guidelines, compliance is defined as 'the conformity with obligations, imposed by a state, its competent authorities and agencies on the regulated community, whether directly or through conditions and requirements, permits, licenses and authorizations' to implement MEAs. Compliance also amounts to 'the fulfilment by the contracting parties of their obligations under a MEA'.[4] Meanwhile, 'environmental law violation' indicates the contravention of national environmental laws.[5]

Compliance methods and processes do not take place in a vacuum, so it is crucial to assess them against the broader context of the legal framework instituted by the specific EA. Clearly, the socioeconomic, political, and cultural context of each signatory influences compliance. Hence, treaty implementation is conditioned by the specific circumstances in which the respective state implements treaty provisions.

A burning question regards the evaluation and effects of IEAs. In the theoretical terrain, scholars distinguish between the impact of a treaty and its effectiveness. Impact refers to the capacity of the treaty to solve the environmental problem, mandating certain behaviours and instituting specific commitments, providing for legal remedies.

Implementation is never perfect or complete. Flaws can be observed across the various subfields of IEL. Treaties may be implemented but fail to appropriately address the environmental problem they mean to alleviate or solve due to a lack of effectiveness.[6] Success or failure in terms of compliance will depend on the manner in which States understand their commitments under the different environmental treaties.

As regards problem-solving functions displayed by IEAs, whether the treaty has resolved the targeted problem is not always self-evident. Gathering of empirical evidence remains key to depicting an accurate landscape of compliance in specific sectors. Results supported by empirical evidence are less common in IEL, but, in certain sectors, they show that there is a gap in understanding how IEL norms are implemented in practice and the level of effectiveness of IEAs.[7]

Compliance methods vary across different IEAs as they include national binding, non-binding and judicial mechanisms. Where the corpus of IEL provides for a specific mechanism there is usually a follow-up procedure instituted

3 UNEP's Compliance and Enforcement Guidelines of Multilateral Environmental Agreements (2002), available at https://wedocs.unep.org/bitstream/handle/20.500.11822/17018/UNEP-guidelines-compliance-MEA.pdf?sequence=1&isAllowed=y, accessed 10 January 2020.

4 UNEP's Compliance and Enforcement Guidelines (2006), available at https://wedocs.unep.org/bitstream/handle/20.500.11822/17018/UNEP-guidelines-compliance-MEA.pdf?sequence=1&isAllowed=y accessed 20 January 2020.

5 Ibid.

6 Lakshman Guruswamy, *International Environmental Law in a Nutshell* (4th edn West 2012), p. 58.

7 UN Environment 2019, Annual Report, available at https://www.unenvironment.org/annual-report/2019/index.php, accessed 1 April 2020.

through an ad-hoc mechanism or traditional international law tools. Environmental quality indicators, often set by the negotiators, along with other indicators observed in the implementation of the treaties, define success or failure in compliance. Reasons for failure and shortfalls of compliance are related to treaty design, and the peculiarities of the specific context in which treaty provisions are implemented.

2 How international environmental law works in practice. International environmental law compliance from a comparative perspective

The increasing volume of treaty-making in IEL has led to the mushrooming of Multilateral Environmental Agreements (MEAs) adopting a variety of means to monitor compliance with treaty provisions and, more generally, IEL. In order to determine the degree of compliance with a particular IEA, the wording of the treaty is of utmost importance as it may reveal the manner in which the specific environmental problem is addressed, the prescriptions embodied therein, its institutional set-up created and the goals which were set. Goal-setting in IEAs becomes crucial to scrutinizing compliance. Targets which are unrealistic, too ambitious, shallow, inadequate or mismatched may result in deficient implementation or lack of compliance. Less ambitious objectives may give the impression that the treaty has been complied with, despite not having been effective in addressing the environmental problem at hand. Equally important is an appropriate incentive system. From an economic standpoint, Barrett argues that, for cooperation to be sustained, States need to set up institutions that can deal with free-riding, and MEAs must be self-enforcing.[8] However, the reaching of an environmental agreement and the commitments set therein do not automatically translate into a necessary change in state behaviour.

There is no settled definition of 'international environmental treaty', 'international environmental agreement' or 'multilateral environmental agreements' as, broadly speaking, these terms are used interchangeably. MEAs designate international treaties signed between three or more states which are open for accession by any state in the international community.[9] It is worth mentioning that the environmental subject matter can be addressed in an ad-hoc environmental treaty as well as in other treaties regulating issues closely related to environmental protection, such as free trade agreements containing a sustainable development or an environmental protection chapter.[10]

---

8 Scott Barrett, 'Self-Enforcing International Environmental Agreements', (1994) 46 *Oxford Economic Papers*, pp. 878–894.

9 André Nollkaemper, 'Compliance Control in International Environmental Law: Traversing the Limits of the National Legal Order' (2002) 13(1) *Yearbook of International Environmental Law*, pp. 165–186.

10 Raezz, Schmied and Voituriez, *The Future of Sustainable Development Chapters in EU Free Trade Agreements* (European Parliament 2018), available at https://www.iddri.org/sites/default/

Taking note of the high number of MEAs concluded in some areas of IEL, one may have the impression that considerable progress has been achieved. However, this proliferation of treaties is not always equivalent to an effective improvement of environmental conditions. The truth is that effectiveness and real improvement depend on the factors that apply to a particular area. For example, in the area of biodiversity, the Convention on International Trade in Endangered Species of Wild Fauna and Flora (CITES) regulates trade in endangered species, setting standards on the hunting and harvest of these species, and coordinates efforts to protect them.[11] The effectiveness of the system relies on the sanctions (in the form of trade restriction measures and the suspension of specific rights and privileges) that can be imposed in cases of non-compliance.[12] Similarly, the effectiveness of international climate change legislation is assessed by the decrease of greenhouse gases (emission reductions), as per the terms of the specific treaties set out in the UN Framework Convention on Climate Change (Kyoto Protocol and Paris Agreement).[13] Finally, the impact of the International Convention for the Regulation of Whaling (ICRW) is measured through its effects on the whaling industry, the population of whales or the implementing measures adopted.[14]

If IEL is the branch of international law (IL) dealing with international environmental problems, how its norms define particular problems conditions compliance and effectiveness. The question of effectiveness lies between international law and international relations domains. The driving forces behind global environmental compliance and governance are not only legal, institutional and policy instruments but also socioeconomic factors. Ultimately, effectiveness depends upon non-legal factors.

To prove efficient, an international environmental agreement should clearly set out the consequences of the breach of treaty provisions.[15] Flawed implementation may occur when the measures to put international environmental rules into effect are inadequate or fail to achieve the objectives set out in the treaty. Extent of compliance with a treaty largely depends on national implementation. Even

files/PDF/Publications/Catalogue%20Iddri/Autre%20Publication/the%20future%20of%20sustainable%20development%20chapters%20in%20EU%20free%20trade%20agreements.pdf accessed 1 April 2020.

11 Convention on International Trade in Endangered Species of Wild Fauna and Flora (CITES), 3 March 1973, 27 UST 1087 (entered into force 1 July 1975).

12 The original text did not foresee any specific enforcement provisions, sanctions or penalties. The system has developed from article XIII and the guidelines adopted by the conference of the Parties, which provide for escalation of cases to and including trade bans.

13 European Union, Climate negotiations, available at https://ec.europa.eu/clima/policies/international/negotiations_en accessed 10 January 2020.

14 The International Convention for the Regulation of Whaling (ICRW) was signed on 2 December 1946 and entered into force on 10 November 1948, available at https://iwc.int/convention accessed 1 April 2020.

15 Mary Ellen O'Connell, 'Enforcement and the Success of International Environmental Law' (1995) 3(1) *Indiana Journal of Global Legal Studies*, Article 4, pp. 47–64, available at http://www.repository.law.indiana.edu/ijgls/vol3/iss1/4 accessed 1 April 2020.

if there is an implicit obligation emanating from the rule *pacta sunt servanda*, treaties may embody content-specific provisions about national implementation, detailing the steps to be taken in order to meet treaty obligations. National implementation ought to take into consideration regional competences, depending on the form of government adopted by the specific State. In federal States, national implementation may mean that regions can implement the same MEA in different manners. In more centralized states, the control over implementation still rests on the central government.

Domestically, the implementation of treaty obligations may imply conferring responsibilities on non-state entities and non-governmental groups as well as private sector actors: for instance, in the forestry sector the 'reducing emissions from deforestation and forest degradation' (REDD) initiative or debt-for-nature swaps (DNS) in the biodiversity regime.[16] DNS represents the agreement that allows a developing country to reduce its debt stock or service in exchange for a commitment to protect nature from the debtor government. The donor (or donors) cancels the debt owned by a developing country's government on the condition that resources from the reduced debt service are invested in conservation projects. The codes of conduct which these companies adopt may also contain some elements for the implementation of an international environmental treaty.[17] Attention should be drawn to compliance beyond national jurisdictions in those areas which are not subject to the sovereignty of any state, such as the Antarctic or the deep-sea bed. Participation of non-traditional actors (vis-à-vis states as traditional actors), such as indigenous peoples or local communities, has begun to represent a common feature of IEL, particularly accentuated with respect to specific regimes, such as biodiversity or climate change.

As the IEL compliance proceedings unravel, distinctive aspects are worth noting. Transnational regulation going beyond the state is now a pervasive feature in IEL which brings in other actors and the regulation of private conduct by non-state actors. Private enforcement of IEL has become widespread across its various regimes or sectors. The business sector has been active in environmental regulation, although diverse visions of international business exist in environmental regulation.[18] The involvement of the private sector is more significant in specific areas of IEL, such as with regard to forestry or the protection of biological diversity, which lie at the intersection between IEL and trade law. Both the Convention on Biological Diversity (CBD) and the Trade-Related Intellectual Property Rights (TRIPS) agreement (negotiated as part of the Uruguay round) consider different aspects of this question. Conceivably, assigning responsibilities

16 Jared E. Knicley, 'Debt, Nature, and Indigenous Rights: Twenty-five Years of Debt-For-Nature Evolution' (2012) 36 *Harvard Environmental Law Review*, pp. 79–122. United Nations, *Debt-for-nature swaps (DNS)*, available at https://www.undp.org/content/dam/sdfinance/doc/Debt%20for%20Nature%20Swaps%20_%20UNDP.pdf accessed 10 January 2020.

17 Stepan Wood, 'Voluntary Environmental Codes and Sustainability', in Benjamin J. Richardson and Stepan Wood (eds), *Environmental Law for Sustainability* (Hart 2006), pp. 229–276.

18 Steven Ratner, Chapter 35. 'Business', in Bodansky, Brunee & Hey, *Handbook of International Environmental Law*, pp. 807–828.

to specific actors under a treaty regime could lead to an increased overall efficiency and a higher compliance rate.

To a greater extent, implementation, effectiveness and impact are taken as synonyms. In strict terms, there is a clear demarcation of the various scopes of these expressions. Impact or effectiveness in solving the environmental problem which specific norms purport to address holds the key to understanding whether IEL norms fulfil their objectives. As an added difficulty, implementation and effectiveness are often assessed without reliance on empirical evidence.

A significant step toward increasing the level of compliance with IEL consists in the adoption of non-compliance procedures or mechanisms. Non-compliance mechanisms in IEL are defined as those proceedings instituted under specific treaties to monitor compliance.

Although not binding, declarations have paved the way towards the adoption of mandatory instruments in IEL.[19] In this evolution, the various specialized conferences organized by the United Nations have brought different elements into the notion of compliance with IEL; such conferences include the 1992 United Nations Conference on Environment and Development (Earth Summit), the 2000 United Nations Millennium Declaration and the 2002 World Summit on Sustainable Development (WSSD).

Cooperation and conflict are both present in IEL compliance processes. States and other relevant stakeholders have taken different stances on the issue. The role of technical mechanisms/advisory bodies in improving compliance with IEL has increased exponentially over recent years. Some IEAs provide for subsidiary bodies tasked with implementation, such as the Open-ended Working Group of the Basel Convention on the Control of Transboundary Movements of Hazardous Wastes and their Disposal.[20] Facilitation and technical assistance can further contribute to ensuring compliance with IEL, as discussed in Chapter 3.

IEL deals with risks on an international level, which relates to the dichotomy between science and precaution. Contemporary IEL displays specific characteristics, leaning towards a more systematic analysis which encompasses elements integrating scientific and legal approaches. Sometimes, available IEL standards are ambiguous in their formulation. This ambiguity might be intended to allow some leeway in the implementation of norms or be unintended but determined by the specific circumstances surrounding implementation.

In terms of the determination of liability, IEL relies on the state responsibility regime under general international law. The presence of some elements of soft law in the design of IEL's legal architecture poses questions about the robustness

---

19 Stockholm Declaration on the Human Environment, June 16, 1972, UN Doc. A/CONF.48/14 & Corr. 1 (1972), 11 *ILM* 1416 (1972).

20 Draft framework for the environmentally sound management of hazardous wastes and other wastes Eighth meeting, Geneva, 25–28 September 2012, Matters related to the work programme of the open-ended Working Group for 2012–2013: Scientific and technical matters: follow-up to the Indonesian-Swiss country-led initiative: developing guidelines for environmentally sound management, UNEP/CHW/OEWG.8/INF/8, 17 August 2012.

of the IEL system. Being conceived as an inter-state legal system, the endorsement of IEL by states varies from one sector to another of IEL. This increasing 'sectoralisation' of IEL is also observed in compliance as specific and relevant environmental problems are addressed through the creation of various bodies of environmental law. Diversity of the solutions adopted is also observed as some sectors of IEL are directly concerned with different situations and regulated by specific legal systems.

Another relevant question regarding the tenor of the decisions made is whether States are embracing the implementation of the various IEL norms. Usually, non-compliance decisions on the international level are adopted by treaty bodies which in many cases lack binding implementation powers. International courts do not entertain jurisdiction to adjudicate over environmental disputes. A similar rationale may augur progress in favour of international courts. Facilitative approaches in IEL may, as a downside, not be able to eliminate any remaining uncertainties. These initiatives have the potential to cause a shift in compliance but require a skilful definition of the obligations alongside the design of appropriate monitoring mechanisms.

Institutions and organisations involved in compliance, international implementing institutions and mechanisms in IEL may differ from those existing within States, which does not mean that they do not fulfil a significant function in the compliance realm. Many have specific functions in the field of compliance, whereas others undertake the task of facilitating the implementation of IEL.

In a broad classification, the following techniques can be distinguished: treaty-based compliance mechanisms, diplomatic avenues, and judicial remedies.[21] Questions surrounding innovative compliance techniques merit closer examination. Procedural questions become crucial in IEL as evidence needs to be gathered to prove basic facts, such as the amount of CO_2 released into the atmosphere, the level of water pollution, the extension of deforestation or the danger of animals or other species becoming extinct.

Methodological aspects deserve further mention. IEL scholarship traditionally portrays law in a positivist manner; interdisciplinary approaches are less common. Compliance is analysed from a doctrinal legal analysis approach based on the examination of the relevant provisions of MEAs, contrasting the norms with available information about observed compliance. The main argument against this approach is that the analysis is based on information available through the mechanisms instituted in the framework of the different MEAs. With this pragmatic focus and its limitations in mind, this approach includes the analysis of state practice, encompassing relevant case law where available. Other theoretical considerations stemming from disciplines such as sociology and political ecology contribute to the analysis of the question of compliance.

---

21 Gerhard Loibl, 'Compliance Procedures and Mechanisms', in M. Fitzmaurice, D. Ong, and P. Merkouris (eds), *Research Handbook on International Environmental Law* (Edward Elgar 2010), pp. 426–429.

Evidently, the effective improvement of environmental quality after the adoption of IEL norms falls beyond the scope of the book. However, the approach addresses the question of effectiveness, analysing the impact on the sector of the environment which the norms purport to improve. Insights into compliance stem from compliance mechanisms' reports and governmental bodies and non-governmental organisations' resolutions on a panoply of questions concerning compliance.

In identifying theories about compliance with international law, Raustiala groups them in terms of rationalist theories, norm-driven theories and liberal theories.[22] Clearly, there are limits to international environmental treaties, as Goldsmith and Posner have underlined.[23] When evaluating compliance with IEL, Ronald Mitchell pinpoints 'comparators' of IEA influence: using behavioural change and counterfactuals, selecting the level of analysis and considering four typologies of behaviour – treaty-induced compliance, coincidental compliance, good faith non-compliance and intentional non-compliance.[24] In assessing compliance with IEL, different IEA projects have a dissimilar influence and demonstrate different endogeneity, leading to different models of actor behaviour.

Private enforcement of IEL norms needs to be put into context. Private actors play a role in the enforcement of EU law as they can assist inter-governmental bodies in ensuring compliance. Far more controversial are cases in which private actors are involved in non-compliance. Traditionally, under international law only States can be held accountable for non-compliance. A different level concerns the possibility of private actors bringing legal claims for environmental harm caused. The politics surrounding compliance and non-compliance with IEL reveal the intricacies of the system, particularly considering the limitations of enforcement in international law. Global environmental politics approaches contribute a different standpoint by emphasizing the interrelations between formal nation-state structures and other actors beyond the State, such as civil society organizations, non-profit entities and the private sector.[25]

In the life-cycle of a specific environmental regime, compliance and control can be also seen as means of dispute avoidance. It should be noted that compliance and control usually entail different levels of conformity with IEL.

---

22 Karl Raustiala, 'Compliance & Effectiveness in International Regulatory Cooperation', 32 *Case Western Reserve Journal of International Law* 387 (2000), available at https://scholarlycommons.law.case.edu/jil/vol32/iss3/2 accessed 1 April 2020.

23 Jack Goldsmith and Eric Posner, *The Limits of International Law* (Oxford University Press 2006).

24 Ronald B. Mitchell, 'Compliance Theory: Compliance, Effectiveness, and Behaviour Change in International Environmental Law', in Daniel Bodansky, Jutta Brunnée, and Ellen Hey (eds), *The Oxford Handbook of International Environmental Law*, pp. 895, 899.

25 See, for instance, T. Hickmann and J.P. Elsässer, 'New Alliances in Global Environmental Governance: How Intergovernmental Treaty Secretariats Interact with Non-state Actors to Address Transboundary Environmental Problems' (2020) *Int Environ Agreements*, available at https://doi.org/10.1007/s10784-020-09493-5 accessed 1 April 2020.

Reference must be made to dispute settlement procedures and qualified approaches to responsibility and liability. In view of the dissimilar levels of compliance with IEL, it is difficult to assess overall compliance with a particular MEA. The situation is more complex than in national law due to the lack of a centralized judicial system operating a compulsory model to deal with non-compliance. From a purely international law perspective, only a few cases involving non-compliance with IEL have been brought before the ICJ specifically addressing the content of States' obligations particularly regarding transboundary environmental harm.

3 Nature of the obligations: binding IEL provisions and soft law. International environmental law principles applicable to the enforcement: a preventative or reactive approach?

In relation to the sources of IEL, international norms are shaped by the various stances taken by States and other actors on specific environmental problems. Following the analysis of article 38 of the Statute of the International Court of Justice, most IEL obligations emanate from legally binding sources, such as international customs, treaties, and general principles of international law.[26]

Treaties remain the predominant mode of regulating environmental problems in IEL through the creation of specific regimes. According to the IEA Database Project, there are more than 3,000 IEAs, leading to what the UN Environment Programme refers to as 'treaty congestion'.[27] States have signed a variety of internationally recognized agreements in the past 50 years, including those related to atmosphere; biodiversity; chemicals, hazardous substances and waste; and land conventions, as well as 196 conventions that are broadly related to issues dealing with water.[28]

From 2015 on we have observed an increasing number of Memoranda of Understanding (MoUs) of a bilateral nature with less binding force. The question of the implementation of treaties in IEL depends on the nature of the specific norms. Self-executing or self-enforcing environmental treaties can be directly applicable.[29] Drawing on previous research on environmental treaties, it is crucial that the drafter of the treaties lays down clear substantive rules of IEL so that the norms can be deployed to foster compliance. Amongst the several factors that induce voluntary compliance with IEL, the appropriate design of treaty mechanisms may determine the success or failure of MEAs.

---

26 Pierre-Marie Dupuy and Jorge Viñuales, 'The Sources of International Environmental Law' in *International Environmental Law* (Cambridge University Press 2015), pp. 33–37.

27 Ronald B. Mitchell, *International Environmental Agreements (IEA) Database (2002–2020)*, available at https://iea.uoregon.edu/one-indicator?field_lineage_value=CITES accessed 1 April 2020.

28 Ibid.

29 Barrett (n 8) at 878–894.

Customary international law, although relevant in the overall legal landscape, is less clear-cut. IEL scholars have noted the inadequacy of custom in regulating novel environmental problems, the difficulty in addressing the rapid pace in its evolution and the need for adaptability and legal certainty.[30] Nonetheless, key areas of international law containing provisions also applicable to IEL compliance are governed by custom. Take, for instance, the no-harm principle crucial in the prevention of transboundary damage and environmental impact assessment, and the State responsibility regime in which codification is based on the compilation of customs.[31] Customary IEL, however, can only bind States if there is a state practice accepted by a significant number of States showing *opinio juris*. States that persistently object are not bound, and lack of consensus can raise questions on validity – in other words, disagreements on whether the precautionary principle is customary law.

Principles of IEL play an important role in securing compliance with IEL as they are relied upon to check compliance in specific sectors of IEL, such as the common law of mankind, sustainable development and global commons. It might be more difficult to rely on embryonic or emerging principles of IEL which are not yet consolidated.

In terms of soft law, a distinction should be made between the legal nature of instruments and their content, which also has consequences on compliance. The feature of 'soft law' refers to the legal status of the instrument as not carrying any legally binding force.[32] In spite of this, the content of the international instrument may or may not be of compulsory observance.[33] The line between soft and hard law is sometimes not that clear, as the ICJ underlined in the Qatar-Bahrain Maritime Delimitation case[34]; the important element is the substance, and the label is not decisive.[35]

For instance, soft IEL has laid down the basis for the evolution of IEL, starting with the 1972 Stockholm Declaration and the 1992 Rio Declaration, which paved the way for the adoption of treaties crucial for contemporary IEL, such as the UNFCCC and the CBD, amongst others. Equally relevant are the 'World Charter for Nature' (1982) or the 'Copenhagen Accord' (2009).[36]

---

30 Dupuy and Viñuales (n 26) at 34.

31 Pierre-Marie Dupuy, Ginevra Le Moli, and Jorge E. Viñuales, *Customary International Law and the Environment*, C-EENRG Working Papers 2018–2 (December 2018), available at https://www.ceenrg.landecon.cam.ac.uk/working-paper-files/CEENRG_WP_19_CustomaryInternationalLawandtheEnvironment.pdf accessed 1 April 2020.

32 Alan Boyle, 'Soft Law in International Law Making', in Malcolm D. Evans (eds), *International Law* (5th edn Oxford University Press 2018), p. 120.

33 Ibid., at 119–137.

34 International Court of Justice Maritime Delamination and territorial questions between Qatar and Bahrain, Jurisdiction and admissibility, judgement ICJ report 1994, 112.

35 Boyle (n 31) at 120.

36 UN. General Assembly, The World Charter for Nature (37th session: 1982–1983), available at https://digitallibrary.un.org/record/39295?ln=es accessed 1 April 2020.

The myriad of IEL norms comes to play in terms of compliance. MEAs contribute to the design of the specific legal framework applicable to the sector in question: for instance, biodiversity or climate change. Bodies created under MEAs have developed quite an extended group of norms, many of them regulating different aspects of compliance. These resolutions, reports and other norms play quite a large role in defining aspects such as reporting, monitoring and control. In some cases this secondary law (vis-à-vis the respective treaty considered as 'primary law') has fleshed out the details of compliance mechanisms which were not explicitly regulated or provided for in the MEA. Expected ways in which international law impacts on state behaviour include legal and policy outputs, outcomes, and impacts. Soft-law mechanisms present the main pitfall of weak supervision and lack of compulsory enforcement in the event of non-implementation within States.

INTERNATIONAL COURT OF JUSTICE

No Harm Principle – *The Threat or Use of Nuclear Weapons case* (1996), paragraph 29

29. The Court recognizes that the environment is under daily threat and that the use of nuclear weapons could constitute a catastrophe for the environment. The Court also recognizes that the environment is not an abstraction but represents the living space, the quality of life and the very health of human beings, including generations unborn. The existence of the general obligation of States to ensure that activities within their jurisdiction and control respect the environment of other States or of areas beyond national control is now part of the corpus of international law relating to the environment.

Source: https://www.icj-cij.org/files/
case-related/95/095-19960708-ADV-01-00-EN.pdf

INTERNATIONAL COURT OF JUSTICE

Environmental Impact and Risk Assessment – *The Gabčíkovo-Nagymaros case* (1997), paragraph 140

140. It is clear that the Project's impact upon, and its implications for, the environment are of necessity a key issue. The numerous scientific reports which have been presented to the Court by the Parties - even if their conclusions are often contradictory - provide abundant evidence that this impact and these implications are considerable.

(Continued)

In order to evaluate the environmental risks, current standards must be taken into consideration. This is not only allowed by the wording of Articles 15 and 19, but even prescribed, to the extent that these articles impose a continuing - and thus necessarily evolving – obligation on the parties to maintain the quality of the water of the Danube and to protect nature.

The Court is mindful that, in the field of environmental protection, vigilance and prevention are required on account of the often irreversible character of damage to the environment and of the limitations inherent in the very mechanism of reparation of this type of damage.

Throughout the ages, mankind has, for economic and other reasons, constantly interfered with nature. In the past, this was often done without consideration of the effects upon the environment. Owing to new scientific insights and to a growing awareness of the risks for mankind – for present and future generations – of pursuit of such interventions at an unconsidered and unabated pace, new norms and standards have been developed, set forth in a great number of instruments during the last two decades. Such new norms have to be taken into consideration, and such new standards given proper weight, not only when States contemplate new activities but also when continuing with activities begun in the past. This need to reconcile economic development with protection of the environment is aptly expressed in the concept of sustainable development.

For the purposes of the present case, this means that the Parties together should look afresh at the effects on the environment of the operation of the Gabcikovo power plant. In particular they must find a satisfactory solution for the volume of water to be released into the old bed of the Danube and into the side-arms on both sides of the river.

Source: https://www.icj-cij.org/en/case/92/judgments

INTERNATIONAL COURT OF JUSTICE

Transboundary harm – *The Pulp Mills case* (2010), paragraph 204

204. It is the opinion of the Court that in order for the Parties properly to comply with their obligations under Article 41 (a) and (b) of the 1975 Statute, they must, for the purposes of protecting and preserving the aquatic environment with respect to activities which may be liable to cause transboundary harm, carry out an environmental impact assessment. As the Court has observed in the case concerning the Dispute Regarding Navigational and Related Rights,

'there are situations in which the parties' intent upon conclusion of the treaty was, or may be presumed to have been, to give the terms used – or some of them – a meaning or content capable of evolving, not one fixed once and for all, so as to make allowance for, among other things, developments in international law' (Dispute Regarding Navigational and Related Rights (Costa Rica v. Nicaragua), Judgment of 13 July 2009, para. 64).

In this sense, the obligation to protect and preserve, under Article 41 (a) of the Statute, has to be interpreted in accordance with a practice, which in recent years has gained so much acceptance among States that it may now be considered a requirement under general international law to undertake an environmental impact assessment where there is a risk that the proposed industrial activity may have a significant adverse impact in a transboundary context, in particular, on a shared resource. Moreover, due diligence, and the duty of vigilance and prevention which it implies, would not be considered to have been exercised, if a party planning works liable to affect the regime of the river or the quality of its waters did not undertake an environmental impact assessment on the potential effects of such works.

Source: https://www.icj-cij.org/en/case/135/judgments

4 Voluntary and forced compliance in international environmental law

A substantial body of literature on compliance has addressed gaps between treaty objectives and failure to implement treaty provisions. Different approaches in the IEL literature have taken into account the evaluation of formal compliance with norms, but few have assessed behavioural change. This entails examining whether relevant actors have changed their behaviour because of the norm or independently due to other factors. A certain action or inaction may be mandated by the IEL, yet the behavioural change observed can be motivated by other reasons. Conversely, voluntary assumption of a behaviour may result in an effective modification of the behavioural pattern previously observed.

A distinction should be drawn between 'voluntary' and 'forced' compliance, with the former cases being not only mandated by the norm but enforced and the latter cases being those in which compliance with the norms takes place spontaneously without the mediation of any compulsory mechanism or implementation.

Forced and voluntary compliance in IEL are two interrelated aspects. The former indicates the binding nature of the mechanisms set out in treaties to secure compliance. To a certain extent, the orientation of state actions determines the compliers with and the violators of the MEAs. In contrast, the latter is articulated through actions that induce compliance without imposing a particular sanction or alternative negative response. There can be a reward or an incentive to influence compliance.

Within the landscape of IEL, there is a growing presence of private actors alongside traditional government and public actors. Examples of voluntary compliance have spread in IEL in recent years. In an attempt to shed light on compliance, these two types of mechanisms prompt two research questions about the effects of IEAs: Are international norms having the desired effect? and are international environmental compliance mechanisms a misfit?

Attribution rules under SR rules leave out the responsibility or accountability of corporations. On the face of the breach of obligations under customary international law (such as for transboundary harm) or treaty commitments, attribution norms mandate connecting the wrongdoing to the State in which the breach has taken place rather than to the corporation. There has been a slow but progressive shift in the international community to generate a set of rules and regimes rooted in civil liability to harness corporate accountability for a breach of environmental law, attributing it to the polluter rather than to the State.[37]

5 Legal cultures and international environmental law compliance. The civil law/common law divide: is there room for other legal cultures in international environmental law?

Legal families (and similar systems) include concepts which permeate IEL. Legal families and national legal systems have become relevant as international and domestic environmental policies have become closer, and the influence of the latter has increased. It is thus crucial to understand how different legal systems play out when it comes to compliance. Ultimately, IEL will be implemented through national legislations and will impact the levels of compliance.

In terms of legal families, different approaches to environmental law may include notions like common law, civil law (the Romano-Germanic or Continental family of law), Islamic law, Asian law or indigenous customs, which are still in frequent use.[38] In the study of Western comparative law systems, authors often include two main systems: common law and civil law.[39] The former is traditionally considered an uncodified form of law which applies in ex-British colonies across the globe. In turn, the latter is understood as a codified form of law, developed in continental Europe and applicable in the ex-colonies of European imperial powers. Both systems can be seen as their respective antithesis: whereas

---

37 Elisa Morgera, *Corporate Accountability in International Environmental Law* (Oxford University Press 2009); Lakshman D. Guruswamy, *International Environmental Law* (4th edn West 2010).

38 O'Connell (n 14).

39 Jaako Husa, *The Future of Legal Families* (2016) Oxford Handbooks Online, available at https://www.oxfordhandbooks.com/view/10.1093/oxfordhb/9780199935352.001.0001/oxfordhb-9780199935352-e-26 accessed 1 April 2020.

common law relies on the doctrine of binding precedent as developed by high courts, civil law draws on Roman law models and the French civil code. Common law offers a different perspective on the application of IEL based on customary law and case law. Civil law systems tend to apply IEL in connection with their traditions. Other legal constructs include customary law systems.

Approaches based only on legal families have been criticized due to a variety of epistemological and methodological problems.[40] One of the main issues has been cultural bias as the concept of legal families draws on Western concepts. Equally, legal families approaches have traditionally focused on private law. In a more nuanced vision of legal families, the elements are ingrained in the specific legal system.

Cultural values influence perceptions about the environment and environmental norms.[41] From this perspective, other systems, such as 'indigenous law' or 'religious law' (Confucian or Islamic law, for instance) have not been taken into consideration.[42] Those legal systems are kept on the margins and often neglected. Gradually, however, they have been incorporated into the analysis of environmental issues, such as right to water and governance of water resources.[43] Special mention must be made to indigenous laws[44] concerning the protection of the environment, including concepts such as 'Mother Earth rights' or 'buen vivir', as a shift in the anthropocentric paradigm that has predominated so far toward the recognition of the rights of nature.[45] This new conceptual framework entails the idea of a deep respect for nature, not only as an object of protection (livelihood) but also as a subject of rights rooted in the conception of a social organisation and cosmovision/spirituality.

Pre-existing complexities embedded in the respective legal systems may then be observed in the compliance with IEL. Environmental problems which transcend the boundaries of the respective national legal systems might be addressed differently depending on the specific domestic law that applies. This is particularly observed in the implementation of environmental obligations under the specific treaty and through the machinery established therein, as in the case

---

40 Geoffrey Samuel, *An Introduction to the Comparative Law Theory and Method* (Hart 2014), pp. 50–53, at 50.
41 Roda Mushkat (ed), *International Environmental Law and Asian Values: Legal Norms and Cultural Influences (Law and Society Series)* (UBC Press 2005).
42 Marylin Johnson Raisch, *Religious Legal Systems in Comparative Law: A Guide to Introductory Research* (2006), available at https://www.nyulawglobal.org/globalex/Religious_Legal_Systems.html#_Buddhist_Law_and_Legal Theory accessed 1 April 2020.
43 Philippe Cullet and Joyeeta Gupta, 'Evolution of Water Law and Policy in India', in Joseph W. Dellapenna and Joyeeta Gupta (eds), *The Evolution of the Law and Politics of Water* (Springer Academic Publishers 2009), p. 159.
44 Jose Aylwin, Matias Meza-Lopehandia, and Nancy Yáñez, *Los pueblos indígenas y el derecho* (Observatorio Ciudadano 2013).
45 Pablo Sólon, 'The Rights of Mother Earth', in Satgar Vishwas (ed), *The Climate Crisis: South African and Global Democratic Eco-Socialist Alternatives* (Wits University Press 2018), pp. 107–130.

of the Ozone Convention. Some treaties, such as environmental framework treaties, can contain obligations and constitute free-standing treaties. Treaties setting up more detailed standards may assist States in the implementation of international obligations in domestic legal systems. Ultimately, legal systems will converge under IEL, giving rise to quite a hybrid system.

COMUNIDADES INDÍGENAS MIEMBROS DE LA ASOCIACIÓN LHAKA HONHAT (NUESTRA TIERRA) V. ARGENTINA, INTER-AM. CT. H.R. (FEB 6, 2020)

Right to a Healthy Environment, Duty to Prevent Environmental Damage and Right to Cultural Identity

203. (…) The right to a healthy environment protects components of (…) the environment, such as forests, seas, rivers, and other natural features, as interests in themselves, even in the absence of certainty or evidence about how it affects individual people" (…) "The question is to protect nature not only because of its 'utility' or 'effects' on human beings but also because of its importance for other living organisms (…) other human rights can also be violated as a consequence of environmental damage."

207. With regard to State obligations related to the right to a healthy environment, in addition to a duty to respect the rights and freedoms set out in the Convention, pursuant to Article 1.1 of the Convention (…) States must prevent violations. This duty comprises the "private sphere" (…) States must establish adequate mechanisms to supervise and control certain activities to guarantee human rights, protecting them from public entities and private individuals.

208. The prevention principle forms part of international customary law and implies the obligation of States to take action and to carry out all the necessary measures *ex ante*. This duty of prevention includes all those measures of a legal, political, administrative, and cultural nature that promote the safeguard of human rights and ensure that eventual violations of those rights are examined and dealt with as wrongful acts that, as such, may result in punishment for those who commit them, together with the obligation to compensate the victims for the negative consequences. This duty to prevent must be fulfilled under the minimum standard of due diligence, which must be appropriate and proportional to the degree of risk of environmental damage. Although it is not possible to list all the measures States should adopt to fulfil these duties, they might include the obligations to (i) regulate; (ii) supervise and monitor; (iii) require and approve environmental impact assessments; (iv) establish contingency plans; and (v) mitigate in cases of environmental damage.

209. Moreover, the Court has noted that different human rights can be affected by environmental damage, and this can occur with greater

intensity in certain groups in vulnerable situations, including indigenous peoples and communities that depend, economically for their survival, fundamentally from environmental resources, [like] the forest areas or river domains. Under International Human Rights Law, States are legally bound to address these vulnerabilities.

240. The Court understands that the right to cultural identity protects the freedom of people, including acting in association or community, to identify with one or various societies, communities, or social groups, to follow a way or lifestyle linked to the culture to which it belongs and to participate in its development. In this sense, the law protects the distinctive features that characterize a social group, without implying denying the historical, dynamic and evolutionary character of culture.

Source: http://www.corteidh.or.cr/docs/casos/articulos/ seriec_400_esp.pdf. Author's translation.

6 Developed and developing states: North-South contrasts

Another noticeable difference in terms of approaches to compliance is the divide between North and South, and how these differences are embedded across compliance practices.[46] Framed as part of the Third World Approaches to International Law (TWAIL), North-South differences are quite pervasive across sub-fields of IEL, such as climate justice, extractive industries, environmental access rights, land grabs, hazardous waste and pollution.[47] Concerns and priority areas for the Global South are specific in IEL being determined by historical elements and current economic features concerning production, supply chains and consumer behaviour.[48]

One of the main challenges that contemporary environmental law faces is balancing competing interests in the quest for a better harmonization between the different branches of international law, such as trade and investment law.

The two case studies below reflect the intricacies of normative models adopted in different regions. In Latin America, the emergence of ideas about environmental constitutionalism brought other dimensions into environmental protection. Rather than being a novel idea, environmental constitutionalism is the result of the evolution of various layers of environmental protection operated over the last three

---

46 Carmen G. Gonzalez, 'Bridging the North-South Divide: International Environmental Law in the Anthropocene' (October 10, 2015). Pace Environmental Law (PELR) Review, Vol. 32, p. 407, 2015; Seattle University School of Law Research Paper No. 16-02, available at SSRN: https://ssrn.com/abstract=2672460.

47 Shawkat Alam, Sumudu Atapattu, Carmen G. Gonzalez, and Jona Razzaque (eds), *International Environmental Law and the Global South* (Cambridge University Press 2015).

48 Sumudu Atapattu and Carmen Gonzalez, 'The North–South Divide in International Environmental Law: Framing the Issues', January 2015, doi: 10.1017/CBO9781107295414.002.

decades, leading to 'the confluence of constitutional law, international law, human rights, and environmental law'.[49] Put simply, environmental constitutionalism reflects the final outcome of the intersections between international law and domestic law in the protection of environmental rights. This is in line with the constitutional and public law theories that emerged in Latin American Constitutions in the 1980s and 1990s when several constitutions were reformed to include the protection of environmental rights. During this period, there was a considerable 'greening' of Latin American constitutions with the inclusion of provisions on the protection of the environment.[50] In its current formulation, environmental constitutionalism could assist in the progressive interpretation of the constitutions and the consideration of climate change as a new threat to the enjoyment of environmental rights.[51]

In the European Union (EU), the implementation of the Habitats and Birds Directive in EU law has proven to be an example of effective implementation. The creation of the European Environment Agency (EEA) in 1994 represented a shift in monitoring of environmental compliance. In its role, the EEA provides sound, independent information on the environment for those involved in developing, adopting, implementing, and evaluating environmental policy as well as the general public.[52] The EEA works in close collaboration with the European Environmental Information and Observation Network (Eionet) and its 32 member countries, gathers data and produces assessments on a wide range of topics related to the environment.

WORLD WILD FUND FOR NATURE

General Practices

WWF Programme Standards (2017)

There are three main overarching practices that apply to most or all of the steps in these standards. Instead of listing them for each step, they are described here.

1 Involve Stakeholders and be accountable to them

In conducting a project, it is important to define and, at every step, involve and be accountable to the appropriate internal and external stakeholders.

---

49 James May and Erin Daly, *Global Environmental Constitutionalism* (Cambridge University Press 2015).

50 Raul Brañes, *El Acceso a La Justicia Ambiental en América Latina* (UNEP 2000). Overall, the author refers to the 'constitucionalismo ambiental latinoamericano' (Latin American environmental constitutionalism).

51 Ezio Costa Cordella, 'La obra comparada de Raul Brañes y la evolucion del derecho ambiental latinoamericano' (2018) *Justicia Ambiental*, p. 20.

52 European Environmental Agency, available at https://www.eea.europa.eu/ accessed 1 April 2020.

You will need to identify key stakeholders independently, and determine with them what roles they might play in design, implementation and monitoring. (...) Implementing this strategy effectively will help to create a sense of ownership of the project beyond WWF during implementation and, ultimately, after the initial project ends. It will also help you to better understand the project's impacts, both positive and negative.

WWF is committed to finding equitable solutions for people and the environment and has agreed social policies on poverty and conservation, indigenous peoples, human rights and gender. You should ensure that both you and your team are familiar with these policies, and convey their potential implications for the project to all partners and primary stakeholders. Ensuring that your project adheres to these policies (see Box 1 below) will help WWF avoid engaging in unethical activities.

It is important that your stakeholder analysis does not consider local communities as a homogenous group. For example, there may be differences between men and women, young and old, ethnic groups etc. in the use and management resources and in decision-making. You should pay particular attention to indigenous and/or marginalized people who might be significantly affected by the project but often have little voice. Conversely you should also consider powerful individuals and organizations who, irrespective of being affected, are by definition influential.

Similarly, you will need to formalise some or your partnerships and work to cultivate them throughout the life of the project, hence maintaining positive and supportive relationships.

Source: https://wwf.panda.org/discover/about_wwf/
how_were_run/programme_standards/

BOX 1. THE KEY ELEMENTS OF ACCOUNTABILITY

Participation: key stakeholders and beneficiaries are involved in the design, implementation and decision making of the work of the project.

Transparency: people affected by the project have timely access to relevant information in an accessible format, in order that they can hold the project to account.

Feedback: the project has defined appropriate and accessible systems to enable the people affected by the project to provide feedback.

Evaluation and Learning: the project is accountable for its performance in delivering the goals of the project. The project is committed to improving the quality of its work through learning and adaptive management. Lessons learned are shared with partners, peers and donors.

Source: http://awsassets.panda.org/downloads/
WWF_Standards_2017-June_30_clean.pdf

BALI GUIDELINES ON PRINCIPLE 10- PUTTING RIO PRINCIPLE 10 INTO ACTION

An Implementation Guide

Guideline 1

Any natural or legal person should have affordable, effective and timely access to environmental information held by public authorities upon request (subject to Guideline 3), without having to prove a legal or other interest.

Guideline 2

Environmental information in the public domain should include, among other things, information about environmental quality, environmental impacts on health and factors that influence them, in addition to information about legislation and policy, and advice about how to obtain information.

Guideline 3

States should clearly define in their law the specific grounds on which a request for environmental information can be refused. The grounds for refusal are to be interpreted narrowly, taking into account the public interest served by disclosure.

Source: UNEP. Available at http://wedocs.unep.org/
handle/20.500.11822/11201

INTERNATIONAL COURT OF JUSTICE

Case Concerning Pulp Mills on The River Uruguay (Argentina v. Uruguay), Judgment of 20 April 2010

173. The Court observes that Article 1, as stated in the title to Chapter I of the 1975 Statute, sets out the purpose of the Statute. As such, it informs the interpretation of the substantive obligations, but does not by itself lay down specific rights and obligations for the parties. Optimum and rational utilization is to be achieved through compliance with the obligations prescribed by the 1975 Statute for the protection of the environment and the joint management of this shared resource. This objective must also be ensured through CARU, which constitutes "the joint machinery" necessary for its achievement, and through the regulations adopted by it as well as the regulations and measures adopted by the Parties.

174. The Court recalls that the Parties concluded the treaty embodying the 1975 Statute, in implementation of Article 7 of the 1961 Treaty, requiring the Parties jointly to establish a regime for the use of the river covering, inter alia, provisions for preventing pollution and protecting and preserving the aquatic environment. Thus, optimum and rational utilization may be viewed as the cornerstone of the system of co-operation established in the 1975 Statute and the joint machinery set up to implement this co-operation.

175. The Court considers that the attainment of optimum and rational utilization requires a balance between the Parties' rights and needs to use the river for economic and commercial activities on the one hand, and the obligation to protect it from any damage to the environment that may be caused by such activities, on the other. The need for this balance is reflected in various provisions of the 1975 Statute establishing rights and obligations for the Parties, such as Articles 27, 36, and 41. The Court will therefore assess the conduct of Uruguay in authorizing the construction and operation of the Orion (Botnia) mill in the light of those provisions of the 1975 Statute, and the rights and obligations prescribed therein.

Source: https://www.icj-cij.org/en/case/135/judgments

LAKE LANOUX ARBITRATION (FRANCE V. SPAIN) (1957) 12 R.I.A.A. 281; 24 I.L.R. 101, ARBITRAL TRIBUNAL, 1 NOVEMBER 16, 1957

2 The Facts. —This arbitration concerned the use of the waters of Lake Lanoux, in the Pyrenees. Briefly, the French Government proposed to carry out certain works for the utilization of the waters of the lake and the Spanish Government feared that these works would adversely affect Spanish rights and interests, contrary to the Treaty of Bayonne of May 26, 1866, between France and Spain and the Additional Act of the same date. In any event, it was claimed that, under the Treaty, such works could not be undertaken without the previous agreement of both parties.

It must first be determined what are the "interests" which have to be safeguarded. A strict interpretation of Article 11 would permit the reading that the only interests are those which correspond with a riparian right. However, various considerations which have already been explained by the Tribunal lead to a more liberal interpretation. Account must be taken of all interests, of whatsoever nature, which are liable to be affected by the works undertaken, even if they do not correspond to a right. Only such a solution complies with the terms of Article 16, with the spirit of the Pyrenees

(Continued)

Treaties, and with the tendencies which are manifested in instances of hydroelectric development in current international practice.

The second question is to determine the method by which these interests can be safeguarded. If that method necessarily involves communications, it cannot be confined to purely formal requirements, such as taking note of complaints, protests or representations made by the downstream State. The Tribunal is of the opinion that, according to the rules of good faith, the upstream State is under the obligation to take into consideration the various interests involved, to seek to give them every satisfaction compatible with the pursuit of its own interests, and to show that in this regard it is genuinely concerned to reconcile the interests of the other riparian State with its own.

Source: https://www.informea.org/sites/
default/files/court-decisions/COU-143747E.pdf

TRAIL SMELTER CASE (UNITED STATES, CANADA), 16 APRIL 1938 AND 11 MARCH 1941 VOLUME III PP. 1905–1982

When a State espouses a private claim on behalf of one of its nationals, expenses which the latter may have incurred in prosecuting or endeavoring to establish his claim prior to the espousal are sometimes included and, under appropriate conditions, may legitimately be included in the claim. They are costs, incidental to damage, incurred by the national in seeking local remedy or redress, as it is, as a rule, his duty to do, if, on account of injury suffered abroad, he wants to avail himself of the diplomatic protection of his State. The Tribunal, however, has not been informed of any case in which a Government has sought before an international jurisdiction or been allowed by an international award or judgment indemnity for expenses by it in preparing the proof for presenting a national claim or private claims which it had espoused; and counsel for the United States, on being requested to cite any precedent for such an adjudication, have stated that they know of no precedent. (...) In the absence of authority established by settled precedents, the Tribunal is of opinion that, where an arbitral tribunal is requested to award the expenses of a Government incurred in preparing proof to support its claim, particularly a claim for damage to the national territory, the intent to enable the Tribunal to do so should appear, either from the express language of the instrument which sets up the arbitral tribunal or as a necessary implication from its provision. Neither such express language nor implication is present in this case.

Source: http://legal.un.org/riaa/cases/vol_III/1905-1982.pdf

INTERNATIONAL COURT OF JUSTICE

Whaling in the Antarctica, ICJ, Judgment of 31 March 2014

58. Taking into account the Preamble and other relevant provisions of the Convention referred to above, the Court observes that neither a restrictive nor an expansive interpretation of Article VIII is justified. The Court notes that programmes for purposes of scientific research should foster scientific knowledge; they may pursue an aim other than either conservation or sustainable exploitation of whale stocks. This is also reflected in the Guidelines issued by the IWC for the review of scientific permit proposals by the Scientific Committee. In particular, the Guidelines initially applicable to JARPA II, Annex Y, referred not only to programmes that "contribute information essential for rational management of the stock" or those that are relevant for "conduct[ing] the comprehensive assessment" of the moratorium on commercial whaling, but also those responding to "other critically important research needs". The current Guidelines, Annex P, list three broad categories of objectives. Besides programmes aimed at "improv[ing] the conservation and management of whale stocks", they envisage programmes which have as an objective to "improve the conservation and management of other living marine resources or the ecosystem of which the whale stocks are an integral part" and those directed at "test[ing] hypotheses not directly related to the management of living marine resources".

Source: https://www.icj-cij.org/files/case-related
/148/148-20140331-JUD-01-00-EN.pdf

Bibliography

Alam, S, Atapattu, S, Gonzalez, Carmen G, and Razzaque, J, (eds), *International Environmental Law and the Global South* (Cambridge University Press 2015).

Atapattu, S and Gonzalez, C, 'The North–South Divide in International Environmental Law: Framing the Issues', January 2015, doi: 10.1017/CBO9781107295414.002.

Aylwin, J, Meza-Lopehandia, M, and Yáñez, N, *Los pueblos indígenas y el derecho* (Observatorio Ciudadano 2013).

Barrett, S, 'Self-Enforcing International Environmental Agreements', (1994) 46 *Oxford Economic Papers*, pp. 878–894.

Boyle, A, 'Soft Law in International Law Making', in Malcolm D. Evans (ed), *International Law* (5th edn, Oxford University Press 2018), p. 120.

Brañes, R, *El Acceso a La Justicia Ambiental en América Latina* (UNEP 2000). Overall, the author refers to the 'constitucionalismo ambiental latinoamericano' (Latin American environmental constitutionalism).

Bruch, C, 'Is International Environmental Law Really "Law"?: An Analysis of Application in Domestic Courts' (2006) 23 *Pace Environmental Law Review*, p. 423.

Costa Cordella, E, 'La obra comparada de Raul Brañes y la evolucion del derecho ambiental latinoamericano' (2018) *Justicia Ambiental*, p. 20.

Cullet, P and Gupta, J, 'Evolution of Water Law and Policy in India', in Joseph W. Dellapenna and Joyeeta Gupta (eds), *The Evolution of the Law and Politics of Water* (Springer Academic Publishers 2009), p. 159.

D'Amato, Anthony, 'Is International Law Really 'Law'?' (2010) Faculty Working Papers, p. 103.

Dupuy, PM and Viñuales, J, 'The Sources of International Environmental Law', in *International Environmental Law* (Cambridge University Press 2015), pp. 33–37.

Dupuy, PM, Le Moli, G, and Viñuales, JE, Customary International Law and the Environment, C-EENRG Working Papers 2018-2 (December 2018), https://www.ceenrg. landecon.cam.ac.uk/working-paper-files/CEENRG_WP_19_CustomaryInternational LawandtheEnvironment.pdf accessed 1 April 2020.

European Environmental Agency, available at https://www.eea.europa.eu/ accessed 1 April 2020.

Goldsmith, J and Posner, E, *The Limits of International Law* (Oxford University Press 2006).

Gonzalez, CG, 'Bridging the North-South Divide: International Environmental Law in the Anthropocene' (October 10, 2015). *Pace Environmental Law (PELR) Review*, Vol. 32, p. 407, 2015; Seattle University School of Law Research Paper No. 16-02, available at SSRN: https://ssrn.com/abstract=2672460.

Guruswamy, L, *International Environmental Law in a Nutshell* (4th edn West 2012), p. 58.

Hickmann, T, and Elsässer, JP, 'New Alliances in Global Environmental Governance: How Intergovernmental Treaty Secretariats Interact with Non-state Actors to Address Transboundary Environmental Problems' (2020) Int Environ Agreements, https:// doi.org/10.1007/s10784-020-09493-5 accessed 1 April 2020.

Husa, J, 'The Future of Legal Families' (2016) Oxford Handbooks Online, available at https:// www.oxfordhandbooks.com/view/10.1093/oxfordhb/9780199935352.001.0001/ox-fordhb-9780199935352-e-26 accessed 1 April 2020.

International Court of Justice Maritime Delamination and Territorial Questions between Qatar and Bahrain, Jurisdiction and Admissibility, Judgement ICJ report 1994.

Johnson Raisch, M, Religious Legal Systems in Comparative Law: A Guide to Introductory Research (2006), available at https://www.nyulawglobal.org/globalex/ Religious_Legal_Systems.html#_Buddhist_Law_and_Legal Theory accessed 1 April 2020.

Knicley, JE, 'Debt, Nature, and Indigenous Rights: Twenty-five Years of Debt-For-Nature Evolution' (2012) 36 *Harvard Environmental Law Review*, pp. 79–122. United Nations, Debt-for-nature swaps (DNS), available at https://www.undp.org/ content/dam/sdfinance/doc/Debt%20for%20Nature%20Swaps%20_%20UNDP.pdf accessed 10 January 2020.

Loibl, G, 'Compliance Procedures and Mechanisms', in M. Fitzmaurice, D. Ong, and P. Merkouris (eds), *Research Handbook on International Environmental Law* (Edward Elgar 2010), pp. 426–429.

May, J and Daly, Erin, *Global Environmental Constitutionalism* (Cambridge University Press 2015).

Mitchell, RB, 'Compliance Theory: Compliance, Effectiveness, and Behaviour Change in International Environmental Law', in Daniel Bodansky, Jutta Brunnée, and Ellen Hey (eds), *The Oxford Handbook of International Environmental Law* (Oxford University Press 2007), pp. 895, 899.

Mitchell, RB, International Environmental Agreements (IEA) Database (2002–2020), available at https://iea.uoregon.edu/one-indicator?field_lineage_value=CITES accessed 1 April 2020.

Morgera, E, *Corporate Accountability in International Environmental Law* (Oxford University Press 2009).

Mushkat, R (ed), International Environmental Law and Asian Values: Legal Norms and Cultural Influences (Law and Society Series) (UBC Press 2005).

Nollkaemper, S, 'Compliance Control in International Environmental Law: Traversing the Limits of the National Legal Order' (2002) 13(1) *Yearbook of International Environmental Law*, pp. 165–186.

O'Connell, ME, 'Enforcement and the Success of International Environmental Law' (1995) 3(1) *Indiana Journal of Global Legal Studies*, Article 4, available at https://www.repository.law.indiana.edu/ijgls/vol3/iss1/4 accessed 1 April 2020.

Raezz, Schmied and Voituriez, The Future of Sustainable Development Chapters in EU Free Trade Agreements (European Parliament 2018), available at https://www.iddri.org/sites/default/files/PDF/Publications/Catalogue%20Iddri/Autre%20Publication/the%20future%20of%20sustainable%20development%20chapters%20in%20EU%20free%20trade%20agreements.pdf accessed 1 April 2020.

Ratner, S, 'Chapter 35. Business', in Bodansky, Brunee & Hey, *Handbook of International Environmental Law* (Oxford University Press 2007), pp. 807–828.

Raustiala, K, 'Compliance & Effectiveness in International Regulatory Cooperation', 32 *Case Western Reserve Journal of International Law* 387 (2000), available at https://scholarlycommons.law.case.edu/jil/vol32/iss3/2 accessed 1 April 2020.

Samuel, G, *An Introduction to the Comparative Law Theory and Method* (Hart 2014), pp. 50–53, at 50.

Solón, P, 'The Rights of Mother Earth', in Satgar Vishwas (ed), *The Climate Crisis: South African and Global Democratic Eco-Socialist Alternatives* (Wits University Press 2018) pp. 107–130.

UN Environment 2019, Annual Report, available at https://www.unenvironment.org/annualreport/2019/index.php, accessed 1 April 2020.

UN. General Assembly, The World Charter for Nature (37th session: 1982–1983), available at https://digitallibrary.un.org/record/39295?ln=es accessed 1 April 2020.

UNEP's Compliance and Enforcement Guidelines (2006), available at https://wedocs.unep.org/bitstream/handle/20.500.11822/17018/UNEP-guidelines-compliance-MEA.pdf?sequence=1&isAllowed=y accessed 20 January 2020.

UNEP's Compliance and Enforcement Guidelines of Multilateral Environmental Agreements (2002), available at https://wedocs.unep.org/bitstream/handle/20.500.11822/17018/UNEP-guidelines-compliance-MEA.pdf?sequence=1&isAllowed=y accessed 10 January 2020.

Wood, S, 'Voluntary Environmental Codes and Sustainability', in Benjamin J. Richardson and Stepan Wood (eds), *Environmental Law for Sustainability* (Hart 2006) pp. 229–276.

2 International environmental law compliance

Theoretical framework, current trends and future scenarios

1 Redefining compliance with international environmental law

Compliance with International Environmental Law (IEL) has focussed on MEAs in order to secure observance of the treaties by individual States and international organisations that may be allowed to become parties to MEAs. Compliance and implementation of treaties are often used interchangeably. As a specific term 'implementation' refers to the measures taken to bring a treaty to life within the respective individual States. In this vein, implementation means not only enacting relevant laws and regulations but also adopting relevant policies as well as other measures and actions required for parties to meet their obligations under an MEA.

This chapter dissects the essential features and specific characteristics of compliance with IEL. It looks at the differences between compliance and enforcement, providing a general framework for international responsibility and liability under various regimes. In an extensive examination of the regimes, the chapter indicates the main trends in terms of mechanisms and approaches to compliance in IEL.

By merely looking at the normative inflation experienced in IEL, one may fall prey to the view that compliance is less of an issue than it used to be. Modern environmental law-making was kick-started by the Earth Summit in Rio de Janeiro in 1992 and Agenda 21, which, despite being a soft-law instrument, led to the adoption of various treaties.[1] At the Conference, the climate and biodiversity treaties embodied the two respective regimes.

Although numerous compliance mechanisms have been set up in the treaties this does not automatically mean effective compliance. A further distinction must be drawn between implementation, including formal implementation and effective implementation on the ground.[2] In identifying several layers of implementation,

---

1 United Nations Conference on Environment and Development, Rio de Janeiro, 3–14 June 1992, Agenda 21, available at https://sustainabledevelopment.un.org/content/documents/Agenda21.pdf accessed 25 March 2020.

2 Malgosia Fitzmaurice and Catherine Redgwell, 'Environmental Non-compliance Procedures and International Law' (2000) 31 *Netherlands Yearbook of International Law*, pp. 35–65.

Guruswamy distinguishes various types of meanings of implementation. 'Formal implementation' is understood as the 'process by which a treaty is incorporated into domestic law through legislative, judicial, or executive action'.[3] In turn, 'compliance' designates 'the extent to which a party has adhered to its treaty obligations by deploying the formal implementing machinery established by the treaty.[4] The third dimension of implementation can also be referred to as material implementation, focussing on effective implementation on the ground by a party to an MEA.[5]

External factors that are shaping compliance with IEL fall into different categories. Alongside the internal or intrinsic factors observed in addressing specific environmental problems, such as air pollution, water pollution, land degradation, deforestation and anthropogenic climate change, new external factors are emerging. Among others, it is worth mentioning the impact of technology and science on environmental compliance. Available scientific evidence has traditionally been relied upon, in line with the application of the precautionary principle. Technological development influences compliance by providing more accurate environmental information.

The various generations of MEAs have addressed and regulated environmental problems in light of scientific evidence and evolution of the technology. Best available technology represents one of the core tools in the definition of compliance with environmental law at the domestic level, and the concept has been distinctly deployed in IEL.[6] Best available technology or best available techniques (BAT), understood as the technology approved by legislators or regulators for output standards of a certain process, is at the centre of pollution prevention and key in the achievement of sustainable development.[7] BAT has also become relevant in other realms, such as in the field of international trade law as regards environmental protection and processes and production methods.[8]

Environmental protection and sustainable development are intertwined in the setting of sustainable development goals. Contemporary law-making shows numerous examples of soft law in the form of action plans, outlining actions to be undertaken by a wide range of actors. Various initiatives have emerged under existing multilateral environmental agreements, establishing links between the different areas.

3 Lakshman D. Guruswamy, *International Environmental Law* (4th edn West 2012) at 56.
4 Ibid., at 57.
5 Ibid.
6 Ray Purdy, 'Satellites: A New Era for Environmental Compliance?' (2006) 3(5) *Journal for European Environmental and Planning Law*, pp. 406–413.
7 OECD, available at https://www.oecd.org/chemicalsafety/risk-management/policies-on-best-available-techniques-or-similar-concepts-around-the-world.pdf accessed 1 April 2020. See also Panos Merkouris, 'The Principle of Sustainable Development and Best Available Technology under International Law', in K. Makuch and R. Pereira (eds), *Environmental and Energy Law* (Wiley-Blackwell 2012), pp. 37–60, 24.
8 Renske A. Giljam, 'Extended Application of 'Best Available Techniques' as a Means to Facilitate Ecological Governance', (2018) 36(2) *Journal of Energy & Natural Resources Law*, pp. 181–208.

Along with formal MEAs, recent years have witnessed the adoption of a series of 'voluntary international agreements', such as in the shape of declaratory provisions or provisions with a hortatory content also involving the private sector. An example of this is Article 6 of the Paris Agreement, which states that '[p]arties recognize that some Parties choose to pursue voluntary cooperation in the implementation of their nationally determined contributions to allow for higher ambition in their mitigation and adaptation actions and to promote sustainable development and environmental integrity'.[9] In specific IEL areas, in the last few decades, institutions have developed guidelines for compliance with regard to sectoral environmental protection. See, for instance, the 2015 Cairo Guidelines and Principles for the Environmentally Sound Management of Hazardous Wastes.[10]

Compliance issues confront States with a series of questions about the fulfilment of international obligations. Obligations of conduct or result, as set out in IEL norms, are required from States under different international environmental regimes. States subject to these obligations are supposed to demonstrate compliance with the norms through the adoption of the necessary measures to fulfil the obligations set forth in the specific MEA. Ultimately, the effectiveness of MEAs relies on the respective contracting states to implement the norms domestically.

What is a source of concern amongst states concerning environmental protection on the international level depends on a myriad of factors. Classical dynamics relating to consistent collective action in relation to global environmental problems can be observed in the articulation of mechanisms and the creation of institutional machinery to monitor compliance. Ensuring compliance and implementation with IEL also involves a question of values, whether their nature be ethical, societal or market-related. These values are interwoven into the legal framework of IEL.

One particularly difficult aspect is the solution of disputes that may arise with regard to imperfect or inadequate compliance with MEAs. Wherever non-compliance with IEA or a dispute arises, States resort to classical means of dispute settlement, scattered throughout various areas of international law. However, there is no permanent settlement mechanisms for the resolution of environmental disputes. Formal methods available to States party to a controversy (art 33 UN Charter) consist of judicial and non-judicial (or diplomatic) methods, the latter offering the benefits of flexibility, cheapness, privacy and freedom to determine the details of the proceedings.[11] Global commons problems bring up different compliance problems, such as ozone depletion, climate change or deep-sea bed exploitation.

9 Paris Agreement, Article 6.
10 Decision 14/30 of the Governing Council of UNEP, of 17 June 1987, available at https://wedocs.unep.org/handle/20.500.11822/29578?show=full accessed 1 March 2020.
11 Patricia Birnie, Alan Boyle, and Catherine Redgwell, *International Law and the Environment* (3rd edn Oxford University Press 2009).

Many deficiencies of the traditional IEL system have become evident. Traditional inter-state dispute settlement is ill-suited to address the question of compliance. Moreover, scholars have pointed out the deficiency of the law of state responsibility to address lack of environmental compliance.[12] The law of state responsibility falls short of responding to the challenges posed by IEL. Environmental harms are widely distributed, and there is no specific incentive to undertake enforcement actions.

Efforts to modernize environmental compliance are evinced by the adoption of new international treaties and additional protocols or agreements to MEAs previously concluded. Implementation relies on measures which States adopt to make international agreements effective in their respective domestic law systems. Although some MEAs are self-executing and do not require the adoption of national legislation, many of them do ask for specific mechanisms. Systems and mechanisms which have remained unused for decades have hereby come to life.

Many scholars have addressed compliance with IEL from different angles. Compliance has traditionally been linked to legal effectiveness, which relates to specific environmental problems that the relevant environmental treaty attempts to solve. Scholars like Bodansky have categorized treaty-based compliance systems in terms of their legal effectiveness as follows: compliance, behavioural effectiveness, and problem-solving effectiveness. Questioning the formal concept of compliance, Bodansky offers several contrasting ways in which to interpret compliance. First, the concept of legal effectiveness, more related to compliance in a material meaning, scrutinizes whether the results obtained are aligned with the legal requirements set out in the specific environmental treaty. In this sense, States obey the obligations laid down in a treaty, providing for measures such as the creation of a permit system for trade in endangered species (under CITES) or instituting reporting obligations on greenhouse gas emissions (under the Kyoto Protocol).

From a formalistic standpoint, a state is compliant as long as it acts consistently with the obligations set forth in the treaty. Clearly, if the obligation is an obligation of result, states will be deemed in compliance when the outcome is achieved, as in the stipulated reduction or curbing of gases.[13] In a second meaning identified by Bodansky, behavioural effectiveness relates to a change in state behaviour influenced by a treaty, even though the state may not formally comply with the wording of the treaty.[14] Finally, from a teleological perspective, problem-solving effectiveness refers to the extent to which a certain treaty contributes to the achievement of environmental goals or to solving an environmental problem.[15]

---

12 Haroldo Machado Filho, 'Looking for Adequate Tools for the Enforcement of Multilateral Environmental Agreements: Compliance Procedures and Mechanisms', European Society of International Law 2018, available at https://esil-sedi.eu/wp-content/uploads/2018/04/Filho.pdf accessed 1 March 2020.
13 Daniel Bodansky, *The Art and Craft of International Environmental Law* (Cambridge University Press 2011) at 63.
14 Bodansky (n 13) at 64.
15 Ibid.

Taking the 1987 Montreal Protocol on Substances that Deplete the Ozone Layer (hereinafter referred to as 'the Montreal Protocol') as an example, Bodansky illustrates the various connotations of compliance as understood in IEL. The main goal set for States is to reduce the consumption and production of Ozone Depleting Substances (ODS) by the required limits. Legal effectiveness resides in the effective reduction of consumption and production of ODS. From a behavioural perspective, it is deemed to be effective only if the reductions are a direct consequence of the Protocol. Finally, the problem-solving effectiveness consists in the actual reversion of the depletion of the stratospheric ozone layer.[16] Equally, the Kyoto Protocol allows for both States and international organisations to become parties to the treaty. In another example, Bodansky identifies diverse layers of effectiveness evaluating the problem-solving effectiveness of CITES.[17] Legal effectiveness is thus different from behavioural effectiveness as the former may not necessarily be induced by the adoption of new environmental standards. Guruswamy further differentiates between effectiveness and the impact of IEL norms.[18] Key contributions from Downs and Raustiala to the IEL literature point out the obstacles in obtaining compliance.[19]

Interdisciplinary theoretical stances, such as political sciences approaches, place emphasis on different elements of the process. Indeed, from a political science perspective, behavioural changes carry more relevance than any potential formal attempt to conform to IEL norms. Other scholars, such as Miles et al., offer evidence-based approaches examining the various environmental regimes and have classified them into separate categories: effective, mid-performance and ineffective regimes.[20] Under the first category, they mention the Sea Dumping of Low-Level Radioactive Waste, Management of Tuna Fisheries in the Pacific and Vienna Convention and Montreal Protocol on Ozone Layer Depletion. Examples of mixed-performance regimes include Land-Based Pollution Control in the North Sea, the Convention on Long-Range Transboundary Air Pollution, Satellite Telecommunication and Management of High Seas Salmon in the North Pacific. Ineffective regimes, by contrast, include the Mediterranean Action Plan, Oil Pollution from Ships at Sea, International Trade in Endangered Species, International Whaling Commission and Convention for the Conservation of Antarctic Marine Living Resources.

Diplomatic means are more political and pragmatic, and non-legalistic; forward-looking, as their goal is to manage environmental problems in order to

---

16 Ibid.
17 Ibid., at 67.
18 Guruswamy (n 3).
19 Alan E. Boyle, 'Saving the World? Implementation and Enforcement of International Environmental Law through International Institutions' (1991) 3(2) *Journal of Environmental Law*, pp. 229–245.
20 Edward L. Miles, Steinar Andresen, Elaine M. Carlin, Jon Birger Skjærseth, Arild Underdal and Jørgen Wettestad, *Environmental Regime Effectiveness Confronting Theory with Evidence* (MIT Press 2001).

achieve a reasonable level of compliance in the future; and non-adversarial, rather than contentious in nature. Characteristically in this approach, compliance and non-compliance is part of a continuum.

In a broader sense, compliance with IEL involves compliance devised through its other branches.[21] Interestingly, motivation for this compliance poses various other questions: Why do states engage in compliance with IEL? Does it really foster compliance, or is it merely reflecting behaviour?[22] What is the desired behaviour? What is expected from the various actors? How can compliance with IEL be induced?

Notably, varying levels of compliance or non-compliance are observed in practice. Thus, there are cases of small and big violations, bare compliance and over-compliance, and compliance and breach. Each regime reflects multiple approaches to these issues, such as the Espoo Convention on Transboundary Environmental Impact Assessment, the Kyoto Protocol, the Basel Convention, the Aarhus Convention on Public Participation, the Cartagena Biosafety Protocol, the London Protocol, the Rotterdam Chemicals Convention and the Stockholm Convention on Persistent Organic Pollutants.

Several parties are involved in the environmental compliance process: the non-compliant States, non-state actors, international organisations, non-governmental organisations and other stakeholders. Implementation is influenced by the structure of the state. Multilevel governance and regional organisations represent another feature in the current landscape for compliance. Given the increasing number of environmental norms, overlaps between international, regional and national levels often occur.

Compliance implies assessing the steps which States have taken to comply with the obligations, procedural or substantive. Flaws in the legal technique and in the wording of the MEAs may condition the implementation. Sanctions are used as deterrents to encourage compliance and punish offenders. Although formal implementation may be measured by determining how States have achieved the stated objectives of the treaty, what is crucial is to address the environmental problems tackled in the MEAs.

2 Fragmentation of compliance monitoring in IEL

Compliance is subject to the obligations established by various MEAs and the actual conduct or results of States subject to these obligations. Implementation

---

21 Alan E. Boyle, 'Relationship between International Environmental Law and Other Branches of International Law', in Daniel Bodansky, Jutta Brunnée, and Ellen Hey (eds), *The Oxford Handbook of International Environmental Law* (Oxford University Press 2008).
22 Andrew T. Guzman, 'A Compliance Based Theory of International Law' (2002) 29(90) *California Law Review*, p. 1823. George W. Downs, David M. Rocke, and Peter N. Barsoom, 'Is the Good News about Compliance Good News about Cooperation?' (1996) 50(3) *International Organization*, pp. 379–406.

and compliance processes in international law are not, however, centralized, and, thus, compliance is not straightforward.

Obligations contemplated in MEAs may overlap with other commitments imposed on states under different treaty regimes.[23]

Considered a feature of contemporary international environmental law, the proliferation of international environmental instruments[24] has created potential incompatibilities.[25] Endogenous incompatibility arises when environmental law treaties regulating different areas of environmental law clash. Exogenous incompatibility arises when international environmental treaties present contradictions with other areas of international law, such as international economic law. Scholars classify these conflicts by distinguishing between normative conflicts and legitimacy conflicts.[26]

Some international environmental treaties are more prone to interactions with other areas of international law, such as the following: the Washington Convention on International Trade in Endangered Species of Wild Fauna and Flora, 3 March 1973; the International Tropical Timber Agreement, 18 November 1983; the International Maritime Convention on the Prevention of Marine Pollution by Dumping of Wates and Other Matter, 29 December 1972; and the Montreal Protocol on Substances that Deplete the Ozone Layer, 6 September 1987.

The type of obligations set forth in environmental treaties, whether procedural or obligations of conduct, may lead to normative conflicts. Beyond the IEL realm, several international treaties envisage obligations with a bearing on the environmental realm. The diversification and expansion of international law has led to the co-existence and overlap of regimes. For example, the obligations set out in the UN Framework Convention on Climate Change are intertwined with other commitments assumed by states under other treaty regimes.[27]

Treaty congestion has been criticized by IEL scholarship, led by Brown Weiss, which has underlined the 'operational inefficiency' deriving from the multiplication of international environmental treaties.[28] This clearly has an impact on international environmental management. In managing fragmentation, various

---

23 Martti Koskenniemi, *Fragmentation of International Law: Difficulties Arising from the Diversification and Expansion of International Law*, Report of the Study Group of the International Law Commission, A/CN.4/L.682 (13 April 2006), available at https://legal.un.org/ilc/documentation/english/a_cn4_l682.pdf accessed 1 March 2020.

24 International Environmental Agreements (IEA) Database Project, 2002–2019, available at https://iea.uoregon.edu accessed 1 April 2020.

25 Edith Brown Weiss, 'International Environmental Law: Contemporary Issues and the Emergence of a New World Order' (1993) 81 *Georgetown Law Journal*, p. 675.

26 Pierre-Marie Dupuy and Jorge Viñuales, *International Environmental Law* (CUP 2015) at 385–386.

27 Panagiotis Delimatsis, *Research Handbook on Climate Change and Trade Law* (Edward Elgar 2016).

28 Brown Weiss (n 25) at 697–699.

strategies have been proposed, such as relying on interpretation tools. Relevant literature has shifted from fragmentation to a more holistic approach to the co-existence of the regimes.

Compliance as a function and as a category responds to different treaty regimes. There are many relevant factors, such as the nature of the activities; the treaty itself; the characteristics of the states; policy factors; information; and the behaviours and attitudes of NGOs, other states and IGOs. Amongst these various legal systems conceived as islands of compliance, fragmentation in the compliance with IEL can be observed. Certain self-contained regimes within IEL, such as biodiversity, bring about more complexity as they encompass other compliance categories.

Environmental law scholars have devised strategies to manage the overlap between two legal regimes in IEL, concerning such areas as the interconnected global environmental threats of biodiversity loss and climate change.[29] The interface between climate and biodiversity exists more as an overlap with some potential conflicts between different regimes. Various cases can be used to illustrate the processes of compliance under other regimes. This phenomenon has been underlined with regard to forest carbon sinks under the Kyoto Protocol and measures to tackle deforestation.

With respect to the multiplicity of regimes, there are several key stakeholders involved in compliance with environmental law. Other regimes, such as trade and investment, comprise environmental provisions that influence implementation and compliance with IEL. For instance, under the trade regime, the Technical Barriers to Trade Agreement (TBT) and the Sanitary and Phytosanitary Agreement (SPS) both broadly encompass environmental provisions.

From a dispute resolution perspective, some scholars have also attributed the increase in fragmentation to international dispute settlement and the features of international environmental litigation that takes place before adjudicative institutions, including permanent courts, ad-hoc arbitral tribunals, regional courts and judicial bodies.[30] Arguably, this particular characteristic of contemporary environmental dispute resolution has led to more fragmentation. In particular, this can be observed in two specific fields: human rights and the trade dispute settlement system. It has been claimed that some judicial and quasi-judicial bodies undermine rules and principles of IEL by following specific purposes of non-environmental regimes rather than applying IEL. Fragmentation in international dispute resolution has to be examined against the backdrop of the recent

---

29 Harro Van Asselt, 'Managing the Fragmentation of International Environmental Law: Forests at the Intersection of the Climate and Biodiversity Regimes' (2012) 44 *International Law and Politics*, p. 1205.

30 Tim Stephens, 'Fragmentation of International Environmental Law', Chapter 10 -Part III – Contemporary Challenges in *International Courts and Environmental Protection* (Cambridge University Press 2009), pp. 304–344, available at https://doi.org/10.1017/CBO97805115 76034.012 accessed 1 April 2020.

expansion of the body of international case law on environmental issues in the human rights and international trade law fields.[31]

Pluralism in IEL is evidenced in the emergence of various specialized regimes set up through rules and institutions. Some commentators have argued that the development of quasi-autonomous legal orders leads to the compartmentalization of IEL, while others propose that the decentralization contributes to community objectives which cannot be reached through general rules.

MEAs which have been widely accepted and ratified by States, such as the Convention on Biological Diversity (CBD), create separate legal regimes. Several problems are intertwined and require an adequate policy response. What is interesting is the question of compliance at the intersection of the different regimes in cases of conflicts and convergence between regimes. Convergence depends on how a particular system accommodates the requirements under the other regime. Studies have focussed particularly on the relationship between the climate and the biodiversity regimes.[32]

Although some environmental problems are interrelated, legal regimes governing them may have evolved separately, and thus the interactions on the international law level are less common. In the face of these differing environmental problems and challenges, convergence between regimes would bring more cooperation and improve compliance.

The field of species, ecosystems and biodiversity constitutes a fertile ground for the analysis of the interactions between the regimes, and top-down and bottom-up regulations. The Convention on International Trade in Endangered Species of Wild Fauna and Flora (CITES) deals with the trade of certain species comprised in the list annexed to the Convention. Differing obligations are stipulated for the categories in appendixes I, II and III.[33] Obligations set out by the treaty apply to these species.

In terms of the interface with other branches of international law, environmental claims have arisen in the context of international economic law disputes in the investment and trade realms. In the investment realm, this includes cases concerning compulsory taking of property by the host state, environmental considerations in the permitting cycle, claims concerning environmental liability and measures ordering reparation for environmental damage and measures concerning renewable energy.[34] In international trade law, the WTO dispute settlement system has witnessed an increase in the number of controversies with

31 Ibid.
32 Van Asselt (n 29) at 1212.
33 CITES, Annexes I, II and III, available at Appendices I, II and III valid from 26 November 2019, available at https://www.cites.org/eng/app/appendices.php accessed 1 April 2020.
34 See cases such as *Santa Elena Compañia del Desarrollo de Santa Elena S.A. v. Republic of Costa Rica*, ICSID Case No. ARB/96/1 Arbitral Award 17 February 2000 and *Chevron v Ecuador*, Corporation v. The Republic of Ecuador, UNCITRAL, PCA Case No. 2009–23 and *Burlington Resources Inc. v. Republic of Ecuador*, ICSID Case No. ARB/08/5 (formerly Burlington Resources Inc. and others v. Republic of Ecuador and Empresa Estatal Petróleos del Ecuador (PetroEcuador)). Kyla Tienhaara, *The Expropriation of Environmental Governance: Protecting*

environmental content. The so-called environmental exceptions laid down in Article 20 paragraphs b and g of the General Agreement on Tariffs and Trade (GATT) have been invoked to justify the adoption of measures otherwise in breach of the trade liberalization principles. These particular types of clashes or conflicts will be examined in detail in another chapter of this book.

One way of anticipating and avoiding conflict is through a sustainability impact assessment of proposed trade and investment agreements during the negotiating period and before they are concluded.[35] Used in the negotiation of international trade and investment treaties, this type of assessment provides a tool to monitor in advance the environmental risks attached to the implementation of treaties frequently used in development cooperation.[36] However, its effectiveness is limited as these types of assessments are not prescribed, being regulated through soft-law norms rather than by stringent international norms.

Through the lenses of compliance, fragmentation and segmentation of the regimes may create normative and practical hindrances to the implementation of IEL. Normative conflicts may arise if the same type of state behaviour is considered lawful under one regime while being in breach of another. Practical problems may thus be generated.

HANDBOOK FOR TRADE SUSTAINABILITY IMPACT ASSESSMENT (2ND EDITION, EUROPEAN COMMISSION 2016)

Definition of SIAs

SIAs are trade-specific and independent ex ante assessments carried out by external consultants simultaneously with major trade negotiations. They assess in depth the potential economic, social, human rights and environmental impacts of the agreement under negotiation. SIAs help to steer the trade negotiations by feeding them with evidence on an ongoing basis.

Trade SIAs consist of two complementary components of equal importance: (i) a robust analysis of economic, social, human rights and environmental impacts, using, among other methods, modelling techniques and

(Continued)

Foreign Investors at the Expense of Public Policy (Cambridge University Press 2009). See, also, Dupuy and Viñuales (n 26) at 385.

35 European Commission, Handbook for Trade Sustainability Impact Assessment, European Commission, External Trade, March 2006, available at https://www.wto.org/english/forums_e/public_forum_e/sia_handbook.pdf accessed 1 April 2020.

36 Jean Hugé, N. Mukherjee, C. Fertel, J.P. Waaub, Thomas Block, Tom Waas, N. Koedam, and F. Dahdouh-Guebas, 'Conceptualizing the Effectiveness of Sustainability Assessment in Development Cooperation' (2015) 7(5) *Sustainability*, pp. 5735–5751.

causal chain analysis. This component is undertaken in a clear and objective manner using state-of-the-art techniques; (ii) a wide consultation process involving stakeholders both in the EU and in the partner country, which provides opportunities for information-gathering and dissemination of results' (Page 9).

Source: https://trade.ec.europa.eu/doclib/docs/
2016/april/tradoc_154464.PDF

3 International responsibility and liability

In IEL, the determination of a breach and the allocation of responsibility raise two different questions. From a strictly terminological viewpoint, the international regime of state responsibility (hereinafter, 'SR') has been alluded to in terms of general international law, whereas liability recalls the domestic law terminology. Liability entails fault liability, strict and absolute liability, and civil liability. A unique feature of IEL involves securing accountability for transboundary environmental harm. A doctrinal debate about fault as an element of the primary obligation in the consideration of the wrongful act may indicate that fault is not necessary in some IEL cases. For instance, in terms of transboundary harm IEL instruments like the Stockholm Declaration do not require intention or negligence as a constitutive element of the wrongful act. IEL scholars have argued that the strict liability regime for environmental harm may emerge independently on the basis of the principles of equity, sovereign equality and good neighbourliness.[37] Strict liability leads to a reversal of the burden of proof, with the possibility for the defending State to still invoke circumstances precluding wrongfulness or liability. At the other end of this spectrum, however, the absolute (or objective) liability regime rules out the possibility of invoking circumstances precluding liability.[38] Authors also mention civil liability (treaty overlay and civil liability litigation), even if few international treaties have established a system along these lines, enabling private individuals to bring a claim within national jurisdiction.[39]

Liability in IEL has been the focus of study by scholars and international institutes with the aim of adopting rules governing liability in IEL.[40] The prevention

37 Birnie, Boyle and Redgwell (n 11) at 218.
38 Alex Kiss and Dinah L. Shelton, 'Strict Liability in International Environmental Law. Law of The Sea', in Tafsir Malick Ndiaye and Rüdiger Wolfrum (eds), *Environmental Law and Settlement of Disputes: Liber Amicorum Judge Thomas A. Mensah* (Brill Academic Publishers 2007). GWU Legal Studies Research Paper No. 345, GWU Law School Public Law Research Paper No. 345, available at SSRN: https://ssrn.com/abstract=1010478 accessed 1 April 2020.
39 Andrea Laura Mackielo, 'Core Rules of International Environmental Law' (2009) 16(1) *ILSA Journal of International & Comparative Law*, Article 11.
40 Institut de Droit International, Session of Strasbourg – 1997, *Responsibility and Liability under International Law for Environmental Damage* (Eighth Commission, Rapporteur: Mr Francisco

system is based on the principle *sic utere tuo ut alienum non laedas*. In inter-state relations, this represents the obligation not to cause injury to another State's territory.[41] These principles evoke values applicable in compliance and enforcement contexts. States' key obligations of prevention, cooperation, notification, restoration and compensation play a fundamental role in ensuring compliance in IEL. Under international law, however, private parties do not hold environmental liability in principle.[42] This represents a clear limitation for the compliance system as the conduct of private parties (be they multinational companies or individual polluters) cannot be considered direct liability in IEL, as cases like *Trail Smelter* and *Pulp Mills* demonstrate.[43] The ICJ case law has demonstrated the diverse interpretations of SR in cases involving environmental damage.[44]

In an attempt to resolve this gap, soft-law norms have emerged in international law in the fields of corporate accountability and corporate social responsibility. IEL principles are at the root of the statement of the responsibility of States to avoid damage to the environment beyond their jurisdiction. In particular, principles such as the precautionary, the preventative and the sustainable development principles embodied in declarations guide the implementation and compliance of IEL. Principles of international law applicable to responsibility and liability are tailored to the specific context of environmental damage. A specific principle concerns inter- and intra-generation responsibility.[45]

Orrego Vicuña), available at https://www.idi-iil.org/app/uploads/2017/06/1997_str_03_en.pdf accessed 1 April 2020. Birnie, Boyle and Redgwell (n 11).

41 Jutta Brunnée, ESIL Reflection Procedure and Substance in International Environmental Law Confused at a Higher Level? (2016) 5(6) ESIL Forum, available at https://esil-sedi.eu/post_name-123/ accessed 1 April 2020. See, also Robert Esposito, The ICJ and the Future of Transboundary Harm Disputes: A Preliminary Analysis of the Case Concerning Aerial Herbicide Spraying (Ecuador v. Colombia), Pace International Law Review. Online Companion, August 2010, at 1.

42 Sandrine Maljean-Dubois, 'International Litigation and State Liability for Environmental Damages: Recent Evolutions and Perspectives' in Jiunn-rong Yeh (ed), *Climate Change Liability and Beyond* (National Taiwan University Press 2017).

43 Xue Hanqin, *Transboundary Damage in International Law* (Cambridge University Press 2003); Phoebe Okowa, *State Responsibility for Transboundary Air Pollution in International Law* (Oxford University Press 2001).

44 International Court of Justice, *Case Concerning Certain Phosphate Lands in Nauru* (Nauru v. Australia). Phosphate mining on Nauru – Responsibility for rehabilitation of worked-out lands – Whether there was joint/ responsibility of/ three States are responsible for the full extent of rehabilitation of worked-out lands, available at https://www.icj-cij.org/files/case-related/80/080-19920626-JUD-01-00-EN.pdf accessed 1 April 2020.

45 Responsibility towards future generations. Pedro Flores y Otros v. Corporacion Del Cobre, Codelco, Division Salvador. Recurso. De Proteccion. Copiapo. Supreme Court Of Chile Rol.12.753.Fs. 641 (1988). The Supreme Court of Chile in Pedro Flores v. Corporación del Cobre, Codelco, Division Salvador 1988, upheld a constitutional environmental right to live in an environment free from contamination in order to stop the deposition of copper mill tailings onto Chilean beaches that were adversely affecting protected marine life.

> ### Declaration of the United Nations Conference on the Human Environment (1972) Principle 21
>
> States have, in accordance with the Charter of the United Nations and the principles of international law, the sovereign right to exploit their own resources pursuant to their own environmental policies, and the responsibility to ensure that activities within their jurisdiction or control do not cause damage to the environment of other States or of areas beyond the limits of national jurisdiction.
>
> ### Rio Declaration on Environment and Development (1992) Principle 2
>
> States have, in accordance with the Charter of the United Nations and the principles of international law, the sovereign right to exploit their own resources pursuant to their own environmental and developmental policies, and the responsibility to ensure that activities within their jurisdiction or control do not cause damage to the environment of other States or of areas beyond the limits of national jurisdiction.

Several different concepts are related to the regime of SR: attribution, causation, reparation and exhaustion of local remedies.[46] Attribution has mainly referred to inter-state claims in which a wrongful act with a negative impact on the environment has taken place. From this perspective, all international obligations with bearing on the environmental realm found in treaty or in customary law can give rise to SR.[47] Some obligations under IEL would be more specific – for instance in terms of reduction of emissions – making it easier to pinpoint whether there was a lack of compliance. Causation, defined as the relationship between the wrongful act and the harmful result, can become particularly controversial under IEL when several factors have contributed towards a harmful outcome.[48] A decisive question at this point is how to assess IEL tools in order to bring the situation to the *status quo ante* or even improve it. The international responsibility presents difficulties when it comes to securing compliance with IEL. In the mindset of a more reactive approach, international responsibility may fulfil the objectives. However, in a preventative approach to environmental damage, it does not fit the pattern associated with an effective operating system.

46 James Crawford, *State Responsibility: The General Part, Cambridge Studies in Comparative and International Law* (Cambridge University Press 2014).
47 Tseming Yang and Robert V. Percival, 'The Emergence of Global Environmental Law' (2009) 36 *Ecology Law Quarterly*, p. 615.
48 Ilias Plakokefalos, 'Causation in the Law of State Responsibility and the Problem of Overdetermination: In Search of Clarity' (2015) 26(2) *European Journal of International Law*, pp. 471–492, available at https://doi.org/10.1093/ejil/chv023 accessed 1 March 2020.

Many criticisms have been raised, pointing at the fact that the SR regime is not fit-for-purpose when it comes to the breach of IEL obligations. Some of the more innovative provisions of the current draft articles of the International Law Commission (ILC) on SR aim at solving these questions, such as the inclusion of *erga omnes* obligations.[49]

As SR might take different forms in times of peace and times of war, the ILC has been working on the draft articles on environmental damages caused in the context of armed conflict.[50] With the proliferation of various types of armed conflicts, the pollution and environmental damage caused as a result have increased, leading to international claims.[51] Amongst other known effects of pollution caused by armed conflicts, there are chemical contaminations, such as that resulting from the bombing of industrial sites in Kosovo (1999), and oil pollution, such as the leak in the Mediterranean Sea during the Israel–Lebanon war (2006).[52] UNEP has closely observed more than 20 post-conflict situations and followed this topic during the last two decades, helping to shape principles that apply to addressing significant environmental harm caused during armed conflict.[53]

Various mechanisms have been used to enhance or induce compliance with IEL under the framework of due diligence and hence avoid SR. The liability of non-state actors has been an elusive matter. In terms of environmental liability, the IEL system offers limited coverage in the regulation of responsibility in the face of transboundary harm or long-range pollution caused by private activities. Using the categories of 'business and human rights approaches', the three obligations of respect, protect and remedy may be functional to the system.[54]

49 Tuomas Palosaari, 'More than Just Wishful Thinking? Existence and Identification of Environmental Obligations Erga Omnes', University of Eastern Finland Law School, Master's Thesis Seminar, 27 March 2018, available at https://epublications.uef.fi/pub/urn_nbn_fi_uef-20180404/urn_nbn_fi_uef-20180404.pdf accessed 1 March 2020.

50 ILC, Chapter VI. Protection of the Environment in Relation to Armed Conflicts, available at https://legal.un.org/ilc/reports/2019/english/chp6.pdf. See also, Conflict and Environment Observatory, *UN Lawyers Approve 28 Legal Principles to Reduce the Environmental Impact of War*, available at https://ceobs.org/un-lawyers-approve-28-legal-principles-to-reduce-the-environmental-impact-of-war/ accessed 1 March 2020.

51 Report and recommendations made by the Panel of Commissioners Appointed to Review the Well Blowout Control Claim. State responsibility – losses occasioned by invasion of another State – Proof of causation – Damage to oil wells – Allegations by Iraq that damage caused by Coalition forces, in E. Lauterpacht, C. J. Greenwood, A. G. Oppenheimer (eds), *International Law Reports*, Volume 109 (1998), p. 479. Reports and recommendations made by the panel available at https://jusmundi.com/en/document/decision/en-well-blowout-control-claim-report-and-recommendations-made-by-the-panel-wednesday-18th-december-1996 1 April 2020.

52 Matilda Lindén, 'Environmental Damage in Armed Conflict To What Extent Do the Remedies Available for Environmental Damage in Armed Conflict Reflect the Polluter Pays Principle? The Cases of the Jiyeh Power Station and the Niger Delta Conflict' (University of Gottenburgh 2017), available at https://gupea.ub.gu.se/bitstream/2077/53076/1/gupea_2077_53076_1.pdf accessed 1 April 2020.

53 UNEP, *Protecting the Environment during Armed Conflict: An Inventory and Analysis of International Law* (UNEP 2009).

54 Timo Koivurova, *Introduction to International Environmental Law* (Routledge 2012).

INSTITUT DE DROIT INTERNATIONAL

Session of Strasbourg – 1997
Responsibility and Liability under International Law for Environmental Damage
Basic Distinction on Responsibility and Liability

Article 1

The breach of an obligation of environmental protection established under international law engages responsibility of the State (international responsibility), entailing as a consequence the obligation to re-establish the original position or to pay compensation.

The latter obligation may also arise from a rule of international law providing for strict responsibility on the basis of harm or injury alone, particularly in case of ultra-hazardous activities (responsibility for harm alone).

Civil liability of operators can be engaged under domestic law or the governing rules of international law regardless of the lawfulness of the activity concerned if it results in environmental damage.

The foregoing is without prejudice to the question of criminal responsibility of natural or juridical persons.

Source: Institut de Droit International, full text available at
https://www.idi-iil.org/app/uploads/2017/06/1997_str_03_en.pdf

INTERNATIONAL COURT OF JUSTICE

Nuclear Tests Case – New Zealand v France
Judgment of 20 December 1974
Questions of jurisdiction and/or admissibility

Atmospheric contamination - Tests resulting in the deposit of radioactive fallout on territory of other States and on high seas – Legality of the nuclear tests – Applicability of absolute responsibility for damage caused

18. As the United Nations Scientific Committee on the Effects of Atomic Radiation has recorded in its successive reports to the General Assembly, the testing of nuclear devices in the atmosphere has entailed the release into the atmosphere, and the consequent dissipation in varying degrees throughout the world, of measurable quantities of radioactive matter. It is

asserted by Australia that the French atmospheric tests have caused some fall-out of this kind to be deposited on Australian territory; France has maintained in particular that the radio-active matter produced by its tests has been so infinitesimal that it might be regarded as negligible, and that such fall-out on Australian territory does not constitute a danger to the health of the Australian population. These disputed points are clearly matters going to the merits of the case, and the Court must therefore refrain, for the reasons given above, from expressing any view on them.

Source: International Court of Justice – https://www.icj-cij.org/
files/case-related/59/059-19741220-JUD-01-00-EN.pdf

INTERNATIONAL COURT OF JUSTICE

Case concerning the Gabčíkovo – Nagymaros Project (Hungary v Slovakia) Judgment of 25 September 1997

State of necessity as a ground for precluding wrongfulness – Article 33 of the Draft Articles on State Responsibility - Environment - "Grave und imminent peril"

40. Throughout the proceedings, Hungary contended that, although it did suspend or abandon certain works, on the contrary, it never suspended the application of the 1977 Treaty itself. To justify its conduct, it relied essentially on a "state of ecological necessity". Hungary contended that the various installations in the Gabčíkovo - Nagymaros System of Locks had been designed to enable the Gabčíkovo power plant to operate in peak mode. Water would only have come through the plant twice each day, at times of peak power demand. Operation in peak mode required the vast expanse (60 km') of the planned reservoir at Dunakiliti, as well as the Nagymaros dam, which was to alleviate the tidal effects and reduce the variation in the water level down-stream of Gabčíkovo. Such a system, considered to be more economically profitable than using run-of-the-river plants, carried ecological risks which it found unacceptable. The Court moreover observes that, when it invoked the state of necessity in an effort to justify that conduct, Hungary chose to place itself from the outset within the ambit of the law of State responsibility, thereby implying that, in the absence of such a circumstance, its conduct would have been unlawful. The state of necessity claimed by Hungary - supposing it to have been established - thus could not permit of the conclusion that, in 1989, it had acted in accordance with its obligations under the 1977 Treaty or that those obligations had ceased to be binding upon it. It would only permit the affirmation that, under the circumstances, Hungary would not incur international responsibility by acting as it did. Lastly, the Court points

(Continued)

out that Hungary expressly acknowledged that, in any event, such a state of necessity would not exempt it from its duty to compensate its partner.

49. The Court will now consider the question of whether there was, in 1989, a state of necessity which would have permitted Hungary, without incurring international responsibility, to suspend and abandon works that it was committed to perform in accordance with the 1977 Treaty and related instruments.

50. In the present case, the Parties are in agreement in considering that the existence of a state of necessity must be evaluated in the light of the criteria laid down by the International Law Commission in Article 33 of the Draft Articles on the International Responsibility of States that it adopted on first reading.

51. The Court considers, first of all, that the state of necessity is a ground recognized by customary international law for precluding the wrongfulness of an act not in conformity with an international obligation. It observes moreover that such ground for precluding wrongfulness can only be accepted on an exceptional basis. The International Law Commission was of the same opinion when it explained that it had opted for a negative form of words in Article 33 of its Draft

> in order to show, by this formal means also, that the case of invocation of a state of necessity as a justification must be considered as really constituting an exception - and one even more rarely admissible than is the case with the other circumstances precluding wrongfulness ...
>
> (ibid., p. 51, para. 40)

Thus, according to the Commission, the state of necessity can only be invoked under certain strictly defined conditions which must be cumulatively satisfied; and the State concerned is not the sole judge of whether those conditions have been met.

52. In the present case, the following basic conditions set forth in Draft Article 33 are relevant: it must have been occasioned by an "essential interest" of the State which is the author of the act conflicting with one of its international obligations; that interest must have been threatened by a "grave and imminent peril"; the act being challenged must have been the "only means" of safeguarding that interest; that act must not have "seriously impair[ed] an essential interest" of the State towards which the obligation existed; and the State which is the author of that act must not have "contributed to the occurrence of the state of necessity".

Those conditions reflect customary international law.

Source: International Court of Justice, 1997, available at https://www.icj-cij.org/files/case-related/92/ 092-19970925-JUD-01-00-EN.pdf

4 Implementation, compliance and enforcement in IEL

Scholars distinguish between different stages in the process of IEL compliance, starting with actions aimed at facilitating compliance and then focussing on the mechanisms and processes through which IEL obligations are implemented.[55] Another relevant differentiation to be drawn here relates to the difference between compliance and enforcement. Traditionally, IEL scholarship has followed the distinction between primary norms, as those imposing or prescribing an action or omission, and secondary norms, as those determining the consequences of a breach of the norm.

The UNEP Guidelines, although of an advisory and non-binding nature, complement without altering the obligations assumed by States in MEAs defining the stages in the compliance process.[56] The Guidelines define 'compliance' in terms of the fulfilment by a State of its obligations under an MEA. According to the guidelines, while 'compliance' reflects the terminology used in an international context, 'enforcement' refers to those process which take place in the national sphere.

Compliance alludes to a process in which State behaviour is scrutinized and benchmarked against the requirements set out in the specific obligations (which can be obligations of content or procedural obligations).[57] A panoply of various actions are comprised in the process of compliance. In IEL, the initial approach was to attach negative consequences to the lack of compliance under SR rules; this has since evolved towards the adoption of mechanisms and procedures dealing with non-compliance, involving information, facilitation and management.

Implementation is a necessary step in the compliance cycle, which encompasses various actions, such as passing laws and regulations, including various enabling activities and steps that a State needs to take within its national territory to ensure the implementation of an MEA. This implies enacting national laws and regulations within the institutional framework, and capacity building and training to enhance enforcement competences and raise public environmental awareness. This often entails strengthening institutional frameworks, allocating responsibilities to national and local agencies, and assigning specific competences to carry out enforcement activities. The implementation stage also includes technical and financial assistance in creating and developing institutions, programmes and action plans oriented towards enforcement.

Enforcement, in turn, has traditionally been understood to take place in the national context, namely due to the specific features of decentralization observed in the international legal system. To undertake enforcement actions as a response to a lack of compliance or partial compliance, IEL relies on national law measures. Enforcement in national law can be shaped differently under national

55 Dupuy and Viñuales (n 26) at 270.
56 UNEP, Guidelines on Compliance with and Enforcement of Multilateral Environmental Agreements, available at https://wedocs.unep.org/bitstream/handle/20.500.11822/17018/UNEP-guidelines-compliance-MEA.pdf?sequence=1&isAllowed=y accessed 1 April 2020.
57 Brunnée (n 41).

norms, including procedures and actions carried out by a State through its competent authorities and agencies, to guarantee compliance through civil, administrative or criminal action.

Enforcement in IEL is limited to specific MEAs in the absence of a centralized system: Its main aim is to compel States to adjust to the behaviour prescribed by the norm within the scope of the respective treaty. Some cases dealing with environmental pollution and application of specific treaties in the field of IEL have reached the ICJ, which has created a chamber to deal with them. However, their number is quite reduced, the examination of the obligations is limited to a case-by-case analysis and the ICJ has not always adopted a clear stance on environmental protection on the international level. This lack of a centralized judicial system to check compliance with IEL is somewhat alleviated by the introduction of several mechanisms under MEAs. Non-compliance procedures (NCPs) instituted in the legal framework of various MEAs have resulted in a quantum leap in terms of compliance, as discussed below.

5 Special regimes. An overview of the main compliance mechanisms in international environmental law

The response to a breach of an IEL obligation has included a range of possibilities, ranging from non-compliance claims to a series of dispute settlement mechanisms, such as negotiation, consultation and quasi-judicial and judicial mechanisms. MEAs have modified this original landscape by introducing other mechanisms which aim to prevent the breach of obligations and assist States in their preparation to ensure compliance. These new mechanisms have added to the traditional dispute resolution mechanisms, creating a network of treaty bodies tasked with compliance and non-compliance procedures. Reporting and information processes are now common across the various MEAs which represent a stage before any formal procedure takes place. In practice, there are as many compliance systems as MEAs observable in IEL.

Incentives, financial mechanisms and technology transfers are used in IEL to foster compliance. Examples are the programs offered by World Bank, the International Development Bank and the International Finance Corporation (IFC). Some of these financial institutions, such as the World Bank, have a mixed record in compliance with IEL. The World Bank has come under scrutiny for funding projects with negative effects on the environment. Due to the pressure put on it by NGOs and activists, the World Bank changed its strategy to assume sustainable commitments, assessing the environmental impacts of the development projects it sponsors. The Strategic Environmental Assessment includes the participation of key stakeholders to give a say to 'those affected by policy, program, and plans'.[58] Clearing house mechanisms have proliferated in MEAs; the main function of these mechanisms is to coordinate information exchange between the parties to the respective treaty. Capacity building and

---

58 World Bank, *Strategic Environmental Assessment, Concept and Practice*, World Bank Environmental Strategy Note N14 (2005).

technology transfer also contribute to compliance. Other facilities at the international level have been established to provide financial and technical assistance to developing countries, promoting environmental protection, and supporting projects in the areas of biodiversity, climate change, international waters, land degradation, the ozone layer and persistent organic pollutants (POPs).

In a brief review of the judicial mechanisms available to settle environmental disputes, one must refer to the role of the International Court of Justice (ICJ) and other international courts and tribunals with a bearing in the area of environmental law, such as the International Tribunal for the Law of the Sea (ITLOS).[59] As stated in the Advisory Opinion on the Legality of the Use by a State of Nuclear Weapons in Armed Conflict, it was made clear that the Court can entertain environmental issues in an ever-changing international landscape. In 1993, the ICJ set up a permanent environmental chamber made up of seven members with the goal of providing a specific forum to decide cases with an environmental dimension. Yet the chamber was never used, and it was abolished in 2006.[60] At this point, it is worth underlining the fact that international environmental litigation takes place in other realms, such as investment and trade courts of law.[61] A detailed examination of the role of international courts and tribunals in international environmental litigation is presented in Chapter 6.

New specialized environmental courts and tribunals established in domestic jurisdictions around the world may indicate that the time is ripe to create a similar court or mechanisms to resort to international conflict resolution processes. Despite the possibility of submitting claims before a growing number of environmental courts and tribunals, their jurisdiction is still confined to territorial borders.[62] The creation of an environmental tribunal at the international level would require a new theoretical model capable of explaining and accommodating environmental adjudication.[63] While there have been initiatives to create an International Environmental Court and other multi-national environmental adjudication bodies, they have not received significant support from States.[64]

59 Tim Stephens, 'International Courts and Environmental Governance', in *International Courts and Environmental Protection* (Cambridge Studies in International and Comparative Law Cambridge University Press 2009), pp. 91–118.

60 International Court of Justice, *Chambers and Committees*, available at https://www.icj-cij.org/en/chambers-and-committees accessed 1 April 2020.

61 Philippe Sands, 'Litigating Environmental Disputes: Courts, Tribunals and the Progressive Development of International Environmental Law', in Tafsir Malick Ndiaye and Rüdiger Wolfrum (eds), *Environmental Law and Settlement of Disputes: Liber Amicorum Judge Thomas A. Mensah* (Brill Academic Publishers 2007), available at http://www.oecd.org/investment/globalforum/40311090.pdf accessed 1 April 2020.

62 Richard Lazarus, 'Pursuing 'Environmental Justice': The Distributional Effects of Environmental Protection (1992–1993) 87 *Northwestern University Law Review*, p. 787.

63 Ceri Warnock, 'Reconceptualising Specialist Environment Courts and Tribunals' (2017) 37(3) *Legal Studies*, pp. 391–417.

64 Ole Pedersen, 'An International Environmental Court and International Legalism' (2012) 24(3) *Journal of Environmental Law*, pp. 547–558.

The legal profession and non-profit organisations have favoured the creation of an international environmental court.[65]

More recently, Informal Environmental Conflict Resolution (IECR) mechanisms have emerged within the overall institutional justice architecture. Recent years have witnessed a proliferation of environmental courts and tribunals which conceivably furthers access to environmental justice, yet IECR and transnational law-making have become more significant.[66]

Most MEAs provide for a panoply of institutional arrangements, ranging from reporting mechanisms, including conferences, to the creation of institutional structures and embryonic international organisations in charge of the implementation of IEL. In a review of the typology of the mechanisms, many MEAs institute a 'Conference of the Parties' (COPs), assisted by a secretariat and sometimes scientific advisory bodies. This can be seen in the case of the COPs under the Vienna Ozone Convention and regular COPS under Chapter 7 of the Montreal Protocol or the Biodiversity Convention. Other examples of regular COPs are the Convention for the Protection of the Marine Environment of the North East Atlantic (OSPAR Convention) and CITES, which establishes a COP meeting at least every two years. The UNFCCC represents a more advanced model as it sets up an annual COP.

Non-compliance procedures (NCP) can address the failure by Contracting Parties in properly implementing their treaty obligations. Examples of NCPs instituted under MEAs include the 1987 Montreal Protocol to the 1985 Vienna Convention on the Protection of the Ozone Layer, the 1991 VOC and 1994 Sulphur Protocols to the 1979 Long-Range Transboundary Air Pollution Treaty, the 1992 Convention for the Protection of the Marine Environment of the North-East Atlantic and the 1997 Kyoto Protocol to the 1992 Framework Convention on Climate Change. All these MEAs create separate mechanisms for compliance, having been established under the treaty with nuances.

NCPs are seen as a response to the inadequacies of the SR regime and a move away from classical international law schemes that focus on material breach of treaty obligations in an attempt to properly address problems of environmental treaty compliance. Since its inception, IEL has been confronted with problems related to the particular nature of international environmental obligations, relating to the constraints in addressing treaty breaches due to a failure to act on the part of the responsible State. A specific shortcoming of the SR system which these NCPs attempt to mitigate is the unfitness of SR in preventing harm, especially with regard to the global commons.

65 Anne Mc Millan, *Time for an International Court for the Environment,* International Bar Association (IBA) 2011, available at https://www.ibanet.org/Article/NewDetail.aspx?ArticleUid=71b817c7-8026-48de-8744-50d227954e04 accessed 1 April 2020.

66 D.C Smith, 'Environmental Courts and Tribunals: Changing Environmental and Natural Resources Law around the Globe' (2018) 36(2) *Journal of Energy & Natural Resources Law,* pp. 137–140.

Table 2.1 Compliance mechanisms in MEAs: an overview

MEA	Compliance Mechanism	Periodicity	Dispute Resolution
UNFCCC	Conference of the Parties (COP)	Yearly	No specific conflict resolution mechanism
OSPAR	Meetings of the Parties (Art 23)	Action Plans	Dispute resolution mechanism of Article 32
CITES	COP (Art XI)	Resolution Conf. 14.3, CITES compliance procedures Submission of CITES annual reports	Negotiation, and by mutual consent, submit the dispute to arbitration, in particular that of the Permanent Court of Arbitration at The Hague (Art XVIII.1 and 2)
CBD	COP	At intervals determined by the parties (Art 26)	Negotiation, good offices, mediation. Subject to consent: Arbitration or Submission to the International Court of Justice (Art 27)

Source: Author's own elaboration.

Below is an overview of the institutional machinery of main MEAs. They have operated the transition from bilateral dispute settlement to multilateral means in different forms: mainly, intergovernmental commissions and meetings of treaty parties which coordinate policies, plans and programmes (Table 2.1).[67]

6 Innovative approaches to compliance: current trends and future scenarios

In defining the concept of innovation in IEL, various elements need to be taken into consideration: the manner in which mechanisms are designed in the legal instruments, the regulatory strategy, the introduction of other mechanisms outside law to reinforce compliance, the approach to liability and the role of the courts. It holds true that innovation depends upon the specific sub-system of IEL in question, e.g. water management, pollution or regulation of chemicals. This translates into various ways in which to understand innovation pertaining to the specific sub-area of IEL. Conversely, what can be defined as innovative in one sub-branch of IEL may not prove effective in another specific theme-area.

For most of the 20th century the overall approach to compliance with IEL has been responsive rather than preventative, focussing on specific sectors in

67 Boyle (n 19) at 230.

which enforcement is crucial. Responsive solutions take into account structures and systems of regulators and regulated sectors. 'Control and command' has been the predominant stance, laws laying down the prescribed standards (such as emissions and technology standards) by which compliance is monitored: a breach of an IEL obligation sets in motion compliance mechanisms.

Against this backdrop, innovation in IEL has the goal of keeping abreast of, preventing and adapting to environmental phenomena.[68] In defining innovation in the compliance with IEL, various aspects are revealed as crucial. The core elements of compliance distil inter-state elements. *Erga omnes* obligations have been hailed as a solution to the non-reciprocal character of environmental law obligations.

Innovation presents a variety of dimensions – social, economic, and technological – that should be integrated into the legal responses and mechanisms geared towards IEL. Whether these new international legal responses fulfil the needs and requirements of the society and environmental protection in what has been called the Anthropocene (an era dominated by human activity's influence on climate and the environment) is still an open question.[69]

Law-makers are confronted with evidence stemming from cases pertaining to non-compliance with IEL. The new legal design of various instruments brings about innovative procedures and mechanisms, which include various slants of innovation. Although, because of their features, NCPs are often treated as innovative mechanisms, there is a considerable overlap between them in some cases, and their effectiveness is disputed.[70] Other approaches that encourage compliance with IEL or enforcement include voluntary co-operation frameworks. Self-regulation emerges as an innovative practice. Within this idea of self-regulation, individual agreements are reached in targeted sectors between governments and specific industries to tackle specific environmental problems.

From the perspective of innovation, the introduction of market mechanisms may prove effective in addressing certain environmental problems. Equally relevant, different forms of liability regimes and measures may offer new methods to address environmental problems on the international level.[71]

In the pursuit of compliance, a recalibration of the IEL system is necessary to strike the right balance between economic progress and environmental protection. Newly independent and developing States' stances on IEL should also be taken into consideration to guarantee equality in international society.

68 Neil Craik, Cameron Jefferies, Sara Seck, and Tim Stephens (eds), *Global Environmental Change and Innovation in International Law* (Cambridge University Press 2018).

69 Louis Kotzé (ed), *Environmental Law and Governance for the Anthropocene* (Bloomsbury 2017).

70 Nils Goeteyn and Frank Maes, 'Compliance Mechanisms in Multilateral Environmental Agreements: An Effective Way to Improve Compliance?' (2011) 10(4) *Chinese Journal of International Law*, pp. 791–826.

71 Barboza 2010:4.

Bibliography

Birnie, P, Boyle, A, and Redgwell, C, *International Law and the Environment* (3rd edn Oxford University Press 2009).

Bodansky, D, *The Art and Craft of International Environmental Law* (Cambridge University Press 2011).

Boyle, AE, 'Saving the World? Implementation and Enforcement of International Environmental Law through International Institutions' (1991) 3(2) *Journal of Environmental Law*, pp. 229–245.

Boyle, Alan E, 'Relationship between International Environmental Law and Other Branches of International Law', in Daniel Bodansky, Jutta Brunnée, and Ellen Hey (eds), *The Oxford Handbook of International Environmental Law* (Oxford University Press 2008), pp. 125–146.

Brown Weiss, Edith, 'International Environmental Law: Contemporary Issues and the Emergence of a New World Order' (1993) 81 *Georgetown Law Journal*, p. 675.

Brunnée, J, 'ESIL Reflection Procedure and Substance in International Environmental Law Confused at a Higher Level?' (2016) 5(6) ESIL Forum, available at https://esil-sedi.eu/post_name-123/ accessed 1 April 2020.

CITES, Annexes I, II and III, available at Appendices I, II and III valid from 26 November 2019, available at https://www.cites.org/eng/app/appendices.php accessed 1 April 2020.

Craik, N, Jefferies, Cameron, Seck, Sara, and Stephens, Tim, (eds), *Global Environmental Change and Innovation in International Law* (Cambridge University Press 2018).

Crawford, J, *State Responsibility: The General Part, Cambridge Studies in Comparative and International Law* (Cambridge University Press 2014).

Delimatsis, P, *Research Handbook on Climate Change and Trade Law* (Edward Elgar 2016).

Downs, George W, Rocke, David M, and Barsoom, Peter N, 'Is the Good News about Compliance Good News about Cooperation?' (1996) 50(3) *International Organization*, pp. 379–406.

Dupuy, Pierre M and Viñuales, Jorge, *International Environmental Law* (CUP 2015), pp. 385–386.

Esposito, Robert, 'The ICJ and the Future of Transboundary Harm Disputes: A Preliminary Analysis of the Case Concerning Aerial Herbicide Spraying (Ecuador v. Colombia)', Pace International Law Review. Online Companion, August 2010, at 1.

European Commission, Handbook for Trade Sustainability Impact Assessment, European Commission, External Trade, March 2006, available at https://www.wto.org/english/forums_e/public_forum_e/sia_handbook.pdf accessed 1 April 2020.

Fitzmaurice, MA and Redgwell, C, 'Environmental Non-compliance Procedures and International Law' (2000) 31 *Netherlands Yearbook of International Law*, pp. 35–65.

Giljam, RA, 'Extended Application of 'Best Available Techniques' as a Means to Facilitate Ecological Governance' (2018) 36(2) *Journal of Energy & Natural Resources Law*, pp. 181–208.

Goeteyn, Nils Frank Maes, 'Compliance Mechanisms in Multilateral Environmental Agreements: An Effective Way to Improve Compliance?' (2011) 10(4) *Chinese Journal of International Law*, pp. 791–826.

Guruswamy, L, *International Environmental Law* (4th edn West 2012).

Guzman, Andrew T, 'A Compliance Based Theory of International Law' (2002) 29(90) *California Law Review*, p. 1823.

Hanqin, Xue, *Transboundary Damage in International Law* (Cambridge University Press 2003).

Hugé, Jean N Mukherjee, Fertel, C, Waaub, JP, Block, Thomas, Waas, Tom, Koedam, N, and Dahdouh-Guebas, F. 'Conceptualizing the Effectiveness of Sustainability Assessment in Development Cooperation' (2015) 7(5) *Sustainability*, pp. 5735–5751.

ILC, Chapter VI. Protection of the Environment in Relation to Armed Conflicts, available at https://legal.un.org/ilc/reports/2019/english/chp6.pdf. See also, Conflict and Environment Observatory, UN lawyers approve 28 legal principles to reduce the environmental impact of war, available at https://ceobs.org/un-lawyers-approve-28-legal-principles-to-reduce-the-environmental-impact-of-war/ accessed 1 March 2020.

Institut de Droit International, Session of Strasbourg – 1997, Responsibility and Liability under International Law for Environmental Damage (Eighth Commission, Rapporteur: Mr Francisco Orrego Vicuña), available at https://www.idi-iil.org/app/uploads/2017/06/1997_str_03_en.pdf accessed 1 April 2020.

International Court of Justice, Chambers and Committees, available at https://www.icj-cij.org/en/chambers-and-committees accessed 1 April 2020.

International Environmental Agreements (IEA) Database Project, 2002–2019, available at https://iea.uoregon.edu accessed 1 April 2020.

Kiss, Alex and Shelton, Dinah L, 'Strict Liability in International Environmental Law. Law of The Sea', in Tafsir Malick Ndiaye and Rüdiger Wolfrum (eds), *Environmental Law And Settlement of Disputes: Liber Amicorum Judge Thomas A. Mensah* (Brill Academic Publishers 2007). GWU Legal Studies Research Paper No. 345, GWU Law School Public Law Research Paper No. 345, available at SSRN: https://ssrn.com/abstract=1010478 accessed 1 April 2020.

Koivurova, T, *Introduction to International Environmental Law* (Routledge 2012).

Koskenniemi, Martti, Fragmentation of International Law: Difficulties Arising from the Diversification and Expansion of International Law, Report of the Study Group of the International Law Commission, A/CN.4/L.682 (13 April 2006), available at https://legal.un.org/ilc/documentation/english/a_cn4_l682.pdf accessed 1 March 2020.

Kotzé, Louis (ed), *Environmental Law and Governance for the Anthropocene* (Bloomsbury 2017).

Lazarus, R, 'Pursuing 'Environmental Justice': The Distributional Effects of Environmental Protection (1992–1993) 87 *Northwestern University Law Review*, p. 787.

Lindén, M, 'Environmental Damage in Armed Conflict to What Extent Do the Remedies Available for Environmental Damage in Armed Conflict Reflect the Polluter Pays Principle? The Cases of the Jiyeh Power Station and the Niger Delta Conflict' (University of Gottenburgh 2017), available at https://gupea.ub.gu.se/bitstream/2077/53076/1/gupea_2077_53076_1.pdf accessed 1 April 2020.

Machado Filho, H, 'Looking for Adequate Tools for the Enforcement of Multilateral Environmental Agreements: Compliance Procedures and Mechanisms', European Society of International Law 2018, available at https://esil-sedi.eu/wp-content/uploads/2018/04/Filho.pdf accessed 1 March 2020.

Mackielo, Andrea Laura, 'Core Rules of International Environmental Law' (2009) 16(1) *ILSA Journal of International & Comparative Law*, Article 11, pp. 257–299.

Maljean-Dubois, Sandrine, 'International Litigation and State Liability for Environmental Damages: Recent Evolutions and Perspectives' in Jiunn-rong Yeh (ed), *Climate Change Liability and Beyond* (National Taiwan University Press 2017), available at https://halshs.archives-ouvertes.fr/halshs-01675506/document accessed 1 April 2020.

Mc Millan, A, Time for an International Court for the Environment, International Bar Association (IBA) 2011, available at https://www.ibanet.org/Article/NewDetail.aspx?ArticleUid=71b817c7–8026-48de-8744–50d227954e04 accessed 1 April 2020.

Merkouris, P, 'The Principle of Sustainable Development and Best Available Technology under International Law', in K. Makuch and R. Pereira (eds), *Environmental and Energy Law* (Wiley-Blackwell 2012) pp. 37–60, 24.

Miles, Edward L, Andresen, Steinar, Carlin, Elaine M, Skjærseth, Jon Birger, Underdal, Arild, and Wettestad, Jørgen, *Environmental Regime Effectiveness Confronting Theory with Evidence* (MIT Press 2001).

OECD, available at https://www.oecd.org/chemicalsafety/risk-management/policies-on-best-available-techniques-or-similar-concepts-around-the-world.pdf accessed 1 April 2020.

Okowa, *Phoebe State Responsibility for Transboundary Air Pollution in International Law* (Oxford University Press 2001).

Palosaari, Tuomas, 'More than Just Wishful Thinking? Existence and Identification of Environmental Obligations Erga Omnes', University of Eastern Finland Law School, Master's Thesis Seminar, 27 March 2018, available at https://epublications.uef.fi/pub/urn_nbn_fi_uef-20180404/urn_nbn_fi_uef-20180404.pdf accessed 1 March 2020.

Pedersen, O, 'An International Environmental Court and International Legalism' (2012) 24(3) *Journal of Environmental Law*, pp. 547–558.

Plakokefalos, Ilias, 'Causation in the Law of State Responsibility and the Problem of Overdetermination: In Search of Clarity' (2015) 26(2) *European Journal of International Law*, pp. 471–492, available at https://doi.org/10.1093/ejil/chv023 accessed 1 March 2020.

Purdy, R, 'Satellites: A New Era for Environmental Compliance?' (2006) 3(5) *Journal for European Environmental and Planning Law*, pp. 406–413.

Sands, P, 'Litigating Environmental Disputes: Courts, Tribunals and the Progressive Development of International Environmental Law', in Tafsir Malick Ndiaye and Rüdiger Wolfrum (eds), *Environmental Law And Settlement of Disputes: Liber Amicorum Judge Thomas A. Mensah* (Brill Academic Publishers 2007), available at http://www.oecd.org/investment/globalforum/40311090.pdf accessed 1 April 2020.

Smith, DC, 'Environmental Courts and Tribunals: Changing Environmental and Natural Resources Law around the Globe' (2018) 36(2) *Journal of Energy & Natural Resources Law*, pp.137–140.

Stephens, T, 'Fragmentation of International Environmental Law', Chapter 10-Part III – Contemporary Challenges in International Courts and Environmental Protection (Cambridge University Press 2009), pp. 304–344, available at https://doi.org/10.1017/CBO9780511576034.012 accessed 1 April 2020.

Stephens, T, 'International Courts and Environmental Governance', in T. Stephens (ed.), *International Courts and Environmental Protection* (Cambridge Studies in International and Comparative Law Cambridge University Press 2009), pp. 91–118.

UNEP, Decision 14/30 of the Governing Council of UNEP, of 17 June 1987, available at https://wedocs.unep.org/handle/20.500.11822/29578?show=full accessed 1 March 2020.

UNEP, Guidelines on Compliance with and Enforcement of Multilateral Environmental Agreements, available at https://wedocs.unep.org/bitstream/handle/20.500.11822/17018/UNEP-guidelines-compliance-MEA.pdf?sequence=1&isAllowed=y accessed 1 April 2020.

UNEP, *Protecting the Environment during Armed Conflict: An Inventory and Analysis of International Law* (UNEP 2009).

United Nations Conference on Environment and Development, Rio de Janeiro, 3–14 June 1992, Agenda 21, available at https://sustainabledevelopment.un.org/content/documents/Agenda21.pdf accessed 25 March 2020.

Van Asselt, H, 'Managing the Fragmentation of International Environmental Law: Forests at the Intersection of the Climate and Biodiversity Regimes' (2012) 44 *International Law and Politics*, p. 1205.

Warnock, C, 'Reconceptualising Specialist Environment Courts and Tribunals' (2017) 37(3) *Legal Studies*, pp. 391–417.

World Bank, Strategic Environmental Assessment, Concept and Practice, World Bank Environmental Strategy Note N14 (2005).

Yang, Tseming and Percival, Robert V, 'The Emergence of Global Environmental Law' (2009) 36 *Ecology Law Quarterly*, p. 615.

3 International environmental law compliance in context I

Tools

1 International environmental compliance: instruments and actors

This chapter focusses on international environmental law (IEL) compliance in context, examining actors and tools. The chapter examines minimum compliance requirements and specific tools set out in MEAs. It deals with the actors and the progress in compliance, also examining cross compliance provisions (depending on the different specialised systems). It examines the practical guidelines on compliance with international legal commitments in the environmental field issued by international organisations.[1]

Treaty provisions may promote implementation and compliance with the norms; set up a completely new compliance system, generating an external supervisory body; or rely on pre-existing organisations to secure compliance. Wherever a treaty creates new mechanisms, institutions and techniques to foster compliance, there is an express (or implicit) conferral of powers on relevant organisations and authorities which may also comprise means to deal with non-compliance or violation of the provisions of treaties.

Factors which have an influence on compliance include *inter alia* self-interest on the part of the addressees of the norms, incentives created under the specific legal framework, implementation promotion mechanisms and tools, early warning systems, legal threats and external pressure derived from non-legal mechanisms.

Given the diverse nature of IEL, in the recent evolution there has been a proliferation of mechanisms and tools which reflect States' consensuses on crucial environmental problems. The sophistication observed in these mechanisms may include intergovernmental tools relying on states' actions without significantly altering state behaviour; more advanced mechanisms geared into MEAs could introduce new tools or even create a new market for environmental products or services, such as the programme REDD ('reducing emissions from deforestation and degradation') or emissions trading systems.

---

1 Abram Chayes and Antonia Handler Chayes, *The New Sovereignty: Compliance with International Regulating Agreements* (Harvard University Press 1995).

In the move from a hard compliance system to a non-compliance system, new stages in the non-compliance processes are observed. Some mechanisms are activated before non-compliance is detected and are aimed at completing a follow-up of the implementation of IEL norms. For this purpose, reporting mechanisms instituted under MEAs communicating information about a particular State's actions in implementing treaty provisions serve to monitor compliance. More formal mechanisms are put in place when a breach of the treaty occurs, requiring the determination of non-compliance and the adoption of measures as a consequence of a behaviour. Facilitation of compliance entails the adoption of a series of measures geared towards assisting State's in preparation wherever necessary to comply with treaty obligations. In turn, managing of non-compliance alludes to all the tools and mechanisms available to address lack of implementation. The legal basis for the establishment of non-compliance mechanisms is often set out in regional and international environmental agreements through an explicit provision ('enabling clause'). This stipulates the creation of a compliance mechanism within a certain period after the treaty comes into effect.[2]

Depending on how institutionalized the regime is and which administrative structure or organization has been chosen, there might be different actors performing roles in controlling the implementation by State Parties and assessing the effects of non-compliance. In each of these regimes, international institutions can have important responsibilities for monitoring the impact of various activities on the quality of the environment.

Monitoring and reporting have become the most-used mechanisms across the various MEAs, with the main treaty bodies creating mechanisms in this regard.[3] As for the evolution of the system, the Montreal Protocol on Substances that Deplete the Ozone Layer, introduced in 1987, represented the first of more advanced systems of compliance control in this particular environmental field. It meant a significant change in the means of ensuring compliance with MEAs, moving from a confrontational scheme based on compliance control to a system articulated around the ideas of cooperation and partnership.[4]

2 Gerhard Loibl, 'Compliance Procedures and Mechanisms', in Malgosia Fitzmaurice, David M. Ong, and Panos Merkouris (eds), *Research Handbook on International Environmental Law* (Edward Elgar 2010), pp. 427–428.
3 United Nations Environment Programme, *Compliance Mechanisms under Selected Multilateral Environmental Agreements* (UNEP 2007), available at https://wedocs.unep.org/bitstream/handle/20.500.11822/7507/-Compliance%20Mechanisms%20under%20selected%20Multilateral%20Environmental%20Agreements-2007761.pdf?sequence=3&isAllowed=y accessed 1 April 2020.
4 Ulrich Beyerlin, Peter-Tobias Stoll and Rüdiger Wolfrum, *Conclusions Drawn from the Conference on Ensuring Compliance with MEAs*, available at https://www.ippc.int/static/media/files/publications/en/1182346189781_conclusionsfrom_MEA_Compliance_conf.pdf accessed 1 April 2020.

The Montreal Protocol system[5] is innovative in several ways. As a non-adversarial mechanism, it encompasses three different institutional bodies in charge of compliance control.[6] From this institutional perspective, their respective functions are interlinked. The Secretariat (also known as the 'Ozone Sectretariat') performs not only a bureaucratic function, as it is in charge of compiling relevant data from the Parties, but also processes the data, analysing them to determine whether there is a lack of compliance.[7] Besides, the Secretariat is endowed with the power to begin an ad-hoc investigation while carrying out its duties, if it finds out that a Party has not fulfilled its obligations.[8] The Implementation Committee, composed of 'Parties', monitors compliance with the obligations. The political body is the Meeting of the Parties, comprising the members of the Protocol, and can take measures ranging from sanctions to assistance. These include adopting interim calls and recommendations: It can award or withhold assistance through the Multilateral Fund or the Global Environment Facility (GEF). The sanctions include the suspension of rights and privileges under the Protocol in trade and transfer of technology. Procedurally, this non-confrontational method of law enforcement may guarantee a better engagement of the Parties with MEAs, leading to better levels of compliance with treaty obligations.

Other systems instituted under MEAs still involve either a single compliance control body or a dual system with different bodies. For instance, under the international climate regime, the UN Framework Climate Convention foresees two separate paths for individuals and collective implementation.[9] Some other significant features of this system consist of the creation of the so-called Subsidiary Body for Implementation (Article 10), which does not possess direct monitoring powers regarding individual parties but instead performs functions in terms of collective implementation by assessing 'the overall aggregated effect of the steps taken by the Parties'.[10] Some issues regarding its inefficiency have been raised, taking into consideration its nature as an open-ended body. Government representatives who are members of this body should be 'experts on matters related to climate change'.[11] Another weakness is that the body does not have any investigative or recommendatory functions but rather examines the information received and assists the Conference of the Parties.

---

5 It comprises the Vienna Convention for the Protection of the Ozone Layer and the Montreal Protocol on Substances that Deplete the Ozone Layer (with all the amendments), including the 2016 Kigali Amendment to the Montreal Protocol. All treaties available at https://ozone.unep.org/sites/default/files/2019-12/The%20Ozone%20Treaties%20EN%20-%20WEB_final.pdf accessed 1 April 2020.

6 UNEP, *Handbook for the Montreal Protocol* (14th ed 2020), available at https://ozone.unep.org/treaties/montreal-protocol#nolink accessed 1 April 2020.

7 UNEP, the Ozone Secretariat, available at https://ozone.unep.org/ accessed 1 April 2020.

8 Montreal Protocol, Article 7.

9 UNFCCC, Articles 8, 9 and 10.

10 UNFCCC, Article 10.2.a.

11 Ibid.

In an overview of the functions performed by various compliance mechanisms observed under MEAs, the following methods can be identified:

- **Data-collection functions:** This function is related to self-reporting obligations on the part of State Parties and could consist of the mere registration of data submitted by governments (annual reports that the Parties themselves prepare on their national implementation) but could also include the outcomes of investigations undertaken by the international body itself.[12]
- **Review functions:** Compliance bodies scrutinise data and information submitted by governments on their performance and/or information obtained by other means. The revision can consist of acknowledging the submissions and tracking the information provided or performing an exhaustive evaluation of the reports, benchmarking them against operating parameters set out in the applicable legal framework.[13]
- **Investigative functions:** Under some MEAs the control body has powers to trigger an investigation if the information received is insufficient or inadequate. The compliance bodies can request additional written information from the respective government. These functions usually include the possibility to pose questions to the representatives of the government under scrutiny. Although some treaties allow compliance bodies to carry out 'on-site inspections', these require the consent of the State to be scrutinised.
- **Recommendatory functions:** Bodies of a political nature are usually tasked with making recommendations after drafting conclusions based on the information provided when there is evidence that the State in question has not fulfilled its obligations. Recommendations can be issued directly or indirectly, publicly or not. The decision to make a report or recommendations available publicly determines the amount of pressure placed on the State to comply (a sort of 'naming and shaming'). Sometimes, the expert or the scientific body issues the recommendations to the political body to address deficient compliance or non-compliance.[14]
- **Execution functions:** This implies adopting measures that are necessary under the relevant treaty that go beyond mere monitoring and evaluating activity. Measures can take different forms, ranging from calls for action to sanctions. Sanctions can be imposed in different forms, such as suspension of rights and membership (wherever applicable) and trade embargos due to

12 Ulrich Beyerlin, Peter-Tobias Stoll and Rüdiger Wolfrum, *Conclusions Drawn from the Conference on Ensuring Compliance with MEAs*, in Beyerlin, Stolll and Wolfrum (eds), *Ensuring Compliance with Multilateral Environmental Agreements: A Dialogue between Practitioners and Academia* (Brill 2006), available at https://www.ippc.int/static/media/files/publications/en/1182346189781_conclusionsfrom_MEA_Compliance_conf.pdf accessed 1 April 2020.
13 INECE, *Principles of Environmental Compliance and Enforcement Handbook International Network for Environmental Compliance and Enforcement*, pages 54 and 57 (INECE April 2009), available at http://themisnetwork.rec.org/uploads/documents/Tools/inece_principles_handbook_eng.pdf accessed 1 April 2020.
14 Ibid.

a lack of environmental compliance. Measures to be taken are not only puni-
tive; there are assistance measures (or sometimes suspending of assistance),
often used when a State lacks the technical capacities, administrative skills
and/or financial means to fulfil its obligations adequately.

These various functions or roles can be performed by one compliance body or
by more than one. Pursuant to the specific MEA's wording the tasks (revision,
investigation, recommendation) can be allocated to institutions of a diverse nature, and tasks will be accomplished by an expert or a scientific body. In order to
guarantee independence and effectiveness, these bodies are composed of highly
qualified individuals acting independently of any governmental influence.

MONTREAL PROTOCOL

Meeting of the Parties

Decisions on non-compliance: Argentina

Decision XIII/21: Compliance with the Montreal Protocol by Argentina

The Thirteenth Meeting of the Parties decided in decision XIII/21:

1 To note that Argentina ratified the Montreal Protocol on 18 September
   1990, the London Amendment on 4 December 1992, the Copenhagen Amendment on 20 April 1995, and the Montreal Amendment on
   15 February 2001. The country is classified as a party operating under
   Article 5(1) of the Protocol and its country programme was approved
   by the Executive Committee in 1994. Since approval of the country programme, the Executive Committee has approved $43,287,750
   from the Multilateral Fund to enable compliance in accordance with
   Article 10 of the Protocol;
2 Argentina's production baseline for Annex A, group I substances is
   2,745.3 ODP-tonnes. Argentina reported production of 3,101 and
   3,027 ODP-tonnes of Annex A, group I substances in 1999 and 2000
   respectively. Argentina responded to the Ozone Secretariat's request
   for data regarding the control period 1 July 1999 to 30 June 2000.
   Argentina reported production of 3,065 ODP-tonnes of Annex A,
   group I controlled substances for the production freeze control period
   of 1 July 1999 to 30 June 2000. As a consequence, for the control period 1 July 1999 to 30 June 2000, Argentina was in non-compliance
   with its obligations under Article 2A of the Montreal Protocol;
3 To request that Argentina submit to the Implementation Committee
   a plan of action with time-specific benchmarks to ensure a prompt

(Continued)

return to compliance. Argentina may wish to consider including in its plan actions to establish production quotas that will freeze production at baseline levels and support the phase-out;

4   To closely monitor the progress of Argentina with regard to the phase-out of ozone depleting substances. To the degree that Argentina is working towards and meeting the specific Protocol control measures, Argentina should continue to be treated in the same manner as a party in good standing. In this regard, Argentina should continue to receive international assistance to enable it to meet these commitments in accordance with item A of the indicative list of measures that might be taken by a Meeting of the Parties in respect of non-compliance. However, through this decision, the parties caution Argentina, in accordance with item B of the indicative list of measures, that in the event that the country fails to return to compliance in a timely manner, the parties shall consider measures, consistent with item C of the indicative list of measures. These measures may include the possibility of actions available under Article 4, such as ensuring that the supply of CFCs (that is the subject of non-compliance) is ceased and that importing parties are not contributing to a continuing situation of non-compliance.

Source: https://ozone.unep.org/treaties/montreal-protocol/
meetings/thirteenth-meeting-parties/decisions/decision-xiii21-
compliance?source=decisions_by_article_topic_relation&args%
5B0%5D=69&parent=2197&nextParent=2198

2 Tools and mechanisms of compliance: a. Hard law and soft-law instruments. b. International agreements c. Market-based mechanisms

A variety of processes and tools in IEL are put forward to implement substantive obligations imposed on States. Mechanisms instituted in IEL are designed to enhance compliance and to disincentivise non-implementation through the state responsibility regime. Most tools in IEL are adopted under both regimes.

Traditionally, the approach has been to respond to a breach of an IEL norm, then resort to judicial mechanisms and other forms of alternative dispute settlement (inquiry, mediation, conciliation and arbitration). Non-compliance mechanisms are quite a recent phenomenon in IEL, modelled upon the mechanism of the Montreal Protocol, which provided the blueprint for other similar mechanisms and tools.[15] Transplants between regimes and regions are also frequent.

15 Antonio Cardesa-Salzmann, 'Constitutionalising Secondary Rules in Global Environmental Regimes: Non-Compliance Procedures and the Enforcement of Multilateral Environmental Agreements' (2012) 24(1) *Journal of Environmental Law*, pp. 103–132.

Contemporary environmental treaty-making reflects the evolution of IEL, indicating a shift from a notion of compliance based on the notion of dispute settlement to a more nuanced stance, with emphasis on prevention and avoidance of non-compliance.[16]

a Hard-law and soft-law instruments

There is a significant literature on the interaction between so-called 'hard' and 'soft' law, much of which describes the relation of mutual support and argues that the 'soft' law relies on 'hard' law or on a 'hard' law framework to be effective. Usually, in IEL States negotiate non-binding legal instruments when it is not possible to reach consensus on binding commitments at the international level or when a binding treaty setting specific legal obligations faces obstacles in the Congress or Parliament. The expectation, then, is that soft-law instruments may address new environmental problems rapidly.

Generally, the distinction between hard law and soft law has had a clear effect on the different types of compliance mechanisms. Hard-law instruments in IEL, designed to ensure compliance with international environmental treaties, include a wide range of elements and techniques.[17] Treaty bodies instituted under specific regimes and management by international organisations are often the tools relied upon.[18]

In contrast, soft-law instruments do not entail compulsory enforcement to secure compliance with IEL. They may act in differing ways, such as incentives or disincentives by putting pressure on the defaulting States. Although they lack mechanisms for enforcement, states will seek to maintain good standing and reputation, and wrongdoing states will try to restore their reputation. Equally, soft law in IEL may lay the groundwork for the adoption of hard law. To illustrate, the Stockholm Conference on the Human Environment, held in 1972, nurtured the idea of prevention of environmental harm and fostered the concept of conservation and sustainable development.[19]

Nevertheless, the differentiation between hard and soft law seems artificial as often MEAs embody both types of norms. Boyle has exhaustively examined the functions which soft-law performs in international law.[20]

16 Alan Boyle, 'Saving the World? Implementation and Enforcement of International Environmental Law through International Institutions' (1991) 3(2) *Journal of Environmental Law*, pp. 229–245.

17 Jon Skjærseth, Olav Stokke and Jørgen Wettestad, 'Soft Law, Hard Law, and Effective Implementation of International Environmental Norms' (2006) 6(3) *Global Environmental Politics*, pp. 104–120.

18 Julio Barboza, *The Environment, Risk and Liability in International Law* (Brill 2010).

19 United Nations Conference on the Human Environment, Stockholm Conference on the Human Environment in 1972, available at https://legal.un.org/avl/ha/dunche/dunche.html accessed 1 April 2020.

20 Alan E. Boyle, 'Some Reflections on the Relationship of Treaties and Soft Law' (1999) 48(4) *International and Comparative Law Quarterly*, pp. 901–913.

The categorisation of international soft-law norms varies greatly. Some non-binding legal processes have been considered as 'elaborative soft law', consisting of authoritative norms referring to the interpretation, elaboration and application of hard law, and providing a general framework for the development of hard-law norms, like the UNFCCC.[21] Soft-law norms can also demonstrate emergent hard law, paving the way (or even calling) for the adoption of legally binding norms in a specific area of IEL, such as the Rio Declaration. An international declaration concerning environmental protection of a hortatory nature may lead by the development of state practice and opinion juris into customary international law. Soft-law norms can be 'hardened' by way of treaty or custom, as happened with environmental access rights and environmental impact assessment in IEL.[22]

In some areas of IEL, soft-law institutions may be more effective than hard-law mechanisms. This is the case in the protection of the marine environment and reduction of transboundary air pollution, amongst others. Soft-law institutions are more advantageous than legally binding ones as they do not require domestic ratification and offer greater flexibility and participation.[23] However, it should be borne in mind that arguably voluntary compliance with soft-law norms does not suffice to transmute soft law into legally binding norms for it falls short of the necessary will.[24] In this event a different law-making process should operate the transformation.

b International agreements

Treaty-negotiations in IEL often become quite lengthy. The international framework highlights the importance of compliance and enforcement with IEL. Reliance on international institutions presents limitations as they should be endowed with appropriate powers and responsibilities under the respective legal framework.

Institutional arrangements for the implementation of MEAs comprise a wide range of mechanisms, as follows: conferences or meetings of the Parties of the specific MEA, treaty Secretariats, advisory bodies and a wide variety of non-compliance procedures/mechanisms (reporting mechanisms tracking progress in the implementation of treaties, financial mechanisms, capacity building programmes). Against this background, the role of international organisations and compliance and enforcement networks in ensuring the effectiveness of the non-compliance procedure is pivotal.

---

21 Christine Chinkin, 'Normative Development in the International Legal System', in Dinah Shelton (eds), *Commitment and Compliance: The Role of Non-binding Norms in the International Legal System* (Oxford University Press 2003), pp. 30–31.
22 Ibid., at 30.
23 Skjærseth, Stokke and Wettestad (n 17), pp. 104–120.
24 Chinkin (n 21) at 31.

Of the different methods to ensure compliance, the following are most often considered by the mainstream literature: interpretation; research; data collection and/or dissemination; registration, reporting obligations and reporting back; assessments (monitoring and/or reporting) and reviews of performance; management by international organizations; and enforcement.

Interpretation is used in some MEAs as a compliance technique in line with the methods set out in the Vienna Convention on the Law of Treaties (VCLT). This is the case in the Montreal Protocol on Substances that Deplete the Ozone Layer, which relies on interpretation to clarify treaty obligations, particularly those included in Annex A.[25] This has enabled, for instance, the inclusion of an Ozone Depletion Potential figure by way of interpretation. The Meeting of the Parties (MOP) even adopted a non-compliance procedure that was not expressly set up in the Protocol, providing for an amicable resolution of disputes through a decision made by the MOP.[26] Equally, other MEAs refer to treaty interpretation as a compliance tool.

In turn, research plays an important role in the definition of technical aspects in order to determine the extent of environmental harm and the impacts of some processes necessary to identify if parties are treaty-compliant. The UNFCC mentions research as a way to establish the causes, effects and evolution of climate change-related events as well as the economic and social effects of ad-hoc policies and strategies (UNFCCC, Articles 4 (g) and 5). The Arctic Convention contemplates research as a way to help conservation. Similarly, the Biodiversity Convention foresees research as a contribution to conservation and sustainable use of biodiversity.[27] A common practice observed is the setting up of subsidiary bodies tasked with research functions, such as the Subsidiary Body on Scientific, Technical, and Technological Advice.[28]

Data collection and dissemination of research can assist in ensuring compliance. The traditional reporting back obligation often includes information sourced through research and data collection. Reporting activities can also be performed by the organisation on behalf of State Parties. All these activities aim to bring compliance issues to the attention of other states and the international organisation.

Reporting is closely related to the obligation to provide assessments and reviews: for instance, the UNFCCC, which allocates this responsibility on contracting States to submit to the COP an overview of the measures to implement the Convention and a detailed description of anthropogenic emissions determining the sources and the removal of carbon sinks (Articles 4 (1)(a) and (j), 12(1)(a) and (b)).

---

25 See also the resolution of controversies regarding the interpretation or application, available at https://unep.ch/ozone/pdf/Montreal-Protocol2000.pdf accessed 1 April 2020.

26 Lakshman Guruswamy, *International Environmental Law in a Nutshell* (4th edn West 2012), p. 74.

27 Biodiversity Convention, Article 12.

28 Biodiversity Convention, Article 25.

Panels of Experts, such as those established under the Montreal Protocol, the UNFCCC and the Biodiversity Convention, are envisaged to simplify the process of treaty amendment. These special scientific bodies are particularly helpful to interpret the protocols and scientific annexes. Parties may employ diplomatic or other means to enforce IEL when a party fails to comply with its obligations.

c Market-based mechanisms

Regulatory and market-based perspectives have determined the evolution of IEL and policy. The evolution has gone from a command-and-control legislative approach to the internalisation of environmental costs. Market-mechanisms can be seen as incentives to entice compliance.

Dissimilar patterns in the evolution of IEL have led to various mechanisms. Initiatives to take more advantage of the potential of market mechanisms have paved the way for the emergence of new types of instruments, which impact on the question of compliance.

The idea is that environmental protection requirements should be made an integral part of the economic process, which induces compliance. Analysing the motivations behind compliance, States decide to abide by IEL for numerous reasons.[29]

The emergence of a new paradigm of compliance with IEL represented the shift from the so-called 'command-and-control' approach to environmental policy instruments that involve the active participation of private parties: for instance, the question of joint implementation and the Clean Development Mechanisms (CDMs).

The shift from command-and-control to market-based instruments experienced in environmental policy instruments might be the result of the goal to internalise external environmental costs.

d Guidelines issued by international and regional organisations

In the quest to ensure compliance with IEL, non-binding guidelines produced by international and regional organisations support States and non-state actors in the implementation of IEL. Although non-binding, they provide actors with relevant insights in terms of implementation and, sometimes, capacity building.

e Environmental compliance networks

Considered a transnational law phenomenon, environmental compliance networks engage various actors involved in compliance with IEL. The International

---

29 Harold Hongju Koh, 'Why Do Nations Obey International Law?' (1997) Faculty Scholarship Series 2101, available at https://digitalcommons.law.yale.edu/fss_papers/2101 accessed 1 April 2020.

Network for Environmental Compliance and Enforcement (INECE) represents an example of a transnational network for assuring environmental compliance with laws designed to protect human health and the environment. INECE is a

> unique trans-governmental network dedicated to the three-fold mission of: raising awareness of the importance of environmental compliance and enforcement; strengthening capacity through the regulatory circle to implement and secure compliance with environmental requirements and developing networks for enforcement and compliance cooperation.[30]

The concept of Transnational Legal Orders (TLO) further assists us in understanding the main features of IECR. In the formulation of Halliday and Shaffer, a TLO 'seeks to produce order in a domain of social activity or an issue area that relevant actors (stakeholders) have construed as a problem of some sort or another'.[31]

A very active network in the international arena is the International Network for Environmental Compliance and Enforcement (INECE) that encompasses environmental compliance and enforcement practitioners devoted to raising awareness of compliance.[32] INECE also operates through regional networks which focus on regional environmental problems.

In Europe, the European Union Network for the Implementation and Enforcement of Environmental Law (IMPEL) was established as an international non-profit association of the environmental authorities of the European Union Member States; acceding and candidate countries of the EU, EEA and EFTA countries; and candidates for joining the European Community.[33]

There are other environmental compliance networks operating in other regions, such as the Americas and Asia.[34] The INECE has created various regional networks to strengthen compliance and enforcement networks at all levels of governance (national, regional and global). Regional networks are spread in Europe, the European Accession countries, Eastern Europe, the Caucasus and central Asian region, Australasia, Asia, East Africa, the Arab region, North Africa, North America and Central America.[35] The main goal of the networks is to enable and encourage compliance through a series of techniques, such as data collection, dissemination and fostering public participation in environmental matters.

---

30 Thomas Hale and David Held (eds), *The Handbook of Transnational Governance: Institutions and Innovations* (Polity Press 2011).
31 Terence C. Halliday and Gregory Shaffer (eds), *Transnational Legal Orders* (Cambridge University Press 2015).
32 INECE consists of a partnership of government and non-government enforcement and compliance practitioners from more than 150 countries. Information available at https://www.inece.org/about/ accessed 1 April 2020.
33 IMPEL has 55 members from 36 countries including all EU Member States, North Macedonia, Serbia, Turkey, Iceland, Kosovo, Albania, Switzerland and Norway.
34 Michael Faure, Peter De Smedt, and An Stas (eds), *Environmental Enforcement Networks: Concepts, Implementation and Effectiveness* (Edward Elgar Publishing 2015).
35 Ibid., at 88.

3 Procedural aspects of compliance: a. Procedural obligations and principles. b. Monitoring. c. Verification

Treaty provisions determine the type of obligations State Parties possess vis-à-vis each other, the type of commitments they are engaged in and the degree to which States are supposed to comply with the commitments under MEAs.

MEAs usually contain some provisions for information exchange. The Secretariat of each regime is usually endowed with the functions of receiving, processing and distributing the relevant data. Moreover, MEAs contain a number of activities to be performed jointly by the State Parties of the respective regime.

Substantive obligations are complemented by procedural duties under the primary norms of the regime. Substantive obligations are determined by treaty law and customary international law, such as the obligation to prevent environmental damage, curb emissions, protect biodiversity, include species on lists or control the transboundary movement of some substances.[36]

a Procedural obligations and principles

The main procedural obligations on the State Parties diversify depending upon the specific MEA and the specific legal framework containing obligations. Under Principle 10 of the Rio Declaration procedural rights consist of access to environmental information, public participation and environmental justice.

The freedom of access to environmental information is key to implementing other rights, such as public participation in environmental matters and access to environmental justice. Access to environmental information as a procedural right implies granting access to relevant environmental information in a range of manners.

The precautionary principle, although substantive, also has a procedural slant, shifting the burden of proof in cases in which there is a risk of environmental harm. These procedural principles, rooted in Principle 10, lead to an increased participation of NGOs and other obligations in the compliance procedure.

Procedural obligations enshrined in environmental treaties are aimed at assisting States in the implementation of substantive obligations by taking national measures and informing them about these by sending information to the respective institutions. The main goal behind providing this information is to create a database for monitoring compliance in addressing the evolution of the measures to regulate the problem. Procedural obligations are the basis upon which

---

36 Montreal Protocol on Substances that Deplete the Ozone Layer, 16 September 1987, Articles 2 to 21, annexes A,B, C and E; United Nations Framework Convention on Climate Change. Convention on International Trade in Endangered Species of Wild Fauna and Flora, 3 March 1973, Articles III–IV. Basel Convention on the Control of Transboundary Movements of Hazardous Wastes and their Disposal, 22 March 1989, Articles 4 and 6. Convention on Biological Diversity, Article 6.

non-compliance mechanisms function; they may vary according to the type of treaty provisions and the treaty bodies instituted.

As observed in the MEAs, state obligations with respect to compliance mechanisms vary significantly, from setting very general procedural obligations to providing information to more sophisticated systems, regulating all the details. Attempts to categorise these different systems may fail as compliance systems can develop over time according to the decisions adopted by the main treaty body.

More general compliance-related obligations foresee the reporting on implementation measures and monitoring of certain environmental variables over time to a treaty body (which might be the Secretariat or the Conference of the Parties): for instance, reporting obligations under the Long-range Transboundary Air Pollution (LRTAP) Convention concerning the reduction of sulphur emissions.[37] Sometimes, environmental treaties set specific deadlines and requirements for the communication of the information. Procedural obligations are further spelled out by asking the respective treaty bodies to verify the data submitted, asking them to complement the information submitted and collect more information on its own standing.

Examples of more detailed compliance mechanisms are those created by the Ramsar Convention. Clearly more complex mechanisms are those established by CITES and the compliance mechanism under the UNFCCC (Article 12).

b Monitoring

The gathering of information about compliance with international environmental standards, which is then fed back to the Secretariat instituted under the respective MEA, is a common mechanism. Reporting activities mainly consist of sending information back, which is then mainly used to monitor national compliance or determine whether the MEA has induced a new behaviour. Reporting requirements may vary from treaty to treaty, with some regimes, such as that in the case of atmospheric pollution, more detailed than others.[38] A lack of proper compliance with reporting requirements may lead to misreporting, which is a grey and borderline area in compliance.

Monitoring concerns the mechanisms for compiling information and reporting on the implementation of obligations. Diverse types of monitoring mechanisms are used in IEL, an area that has remained relatively undeveloped in relation to MEAs.[39]

---

37 1985 Helsinki Protocol on the Reduction of Sulphur Emissions or their Transboundary Fluxes by at least 30 per cent (Protocol on Sulphur emissions), Articles 4 and 6, available at https://www.unecce.org/env/lrtap/sulf_h1.html accessed 1 April 2020.

38 Jørgen Wettestad, 'Monitoring and Verification', in Daniel Bodansky, Jutta Brunnée, and Ellen Hey (eds), The *Oxford Handbook of International Environmental Law* (Oxford University Press 2008), pp. 975–976.

39 Philippe Sands, Jacqueline Peel, Adriana Fabra and Ruth MacKenzie, *Principles of International Environmental Law* (3rd edn CUP 2012).

Monitoring consists of the measurement over time of the quality of the environment against pre-established standards and activities, and the effects of such activities.

Despite transplants and mutual or reciprocal influences, monitoring systems respond to the nature of the environmental problem they relate to. Continuous emissions monitoring systems (CEMS) are common in the area of air pollution to control the emissions of chlorofluorocarbons (CFCs). The quest for transparency in monitoring refers to broadening the participation of civil society.

c *Verification*

Verification is an elusive concept in IEL compliance, sometimes deemed a synonym of monitoring: in this book it designates processes and mechanisms used to establish whether a State Party is in compliance with its obligations under the IEL.[40] Enforcement follows if, as a result of the verification process there is a determination of non-compliance with, infringement or breach of the obligations set by the MEA. A variety of differing verification regimes are observed in IEL, especially in the field of air pollution.

Scrutinising the effectiveness of MEAs entails the study of how compliance is verified. International agreements with a proper verification regime in place are more likely to succeed in both negotiation and implementation. The process of verification provides transparency and adds confidence to existing formal and informal agreements, fostering future cooperation and compliance. Beyond compliance with the specific agreement, verification processes produce information that can constitute the technical basis for future agreements and build consensus around key topics.

Verification covers the performance of investigative functions by treaty bodies. Verification is particularly relevant under the climate change regime, being one of the elements of the triad of 'measuring, reporting and verification' obligations.

Data are furnished by the same governments they are supposed to control. More or less independent sources of information, such as NGOs or media, may be helpful, especially in cases where governments try to sidestep their obligations or deliver no data at all.[41]

Under the Ramsar Convention, a mechanism for the communication and verification of information concerning protected sites is in place. The treaty body which deals with communications possesses broader powers, including the power to verify the information submitted, the power to request additional information and the power to collect independent information *proprio motu* by using other means.

---

40 Jesse H. Ausubel and David G. Victor, 'Verification of International Environmental Agreements' (1992) 17 *Annual Review of Energy and the Environment*, pp. 1–43.

41 Winfried Lang, 'Compliance Control in International Environmental Law: Institutional Necessities' (1996) 56 ZAOERV, available at https://www.zaoerv.de/56_1996/56_1996_3_a_685_695.pdf accessed 1 April 2020.

MONTREAL PROTOCOL

Decision XVII/22: Non-compliance with data-reporting requirements for the purpose of establishing baselines under Article 5, paragraphs 3 and 8 ter (d)

The Seventeenth Meeting of the Parties decided in Dec. XVII/22:

1 To note that Serbia and Montenegro has not reported data for one or more of the years which are required for the establishment of baselines for Annexes B and E to the Protocol, as provided for by Article 5, paragraphs 3 and 8 ter (d);

2 To note that that places Serbia and Montenegro in non-compliance with its data-reporting obligations under the Montreal Protocol until such time as the Secretariat receives the outstanding data;

3 To stress that compliance by Serbia and Montenegro with the Montreal Protocol cannot be determined without knowledge of those data;

4 To acknowledge that Serbia and Montenegro has only recently ratified the amendments to the Protocol to which the data-reporting obligation relates, but also to note that it has received assistance with data collection from the Multilateral Fund for the Implementation of the Montreal Protocol through the Fund's implementing agencies;

5 To urge Serbia and Montenegro to work together with the United Nations Environment Programme under the Compliance Assistance Programme and with other implementing agencies of the Multilateral Fund to report data as a matter of urgency to the Secretariat and to request the Implementation Committee to review the situation of Serbia and Montenegro with respect to data reporting at its next meeting.

Source:https://ozone.unep.org/treaties/montreal-protocol/meetings/seventeenth-meeting-parties/decisions/decision-xvii22-non

4 Compliance assistance: a. Financial mechanisms. b. Capacity building. c. Transfer of technology

During the process of compliance to implement international environmental obligations, there are different stages, such as information, facilitation and management. In the case of environmental damage, the final stage is enforcement, leading to reparation. The category of financial assistance evidences a new approach to compliance, unveiling different possibilities to assist States in fulfilling their obligations.

There is a variety of techniques concerning information gathering/reporting, the determination of damage and dealing with the specific consequences. Sometimes, the compliance processes have a preliminary stage that consists in compliance assistance. This is a strategic approach aligned with the prevention of a breach and of environmental damage. These mechanisms tackle the question of non-compliance before a problem of financial and technological capacity occurs.[42] Costs and technical expertise necessary to ensure compliance with MEAs may not be available in all States. Ideally, in terms of efficiency, the costs of compliance should be reduced.

All the different techniques can be grouped as 'compliance facilitation' and include capacity building, facilitating the creation of the necessary infrastructure for the implementation of environmental obligations; technical and financial assistance, mainly addressing developing States as well as efficiency; and minimising costs of compliance (for both developed and developing States). The diversity of mechanisms is such that no detailed categorisation is available, but broadly, the mechanisms can be divided into financial mechanisms, capacity building techniques and transfer of technology.[43]

Techniques to facilitate IEL compliance are multidimensional, involving legal aspects but also political and economic dimensions. These techniques are included below as innovative approaches adopted by environmental treaties. Technical assistance in the shape of capacity building and technology transfer is used to enhance compliance skills and capabilities. Various mechanisms are referred to in the provision of financial and economic assistance through development aid, environmental funds, technology transfer and capacity building, among others. In practice, many international environmental treaties provide for a mix of these different instruments. To facilitate the analysis of their specific contribution to IEL compliances, these different mechanisms are presented in separate sections.

a Financial mechanisms

Financial assistance has been included as an important technique in the implementation of MEAS, including public, private or public-private mechanisms. Chapter 37 of Agenda 21 refers to '(t)echnical cooperation, including that related to technology transfer and know-how, [which] encompasses the whole range of activities to develop or strengthen individual and group capacities and capabilities'.[44]

---

42 Pierre-Marie Dupuy and Jorge Viñuales, 'The Sources of International Environmental Law' in *International Environmental Law* (Cambridge University Press 2015), p. 271.

43 Frederick M. Abbott, 'Innovation and Technology Transfer to Address Climate Change: Lessons from the Global Debate on Intellectual Property and Public Health' (2009). ICTSD Programme on IPRs and Sustainable Development, Issue Paper No. 24, FSU College of Law, Public Law Research Paper No. 383, FSU College of Law, Law, Business & Economics Paper No. 09–18, available at SSRN: https://ssrn.com/abstract=1433579 or http://dx.doi.org/10.2139/ssrn.1433579 accessed 1 April 2020.

44 Agenda 21, Chapter 37, Rio de Janerio, Brazil, 3 to 14 June 1992.

An example of this is the Environment Fund set up under the UNEP, which is made up of contributions by Member States. The Fund provides a comprehensive worldwide framework for funding, focussing on the environmental dimensions of the 2030 Agenda.[45]

Each MEA has established a specific financial mechanism not only to support the implementation efforts of the State Parties but also to undertake projects that enhance the implementation of MEAs.

Financial assistance has spread quickly in IEL after the acknowledgement that developing country parties to MEAs may face significant costs as a result of implementing measures. Costs may make it difficult for States to undertake measures and change their behaviour. This acknowledgment led to the inclusion of provisions of a financial mechanism within MEAs. Some MEAs also include rules that govern the different financial mechanisms.

Under MEAs there are a plethora of financial of mechanisms with different formats:

- Trust Funds are a common format of these mechanisms adopted under the framework of regional conventions and MEAs. An example of this is the Regional Seas Conventions negotiated under the auspices of UNEP. These Trust Funds provide seed money to implement actions that are intended to enhance the capacity building of the parties in order to implement international environmental treaties.
- The Global Environmental Facility (GEF) operates as the financial mechanism for the Convention on Biological Diversity ('CBD') and the United Nations Framework Convention on Climate Change ('UNFCCC'). The GEF assists parties from developing countries with access to financial support to cover incremental costs resulting from the implementation of the respective MEA at the national level and the trans-boundary level. In addition, GEF Funds projects in certain focal areas, such as ozone depletion, climate change, biodiversity, shared water resources, desertification and chemicals.
- Other Funds: Under the UNFCCC and the Kyoto Protocol three new Funds to promote compliance by developing countries were established.

b Capacity building

Effective implementation as the main goal of IEL requires capacity building in the form of personnel training, expert assistance, infrastructure and reinforcements of the administrative structure. Under the framework of sustainable development and 'good environmental governance' capacity building at all levels, one of the main aims is fostering the participation of existing institutions and processes, and stakeholders.[46]

45 UN Environment Programme, *About the UN Environment Programme*, available at https://www.unenvironment.org/about-un-environment/what-we-do accessed 1 April 2020.
46 UN, *Environmental Law Capacity Building Programme for Sustainable Development*, available at https://sustainabledevelopment.un.org/partnership/?p=1523 accessed 1 April 2020.

This mechanism has traditionally been contained in environmental treaties and in other similar treaties, such as the World Heritage Fund that was created to assist State Parties in identifying sites of outstanding value, including those of natural value.[47] This approach is by no means confined to cultural heritage and is then applied in IEL.

The application of the 'common but differentiated responsibilities' principle led to different obligations for developed and developing countries, requiring that developed countries take the lead in protecting the ozone layer and stopping the use of ozone-depleting substances.

Principle 7 of the Rio Declaration, listing some basic principles of IEL, establishes:

> States shall cooperate in a spirit of global partnership to conserve, protect, and restore the health and integrity of the Earth ecosystem. In view of the different contributions to global environmental degradation, States have common but differentiated responsibilities. The developed countries acknowledge the responsibility that they bear in the international pursuit of sustainable development in view of the pressures their societies place on the global environment and of the technologies and financial resources they command.[48]

Mechanisms providing financial, technical and technological assistance to developing countries to support them in building up their environment management capacity are numerous; they have been incorporated into international environmental treaty practice.

c Technology transfer

Technology transfer ('TT' or 'Tech Trans') is of the utmost importance for developing countries in the IEL and is vital for global environmental governance. Many horizontal UN goals and instruments, as well as various MEAs, embody specific provisions on the transfer of technology, including transfer of intellectual property rights or technical expertise to the public or private sectors.

For example, Agenda 21 in Chapter 34, addressing 'environmentally sound technologies', refers repeatedly to the need to 'strengthen the technical and institutional capacity in developing countries'.[49] TT entails more complex support operations that entail a certain level of financial assistance, provision of technologies and the transfer of intellectual property rights ('IPRs') relating to patents and licences, raising questions of competitiveness and trade issues.

---

47 International Assistance, *Acting for World Heritage worldwide*, available at https://whc.unesco.org/en/intassistance accessed 1 April 2020.
48 1992 Rio Declaration, Principle 7.
49 Agenda 21, Chapter 34.

The conditions for and the state of technology transfer depend upon the sector: for instance, traditionally, this has been the case in conservation and sustainable use of biodiversity, climate change and the control of persistent organic pollutants.[50] Other examples of technical assistance are foreseen in the Montreal Protocol financed by its Multilateral Fund, particularly after the 'London Amendment' which established it and introduced a provision on the 'transfer of technology'.[51] Although there is a financial component to the technology transfer, the spirit of the reform was intended to make the treaty more inclusive and take more States on board, particularly developing and emerging countries, assisting them with the substitution of controlled substances. Therefore, the amendment allowed sufficient time for these countries to gradually convert their industrial infrastructure into the new system, allowing for the phase out of the previously used substances, with the help of financial assistance and transfer of IPRs. To deal with some issues more effectively, compulsory licences to use IPRs in the development of specific mechanisms are common, like those adopted in the climate change regime.

5 Spaces for voluntary compliance

States obey international law for multiple reasons, particularly when there is a binding norm mandating a certain behaviour so that the threat of the sanction functions as a deterrence. Under 'soft' IEL, voluntary commitments undertaken by States are based on their willingness to take on environmental commitments.[52] In some sectors, these voluntary commitments are widely spread, such as in the global climate change regime or in other areas of regional importance, such as waste management. In an attempt to define voluntary compliance, it is conceived as an alternative to inter-state or state-imposed regulations on a state or a company's behaviour.[53] Proponents of voluntary compliance draw attention to the flexibility that it allows, enabling States to better adapt to changing circumstances. Along with the States, international enterprises have developed

50 Christian Prip, G. Kristin Rosendal, and Morten Walløe Tvedt, *The State of Technology Transfer Obligations in Global Environmental Governance and Law: Biodiversity Conservation and Sustainable Use,* available at https://www.sprep.org/attachments/VirLib/Global/state-technology-transfer.pdf accessed 1 April 2020.

51 *The London Amendment (1990): The Amendment to the Montreal Protocol Agreed by the Second Meeting of the Parties (London, 27–29 June 1990)*, Article 10, available at https://ozone.unep.org/treaties/montreal-protocol/amendments/london-amendment-1990-amendment-montreal-protocol-agreed accessed 1 April 2020.

    2. b. Amendment to the Montreal Protocol on Substances that Deplete the Ozone Layer, London, 29 June 1990. The amendment was adopted by Decision II/2 of 29 June 1990 at the Second Meeting of the Parties to the Montreal Protocol on Substances that Deplete the Ozone Layer, available at https://treaties.un.org/Pages/ViewDetails.aspx?src=TREATY&mtdsg_no=XXVII-2-b&chapter=27&clang=_en accessed 1 April 2020.

52 Koh (n 29).

53 Marcia Gelpe, 'Environmental Enforcement: Encouraging Voluntary Compliance with Environmental Laws' (1996) 19(1) *Israel Environment Bulletin*, p. 5756.

a predominant role in promoting voluntary compliance with international environmental obligations.

What are the main reasons for voluntary compliance with IEL? Compliance with international accords through binding legal mechanisms is often imperfect and concerns only States (so far) operating on the international level. The inadequate choice of proper enforcement of national environmental laws and regulations often leads to lack of implementation.[54] This broader approach to compliance emphasises the adoption of voluntary commitments in paving the way for the adoption of more stringent commitments imposed by binding norms. Some international environmental instruments already rely on voluntary compliance by the parties, such as in the climate change regime.

Examples of voluntary compliance are disseminated throughout the areas of IEL, particularly in forestry and air pollution.[55] Based on the experience obtained through the voluntary approaches used in some sectors, these approaches can expand to cover other areas of IEL. Differences in the approach taken by different sectors bring various implications to IEL as a whole. The underlying causes for these mechanisms are the need to enhance implementation and compliance with IEL. In international law, clearly, States exercising their sovereignty can take on voluntary commitments to address IEL issues.

Voluntary approaches present several challenges: namely coverage, transparency and credibility of the mechanisms. Furthermore, other issues concern the monitoring and sanctions for non-compliance. Based on the experiences of voluntary compliance so far it is possible to draw more general lessons to improve environmental performance and compliance with IEL. In the context of other branches of international law, several voluntary compliance projects have been undertaken to Fund, for instance, emission reduction technologies or mechanisms.

Voluntary commitments are thought to provide greater flexibility than traditional legally binding commitments; States enjoy more flexibility in order to tackle specific or new environmental problems as they arise. On average, transaction costs are significantly less. Leading by example, through the assumption of voluntary commitments under non-binding legal instruments, States can set expectations about the way in which States and other actors should behave, fostering common values.

Consensus on non-binding legal instruments is easier to achieve in IEL, as demonstrated by the climate change regimen and environmental sustainability. Examples of this are the voluntary commitments made by States to control

54 Geoffrey Palmer, 'New Ways to Make International Environmental Law' (1992) 86(2) *The American Journal of International Law*, pp. 259–283.
55 Neil Gunningham and Darren Sinclair, 'Voluntary Approaches to Environmental Protection: Lessons from the Mining and Forestry Sectors', OECD Global Forum On International Investment Conference on Foreign Direct Investment and the Environment – Lessons to be Learned from the Mining Sector, 7–8 February 2002, available at https://www.oecd.org/env/1819792. pdf accessed 1 April 2020.

greenhouse gases (GHGs), as demonstrated by the Copenhagen Agreements,[56] and to adopt measures promoting sustainability, lacking a binding legal instrument.

Voluntary compliance can be a win for all the parties involved, creating more transparency and accountability. Environmental impact assessments make voluntary compliance procedures transparent and more rights-based, including public participation. Engaging the community is key when approving large projects. It means having a multi-pronged approach to compliance, including all the possible avenues to guarantee IEL implementation.

One of the controversial aspects is how to strengthen environmental compliance and enforcement in the event of a breach: for instance, when pollution incidents occur. As possible solutions, one can require an independent environmental review of actions. Environmental compliance certificates could also contribute to fostering the implementation of environmental norms. Another related controversial issue concerns the wording in which the voluntary commitments are formulated, which could turn them into unenforceable commitments. 'Loose wording' often leads to less enforceable commitments. There may be weakness in the norms regulating voluntary compliance or a lack of appropriate legal framework to regulate compliance. To reduce, minimise or avoid lack of compliance, different organisations should follow up on projects or voluntary commitments.

There are certain similarities between the different models of voluntary compliance, and some lessons can be learned from each other.[57] There may be inter-governmental aspects across similar types of projects, even in transboundary cases. Technology can influence regulations, and it is possible to use technology to drive change and provide significant compliance. Data systems should allow for a proper follow-up on the different processes of voluntary compliance. It is worth asking about the role which NGOs and agencies play in compliance. NGOs can facilitate data for institutions to make a follow-up. Indigenous peoples and indigenous communities should have the opportunity to participate in voluntary compliance projects that involve them. This can include working to build these relationships, communicate with the various stakeholders and develop a voluntary compliance cycle. Another significant feature is the power to form the conditions and commitments, and decide on the language and whether it is enforceable. Equally important is determining who does the checking and how the veracity of data is ensured. There are different degrees of innovation observed in different IEL provisions. Voluntary compliance demonstrates that IEL never stands still; it always changes.

---

56 Agreement adopted at the Climate Conference in Copenhagen, Denmark, in December 2009.

57 Harold K. Jacobson and Edith Brown Weiss, 'Strengthening Compliance with International Environmental Accords: Preliminary Observations from a Collaborative Project' (1995) 1(2) *Global Governance*, pp. 119–148.

Bibliography

Abbott, Frederick M, 'Innovation and Technology Transfer to Address Climate Change: Lessons from the Global Debate on Intellectual Property and Public Health' Issue Paper No. 24 (2009), available at https://www.files.ethz.ch/isn/104368/2009_06_innovation_and_technology_transfer.pdf accessed 1 April 2020.

Ausubel, Jesse H and Victor, David G, 'Verification of International Environmental Agreements' (1992) 17 *Annual Review of Energy and the Environment*, pp. 1–43.

Barboza, J, *The Environment, Risk and Liability in International Law* (Brill 2010).

Beyerlin, U, Stoll, Peter-Tobias and Wolfrum, Rüdiger, Conclusions Drawn from the Conference on Ensuring Compliance with MEAs, available at https://www.ippc.int/static/media/files/publications/en/1182346189781_conclusionsfrom_MEA_Compliance_conf.pdf accessed 1 April 2020.

Boyle, A, 'Saving the World? Implementation and Enforcement of International Environmental Law through International Institutions' (1991) 3(2) *Journal of Environmental Law*, pp. 229–245.

Boyle, A, 'Some Reflections on the Relationship of Treaties and Soft Law' (1999) 48(4) *International and Comparative Law Quarterly*, pp. 901–913.

Cardesa-Salzmann, A, 'Constitutionalising Secondary Rules in Global Environmental Regimes: Non-Compliance Procedures and the Enforcement of Multilateral Environmental Agreements' (2012) 24(1) *Journal of Environmental Law*, pp. 103–132.

Chayes, A and Handler Chayes A, *The New Sovereignty: Compliance with International Regulating Agreements* (Harvard University Press 1995).

Chinkin, C, 'Normative Development in the International Legal System' in Dinah Shelton (ed.), *Commitment and Compliance: The Role of Non-binding Norms in the International Legal System* (Oxford University Press 2003), pp. 30–31.

Dupuy, Pierre M and Vinuales, Jorge, 'The Sources of International Environmental Law.' in PM Dupuy and J Vinuales (eds.), *International Environmental Law* (Cambridge University Press 2015), p. 271.

Faure, Michael, De Smedt, Peter, Stas, An, (eds), *Environmental Enforcement Networks: Concepts, Implementation and Effectiveness* (Edward Elgar Publishing 2015).

Gelpe, Marcia, 'Environmental Enforcement: Encouraging Voluntary Compliance with Environmental Laws' (1996) 19(1) *Israel Environment Bulletin*, p. 5756.

Gunningham, Neil and Sinclair, Darren, 'Voluntary Approaches to Environmental Protection: Lessons from the Mining and Forestry Sectors', OECD Global Forum On International Investment Conference on Foreign Direct Investment and the Environment – Lessons to be Learned from the Mining Sector, 7–8 February 2002, available at https://www.oecd.org/env/1819792.pdf accessed 1 April 2020.

Guruswamy, L, *International Environmental Law in a Nutshell* (4th edn West 2012), p. 74.

Hale, Thomas and Held, David, (eds), *The Handbook of Transnational Governance: Institutions and Innovations* (Polity Press 2011).

Halliday, Terence C and Shaffer, Gregory, (eds), *Transnational Legal Orders* (Cambridge University Press 2015).

ICTSD Programme on IPRs and Sustainable Development, Issue Paper No. 24, FSU College of Law, Public Law Research Paper No. 383, FSU College of Law, Law, Business & Economics Paper No. 09–18, available at SSRN: https://ssrn.com/abstract=1433579 or http://dx.doi.org/10.2139/ssrn.1433579 accessed 1 April 2020.

INECE, Principles of Environmental Compliance and Enforcement Handbook International Network for Environmental Compliance and Enforcement, pages 54 and 57

(INECE April 2009), available at http://themisnetwork.rec.org/uploads/documents/Tools/inece_principles_handbook_eng.pdf accessed 1 April 2020.

Jacobson, Harold K and Weiss, Edith Brown, 'Strengthening Compliance with International Environmental Accords: Preliminary Observations from a Collaborative Project' (1995) 1(2) *Global Governance*, pp. 119–148.

Koh, Harold Hongju, 'Why Do Nations Obey International Law?' (1997) Faculty Scholarship Series 2101, available at https://digitalcommons.law.yale.edu/fss_papers/2101 accessed 1 April 2020.

Lang, Winfried, 'Compliance Control in International Environmental Law: Institutional Necessities' (1996) 56 ZAOERV, available at https://www.zaoerv.de/56_1996/56_1996_3_a_685_695.pdf accessed 1 April 2020.

Loibl, G, 'Compliance Procedures and Mechanisms', in Malgosia Fitzmaurice, David M Ong, and Panos Merkouris (eds), *Research Handbook on International Environmental Law* (Edward Elgar 2010), pp. 427–428.

Palmer, Geoffrey, 'New Ways to Make International Environmental Law' (1992) 86(2) *The American Journal of International Law*, pp. 259–283.

Prip, C, Rosendal, G Kristin, and Tvedt, Morten Walløe, The State of Technology Transfer Obligations in Global Environmental Governance and Law: Biodiversity Conservation and Sustainable Use, available at https://www.sprep.org/attachments/VirLib/Global/state-technology-transfer.pdf accessed 1 April 2020.

Sands, Philippe, Peel, Jacqueline, Fabra, Adriana, and MacKenzie, Ruth, *Principles of International Environmental Law* (3rd edn CUP 2012).

Skjærseth, J, Stokke, Olav, and Wettestad, Jørgen, 'Soft Law, Hard Law, and Effective Implementation of International Environmental Norms' (2006) 6(3) *Global Environmental Politics*, pp. 104–120.

UN Environment Programme, About the UN Environment Programme, available at https://www.unenvironment.org/about-un-environment/what-we-do accessed 1 April 2020.

UN, Environmental Law Capacity Building Programme for Sustainable Development, available at https://sustainabledevelopment.un.org/partnership/?p=1523 accessed 1 April 2020.

UNEP, *Handbook for the Montreal Protocol* (14th ed 2020), available at https://ozone.unep.org/treaties/montreal-protocol#nolink accessed 1 April 2020.

UNEP, the Ozone Secretariat, available at https://ozone.unep.org/ accessed 1 April 2020.

United Nations Conference on the Human Environment, Stockholm Conference on the Human Environment in 1972, available at https://legal.un.org/avl/ha/dunche/dunche.html accessed 1 April 2020.

United Nations Environment Programme, Compliance Mechanisms under Selected Multilateral Environmental Agreements (UNEP 2007), available at https://wedocs.unep.org/bitstream/handle/20.500.11822/7507/-Compliance%20Mechanisms%20under%20selected%20Multilateral%20Environmental%20Agreements-2007761.pdf?sequence=3&isAllowed=y accessed 1 April 2020.

Wettestad, Jørgen, 'Monitoring and Verification', in Daniel Bodansky, Jutta Brunnée, and Ellen Hey (eds), *The Oxford Handbook of International Environmental Law* (Oxford University Press 2008), pp. 975–976.

4   International environmental law compliance in context II

Actors

1 Introduction

Actors in international environmental law (IEL) compliance have evolved to include a wide range of non-state actors. However, the latter still play a limited formal role in compliance with IEL. Both individually and together, these numerous factors represent challenges for the international environmental governance system.

International law subjects operating in the field of environmental law continue to be predominantly States, but they now also include the ever-growing and prominent participation of other subjects, such as corporations, international non-governmental organisations, local communities and indigenous peoples. This is a topic at the intersection of IEL and international environmental politics which has contributed various theories about environmental actors, providing different nuances.[1]

As regards compliance, coordination and cooperation between the various actors is crucial. The legal design, the institutional setting and the wording of MEAs are still state-centric, with more openness to participation of non-state actors in the new generation of contemporary treaties. With that caveat in mind, this chapter analyses the part the various actors play in shaping IEL compliance.

2 The 'traditional actors' vs 'other actors'

Actors in IEL perform various functions in the areas of governance, law-making, policymaking and decision-making (including compliance procedures). Within the institutional framework of global environmental governance, it is still international institutions that are mainly in charge of normative development.[2]

---

1 Andrew Hurrell and Benedict Kingsbury, *The International Politics of the Environment: Actors, Interests, and Institutions* (Clarendon Press 1992).
2 Helen Hey, 'International Institutions', in Daniel Bodansky, Jutta Brunnée, and Ellen Hey (eds), *The Oxford Handbook of International Environmental Law* (Oxford University Press 2008), pp. 755–765.

a States and non-state actors

States, alongside international organisations, as derivative subjects of international law, have been considered the classical actors in the IEL realm, including compliance.[3] Increasingly important, however, are international organisations or international institutions. The evolution of the concept of international legal personality (ILP) has had many turning points. Based on the principle of equality amongst States, compliance with IEL presents remarkable differences between developed and developing States, which is translated into the application of the principle of common but differentiated responsibilities.[4]

Despite being involved in environmental law processes and performing activities which entail harm for the environment, non-state actors are not directly accountable for fulfilling international obligations pertaining to the protection of the environment. In principle, only States and international organisations (wherever this is provided for) respond internationally in cases of non-compliance. Some attempts have been made to allocate responsibilities to non-state actors in the event of major environmental damages or cases of transboundary pollution by articulating both hard and soft-law solutions.[5]

Since much emphasis is placed on the obligations to be fulfilled by international law subjects in IEL, it is worth looking at how international personality is regulated. Theories about international legal personality are also applicable in the field of IEL, with some nuances.[6]

Many activities which can cause transboundary environmental harm originate in private parties' actions or omissions that result in non-compliance. Whereas states as 'traditional actors' have continued to be direct addressees of IEL obligations, other non-state actors have emerged in different areas playing an increasing role in standard-setting and implementation of IEL norms. Due diligence obligations point to the accountability of non-state actors: particularly that of multinational corporations.[7]

The definition and attribution of obligations in IEL can be broad in scope. In the corpus of IEL, compliance issues are mostly stipulated through international

---

3 Thilo Marauhn, Chapter 31 'Changing Role of the State', in Daniel Bodansky, Jutta Brunnée, and Ellen Hey (eds), *The Oxford Handbook of International Environmental Law* (Oxford University Press 2008), pp. 729–746.

4 Duncan French, 'Developing States and International Environmental Law: The Importance of Differentiated Responsibilities' (2000) 49(1) *The International and Comparative Law Quarterly*, pp. 35–60.

5 André Nollkaemper, 'Responsibility of Transnational Corporations in International Environmental Law: Three Perspectives', in Gerd Winter (ed), *Multilevel Governance of Global Environmental Change – Perspectives from Science, Sociology and the Law* (Cambridge University Press 2006), pp. 179–199.

6 J.E. Nijman, *The Concept of International Legal Personality, An Inquiry into the History and Theory of International Law* (T.M.C. Asser Press 2004).

7 See for instance, the Draft UN treaty on transnational corporations and human rights, available at https://www.ohchr.org/Documents/HRBodies/HRCouncil/WGTransCorp/OEIGWG_RevisedDraft_LBI.pdf accessed 1 March 2020.

conventional law, i.e. sectoral treaties regulating various environmental problems. The vagueness in the formulation of the norm can facilitate compliance by different actors or lower the bar required for States to adjust their conduct to the expected goal set in the norm. Low compliance may originate from setting ambitious treaty goals without providing the means to achieve them. On the other hand, allowing too much flexibility in reaching the targets may give actors a false expectation of compliance. This is illustrated by the targets set in the 1960s by the International Whaling Commission (IWC), formed under the International Whaling Convention, which adopts regulations and sets quotas on the number of whales that can be killed.[8]

IEL is made up of sector-specific norms, being highly fragmented with regard to the different environmental sectors and vertically between the various government levels. Consequently, compliance with IEL is fragmented, multi-layered and takes place on different levels. These problems are common to the various legal systems which constitute the IEL system. Equally, some non-state processes in the area of environmental protection, such as standard-setting, which are related to compliance have been excluded from formal law-making in terms of sources of IEL. The diverse functions performed in national law by domestic institutions cannot be exactly mimicked in the international law realm: law-making, law-interpreting, law-implementing and law-enforcing roles have no equivalent in IEL.

Putting all this in an environmental context, most actors in IEL continue to be States in all the various IEL realms, from law-making to policymaking, including compliance. The most widely held view in IEL is that states are the ones responsible in cases of non-compliance, but, progressively, non-state actors may be held accountable for activities that cause transboundary harm to the environment. Here, there is a sharp contrast between domestic law and international law as the former provides for liability for non-compliance by private parties.

National environmental agencies or equivalent national departments have emerged in the landscape of compliance. Although these agencies and governmental bodies do not respond directly, they are tasked with the implementation of MEAs, key to ensuring compliance. Actors in the implementation of international environmental obligations include government officials, legal advisers and domestic courts.

Other grassroots initiatives in IEL have shifted the focus to non-state actors, such as under certain regimes.[9] For instance, the CBD provides for the participation of indigenous peoples and other communities in benefit-sharing agreements.

---

8 International Whaling Convention, *History and Purpose*, available at https://iwc.int/history-and-purpose accessed 1 March 2020.
9 Nicolas Pauchard, 'Access and Benefit Sharing under the Convention on Biological Diversity and Its Protocol: What Can Some Numbers Tell Us about the Effectiveness of the Regulatory Regime?' (2017) 6 *Resources*, p. 11.

Compliance with IEL can take place on the domestic or on the international level. It seems that there is a preference for international or domestic courts, as seen in some cases of damage caused by pollution of international watercourses, which may determine the application of different standards of liability.[10]

International institutions and organisations (with universal and regional scope) undertake various functions in IEL compliance. The different roles of international institutions in global environmental governance also shape contemporary IEL. The controversial question which arises regards the restrictions faced in IEL compliance and the weaknesses of accountability under international law.

Global organisations, like the United Nations (UN), which did not originally have any specific bearing on the field of environmental law have expanded their scope to include environmental protection. Other international organisations which do not institute an organ tasked with the protection of the environment have increased their action in the international environmental law realm.

In terms of the specialized agencies of the UN, although none of them has been endowed with compliance attributions in the field of IEL, some of them have interpreted their constituent treaties to include environmental competence. Amongst other agencies which have interpreted the treaties to encompass environmental functions, there are: the Food and Agricultural Organisation (FAO), the International Labour Organisation (ILO); the World Health Organisation (WHO); the World Meteorological Organisation (WMO); the International Maritime Organization (IMO); and the UN Educational, Scientific and Cultural Organisation (UNESCO).

Other UN bodies also play a role in advancing environmental protection, such as the UN Development Programme (UNDP), UN Institute for Training and Research (UNITAR) and the UN Conference on Trade and Development (UNCTAD), and the Commission on Sustainable Development (CSD).

Since its creation by a General Assembly resolution, the United Nations Environment Programme (UNEP) has performed coordination functions without really possessing executive powers to implement the norms.[11] In broader terms, its function is on a persuasive level, convincing states of the need for environmental action, offering expertise and advice, and sponsoring treaties.

Regional organisations which include in their respective mandates the protection of the environment have emerged on a regional scale, such as the European Union, the Organisation of American States, the African Union and the Association of Southeast Asian Nations (ASEAN). Regional organizations have included an environmental body in their institutional setting, creating a variety of environmental regimes on that level, such as biodiversity or climate change.

---

10 Patricia Birnie, Alan Boyle, and Catherine Redgwell, *International Law and the Environment* (3rd edn Oxford University Press 2008) p. 219.

11 UNEP, *About UN Environment Programme*, available at https://www.unenvironment.org/about-un-environment accessed 1 March 2020.

On the normative level of compliance, the classical vertical command and control power structure governing domestic policies cannot be replicated on the international level. Authority to secure compliance rests on state consent, based on the power of co-equal States.

What is a compliant actor, and what is a non-compliant actor? In terms of 'legal effectiveness', compliance is assessed on the basis of the obligations which IEL rules allocate to actors (obligation of conduct, to do or to abstain from doing, or of the resulting effect on states or other non-state actors). Failure to meet obligations leads to non-compliance procedures and, sometimes, to dispute settlement in IEL. In the climate change regime, under the Paris Agreement, States are required to submit their pledges (Nationally Determined Contributions).[12] Previously, in light of the Kyoto Protocol, the European Union was obliged to curb greenhouse gases emissions by 8% from 1990 in the 2008–2012 period. Pursuant to Article 4.1(b) of the UN Framework Convention on Climate Change (UNFCCC), States are required to formulate national climate programs, 'taking into account their specific national and regional development priorities, objectives and circumstances'.[13]

The overarching aim of IEL compliance is to instil a new model of action and motivate behavioural change which includes all actors of international law.

b States, sub-state entities and national environmental agencies

In many sectors of environmental law, we find broadly formulated rules which need to be implemented in the respective domestic legal systems, also requiring the adoption of legal and policy measures. On the operational level, this implies the involvement of sub-state divisions. To provide guidance on the implementation of IEL, some national agencies have adopted compliance guidelines or compliance codes of practice.[14] The whole architecture of IEL rests on national implementation for MEAs, and other international environmental treaties impose obligations on States which have the main obligation of putting IEL norms into effect.[15] Ultimately, the effectiveness of MEAs such as those concluded in the area of air pollution or biodiversity depends on the degree of implementation of the norms in the national sphere. Consider, for instance, the permitting process under CITES, which mandates the creation of national permitting schemes to limit trade in endangered species.

The role of National Environmental Agencies in compliance with IEL should not be overlooked. On the international level, States have the primary responsibility for compliance with IEL. On a domestic level, however, we observe the

---

12 UNFCCC, *Nationally Determined Contributions (NDCs)*, available at https://unfccc.int/ nationally-determined-contributions-ndcs accessed 1 March 2020.
13 UNFCCC, art Article 4.1(b).
14 Code of Practice – Environmental Information Regulations 2004, February 2005, available at https://ico.org.uk/media/for-organisations/documents/1644/environmental_information_ regulations_code_of_practice.pdf accessed 1 March 2020.
15 Daniel Bodansky, *The Art and Craft of International Environmental Law* (Cambridge University Press 2011) at 208.

different branches of government depending on the system a federal or a unitary system or on their having a decentralised or a centralised system.[16] National courts have increasingly developed an approach to implementing IEL norms in the domestic arena. To enhance coordination, internally, States set up ad-hoc committees to resolve implementation issues. In the European Union, national parliaments play a role in ensuring compliance in accordance with the subsidiarity and proportionality principles.

In terms of the implementation of the various types of IEL commitments, there are differences concerning procedural and substantive obligations, and regarding voluntary compliance. The manner in which adopted IEL legal rules are implemented and how compliance is controlled at sub-state level is also crucial to ensuring effective implementation.

Party States implement treaty provisions according to their respective national implementation systems, enforceable through judicial or quasi-judicial bodies. Some States follow a decentralized model of IEL. Separate compliance committees have been established under MEAs. Some treaties have a relatively advanced compliance mechanism. MEAs establish remedies that are available in the case of non-compliance with national legislation or practice. Periodic inspections in order to verify compliance need the input of national governments. One can distinguish between legislative implementation and executive/administrative implementation.

With regard to reporting, national environmental agencies perform a key function in compliance with IEL. As a rule, the local and regional levels are not directly represented in international negotiations. Environmental regulations in the domestic sphere implement various aspects of MEAs, which, ideally, should aim to achieve effectiveness, efficiency, and transparency.[17]

SCOTTISH ENVIRONMENT PROTECTION AGENCY (SEPA)

Compliance assessment scheme guidance manual

3 The compliance matrix

   3.1 The scheme distinguishes between conditions that relate directly to the environment and those which relate to management requirements that ensure appropriate environmental protection. These two types of conditions are referred to as:

     - Environmental Limit Conditions (ELCs);
     - Environmental Management Conditions (EMCs).

(Continued)

---

16 Ibid., at 210 and 211.
17 Neil Gunningham, 'Enforcing Environmental Regulation' (2011) 23(2) *Journal of Environmental Law*, pp. 169–201, available at https://doi.org/10.1093/jel/eqr006 accessed 2 May 2020.

3.2 SEPA considers both types of conditions to be equally important and has developed a compliance matrix made up of six compliance bands (...):
- excellent
- good
- broadly compliant
- at risk
- poor
- very poor

These bands allow the compliance assessment for an activity to be tracked year on year.

3.3 The matrix has been designed to:
- provide an excellent result for activities with no breaches, i.e. full compliance with environmental limits and high performance on environmental management attributes;
- highlight very poor activities where there are breaches of environmental limits as well as low management performance;
- assign activities where environmental management is assessed as having low performance level as:
- at risk if there have been no ELC breaches and- poor or very poor if there have also been breaches of ELC limits;
- assign either a broadly compliant or good overall band to activities where there are only minor breaches or non-compliances.

3.4 Assessment rules have been developed to determine gross, significant, and repeated minor breaches for ELCs, as well as high, medium and low performance for EMCs. However, breaches of ELCs or non-compliances with EMCs do not necessarily translate into an environmental impact. For example: an effluent discharge to a river that exceeded the licensed limits would be counted as a breach even though it may have caused no environmental impact because the river was in spate.

3.5 The overriding concern in developing these rules has been to promote consistency and fairness across regulatory regimes. For this reason, SEPA has set generic rules for assessing gross and significant breaches as well as repetitions of a minor breach. Some regimes have different or specific additional rules due to fundamental differences in the type of activity, licensing regime or process control expected.

3.6 The scheme takes account of good management practice whether or not it is implemented as part of a formal accredited Environmental Management System (EMS).

3.7 Overall compliance is considered satisfactory where the overall compliance assessment is Excellent, Good or Broadly compliant and unsatisfactory where the overall compliance assessment is Very Poor, Poor or At Risk. SEPA will direct and prioritise resources to move sites from unsatisfactory to satisfactory compliance.

Source: https://www.sepa.org.uk/media/368671/
compliance_scheme_manual.pdf

EUROPEAN UNION

Environmental Compliance Assurance

What is environmental compliance assurance?

The European Union has put in place rules to provide society with environmental benefits that include clean water, breathable air and a healthy nature. A recent Eurobarometer survey shows that an overwhelming majority of Europeans want the EU to make sure that these rules are applied across Europe.

Environmental compliance assurance describes all the ways in which public authorities promote, monitor and enforce compliance with such rules. It is part of environmental governance.

Promote means helping businesses and others to comply;

Monitor means using inspections and other checks to collect information about levels of compliance and provide solid evidence for enforcement;

Enforce means stopping those who disregard the rules, sanctioning them and obliging them to rectify the damage.

Promotion covers awareness-raising, guidance and advice. Monitoring covers routine environmental inspections, police investigations and environmental audits by public audit bodies. It also includes examination of complaints from the public. Enforcement covers audit recommendations, official warnings, cease-and-desist orders, administrative fines, criminal prosecutions and demands to take remedial action. Interventions may vary according to what works best.

Source: https://ec.europa.eu/environment/legal/
compliance_en.htm

3 The 'strategic players': a. Multinational corporations. b. International non-governmental organisations

Under the category of non-state actors, international subjects such as multinational corporations or enterprises (MNCs) and international non-governmental organisations (INGOs) have a role in compliance with IEL. Often seen as the antipodes of IEL compliance, both non-state actors and the MNCs and INGOs have evolved in their respective roles. Where there are no formal international regulations, some global companies develop global standards, forming part of the so-called soft-law.

a Multinational corporations (MNCs) and compliance with IEL

Private sector organisations are shaping IEL norms: different IEL areas have experienced their influence in the regulation of different areas.[18] Among the various private sector actors, businesses and particularly Multinational Corporations (MNCs) have become more influential, being involved in various IEL processes.[19] There has been a shift from corporations considered as an object of environmental regulation to their more active participation in IEL making and implementation and compliance procedures.

MNCs are also subject to direct obligations under IEL by application of the polluter pays principle under civil liability conventions, such as MARPOL or the Basel Convention.[20] States continue to be the main addressees of IEL, but increasingly norms are setting obligations or standards for the private sector which require their compliance and proper communication and coordination with the respective State. Notwithstanding, the wording of international environmental treaties does not allude to 'direct corporate liability'.[21]

MNCs have gained notoriety in international law as they have increased their reach in international trade and investment agreements, which often encompass environmental protection or sustainable development clauses.[22] Equally important, MNCs have direct access to international alternative dispute resolution for the settlement of investment disputes with a bearing on environmental issues.[23]

A burgeoning literature on the international accountability of MNCs in IEL puts the focus on duties.[24] The adoption of soft-law OECD guidelines for MNCs[25] and the Business and Human Rights principles which regulate them constitutes a piecemeal development. According to the so-called Ruggie Principles, respect, protect and remedy are basic obligations in the framework of

---

18 Steven R. Ratner, 'Business', in Daniel Bodansky, Jutta Brunnée, and Ellen Hey (eds), *The Oxford Handbook of International Environmental Law* (Oxford University Press 2012).
19 Neil Gunningham, Robert A. Kagan and Dorothy Thornton, *Shades of Green-Business, Regulation, and Environment* (Stanford University Press 2003).
20 Ratner (n 18) at 813.
21 Ibid., at 814.
22 On the issue see Peter Muchlinski, *Multinational Enterprises and the Law* (2nd edn Oxford University Press 2007). Elisa Morgera, *Corporate Accountability in International Environmental Law* (Oxford University Press 2009).
23 Pierre-Marie Dupuy and Jorge E. Viñuales (eds), *Foreign Investment and the Environment in International Law* (Cambridge University Press 2013).
24 David Ong, 'The Impact of Environmental Law on Corporate Governance: International and Comparative Perspectives' (2001) 12(4) *European Journal of International Law*, pp. 685–726.
25 OECD, Guidelines for Multinational Enterprises, http://mneguidelines.oecd.org/annualreportsontheguidelines.htm accessed 1 March 2020.

business and human rights.[26] Efforts to guarantee an environmentally sound corporate conduct have ultimately created a web of soft-law norms with an attempt to codify International Business and Human Rights (IBHR) by adopting a comprehensive treaty.[27]

The IBHR framework provides for an analytical framework based on the safeguard of fundamental rights, comprising environmental rights. Self-regulation on the part of MNCs, expressed in the adoption of codes of conduct, adds in another layer of complexity.

OFFICE OF THE UNITED NATIONS HIGH COMMISSIONER FOR HUMAN RIGHTS

HRC, 17th, 06/07/2011, A/HRC/RES/17/4

Guiding Principles on Business and Human Rights

(...) stressing that the obligation and the primary responsibility to promote and protect human rights and fundamental freedoms lie with the State,

Emphasizing that transnational corporations and other business enterprises have a responsibility to respect human rights,

Recognizing that proper regulation, including through national legislation, of transnational corporations and other business enterprises and their responsible operation can contribute to the promotion, protection and fulfilment of and respect for human rights and assist in channelling the benefits of business towards contributing to the enjoyment of human rights and fundamental freedoms,

Concerned that weak national legislation and implementation cannot effectively mitigate the negative impact of globalization on vulnerable economies, fully realize the benefits of globalization or derive maximally the benefits of activities of transnational corporations and other business enterprises, and that further efforts to bridge governance gaps at the national, regional and international levels are necessary,

Recognizing the importance of building the capacity of all actors to better manage challenges in the area of business and human rights,

1   Welcomes the work and contributions of the Special Representative of the Secretary-General on human rights and transnational corporations

(Continued)

---

26 UN, 'Protect, Respect and Remedy' Framework and Guiding Principles, available at https://www.business-humanrights.org/en/un-secretary-generals-special-representative-on-business-human-rights/un-protect-respect-and-remedy-framework-and-guiding-principles accessed 1 March 2020.
27 OEIGWG Chairmanship Revised Draft 16.7.2019, Legally Binding Instrument To Regulate, In International Human Rights Law, The Activities Of Transnational Corporations And Other Business Enterprises, available at https://www.ohchr.org/Documents/HRBodies/HRCouncil/WGTransCorp/OEIGWG_RevisedDraft_LBI.pdf accessed on 1 March 2020.

and other business enterprises, and endorses the Guiding Principles on Business and Human Rights: Implementing the United Nations "Protect, Respect and Remedy" Framework, as annexed to the report of the Special Representative (…).

Source: https://www.ohchr.org/documents/publications/
guidingprinciplesbusinesshr_en.pdf

b International non-governmental organisations (INGOs) as actors in IEL

International or global non-governmental organisations (INGOs) have increasingly developed and diversified their functions in IEL, playing a substantive role in various areas.[28]

The endorsement they receive through formal IEL by being accredited before the UN enables them to take part in some relevant international environmental processes.[29] The legal standing of NGOs and the consultative status attributed to them facilitates their involvement in the treaty negotiation of MEAs. Revisions and reflections about the notion of compliance come from the World Summit on Sustainable Development (WSSD).[30]

Global NGOs perform diverse functions in compliance with IEL, some of which are more formal than others. Greenpeace engages in several campaigning and advocacy activities that enhance compliance with IEL. The World Conservation Union (IUCN) acts as a hybrid organization which comprises a bunch of non-governmental organisations working on nature conservation.[31] The red list system raises awareness about species at risk of extinction.[32] The Earth Council Alliance performs a relevant role in the field of sustainable development and environmental justice.[33]

Organisations exerting a large function in IEL, such as Greenpeace, the World Wildlife Fund (WWF) or the International Union for the Conservation of Nature (IUCN), belong to a network of organisations operating on national and international spheres, which have developed an important role in raising public awareness about environmental problems and exerting

---

28 Tullio Treves and Alessandro Fodella (eds), *Civil Society, International Courts and Compliance Bodies* (TMC Asser Press 2005).

29 UNEP. List of accredited organizations, available at https://www.unenvironment.org/civil-society-engagement/accreditation/list-accredited-organizations accessed 1 March 2020.

30 United Nations, World Summit on Sustainable Development (WSSD), Johannesburg Summit, Johannesburg, South Africa 26 August – 4 September 2002, available at https://sustainabledevelopment.un.org/milesstones/wssd accessed 1 March 2020.

31 Information about IUCN, which was established in 1964, is available at https://www.iucn.org/ accessed 1 March 2020.

32 IUCN, Red list, available at https://www.iucnredlist.org/ accessed on 1 March 2020.

33 Earth Council, available at https://earthcouncilalliance.org/ accessed on 1 March 2020.

pressure on various actors. International NGOs are essential in achieving an effective system of compliance with international law, as representative of the public interest. NGOs have contributed to environmental summits and declarations on environmental rights, coordinating actions. NGOs are some of the stakeholders highlighting crucial areas for environmental protection at the international level and creating a new mode of global environmental governance. There are still many difficulties that impinge on NGOs' participation in compliance; the challenge lies in the removal of these obstacles to extend the decentralisation of global environmental governance to fully include other stakeholders.

4 International organisations and international environmental law compliance

International organisations contribute to formulating and implementing environmental policies and strategies that foster compliance in a variety of ways. A wide range of international organisations possess these functions in the sphere of environmental protection.

Against this background, UNEP has developed a critical function in setting IEL rules. Broadly formulated rules and guidelines adopted by UNEP provide the respective sector with discretion in balancing environmental concerns against targets when laying down regulations and devising international environmental policy. The principles of environmental law guide international environmental policy to interpret and apply IEL more consistently.

a United Nations Environment Programme (UNEP)

The UN General Assembly established UNEP as a subsidiary body. UNEP, now UN Environment, presents an umbrella for intergovernmental cooperation addressing sectoral environmental protection internationally. Initially established as a programme, with no separate legal personality, its tasks in the field of IEL compliance have grown exponentially.

Several MEAS allocate to UNEP the tasks of implementation, regulation of capacity and technical aspects, performance of inspections and initiating enforcement proceedings. UNEP coordinates actions orientated to the fulfilment of obligations in cooperation with other international organisations and finance mechanisms. Its main task is to foster the advancement and enhancement of the implementation of agreed international norms and policies, monitoring compliance with environmental principles and fostering the implementation of international agreements.[34]

---

34 UNEP, *The Role of UNEP in the Development of Guidelines on Compliance and Enforcement of Multilateral Environmental Agreements* (UNEP Secretariat 2000), available at https://digitallibrary.un.org/record/436919?ln=en 1 April 2020.

UNEP

Guidelines on Compliance with and Enforcement of Multilateral Environmental Agreements[35]

2 Effective participation in negotiations

11. To facilitate wide and effective participation by States in negotiations, the following actions may be considered:

a   Assessment of whether the issue to be addressed is global, regional or subregional, keeping in mind that, where appropriate, States could collaborate in regional and subregional efforts to promote implementation of multilateral environmental agreements;

b   Identification of countries for which addressing an environmental problem may be particularly relevant;

c   Establishment of special funds and other appropriate mechanisms to facilitate participation in negotiations by delegates from countries requiring financial assistance;

d   Where deemed appropriate by States, approaches to encourage participation in a multilateral environmental agreement, such as common but differentiated responsibilities, framework agreements (with the content of the initial agreement to be further elaborated by specific commitments in protocols), and/or limiting the scope of a proposed multilateral environmental agreement to subject areas in which there is likelihood of agreement;

e   Transparency and a participatory, open-ended process.

Source: https://wedocs.unep.org/bitstream/handle/
20.500.11822/17018/UNEP-guidelines-compliance-
MEA.pdf?sequence=1&isAllowed=y

---

b Specialised agencies

Some international organisations and organisms perform implementation functions (supervising monitoring, revising and promoting compliance) in IEL in a multi-layered system.[36]

Specialized agencies in the UN system have performed in the field of environmental protection as well. The FAO provides access to valuable information about the status of the environment in different sectors, such as water or climate

---

35 UNEP, Guidelines on Compliance with and Enforcement of Multilateral Environmental Agreements, available at https://wedocs.unep.org/bitstream/handle/20.500.11822U/31773/English.pdf?sequence=1&isAllowed=y 1 March 2020.

36 Boyle, Birnie and Redgwell (n 10) at 45. Alan Boyle and Christine Chinkin, *The Making of International Law* (Oxford University Press 2007) Chapter 3.

change, which contributes to transparency and monitoring and improving environmental compliance.[37] Other agencies comprise in their mission environmental objectives, such as the International Maritime Organisation, the International Atomic Energy Agency and the World Meteorological Organisation.[38]

In terms of compliance, these international agencies provide expertise and technical knowledge, and offer a forum for negotiations, multilateral discussions, inter-governmental cooperation and information exchange between partners and stakeholders.

The Global Environment Facility (GEF) comprises 18 agencies which address some of the most pressing environmental issues related to biodiversity, climate change, land degradation, chemicals and international waters.[39] All the tasks performed by these agencies are interwoven into the fabric of IEL compliance: they contribute to safeguarding global commons and foster compliance with IEL.

5 Regional systems: regional integration and cooperation organisations as actors in IEL compliance

Implementation of international environmental agreements presents distinctive features across the regions. Whether a state effectively implements its obligations under an MEA depends mainly on resource availability, capabilities and regional and domestic priorities. Often conditioned to the economic aspects, environmental protection is sometimes considered less of a priority. Regional variants demonstrate difficulties in achieving harmonisation in IEL compliance and securing similar environmental standards across states and regions. Conversely, regional approaches enrich IEL by incorporating what are considered priority areas for compliance, tailoring the measures to the specific needs of the regions in question. Often, one observes a complete network of MEAs and regional environmental agreements with a specific regional scope which does not necessarily translate into effective implementation. Regional environmental governance offers a diversity of scenarios: from a strong role performed by the European Union and UNECE which has yielded some successful outcomes to a weaker role played by other regional counterparts. Notwithstanding the differences, regional initiatives reflect consensus about specific aspects of IEL compliance. Some MEAs resonate more with particular regions, like in the case of biodiversity, which also has an impact on compliance with that particular set of norms or area of IEL.

---

37 See Food and Agriculture Organisation, Aquastat – FAO's Global Information System on Water and Agriculture, available at http://www.fao.org/aquastat/en/ accessed 1 March 2020.
38 In environmental protection, the Global Atmosphere Watch (GAW) programme offers updated and specialised information about some of the environmental media, https://public.wmo.int/en/our-mandate/focus-areas/environment accessed 1 March 2020.
39 The Global Environment Facility (GEF) was established through the 1992 Rio Earth Summit. https://www.thegef.org/ accessed 1 March 2020.

Another remarkable development is the geographical expansion of environmental treaties initially concluded in and for a particular region to then be opened to ratification by states outside the region as happens with the UNECE conventions. This expansion wave co-exists with another trend: to conclude environmental treaties to address specific regional environmental concerns, an example of which is the Escazú Agreement, with its provision on the protection of environmental defenders. The latter is also an example of a 'closed' environmental treaty as it rules out the possibility of other states outside the subregion (Latin America and the Caribbean) joining in.[40]

a Europe: United Nations Economic Commission for Europe (UNECE)

Some regional organisations also take a leading role in international negotiations in different environmental areas closely linked to compliance. Not all of them display the same level of development when it comes to IEL compliance. What is decisive is the type of competences attributed to the bodies of the international organisation to monitor the fulfilment of the obligations imposed under MEAs or ad-hoc regional treaties.

In the European Union (EU), the regional organisation did not initially possess competence under EU primary law to regulate or ensure compliance with IEL.[41] The further development of EU environmental law has been prompted by the adoption of legal instruments, which is the outcome of the joint collaboration between the acting institutions and their binding force vis-à-vis Member States.

EU secondary law has served as the vehicle to implementing MEAs in Member States. Following the shared competence system in the EU, Member States have responsibilities in both the implementation of specific EU law and obligations, and the specific implementation of obligations imposed in MEAs on both the EU and Member States.

In environmental compliance, the EU has issued Guidelines and Documents that Member States should observe in certain environmental areas: biodiversity,[42] conservation and climate change.[43] In these areas, the strategies reflect the

---

40 Third-states can become observers but are not allowed to become parties.

41 Anthony R. Zito, Charlotte Burns and Andrea Lenschow, 'Is the Trajectory of European Union Environmental Policy Less Certain?' (2019) 28(2) *Environmental Politics*, pp. 187–207. Tanja A. Börzel and Aron Buzogány, 'Compliance with EU Environmental Law. The Iceberg Is Melting' (2019) *Environmental Politics* 28(2), pp. 315–341.

42 European Union, *Biodiversity Strategy*, available at https://ec.europa.eu/environment/nature/biodiversity/strategy/index_en.htm accessed 1 March 2020.

43 European Commission, *Halting the Loss of Biodiversity; Conservation of Wild Birds Conservation of Natural Habitats and of Wild Flora and Fauna* (20 May 2020), available at https://ec.europa.eu/international-partnerships/news/reinforcing-europes-resilience-halting-biodiversity-loss-and-building-healthy-and-sustainable_en#:~:text=The%20European%20Green%20Deal%20is,-climate%20change%20and%20biodiversity%20together accessed 1 April 2020.

commitments taken by the EU and Member States within international environmental treaties.

For each strategy, the EU sets targets, giving Member States a window of time. The system in place to check compliance through the usual mechanism is monitored by the Commission.[44] Consequently, it is ensured that Member States are implementing EU environmental norms in their respective national legal systems. EU environmental policy and law are aligned with IEL commitments.

The central legally binding instruments remain the directives and, in smaller number, regulations. The Union legislator reserves the adoption of regulations mainly to implement international environmental treaties, as with regard to the so-called 'Aarhus Regulation'.[45] MEAs are incorporated into EU environmental law, forming part of EU law. In terms of the directives, it is primarily a question of implementation. Accordingly, an environmental treaty is one by which Member States are obliged to meet certain obligations.

Another main tool in the design of EU environmental policy is the EU Environment Action Plan, which sets the goals that must be met by all Member States over a period of years.[46]

The EU as an international organisation has become a contracting party to many MEAs and regional environmental conventions. Moreover, it is leading several of the discussions in the environmental arena. The Aarhus Convention is probably the paradigmatic case in terms of compliance as the EU is directly obliged to honour its terms, being subject to the compliance mechanisms instituted therein.[47] There is a plethora of EU soft-law legal instruments on the issue of compliance with the Aarhus Convention. The Aarhus Convention Compliance Committee ('the ACCC') often deals with access to environmental justice vis-à-vis the EU ('the Union').

EU Commission infringement cases have pointed out the extent to which Member States are complying with IEL, be it in terms of the fulfilment of the obligations assumed under international environmental treaties or the implementation of EU environmental law. Cases also underline the main deficiencies

---

44 Maria Lee, *EU Environmental Law, Governance and Decision-Making* (2nd edn Bloomsbury 2014).

45 Regulation (EC) No 1367/2006 of the European Parliament and of the Council of 6 September 2006 on the application of the provisions of the Aarhus Convention on Access to Information, Public Participation in Decision-making and Access to Justice in Environmental Matters to Community institutions and bodies, https://eur-lex.europa.eu/legal-content/EN/TXT/?uri=celex%3A32006R1367 accessed 1 April 2020.

46 European Union, *Environment Action Programme to 2020*, available https://ec.europa.eu/environment/action-programme/ accessed 1 March 2020.

47 Commission Report published on EU implementation of the Aarhus Convention in the area of access to justice in environmental matters. 'Study on EU implementation of the Aarhus Convention in the area of access to justice in environmental matters is published'. Results published on public consultation on 'EU implementation of the Aarhus Convention in the area of access of justice in environmental matters'. Staff Working Document – EU implementation of the Aarhus Convention in the area of access to justice in environmental matters, https://ec.europa.eu/info/law/better-regulation/initiatives/ares-2018-2432060_en accessed 1 March 2020.

in implementation. Some have addressed environmental protection in light of the protection of other freedoms. *Danish Bottles,*[48] *Preussen Elektra* and *Marismas de Santoña* have established the basis of environmental protection in the European Union.[49] Cases have determined the rules that govern the balance between the freedom of circulation and environmental protection or cases of non-compliance with EU law. The Court has reminded Member States of their obligations under IEL and EU environmental law. Furthermore, MEAs obligations have been seen in light of EU principles of environmental law.

The EU's approach seems to be advanced and presents opportunities to participate in negotiations and discussions on various issues; however, there are still many questions which surround the future of the system, such as those posed by non-compliance or the withdrawal of Member States.[50] Undoubtedly, the significant contribution of the EU to good international governance is evinced also in the area of compliance. To some extent, problems observed in the implementation in the EU are not unique to the Member States' domestic legal systems.

REPORT ON EUROPEAN UNION IMPLEMENTATION OF THE AARHUS CONVENTION IN THE AREA OF ACCESS TO JUSTICE IN ENVIRONMENTAL MATTERS

Applicants: who is entitled to administrative or judicial review?

Standing may be granted directly before EU bodies or the CJEU (under the Aarhus Regulation or Articles 263(4) and 277 TFEU) or via national courts (Article 267 TFEU).

The Aarhus Regulation grants standing to environmental NGOs, but not to individuals. Its mechanism is 'meant to facilitate for "qualified entities" access to justice which those entities would not have under Article 263(4) TFEU as interpreted by the Court'. The following question arises: does the exclusion of individuals in the Aarhus Regulation affect overall compliance by the EU with the Aarhus Convention?

Article 9(3) provides that 'members of the public' are to have access to review. Its Article 2(4) defines 'the public' as 'one or more natural or legal

---

48 Judgment of the Court of 20 September 1988. Commission of the European Communities v Kingdom of Denmark. Free movement of goods – Containers for beer and soft drinks. Case 302/86.European Court Reports 1988 -04607 https://www.ecolex.org/details/court-decision/commission-v-denmark-1654df7c-8af9-483c-8220-9752cf0cfc67/accessed 1 March 2020.

49 European Union, *Leading Cases of the European Court of Justice – EC Environmental Law,* available at https://ec.europa.eu/environment/legal/law/pdf/leading_cases_en.pdf accessed 1 March 2020.

50 Richard Macrory, 'Environmental Law in the United Kingdom Post Brexit' (2019) 19 *ERA Forum*, pp. 643–657.

persons, and, in accordance with national legislation or practice, their associations, organizations or group'. It is to be noted that the Convention speaks of 'members of the public' rather than 'the members of the public', suggesting that not every person need be given review possibilities in all circumstances. Furthermore, the Convention also employs the concept of 'the public concerned' to limit the scope of the right of review in certain circumstances.

If Article 9(3) of the Convention were considered as requiring access to justice across the board, such a broad interpretation would be tantamount to imposing on Parties the establishment of an 'actio popularis', which the ACCC itself has expressly declared in previous cases as not being what the Convention requires.

Article 9(3) of the Aarhus Convention does not, therefore, oblige Parties to grant every member of the public unconditional access to every review procedure. Article 9(3) aims.

Source: https://ec.europa.eu/environment/aarhus/pdf/
Commission_report_2019.pdf

b The Americas

In the Americas, environmental protection has also come under the scope of different regional organisations. Although not originally tasked with this competence, the Organisation of American States (OAS) has been performing a coordination role in the area of environmental protection. The UN Economic Commission for Latin America and the Caribbean (UNECLAC) deserves special mention as it grew from maintaining a sustainable development stance (which revolved around the economic issues) to an approach more focussed on environmental protection and encompassing access rights, as witnessed in the adoption of the Escazú Agreement. Several other subregional organisations play a role in securing compliance with IEL. However, it must still be emphasised that these are inter-governmental initiatives whose level of institutional coordination and legal development is not yet comparable to the progress attained in the EU.

With a regional scope, the OAS was not initially endowed with the role of environmental protection, but the pervasiveness of environmental degradation in the continent placed environmental issues on the agenda. In terms of its role in compliance with IEL, OAS supports Member States in the design and implementation of policies, and with projects to integrate environmental priorities into poverty alleviation and socioeconomic development goals.[51]

---

51 OAS, Department of Sustainable Development, available at http://www.oas.org/en/sedi/dsd/ accessed 1 April 2020.

Within the framework of the Department of Sustainable Development, OAS Member States are cooperating on integrated water resources management; energy and climate change mitigation; risk management and adaptation to climate change; sustainable cities, biodiversity and sustainable land management; environmental law; policy and good governance; and sustainable development.[52]

Specifically, the implementation of MEAs and environmental treaties at the hemispheric level has been discussed in international meetings and conferences on key issues, such as on the Environmental Rule of Law in the Americas, which assist States in the implementation of IEL norms.[53] Environmental cooperation also includes implementation activities. Several pitfalls in IEL implementation are observed in the region. The organization undertakes the mandate in biodiversity protection, strengthening environmental law and management of water resources, raising awareness about climate change-related issues and promoting sustainability. Despite the lack of continuity and a proper follow-up mechanism, the summits of the Americas comprised a mandate concerning environmental protection.[54]

Perhaps better known for its role in social and economic development, the United Nations Economic Commission for Latin America and the Caribbean (ECLAC) has promoted environmental protection in Latin America and the Caribbean with an emphasis on how to properly channel economic progress, making it compatible with higher levels of environmental compliance.

ECLAC has addressed environmental issues comprehensively; stressing the connection with sustainable development; providing information on the socioeconomic effects of the lack of implementation of environmental protection norms; assessing environmental performance; putting forward economic policies that foster environmental protection and promoting access to environmental information; and increasing public participation with regard to environmental issues.[55]

The first regional agreement on Principle 10 of the Rio Declaration, the Escazú Agreement, and LAC's first environmental treaty were proposed at the UN Conference on Sustainable Development (Rio+20). Ahead of the adoption of the text, ECLAC coordinated the activities and negotiations around Principle 10.[56] The treaty was opened for signature on 27 September 2018; it is in process of ratification and will enter into force on 22 April 2021.

---

52 Ensuring and promoting sustainable development – which entails balancing economic growth, social equity and environmental protections throughout the Western Hemisphere – is one of the core objectives of the OAS. OAS, *Sustainable Development*, available at http://www.oas.org/en/topics/sustainable_development.asp accessed 1 April 2020.

53 OAS, Environmental rule of Law in the Americas http://www.oas.org/en/topics/environment.asp accessed 1 April 2020.

54 Summits of the Americas-Secretariat, *Follow-up and Implementation: Mandates*, available at http://www.summit-americas.org/sisca/env.html accessed 1 April 2020.

55 Sustainable development and human settlements, available at https://www.cepal.org/en/work-areas/sustainable-development-and-human-settlements accessed 1 April 2020.

56 UNECLAC/CEPAL, Observatorio del Principio 10 en América Latina y el Caribe, available at https://observatoriop10.cepal.org/en accessed 1 April 2020.

In other subregional organisations or regional integration, such as the Central American Integration System, the Caribbean Community (CARICOM), the Organisation of Eastern Caribbean States (OECS), the Andean Community and the Common Market of the South, some efforts have been undertaken to implement MEAs. These subregional organisations have developed their own role in compliance and preparedness, stressing the priorities for the respective region, and providing institutional and capacity building to member states.

Under these subregional processes compliance-related activities vary; they range from the adoption of plans and strategies to implement a specific MEA in the region to the adoption of regional or subregional environmental treaties. An example of the former is the Andean Community strategy in the field of biodiversity.[57] Another type of compliance-related activity is the adoption of ad-hoc regional environmental treaties with a subregional scope.[58] In the framework of subregional organisations, there have been initiatives such as the creation of 'observatories' to monitor environmental compliance.

Even if the Caribbean Community (CARICOM) has a more prominent function in the field of economic integration, the Organisation of Eastern Caribbean States (OECS) has developed a clear role in MEAs' implementation and monitoring compliance.

In Central America, the general legal framework for environmental cooperation and the starting point is the Central American Alliance for Sustainable Development (ALIDES), which introduced a comprehensive regional approach to environmental protection.[59] This included the Central American Environmental Observatory and the creation of a Central American Commission for Environment and Development as subregional bodies instituted in the framework of the Inter-American System of Integration (SICA). Since Central America is a region vulnerable to climatic events, this also included the creation of a regional centre to prevent environmental damage, tasked with the function of preventing such damage (CEPREDENAC).[60] Central American regional plans, programmes and strategies are designed to address specific environmental challenges, such as protection of biodiversity or preparedness to reduce climate change vulnerabilities.[61]

57 Comunidad Andina, *Estrategia Regional de Biodiversidad para los paí'ses del tro'pico andino* (Secretari'a General 2005), available at https://www.cbd.int/doc/nbsap/rbsap/comunidad-andina-rbsap.pdf accessed 1 April 2020.

58 MERCOSUR, Acuerdo marco sobre medio ambiente del Mercosur (2001 MERCOSUR Framework Environment Agreement), available at http://integracionsur.com/wp-content/uploads/2016/11/MercosurAcuerdoMarcoMedioAmbiente01.pdf accessed 1 April 2020.

59 Marie-Claire Cordonier Segger and Renee Gift, 'The Americas' Environmental and Sustainable Development Law', in Shawkat Alam and Erika J. Techera (eds), *Routledge Handbook of International Environmental Law* (Routledge 2012), p. 455. B. Olmos Giupponi, *Rethinking Free Trade, Economic Integration and Human Rights in the Americas* (Hart 2016).

60 Coordinación para la Prevención de los Desastres en América Central y República Dominicana (CEPREDENAC), available at https://www.cepredenac.org/quienes-somos accessed 1 April 2020.

61 Central American Integration System (SICA), *Estrategia Regional Ambiental Marco 2015–2020*, available at https://www.sica.int/ccad/eram/index.aspx accessed 1 April 2020.

Although not a specific environmental law forum, the Inter-American Human Rights System (IAHRS) has offered the possibility to discuss IEL compliance in aspects related to the protection of human rights, in particular referring to indigenous peoples' rights and protection of environmental defenders, and in the field of the safeguarding of the free, prior and informed consent (FPIC) of indigenous peoples. In an overall appraisal of environmental protection at the regional level, the Commission and the Court of the IAHRS have developed through case law the related rights to consultation and the protection of the environment. In particular, they have clarified the conflicting rights involved and identified the idea that indigenous communities should have the right to FPIC, control over and even in some cases consent to the development of natural resources, including the territories where these are situated. Furthermore, they should have the right to restoration of the *status quo ante* where harmful effects have occurred. However, the Court has yet to take the further step of defining whether FPIC has the nature of a *jus cogens* norm. Also, there remains a long road to travel between ruling that reparation must take place and ensuring that it is done.

In the Americas, all subregional institutional frameworks remain intergovernmental, which indicates that Member States still take a more 'diluted' legal stance on the implementation of IEL norms.

c Africa

Environmental resources are plentiful in Africa, a reservoir of biological diversity facing many environmental and ecological challenges. Compliance with IEL in Africa has gone through various stages, marked by the adoption of international legal instruments, the setting up of the regional institutional framework and the development of an incipient specific regional case law. A multitude of factors come together in the implementation of MEAs in Africa, many of which concern capacity building; having appropriate skills; and availability of resources in key sectors, such as biodiversity conservation or combating desertification.[62] MEAs in Africa face several challenges in their implementation, displaying different types of non-compliance with environmental norms on the continent.[63] Against this backdrop, the African Union's role in the adoption of different instruments devoted to environmental protection could be pivotal, adding to multilateral efforts.

---

62 Kevin R. Jones, 'Multilateral Environmental Agreements in Africa: Efforts and Problems in Implementation' (2003) 3 *International Environmental Agreements: Politics, Law and Economics*, pp. 97–135. Kannan Ambalam, 'Challenges of Compliance with Multilateral Environmental Agreements: The Case of the United Nations Convention to Combat Desertification in Africa' (2014) 5 *Journal of Sustainable Development Studies*, pp. 145–168.

63 Cliffe Denker Hofmeyr, 'African Environmental Compliance', 5 October 2012, available at https://www.cliffedekkerhofmeyr.com/en/news/press-releases/2012/africa-group/african-environmental-compliance.html accessed 1 April 2020.

The development of a fully-fledged system for environmental protection in Africa rests also on the adoption of regional environmental protection treaties focussed on the conservation of natural resources.[64]

Another dimension for securing environmental compliance is through the regional human rights system.[65] The African Commission on Human and Peoples' Rights ('ACHPR') has also referred to environmental protection in the context of Free, Prior and Informed Consent (FPIC), although in a different legal setting.[66] In the Advisory Opinion on the adoption of UNDRIP, issued by the ACHPR, other points were raised for discussion. Specifically, concerning FPIC, the ACHPR observed the convergence and similarities between UNDRIP and regional law adopted by the African Union, mentioning as an example the African Convention on the Conservation of Nature and Natural Resources, whose major objective is 'to harness the natural and human resources of our continent for the total advancement of our peoples in spheres of human endeavour' (preamble) and which is intended 'to preserve the traditional rights and property of local communities and request the prior consent of the communities concerned in respect of all that concerns their access to and use of traditional knowledge', which is similar to the provisions of Article 10, 11(2), 28(1) and 32 of UNDRIP.[67]

Comparing this approach with the protection of environmental rights in the IASHR, the latter has progressively developed a specific case law on environmental protection.[68] However, the degree of protection is not analogous to that which it has achieved in Inter-American Human Rights law.[69] The reason may be that, as Udombana recalls, 'determining Africa's indigenous peoples has been largely controversial which has also had an impact on environmental protection broadly considered'.[70] The ACHPR's definition comprises

> those particular groups who have been left on the margins of development and who are perceived negatively by dominating mainstream development, whose cultures and ways of life are subject to discrimination and contempt and whose existence is under threat of extinction.[71]

64 African Convention on the Conservation of Nature and Natural Resources, concluded on 15 September 1968; in force since 16 June 1969. Available from the OAU/AU Treaties, Conventions, Protocols & Charters. Revised African Convention on the Conservation of Nature and Natural Resources, adopted on 7 March 2017. Date of last signature: February 04, 2019.

65 African Charter on Human and Peoples' Rights, June 01, 1981 October 21, 1986 May 19, 2016 Status List AU/AU Treaties, Conventions, Protocols & Charters.

66 G. Lynch, 'Becoming Indigenous in the Pursuit of Justice: The African Commission on Human and Peoples' Rights and the Endorois' (2012) 111(442) *African Affairs (Lond)*, pp. 24–45.

67 African Commission, *Advisory Opinion on UNDRIP (2007)*, para. 35, accessed 1 April 2020.

68 Inter-Am. C.H.R., *Maya Indigenous Communities v. Belize*, Case 12.053, Report No. 78/00, OEA/Ser.L/V/II.111, doc. 20, rev. (2000), para. 197(1).

69 Jim Igoe, 'Becoming Indigenous Peoples: Difference, Inequality, and the Globalization of East African Identity Politics' (2006) 105(420) *African Affairs*, pp. 399–420.

70 Nsongurua Udombana, 'Reparations and Africa's Indigenous Peoples', in F. Lenzerini (ed), *Reparations for Indigenous Peoples International and Comparative Perspectives* (Oxford University Press 2009), pp. 389–407, at 392.

71 ACHPR, *Indigenous Peoples in Africa: The Forgotten Peoples?* (African Commission, Banjul 2006), p. 11.

In particular, the ACHPR has considered that the right to consultation may be seen as a 'subset of the self-determination or self-management provisions of the African Charter, especially when held in the light of (...) ILO No. 169'.[72] Despite this affirmation, 'the majority of African States remained unenthusiastic about the idea of the right to consultation'.[73] However, it is acknowledged that the right to consultation is particularly crucial, taking into consideration that '[m]any indigenous Africans have been forcibly evicted or displaced due to the so-called large-scale development projects – dam building, energy projects'.[74] There is a narrower and indirect protection granted by national constitutions which guarantees the right to participate in governmental affairs and decision-making processes.[75]

In *Social and Economic Rights Action Center and Center for Economic and Social Rights* v. *Nigeria No. 155/96*, the ACHPR reaffirmed the obligation to '"respect, protect, promote, and fulfil" human rights (...) the four levels require States to both positively and negatively adhere to these duties and can be found in the African Charter'.[76] In the *Endorois* case, concerning forcible evictions, the ACHPR examined whether the State of Kenya's creation of a 'Game Reserve', which displaced some members of the Endorois indigenous community from their ancestral land and restricted the community's access to it, was consistent with respect for the indigenous community's rights to their ancestral lands and resources.[77] The ACHPR explained that, in these types of cases, a State's limitations on rights must be proportionate to a legitimate need and should be the least restrictive measures possible.[78] The ACHPR argued that 'even if the Game Reserve was a legitimate aim and served a public need, it could have been accomplished by alternative means proportionate to the need'.[79] It thus concluded, that Kenya,

> [b]y forcing the community to live on semi-arid lands without access to medicinal salt licks and other vital resources for the health of their livestock, (...) *had* created a major threat to the Endorois pastoralist way of life (...) *thus* the very essence of the Endorois' right to culture has been denied, rendering the right, to all intents and purposes, illusory.[80]

---

72 Jide James-Eluyode, 'The Blurred Lines: Analysing the Dynamics of States' Duty and Corporate Responsibility to Consult in Developing Countries' (2015) 23(3) *African Journal of International and Comparative Law*, pp. 405–409.

73 Ibid.

74 Udombana (n 70) at 399.

75 James-Eluyode (n 72) 412.

76 African Commission of Human Rights, *Social and Economic Rights Action Center and Center for Economic and Social Rights* v. *Nigeria No. 155/96*, 27 May 2002, para. 44.

77 African Commission of Human Rights, 276/03 *Centre for Minority Rights Development (Kenya) and Minority Rights Group (on behalf of Endorois Welfare Council) / Kenya*, 25 November 2009.

78 Ibid., para. 100.

79 Ibid., para. 101.

80 Ibid., para. 251 (the text in italics is added).

The ACHPR has also recognised FPIC in discussion but has yet to realise the extent of related protection achieved under IAHRS because of, among other things, the difficulty of identifying Africa's indigenous peoples. However, a right to participation has been accepted, as has, in some circumstances, a right to consultation. The concepts of legitimate need and proportionality have also been recognised by the Commission as relevant to decision-making in cases of environmental conservation.

d Asia

As a large region, Asia presents diverse geographical areas and several environmental challenges.[81] Improving the effectiveness of IEL is linked to advancing development in the region. The task of ensuring compliance with IEL in Asia is shared by various organisations and entities. In terms of geographical areas, one can identify: Asia Pacific, South-East Asia, East Asia, Central Asia, South Asia and South-West Asia (also known as the Middle East), and sometimes also Australia, New Zealand and the island states of the South-West Pacific.[82] Various international environmental institutions, including IOs and Non-Governmental Organisations (NGOs), operate in each subregion to address its many environmental challenges.[83]

Amongst them, there is the acceleration of the rate of biodiversity loss, together with air pollution and the effects of climate change in the region, deforestation and desertification.[84] Effective legal frameworks, coupled with institutions empowered to ensure implementation, provide the critical enabling environment necessary to deliver internationally agreed environmental goals under MEAs. While most Asian countries have developed suitable environmental legal frameworks at different levels, effective implementation remains a crucial challenge for almost as many States. One of the main problem remains the weakness of the rule of law in the implementation.[85]

Joint efforts with the Asian Development Bank have facilitated the implementation of MEAs in the Asia-Pacific Region in order to protect the global

81 Ben Boer, 'The Rise of Environmental Law in the Asian Region' (1999) 32 *University of Richmond Law Review*, p. 1503, available at http://scholarship.richmond.edu/lawreview/vol32/iss5/4 accessed 1 April 2020.

82 Ben Boer, Ross Ramsay, and Donald R. Rothwell, *International Environmental Law in the Asia Pacific* (Kluwer Law International 1998).

83 Gregory L. Rose, *Gaps in the Implementation of Environmental Law at the National, Regional and Global Level* (UNEP 2011).

84 Roda Mushkat, 'International Environmental Law in the Asia-Pacific Region: Recent Developments' (1989) 20(1) *California Western International Law Journal (CWSL)*, pp. 1–20.

85 Wai-Hang Yee, Shui-Yan Tang and Carlos Wing-Hung Lo, 'Regulatory Compliance When the Rule of Law Is Weak: Evidence from China's Environmental Reform' (2016) *Journal of Public Administration Research and Theory*, pp. 95–112. A. Raine and E. Pluchon, 'UN Environment—Advancing the Environmental Rule of Law in the Asia Pacific' (2019) 3(1) *Chinese Journal of Environmental Law*, pp. 117–126, available at https://doi.org/10.1163/24686042-12340037 accessed 1 April 2020.

environment and public health. The development of IEL in Asia Pacific is multifaceted, comprising various aspects of environmental law in the specific State and occasionally the states of South and Central Asia. The whole picture of implementation of MEAs is complemented by a variety of action plans.[86]

The effect of IEL is dependent upon the implementation of the MEAs and has different dimensions: global, regional and subregional environmental law. The different manners in which certain States and groups of States have implemented IEL norms domestically have led to an uneven development with some subregions reaching significant achievements. These areas include, *inter alia*, preservation of heritage, biodiversity and conservation of the marine environment. Overall, the interaction between international and regional environmental law has fostered the environmental protection development of IEL within the region. The various forces shaping the development of international and regional schemes for environmental governance are constantly interacting. There is a long-term objective to achieve ecological, social and economic sustainability.

ASIAN DEVELOPMENT BANK

Environmental Assessment Guidelines 2003

XIX Multilateral Environmental Agreements

319. In the last few years, ADB has played a facilitating role in the context of multilateral environmental agreements (MEAs), including treaties, conventions, and protocols, particularly to support its regional cooperative efforts. The following criteria help determine where ADB assistance can be particularly helpful to DMCs: (i) ADB will concentrate on thematic areas in which it has already acquired expertise, instead of trying to build capacities in new areas; (ii) ADB will focus its participation on MEAs that have clearly identified roles for multilateral development banks; (iii) ADB participation will make a significant contribution to implementing the MEA within specific DMCs or at the subregional or regional level; and (iv) ADB participation will respond to DMC priorities for the relevant MEA. The precise nature of ADB operations in any DMC will be determined through the CSP process, and special attention will be paid to interventions that (i) deliver significant local level benefits as well as global environmental outcomes, (ii) assist vulnerable groups and countries to adapt to global environmental changes, and (iii) facilitate the mobilization of additional resources financial mechanisms of the respective MEA.

---

86 Karina Zhanel, *Review of Implementation of The International Environmental Conventions in Central Asia*, CAREC Environmental Management Programme Specialist, 14.08.2018, available at http://carececo.org/publications/Review%20of%20the%20implementation%20of%20 MEAs%20in%20CA.pdf accessed 1 April 2020.

XX *Environmental Auditing*

322. Environmental audit is a process to review the effectiveness of environmental management. Its objectives are to (i) determine whether a company complies with all regulatory and environmental performance standards, or other management requirements for their operations; and (ii) ensure conformity with environmental assessment requirements, and test the accuracy of the assessment. It entails a systematic, documented and periodic review of either a company's operation or project implementation. Therefore, its results could be very useful to improve company or project management performance.

Source: Asian Development Bank https://www.adb.org/sites/
default/files/institutional-document/32635/files/
environmental-assessment-guidelines.pdf

GREENPEACE SOUTH-EAST ASIA

Philippines' Supreme Court, Segovia et., al. vs. the Climate Change Commission, ey., al., G.R. No. 211010, 7 March 2017

In summary, what we, the Petitioners, are saying, is that the production of fossil fuels by the Carbon Majors has been found to be primarily responsible for large amounts of greenhouse gases. The concentration of said gases, especially carbon dioxide in the atmosphere, causes climate change. An estimated 25–30% of the carbon dioxide already emitted by these activities has been absorbed by the oceans, causing ocean acidification.

The adverse impacts of climate change and ocean acidification brought harm or pose the threat of harm to people, on top of or in addition to damage resulting from natural disasters. These harms resulting from the impacts of climate change and ocean acidification affect the exercise and enjoyment of Filipinos' human rights (...) (a) to life; (b) to the highest attainable standard of physical and mental health; (c) to adequate food; (d) to water (e) to sanitation; (f) to adequate housing; (g) to self-determination; and (h) the human rights of marginalized and disadvantaged groups particularly vulnerable to the effects of climate change, including (1) women; (2) children; (3) persons with disabilities; (4) those living in extreme poverty; (5) indigenous peoples; (6) displaced persons; and, (7) workers; as well as the right of Filipinos to development. Whether or not the Respondent Carbon Majors should be held accountable for the human rights implications of climate change and ocean acidification is what we ask the Honourable Commission.

(Continued)

Why do we ask?

Because the victims must be given remedies, those responsible for climate change and ocean acidification and associated human rights impacts must be held accountable, and the threats of future harms resulting from climate change and ocean acidification must be addressed, remedied, and prevented.

The recognition of the Human Rights Council, OHCHR, and the parties to the UNFCCC that climate change impedes the full and effective enjoyment of human rights protected by the most fundamental international human rights conventions provides a framework for the requested investigation of the Honourable Commission.

This investigation will further bolster the country's leadership position on human rights in the UNFCCC negotiations and at the Human Rights Council. At the 20th Conference of the Parties to the UNFCCC held in Lima, Peru, the Philippines made interventions calling for references to human rights, rights of indigenous peoples, and gender in the 2015 climate agreement. In its high-level ministerial statement, the Philippines reflected on the rights implications of a climate deal (or lack thereof), stating: 'losing the credibility of the UN multilateral process is not only an insult to diplomacy but a complete disregard to human rights'.

The Government of the Philippines joined 17 other countries in signing the Geneva Pledge on Human Rights and Climate Change in February 2015. This demonstrates the Philippines' commitment to 'promote and respect human rights in our climate actions'.

With the mounting evidence of the Carbon Majors holding us back on climate progress, it is essential for the Honourable Commission to act now and establish the responsibility of the Carbon Majors, which will be seen as a strong signal for future climate negotiations and other actions.

So we pray for remedies. Hindi po dapat na kami ay mauuwi lamang sa pagbibilang okaya'y mapapabilang na lamang sa mga biktima ng climate change.

Prayer

WHEREFORE, premises considered, Petitioners most respectfully pray that the Honourable Commission on Human Rights take the following actions:

1   Conduct an investigation into the human rights implications of climate change and ocean acidification and the resulting rights violations in the Philippines, and whether the investor-owned Carbon Majors have breached their responsibilities to respect the rights of the Filipino people;

2 Monitor people and communities acutely vulnerable to the impacts of climate change;

3 Recommend that policymakers and legislators develop and adopt clear and implementable objective standards for corporate reporting of human rights issues in relation to the environment, with special regard for current and future climate change impacts and GHGs from fossil fuel products;

4 Recommend that policymakers and legislators develop and adopt effective accountability mechanisms that victims of climate change can easily access in instances of violation or threat of violation;

5 Notify the investor-owned Carbon Majors and request the submission of plans on how such violations or threats of violation resulting from the impacts of climate change will be eliminated and remedied and prevented in the future; and

6 Recommend that the President call upon other States, especially where the investor owned Carbon Majors are incorporated, to take steps to prevent, remedy, or eliminate human rights violations or threats of violations resulting from the impacts of climate change, or seek a remedy before international mechanisms.

Petitioners further pray for such other just and equitable reliefs under the premises.

Source: http://blogs2.law.columbia.edu/climate-change-litigation/wp-content/uploads/sites/16/non-us-case-documents/2015/20150512_Case-No.-CHR-NI-2016-0001_petition.pdf

Bibliography

ACHPR, *Indigenous Peoples in Africa: The Forgotten Peoples?* (African Commission, Banjul 2006), p. 11.

African Charter on Human and Peoples' Rights, June 01, 1981 October 21.

African Commission, Advisory Opinion on UNDRIP (2007), para. 35, accessed 1 April 2020.

African Commission of Human Rights, 276/03 Centre for Minority Rights Development (Kenya) and Minority Rights Group (on behalf of Endorois Welfare Council) / Kenya, 25 November 2009.

African Commission of Human Rights, Social and Economic Rights Action Center and Center for Economic and Social Rights v. Nigeria No. 155/96, 27 May 2002, para. 44.

African Convention on the Conservation of Nature and Natural Resources, concluded on 15 September 1968; in force since 16 June 1969, available from the OAU/AU Treaties, Conventions, Protocols & Charters. Revised African Convention on the Conservation of Nature and Natural Resources, adopted on 7 March 2017.

Ambalam, K, 'Challenges of Compliance with Multilateral Environmental Agreements: The Case of the United Nations Convention to Combat Desertification in Africa' (2014) 5 *Journal of Sustainable Development Studies*, pp. 145–168.

Birnie, P, Boyle, A, and Redgwell, C, *International Law and the Environment* (3rd edn Oxford University Press 2008), p. 219.

Bodansky, D, *The Art and Craft of International Environmental Law* (Cambridge University Press 2011), p. 208.

Boer, B, Ramsay, R, and Rothwell, DR, *International Environmental Law in the Asia Pacific* (Kluwer Law International 1998).

Boer, B, 'The Rise of Environmental Law in the Asian Region' (1999) 32 *University of Richmond Law Review*, p. 1503, available at http://scholarship.richmond.edu/lawreview/vol32/iss5/4 accessed 1 April 2020.

Börzel, Tanja A, and Buzogány, Aron, 'Compliance with EU Environmental Law. The Iceberg Is Melting' (2019) 28(2) *Environmental Politics*, pp. 315–341.

Boyle, A and Chinkin, C, *The Making of International Law* (Oxford University Press 2007) Chapter 3.

Central American Integration System (SICA), Estrategia Regional Ambiental Marco 2015–2020, available at https://www.sica.int/ccad/eram/index.aspx accessed 1 April 2020.

Comunidad Andina, Estrategia Regional de Biodiversidad para los Países del Trópico Andino (Secretaría General 2005), available at https://www.cbd.int/doc/nbsap/rbsap/comunidad-andina-rbsap.pdf accessed 1 April 2020.

Cordonier Segger, MC and Gift, R, 'The Americas' Environmental and Sustainable Development Law', in S Alam and EJ Techera (eds), *Routledge Handbook of International Environmental Law* (Routledge 2012), pp. 856–874.

Dupuy, PM and Viñuales, JE (eds), *Foreign Investment and the Environment in International Law* (Cambridge University Press 2013).

Earth Council, available at https://earthcouncilalliance.org/ accessed on 1 March 2020.

Eluyode, Jide James, 'The Blurred Lines: Analysing the Dynamics of States' Duty and Corporate Responsibility to Consult in Developing Countries' (2015) 23(3) *African Journal of International and Comparative Law*, pp. 405–409.

European Commission, Halting the loss of biodiversity; Conservation of Wild Birds Conservation of Natural Habitats and of Wild Flora and Fauna (20 May 2020), available at https://ec.europa.eu/international-partnerships/news/reinforcing-europes-resilience-halting-biodiversity-loss-and-building-healthy-and-sustainable_en#:~:text=The%20European%20Green%20Deal%20is, climate%20change%20and%20biodiversity%20together accessed 1 April 2020.

European Union, Biodiversity Strategy, available at https://ec.europa.eu/environment/nature/biodiversity/strategy/index_en.htm accessed 1 March 2020.

European Union, Environment Action Programme to 2020, available at https://ec.europa.eu/environment/action-programme/ accessed 1 March 2020.

European Union, Leading Cases of the European Court of Justice – EC Environmental Law, available at https://ec.europa.eu/environment/legal/law/pdf/leading_cases_en.pdf accessed 1 March 2020.

Food and Agriculture Organisation, Aquastat – FAO's Global Information System on Water and Agriculture, available at http://www.fao.org/aquastat/en/ accessed 1 March 2020.

French, D, 'Developing States and International Environmental Law: The Importance of Differentiated Responsibilities' (2000) 49(1) *The International and Comparative Law Quarterly*, pp. 35–60.

Global Environment Facility (GEF) was established through the 1992 Rio Earth Summit, available at https://www.thegef.org/ accessed 1 March 2020.

Gunningham, N, 'Enforcing Environmental Regulation' (2011) 23(2) *Journal of Environmental Law*, pp. 169–201, available at https://doi.org/10.1093/jel/eqr006 accessed 2 May 2020.

Gunningham, N, Kagan, Robert A, and Thornton, Dorothy, *Shades of Green-Business, Regulation, and Environment* (Stanford University Press 2003).

Hey, H, 'International Institutions', in Daniel Bodansky, Jutta Brunnée, and Ellen Hey (eds), *The Oxford Handbook of International Environmental Law* (Oxford University Press 2008), pp. 755–765.

Hofmeyr, Cliffe Denker, 'African Environmental Compliance', 5 October 2012, available at https://www.cliffedekkerhofmeyr.com/en/news/press-releases/2012/africa-group/african-environmental-compliance.html accessed 1 April 2020.

Hurrell, A, and Kingsbury, Benedict, *The International Politics of the Environment: Actors, Interests, and Institutions* (Clarendon Press 1992).

Igoe, J, 'Becoming Indigenous Peoples: Difference, Inequality, and the Globalization of East African Identity Politics' (2006) 105(420) *African Affairs*, pp. 399–420.

Inter-Am. C.H.R., Maya Indigenous Communities v. Belize, Case 12.053, Report No. 78/00, OEA/Ser.L/V/II.111, doc. 20, rev. (2000), para. 197(1).

International Whaling Convention, History and purpose, available at https://iwc.int/history-and-purpose accessed 1 March 2020.

IUCN, Information about IUCN, which was established in 1964, is available at https://www.iucn.org/ accessed 1 March 2020.

IUCN, Red list, available at https://www.iucnredlist.org/ accessed on 1 March 2020.

Jones, KR, 'Multilateral Environmental Agreements in Africa: Efforts and Problems in Implementation' (2003) 3 *International Environmental Agreements: Politics, Law and Economics*, pp. 97–135.

Lee, M, *EU Environmental Law, Governance and Decision-Making* (2nd edn Bloomsbury 2014).

Lynch, G, 'Becoming Indigenous in the Pursuit of Justice: The African Commission on Human and Peoples' Rights and the Endorois' (2012) 111(442) *African Affairs* (Lond), pp. 24–45.

Macrory, R, 'Environmental Law in the United Kingdom Post Brexit' (2019) 19 *ERA Forum*, pp. 643–657.

Marauhn, T, Chapter 31 'Changing Role of the State', in Daniel Bodansky, Jutta Brunnée, and Ellen Hey (eds), *The Oxford Handbook of International Environmental Law* (Oxford University Press 2008), pp. 729–746.

MERCOSUR, Acuerdo marco sobre medio ambiente del Mercosur (2001 MERCOSUR Framework Environment Agreement), available at http://integracionsur.com/wp-content/uploads/2016/11/MercosurAcuerdoMarcoMedioAmbiente01.pdf accessed 1 April 2020.

Morgera, E, *Corporate Accountability in International Environmental Law* (Oxford University Press 2009).

Mushkat, R, 'International Environmental Law in the Asia-Pacific Region: Recent Developments' (1989) 20(1) *California Western International Law Journal* (CWSL), pp. 1–20.

Nijman, JE, *The Concept of International Legal Personality, An Inquiry into the History and Theory of International Law* (T.M.C. Asser Press 2004).

Nollkaemper, A, 'Responsibility of Transnational Corporations in International Environmental Law: Three Perspectives', in Gerd Winter (ed), *Multilevel Governance of Global Environmental Change – Perspectives from Science, Sociology and the Law* (Cambridge University Press 2006), pp. 179–199.

OAS, Department of Sustainable Development, available at http://www.oas.org/en/sedi/dsd/ accessed 1 April 2020.

OAS, Environmental Rule of Law in the Americas, available at http://www.oas.org/en/topics/environment.asp accessed 1 April 2020.

OECD, Guidelines for multinational enterprises, available at http://mneguidelines.oecd.org/annualreportsontheguidelines.htm accessed 1 March 2020.

OEIGWG Chairmanship Revised Draft 16.7.2019, Legally Binding Instrument to Regulate, in International Human Rights Law, the Activities of Transnational Corporations and Other Business Enterprises, available at https://www.ohchr.org/Documents/HRBodies/HRCouncil/WGTransCorp/OEIGWG_RevisedDraft_LBI.pdf accessed on 1 March 2020.

Olmos Giupponi, B, *Rethinking Free Trade, Economic Integration and Human Rights in the Americas* (Hart 2016).

Ong, David, 'The Impact of Environmental Law on Corporate Governance: International and Comparative Perspectives' (2001) 12(4) *European Journal of International Law*, pp. 685–726.

Pauchard, N, 'Access and Benefit Sharing under the Convention on Biological Diversity and Its Protocol: What Can Some Numbers Tell Us about the Effectiveness of the Regulatory Regime?' (2017) 6 *Resources*, p. 11.

Raine, A and Pluchon, E, 'UN Environment—Advancing the Environmental Rule of Law in the Asia Pacific' (2019) 3(1) *Chinese Journal of Environmental Law*, pp. 117–126, available at https://doi.org/10.1163/24686042-12340037accessed 1 April 2020.

Ratner, S, 'Business', in Daniel Bodansky, Jutta Brunnée, and Ellen Hey (eds), *The Oxford Handbook of International Environmental Law* (Oxford University Press 2012), pp. 807–828.

Rose, GL, *Gaps in the Implementation of Environmental Law at the National, Regional and Global Level* (UNEP 2011).

Treves, Tullio and Fodella, Alessandro, (eds), *Civil Society, International Courts and Compliance Bodies* (TMC Asser Press 2005).

Udombana, N, 'Reparations and Africa's Indigenous Peoples', in F. Lenzerini (ed), *Reparations for Indigenous Peoples International and Comparative Perspectives* (Oxford University Press 2009), pp. 389–407, at 392.

UN, 'Protect, Respect and Remedy' Framework and Guiding Principles, available at https://www.business-humanrights.org/en/un-secretary-generals-special-representative-on-business-human-rights/un-protect-respect-and-remedy-framework-and-guiding-principles accessed 1 March 2020.

UNECLAC, Observatorio del Principio 10 en América Latina y el Caribe, available at https://observatoriop10.cepal.org/en accessed 1 April 2020.

UNEP, About UN Environment Programme, available at https://www.unenvironment.org/about-un-environment accessed 1 March 2020.

UNEP, Guidelines on Compliance with and Enforcement of Multilateral Environmental Agreements, available at https://wedocs.unep.org/bitstream/handle/20.500.11822U/31773/English.pdf?sequence=1&isAllowed=y 1 March 2020.

UNEP, List of Accredited Organizations, available at https://www.unenvironment. org/civil-society-engagement/accreditation/list-accredited-organizations accessed 1 March 2020.

UNEP, The Role of UNEP in the Development of Guidelines on Compliance and Enforcement of Multilateral Environmental Agreements (UNEP Secretariat 2000), available at https://digitallibrary.un.org/record/436919?ln=en 1 April 2020.

UNFCCC, Nationally Determined Contributions (NDCs), available at https://unfccc. int/nationally-determined-contributions-ndcs accessed 1 March 2020.

United Nations, World Summit on Sustainable Development (WSSD), Johannesburg Summit, Johannesburg, South Africa.

Yee, Wai-Hang, Tang, Shui-Yan, and Lo, Carlos Wing-Hung, 'Regulatory Compliance When the Rule of Law Is Weak: Evidence from China's Environmental Reform' (2016) 26(1) *Journal of Public Administration Research and Theory*, pp. 95–112.

Zhanel, K, Review of Implementation of the International Environmental Conventions in Central Asia, CAREC Environmental Management Programme Specialist, 14.08.2018, available at http://carececo.org/publications/Review%20of%20the%20 implementation%20of%20MEAs%20in%20CA.pdf accessed 1 April 2020.

Zito, A, Burns Charlotte, and Lenschow, Andrea, 'Is the Trajectory of European Union Environmental Policy Less Certain?' (2019) 28(2) *Environmental Politics*, pp. 187–207.

Part 2

New features of compliance with international environmental law

5 Intersections, interactions, and conflicts

1 Introduction

Compliance with international environmental law (IEL) provide fertile ground for intersections with other areas of international law. Indeed, the interface between compliance with IEL and commitments undertaken by States in other areas of IL are expressed in either positive or negative interactions. In positive terms, there are synergies or mutual reinforcements, and in negative terms, conflicts or mutually excluding regimes may arise. In one way or another, the numerous existing interactions demonstrate that IEL compliance is multifaceted, and it takes place at different levels (local, regional, national, international, and transnational), the result of different dynamics.

In ensuring compliance with IEL, other branches of international law become relevant, such as international economic law, international energy law and international human rights law. These are the areas of international law in which the interactions with IEL are more accentuated.

Interfaces between IEL and other branches of IL also exist. The international legal body of cultural heritage law offers interesting ramifications as there is a cultural dimension in the international protection of the environment, particularly in what concerns the international legal framework for the protection and safeguarding of intangible cultural heritage (ICH).[1] Equally important are the interlinkages between IEL and the emerging area of animal law which are gaining more significance. Other sub-fields of international law, such as international intellectual property (IP) law also have implications for IEL in terms of international patent protection and technological innovation.[2]

---

1 See Lucas Lixinski, *Intangible Cultural Heritage in International Law* (Oxford University Press 2013). Lisa Rogers, 'Intangible Cultural Heritage and International Environmental Law: The Cultural Dimension of Environmental Protection' (2017) 29 *Historic Environment*, pp. 30–43.

2 See Pierre-Marie Dupuy and J. Viñuales, 'Intellectual Property Rights and the Environment', in *International Environmental Law* (Oxford University Press 2015), pp. 403–413. Claudio Chiarolla, 'Intellectual Property from a Global Environmental Law Perspective: Lessons from Patent Disclosure Requirements for Genetic Resources and Traditional Knowledge' (2019) 8(3) *Transnational Environmental Law*, pp. 503–521.

Keeping with the purpose of the book, the focus will be placed on the areas in which more interactions in terms of compliance are observed. To this end, the following sections address these various interactions, illustrating the analysis with cases.

2 Compliance with international environmental law and relations between international law regimes

Compliance with IEL obligations may turn out to be a matter for other areas of international law. Clear-cut cases of compliance, falling solely within the boundaries of IEL are far less common than cases in which different branches of international law are intertwined. Sometimes, the fulfilment of environmental obligations is not as unequivocal as it may seem.

Relationships between IEL and different regimes set up in other areas of law with an impact on the environmental realm may lead to cooperation or conflict. In some specific sectors, such as biodiversity, there is often an overlap between the objectives and the norms of the various regimes. Legal techniques to harmonise the different areas of law include interpretation methods provided by the Vienna Convention on the Law of Treaties (VCLT).

It is fair to say that in IEL there has been a transition from the 'silo structure' of compliance (constrained to the boundaries of a particular regime) to a more balanced and interrelated structure which takes into consideration interactions with other relevant regimes.

The main building blocks of IEL show deep connections to other branches of international law. Principle 12 of the Rio Declaration fostered the inclusion of sustainable development as a cross-cutting issue in international law by proclaiming that '[s]tates should cooperate to promote a supportive and open international economic system that would lead to economic growth and sustainable development in all countries, to better address the problems of environmental degradation'.[3]

The notion of sustainable development, a core concept in IEL, is far from static. Rather the opposite: The content, scope and application have varied according to the different states in the evolution of IEL.[4] The sustainable development principle has been considered as the central principle in IEL, even though its elusive nature fluctuates between being a merely programmatic principle and being a binding principle.[5]

Many environmental problems are cross-sectoral, which conditions the manner in which they are addressed. In addressing some crucial environmental problems such as climate degradation consistently, international law seems to be too

---

3 Rio Declaration on Environment and Development, Principle 12, available at https://www.cbd.int/doc/ref/rio-declaration.shtml accessed 1 March 2020.
4 Jorge E. Viñuales, 'Sustainable Development', in L. Rajamani and J. Peel (eds), *The Oxford Handbook of International Environmental Law* (2nd edn, Oxford University Press 2019), available at https://www.ceenrg.landecon.cam.ac.uk/working-paper-files/wp20 accessed 1 March 2020.
5 Jorge E. Viñuales, 'The Rise and Fall of Sustainable Development', 22(1) *Review of European Community and International Environmental Law* (2013), pp. 3–13.

fragmented. Although the chapter places the emphasis on the relationship between the various areas of international law and the links to compliance, it also provides a detailed analysis of the specific sectors of IEL.

Given the complexities of the current regimes, some common features can be identified across the different sectors. First, there are some shared obstacles to global cooperation, represented by conflicting priorities, e.g. how to strike the balance between trade liberalisation and environmental protection. These conflicting priorities are not necessarily legal priorities; rather, they are political and policy-oriented priorities. Second, having overcome the idea of fragmentation in international law, one needs to acknowledge that what works well in one area may not work well in other areas. This may depend on the regulatory theories/approaches taken and the evidence available to adjudicate cases. Third, the problem is not only compliance with the norm but also the effectiveness of a particular regime. In terms of the climate change regime, for instance, how the different emissions trading schemes effectively contribute to cutting down emissions. Fourth, there is a certain stagnation in the institutions that govern global environmental law and, therefore, necessitating radical changes in the structure of IEL.

Cross-fertilisation in IEL compliance by reference to other areas of international law brings its own challenges within various global environmental regimes. Network regulations and the system of international courts and tribunals help to deal with collective action problems on certain occasions, as observed in the climate change regime, but presents numerous shortcomings when it comes to other areas such as marine pollution.[6]

3 Trade, international environmental law and sustainable development

IEL often interacts with the world trading system (the regime instituted through the WTO normative system), which covers, under the same institutional architecture, the pre-existing General Agreement on Tariffs and Trade (GATT) 'disciplines'.[7] Seemingly, these regimes are at odds as trade liberalisation may be in conflict with environmental protection measures that may restrict trade in certain goods. The adoption of certain international trade instruments has proven to be an uplift for environmental protection, such as the Doha Development Agenda.[8]

The consideration given to environmental issues in the trade realm increased following the Rio Agreement 1992,[9] which placed attention on the reconciliation of development and the environment, representing a turning point for this relationship and paving the way for a new era in the environment-trade debate.[10]

6 Michael Bowman, Peter Davies and Catherine Redgwell, *Lyster's International Wildlife Law* (2nd edn, Cambridge University Press 2010).
7 Peter Van den Bossche and Werner Zdouc, *The Law and Policy of the World Trade Organization: Text, Cases and Materials* (4th edn, Cambridge University Press 2017).
8 WTO, The Doha Round, available at https://www.wto.org/english/tratop_e/dda_e/dda_e. htm accessed 1 March 2020.
9 The Rio Declaration on Environment and Development 1992.
10 S. Charnovitz, "The WTO's Environmental Progress" (2007) 10(3) *JIEL*, pp. 685–706.

This was also reflected during the Uruguay Round of negotiations (1986–1994) with the introduction of modifications to the Standards Code and the Technical Barriers to Trade (TBT) Agreement.[11] Moreover, environmental protection has been addressed in other disciplines, such as the General Agreement on Trade in Services (GATS), the Agreement on the Application of Sanitary and Phytosanitary Measures (SPS), the Agreement on Subsidies and Countervailing Measures (SCM) and the Trade-Related Aspects of Intellectual Property Rights Agreement (TRIPS).[12] A quantum leap with regard to international trade and environment occurred with the adoption of the Marrakesh Agreement, establishing the WTO.[13] Along with the addition of sustainable development to the Preamble,[14] the Marrakesh Agreement instituted the CTE (a permanent WTO Committee operating in Trade and Environment). This Committee has been more prominent than its predecessor, the EMIT.[15]

The interface between trade and environment also became the focus of the WTO adjudicating bodies, including both the panels and the AB.[16] Overall, the WTO has developed a considerably jurisprudential approach in this regard compared to its predecessor under the GATT, which hardly addressed or invoked environmental principles.[17]

a Compliance with international environmental law from the standpoint of international trade law and vice versa

Commentators argue that the WTO's key principle of non-discrimination through seeking the efficient allocation of resources may have positive effects or externalities for the environment. Clearly, the attainment of sustainable development is one of the main objectives of the multilateral trading system, as

11 WTO, Sustainable Development, available at https://www.wto.org/english/tratop_e/envir_e/ sust_dev_e.htm accessed 1 April 2020).

12 WTO, "Early Years: Emerging Environment Debate in GATT/WTO"(World Trade Organization 2019), available at https://www.wto.org/english/tratop_e/envir_e/hist1_e.htm accessed 1 March 2020; Will Martin and L. Alan Winters, *The Uruguay Round Widening and Deepening the World Trading System* (The World Bank 1995) p. 2.

13 Agreement Establishing the World Trade Organization 1994; Charnovitz (n 10) at 685–706.

14 Agreement Establishing the World Trade Organization 1994, Preamble; Richard Baron and Justine Garrett, 'Trade and Environment Interactions: Governance Issues' OECD Background paper for the 35th Round Table on Sustainable Development 2017, available at http://www.oecd. org/sd-roundtable/papersandpublications/Trade%20and%20Environment%20Interactions%20 FINAL.pdf accessed 1 March 2020.

15 MC, *Marrakesh Ministerial Decision on Trade and Environment*, MTN. TNC/45 (MIN) (14 April 1994); Dominic Gentile, "International Trade and the Environment: What Is the Role of the WTO?" (2009) 19(1) *FELW*, pp. 195–230; WTO, 'The Committee on Trade and Environment' (World Trade Organization 2019), available at https://www.wto.org/english/tratop_e/ envir_e/wrk_committee_e.htm accessed 1 March 2020.

16 Understanding on Rules and Procedures Governing the Settlement of Disputes (DSU) 1995, Article 17; WTO Secretariat, *A Handbook on the WTO Dispute Settlement System* (CUP 2004), pp. 12–16.

17 Michael M. Weinstein and Steve Charnovitz, 'The Greening of the WTO' (2001) 80(6) *Foreign Affairs*, pp. 147–156.

stated in the Preamble to the Marrakesh Agreement, which also refers to the need to protect and preserve the environment.[18] Interpreting this interface as a mutually beneficial relationship between regimes responds to the logic of harmony in achieving sustainable development, which may be supported by some international trade law cases.[19]

As background, the 1992 United Nations Conference on Environment and Development had already recognized the contribution the multilateral trading system could make to sustainable development.[20] The emerging architecture resulting from the entry into force of the Marrakesh Agreement envisages sustainable development as a central principle.[21] In turn, the Doha Development Agenda (DDA), a constituting element of the last trade round, focusses on the balanced achievement of development.[22]

In terms of assessing the harmful effects to identify and understand the hidden risks of trade activities, environmental exceptions were already allowed under Article XX (b and g) of the GATT.[23] Through the lenses of trade, broadly speaking, this article allows for compliance with environmental law (both international and domestic legal systems) to be invoked to justify some derogations under the international trade law regime. Conversely, compliance with international trade norms may pose challenges in terms of environmental governance; take, for instance, tensions encountered in international trade treaties negotiations between trade liberalisation and environmental protection. Within the WTO dispute settlement various environmental issues were discussed, such as policies aimed at reducing the consumption of cigarettes; the protection of dolphins; reduction of risks to human health posed by asbestos; and minimisation of risks to human, animal and plant life and health arising from the accumulation of re-treaded tyres (under Article XX(b)) as well as policies aimed at the conservation of tuna, salmon, herring, dolphins, turtles and clean air (under Article XX(g)).

Based on risk assessment, measures protecting the environment must be proportional and necessary; this requirement is also set out in the Sanitary and Phytosanitary Measures (SPS) Agreement[24] and the Technical Barriers to Trade

---

18 World Trade Organisation, *Sustainable Development*, available at https://www.wto.org/english/tratop_e/envir_e/sust_dev_e.htm accessed 1 April 2020.

19 Pierre-Marie Dupuy and J. Vinuales, *International Environmental Law* (CUP 2015), pp. 394–395.

20 WTO, Sustainable Development, available at https://www.wto.org/english/tratop_e/envir_e/sust_dev_e.htm accessed 1 March 2020.

21 1994 Marrakesh Agreement Establishing the World Trade Organisation. Done at Marrakesh on 15 April 1994. Entry into force: 1 January 1995, available at https://www.wto.org/english/docs_e/legal_e/04-wto_e.htm accessed 1 April 2020.

22 WTO, *Subjects Treated under the Doha Development Agenda*, available at https://www.wto.org/english/tratop_e/dda_e/dohasubjects_e.htm accessed 1 April 2020.

23 GATT, Article XX.

24 The WTO Agreement on the Application of Sanitary and Phytosanitary Measures (SPS Agreement) was adopted during the 1986-94 Uruguay Round and entered into force with the establishment of the World Trade Organization on 1 January 1995. WTO, 'Understanding the WTO Agreement on Sanitary and Phytosanitary Measures', available at https://www.wto.org/english/tratop_e/sps_e/spsund_e.htm accessed 1 April 2020.

(TBT) Agreement.[25] WTO dispute settlement bodies have taken a case-by-case approach, examining the fulfilment of the requirements of the chapeau, which are even more difficult to prove. In line with the chapeau, measures must not constitute a 'means of arbitrary or unjustifiable discrimination' or a 'disguised restriction on international trade'.[26] For these reasons, rules of the multilateral trading system may be seen as a stumbling block to compliance with IEL, and vice versa.

From the international trade law standpoint, several environmental goods and services have an economic value. Also, numerous environmental problems present uncertainties, and many environmental goods and services are considered public goods. In many cases, environmental goods and services cannot be priced in order to be considered under international trade rules, or their protection may clash with international trade law.

When faced with a controversy between these two fields of international law, the WTO dispute settlement bodies (panels and Appellate Body) have conducted a balancing test, weighing up the interests at stake. Wherever the environmental exception is invoked, both the panels and the Appellate Body perform a proportionality test. Environmental risk assessment processes in international trade law follow the precautionary principle.[27] The test also involves environmental cost-benefit analysis (CBA) which is applied to policies aiming to improve environmental protection or to actions that have an impact on the natural environment as an indirect consequence.[28]

Trade-related measures are also frequent in MEAs, such as in the 1973 Convention on Trade in Endangered Species (CITES).[29] Ensuring compliance through trade restrictions to protect the environment is often used as a tool in other international environmental treaties, such as the 1987 Protocol for the Protection of the Ozone Layer, or under those treaties relating to the transboundary movement of hazardous waste regime, such as the 1989 Basel Convention on the Control of Transboundary Movement of Hazardous Wastes and the 2001 Rotterdam Convention on the Prior Informed Consent Procedure

25 Technical Barriers to Trade (TBT) Agreement was also adopted during the 1986–94 Uruguay Round, available at https://www.wto.org/english/tratop_e/tbt_e/tbt_e.htm#:~:text=The%20 Technical%20Barriers%20to%20Trade,create%20unnecessary%20obstacles%20to%20trade accessed 1 April 2020.

26 Lorand Bartels, 'The Chapeau of the General Exceptions in the WTO GATT and GATS Agreements: A Reconstruction' (2015) 109 *American Journal of International Law*, p. 95, available at SSRN: https://ssrn.com/abstract=2557971 or http://dx.doi.org/10.2139/ssrn.2557971 accessed 1 April 2020.

27 Markus W. Gehring and Marie-Claire Cordonier Segger, *Precaution in World Trade Law: The Precautionary Principle and Its Implications for the World Trade* Organization (CISDL 2002), available at https://www.cisdl.org/wp-content/uploads/2018/05/Precaution-in-World-Trade-Law-2003.pdf accessed 1 April 2020.

28 OECD, Cost-Benefit Analysis and the Environment: Further Developments and Policy Use, OECD Publishing, (2018 Paris), available at https://doi.org/10.1787/9789264085169-en.

29 CITES, Appendices I, II and III. CITES, Howe CITES Works, available at https://www.cites.org/eng/disc/how.php accessed 1 April 2020.

for Certain Hazardous Chemicals and Pesticides in International Trade.[30] In addition, CITES uses trade criteria to determine the level of protection.[31] Space precludes a more detailed analysis of other cases, but these examples seem to demonstrate a positive interaction and mutual support between the regimes with environmental protection as a combined effect of these tools.[32]

b Environmental compliance in international trade law jurisprudence

The jurisprudence of the WTO dispute settlement system offers some interesting elements for the discussion on the relationship between trade liberalisation and the protection of the environment. Extra-territorial effects of environmental regulations were at issue in some of the highly debated trade controversies, such as *Shrimp-Turtle*[33] and *Tuna fish-Dolphin*.[34] In the *Re-treaded tyres case*, although they did not include any specific reference to sustainable development, Brazil contended that these decisions recognized that the importation of used tyres entailed environmental risks.[35]

The environmental exception in the world trading system provided for in Article XX of the GATT in three different types (recitals a, b and g) has been often invoked in cases brought before WTO dispute settlement mechanisms, presenting an evolution in terms of compliance or clashes between the different regimes.[36] In various cases before the WTO panels, parties have invoked the environmental exception in the relationship between developing and developed countries, as in the retreaded tyres cases.[37] In the notorious Shrimp/Turtles case the environmental protection was recognised as a possible exception to

---

30 The Basel Convention on the Control of Transboundary Movements of Hazardous Wastes and their Disposal was adopted on 22 March 1989, available at http://www.basel.int/TheConvention/Overview/tabid/1271/Default.aspx accessed 1 April 2020.

31 The Conference of the Parties (CoP), which is the supreme decision-making body of the Convention and comprises all its Parties, has agreed in Resolution Conf. 9.24 (Rev. CoP17) on a set of biological and trade criteria to help determine whether a species should be included in Appendices.

32 Riccardo Pavoni, 'Mutual Supportiveness as a Principle of Interpretation and Law-Making: A Watershed for the 'WTO-and-Competing-Regimes' Debate?' (2010) 3 *European Journal of International Law*, pp. 649, 654–655.

33 United States—Import Prohibition of Certain Shrimp and Shrimp Products- WTO case Nos. 58 (and 61). Ruling adopted on 6 November 1998.

34 United States—Restrictions on Imports of Tuna, the 'tuna-dolphin' case, ruling not adopted, circulated on 3 September 1991. Case brought by Mexico et al. United States—Restrictions on Imports of Tuna, "son of tuna-dolphin", ruling not adopted, circulated on 16 June 1994.

35 WTO, *DS332: Brazil-Measures Affecting Imports of Retreaded Tyres*, available at https://www.wto.org/english/tratop_e/dispu_e/cases_e/ds332_e.htm accessed 1 April 2020.

36 John Carter Morgan III, 'Fragmentation of International Environmental Law and the Synergy: A Problem and a 21st Century Model Solution' (2017) 18 *Vermont Journal of Environmental Law*, p. 133.

37 Dispute Settlement: Dispute DS332. Brazil – Measures Affecting Imports of Retreaded Tyres, available at http://www.wto.org/english/tratop_e/dispu_e/cases_e/ds332_e.htm accessed 10 January 2015.

trade, although the Apellate Body declared that the measure in question was not covered by it because it was arbitrary and discriminatory.

When it came to the protection of animal welfare (broadly considered part of environmental law), the WTO has generated more controversy as seen in the *EC-Seal Products* case.[38] The EU argued the case under the moral exception in favour of animal welfare, indicating that EU citizens were concerned with the welfare aspects of seal hunting and the marketing of the products, thus banning trade in seal products but contemplating some exceptions.[39] The regulation at issue, Regulation (EC) No 1007/2009 on trade in seal products, failed to comply with the test under the chapeau in this case.

To reinforce environmental protection in the international trade regime during the litigation before the WTO dispute settlement body, non-state actors and third States have been offered the possibility to submit amicus curiae briefs, as happened in the controversy surrounding re-treaded tyres.[40]

APELLATE BODY

United States — Import Prohibition of Certain Shrimp and Shrimp Products

WTO case Nos. 58 (and 61). Ruling adopted on 6 November 1999

185. In reaching these conclusions, we wish to underscore what we have not decided in this appeal. We have not decided that the protection and preservation of the environment is of no significance to the Members of the WTO. Clearly, it is. We have not decided that the sovereign nations that are Members of the WTO cannot adopt effective measures to protect endangered species, such as sea turtles. Clearly, they can and should. And we have not decided that sovereign states should not act together bilaterally, plurilaterally or multilaterally, either within the WTO or in other international fora, to protect endangered species or to otherwise protect the environment. Clearly, they should and do.[41]

---

38 WTO Dispute Settlement. DS400: European Communities — Measures Prohibiting the Importation and Marketing of Seal Products, available at https://www.wto.org/english/tratop_e/dispu_e/cases_e/ds400_e.htm accessed 1 April 2020.

39 Lukasz Adam Gruszczynski, "EC – Seal Products Case: Public Morality Meets the World Trade Court" (2014) 3(1–2) *Polish Review of International and European Law*, pp. 101–119, available at https://ssrn.com/abstract=3098942 accessed 1 April 2020.

40 Various NGOs acted as Third Participants in the proceedings: Associação de Combate aos Poluentes (ACPO), Brazil; Associação de Proteção ao Meio Ambiente de Cianorte (APROMAC), Brazil; Centro de Derechos Humanos y Ambiente (CEDHA), Argentina; Center for International Environmental Law (CIEL), United States and Switzerland; Conectas Direitos Humanos, Brazil; Friends of the Earth Europe, Belgium; The German NGO Forum on Environment and Development, Germany; Justiça Global, Brazil; and Instituto O Direito por Um Planeta Verde, Brazil.

41 United States—Import Prohibition of Certain Shrimp and Shrimp Products. WTO case Nos. 58 (and 61). Ruling adopted on 6 November 1998.

WTO – Dispute Settlement – DS135: European Communities – Measures Affecting Asbestos and Products Containing Asbestos

Despite finding a violation of Article III, the Panel ruled in favour of the European Communities. Under Article III (which requires countries to grant equivalent treatment to like products) the Panel found that the EC ban constituted a violation since asbestos and asbestos substitutes had to be considered "like products" within the meaning of that Article. The panel argued that health risks associated with asbestos were not a relevant factor in the consideration of product likeness. However, the Panel found that the French ban could be justified under Article XX (b). In other words, the measure could be regarded as one which was "necessary to protect animal, human, plant life or health." It also met the conditions of the chapeau of Article XX. It therefore ruled in favour of the European Communities.

Dispute Settlement – DS332: Brazil — Measures Affecting Imports of Re-treaded Tyres

On 3 December 2007, the Appellate Body report was circulated to Members. The Appellate Body: upheld the Panel's finding that the import ban can be considered "necessary" within the meaning of Article XX(b) and is thus provisionally justified under that provision and found that the Panel did not breach its duty under Article 11 of the DSU to make an objective assessment of the facts.

(...) reversed the Panel's findings that the MERCOSUR exemption would result in the import ban being applied in a manner that constitutes unjustifiable discrimination and a disguised restriction on international trade only to the extent that it results in volumes of imports of retreaded tyres that would significantly undermine the achievement of the objective of the import ban; reversed the Panel's findings that the MERCOSUR exemption has not resulted in arbitrary discrimination and that the MERCOSUR exemption has not resulted in unjustifiable discrimination; and found instead that the MERCOSUR exemption has resulted in the import ban being applied in a manner that constitutes arbitrary or unjustifiable discrimination within the meaning of the chapeau of Article XX; reversed the Panel's findings that the imports of used tyres under court injunctions have resulted in the import ban being applied in a manner that constitutes unjustifiable discrimination and a disguised restriction on international trade only to the extent that such imports have taken place in volumes that significantly undermine the achievement of the objective of the import ban; and found instead that the imports of used tyres under court injunctions have resulted in the import ban being applied in a manner that constitutes arbitrary or unjustifiable discrimination within the meaning

(Continued)

of the chapeau of Article XX; and AB Award - WT/DS332/AB/R (...) with respect to Article XX of the GATT 1994, the Appellate Body upheld, albeit for different reasons, the Panel's findings that the import ban is not justified under Article XX of the GATT 1994.

1 The Necessity Analysis

9. The European Communities claims that the Panel erred in finding that the import prohibition on retreaded tyres imposed by Brazil (the "Import Ban") was necessary to protect human, animal, or plant life or health, within the meaning of Article XX(b) of the GATT 1994. The European Communities requests the Appellate Body to reverse this finding and to find, instead, that the Import Ban is not "necessary" within the meaning of Article XX(b).

B Arguments of Brazil – Appellee

1 The Necessity Analysis

Para 52. Brazil maintains that the Panel properly found that the Import Ban was "necessary" to protect human, animal, or plant life or health within the meaning of Article XX(b) of the GATT 1994, and therefore requests the Appellate Body to uphold this finding.

a The Contribution Analysis

Para 53. First, Brazil argues that the Panel correctly assessed the contribution made by the Import Ban to the achievement of its objective. The paragraphs set out in Article XX focus on the measure, as such, while the chapeau focuses also on the application of the measure. Therefore, actual contribution is not relevant to the analysis under paragraph (b) of Article XX, and the Panel applied the correct legal standard in using phrases such as "can contribute" and "capable of contributing". Such a standard is also particularly appropriate given that some measures—for example, environmental measures—may not have immediate effect. The Panel's approach was in line with "virtually all" other cases that have examined a measure's contribution under paragraphs (b) and (d) of Article XX of the GATT 1994 or under Article XIV of the General Agreement on Trade in Services (the "GATS"). This is the case whether the risk sought to be avoided is direct or indirect. Brazil adds that the need to undertake the weighing and balancing exercise also illustrates that the European Communities cannot be correct. If a panel were required to assess the extent of a measure's actual contribution, it would have to do the same for alternative measures in order to compare them. Yet, this is impossible, because an alternative measure is one that has not yet been realized. That the Panel was not, as the European Communities claims, required to quantify the Import Ban's contribution to reducing waste tyre volumes is confirmed in the Appellate Body Report in EC – Asbestos, where the Appellate Body held that "a risk may be evaluated either in quantitative or qualitative terms". Brazil also expresses its understanding that, according to existing case law, if the measure can make a contribution to its objective, and no reasonably available alternatives exist, then the measure is "necessary".

Para 65 (...) "Brazil rejects as a 'blatant misrepresentation' the European Communities' argument that the Panel's finding necessarily implies that mere compliance with any international agreement would exclude the existence of arbitrary discrimination, particularly given that the Panel expressly stated that its finding was limited to the "specific circumstances of the case". Furthermore, the European Communities' systemic concerns in this respect are contrary to the well-established precept under general international law that "bad faith on the part of States is not to be presumed", and it is "absurd" to suggest that a WTO Member would conclude an agreement under Article XXIV for purposes of circumventing the requirements of the chapeau of Article XX.

Para 78. Brazil contends that the European Communities has failed to rebut Brazil's prima facie demonstration that MERCOSUR is consistent with the requirements of Article XXIV: 5 and 8. The fact that the CRTA and the Committee on Trade and Development did not reach the conclusion that MERCOSUR is in compliance with Article XXIV does not suggest that MERCOSUR is inconsistent with Article XXIV, in particular, because Members' measures are presumed WTO-consistent until sufficient evidence is presented to prove the contrary, and because the CRTA has only once concluded that a regional trade agreement was compatible with the GATT 1994'.

Source: WTO https://www.wto.org/english/tratop_e/
dispu_e/cases_e/ds332_e.htm

4 Investment and environmental protection: the sustainable development equation

The interface between international investment law (IIL) and IEL have been surrounded by heated scholarly debates that indicate the controversial nature of the relationships between these two international law fields. Usually, the debate has revolved around sustainable development and its legal implications for IIL as another specialised branch of international law.[42] Developing States, particularly, are faced with a challenge: how to strike the balance between achieving sustainable development and granting foreign investors protection.

42 Patricia Birnie, Alan Boyle, and Catherine Redgwell, *International Law and the Environment* (3rd edn Oxford University Press 2009), p. 115.

It has long been argued that IIL will bring in the risk of a 'regulatory chill', which may lead governments to waive the adoption of legitimate regulatory measures for the environment, health or natural resources. In terms of compliance, this represents a 'balancing exercise'; States should also address the perceived threat that investment protection agreements will hinder the safeguard of the environment and their powers to adopt, maintain or enforce any measure they consider appropriate to ensure that investments are compatible with environmental concerns.

Scholars have referred to the interference of foreign investors that may circumvent controls and end up reducing the margin of manoeuvre of the host State as an 'expropriation of environmental governance'.[43] A long-standing idea is that, in a globalised world, multinational companies may exploit natural resources in other (less-developed) States, even being considered as 'global corporate predators'.[44] These tensions between IIL and IEL are embodied in concepts such as 'regulatory chill' and 'pollution havens' (investors from developed States vis-à-vis developing host-States).

Regulatory chill is a term that has been used in the relevant literature, even though its exact meaning is difficult to grasp. In this light, investment arbitration would represent a threat or a restriction to governments and their capability to freely operate in the policy space.[45] According to the regulatory chill theory, case law would demonstrate that investment arbitration hampers the government's right to regulate, leading to a risk of 'regulatory chill'. Environmental protection can be relaxed in many states to achieve other advantages. The concept of 'pollution havens' is not free from controversy.[46] It has been defined as a situation in which any State with less strict environmental standards attracts more investments, creating a 'pollution haven'. But this definition 'would be misleading because countries cannot, in general, be expected to have the same environmental standards all over the world—regardless of whether they want to attract foreign capital'.[47]

43 K. Tienhaara, *The Expropriation of Environmental Governance* (Cambridge University Press 2009).

44 D.R. Loritz, 'Corporate Predators Attack Environmental Regulations: It's Time to Arbitrate Claims Filed under NAFTA's Chapter 11' (2000) 533 *Loyola Los Angeles International & Comparative Law Review*, p. 533.

45 K. Tienhaara, 'Regulatory Chill and the Threat of Arbitration: A View from Political Science (October 28, 2010)', in Chester Brown and Kate Miles (eds), *Evolution in Investment Treaty Law and Arbitration* (Cambridge University Press 2011), available at SSRN: http://ssrn.com/abstract=2065706 accessed 1 April 2020.

46 E. Neumayer, 'Pollution Havens: An Analysis of Policy Options for Dealing with an Elusive Phenomenon' (2001) 10(2) *Journal of Environment & Development*, pp. 147–177.

47 See Bradley J. Condon and T. Sinha, *The Role of Climate Change in Global Economic Governance* (OUP 2013); Tim Stephens, *International Courts and Environmental Protection* (CUP 2009); Sophie Thoyer and Benoit Martimort-Asso, *Participation for Sustainability in Trade* (Ashgate – Global Environmental Governance Series 2007); Timothy Swanson and Sam Johnston, *Global Environmental Problems and International Environmental Agreements-The Economics of International Institution Building* (Edward Elgar 1999) and Jochem Wiers, *Trade and Environment in the EC and the WTO* (Europa Law Publishing 2003).

Nevertheless, globalisation may have some positive impacts on environmental policy, such as convergence of good practices; an increased coordinated action to address international environmental problems under multilateral environmental agreements; and enhanced interactions between civil society groups, which can communicate and co-operate with each other to exert pressure on policymakers and business groups.[48]

To offset possible environmentally harmful effects, international investment agreements (IIAs) include provisions on the right to regulate and references to MEAs to ensure that environmental standards do not fade away. Public welfare objectives are often included in different model BITs (such as the US Model BIT). The 'right to regulate' alludes to a State's sovereign power, under international and domestic law, to enact domestic legislation and adopt measures necessary to protect the public interest within its jurisdiction.

The right to regulate ties in with the doctrine of police powers, according to which, host States may adopt legitimate regulatory measures affecting foreign investors that under certain conditions would not amount to an illegal taking of property.[49] In a strict interpretation, the 'right to regulate' would prevent investment arbitration claims from affecting state sovereignty. International arbitration shows a three-step 'test' used to determine the legality of the right to regulate which comprises three elements that must be present: the existence of public interest, proportionality of the measure and degree of interference with property rights.[50]

This test is often performed in cases dealing with the environmental consequences of large-scale resource exploitation involving public interest.[51] Several cases have sparked criticism against international arbitration, particularly those brought before the International Centre for the Settlement of Investment Disputes (ICSID) and other Investor-to-State Dispute Settlement (ISDS) fora comprising public interest and environmental protection.[52] The notion of public interest stems from different sources and varies from case to case.[53]

Case law arising under the North America Free Trade Agreement (NAFTA) also involved compliance with environmental law obligations. In *Tecmed v*

48 Eric Neumayer, *Greening Trade and Investment: Environmental Protection without Protectionism* (Earthscan 2001).

49 J.R. Marlles, 'Public Purpose, Private Losses: Regulatory Expropriation and Environmental Regulation in International Investment Law' (2007) 16 *Journal of Transnational Law and Policy*, p. 275.

50 *Methanex Corporation*, Award on Jurisdiction. Nafta/Uncitral Case between Ethyl Corporation and the Government of Canada, 24 June 1998, available at http://www.naftalaw.org/disputes_canada_ethyl.htm accessed 1 April 2020.

51 B.J. Condon, 'Treaty Structure and Public Interest Regulation in International Economic Law' (2014) 17(2) *Journal of International Economic Law*, p. 333.

52 R. Rao, 'Facing Arbitration for Environmental Regulation' (2005) 5(1) *Sustainable Development Law & Policy*, p. 66.

53 D.A. Gantz, 'Global Trade Issues in The New Millennium: Potential Conflicts between Investors Rights and Environmental Regulation Under Nafta's Chapter XI' (2001) 33 *George Washington International Law Review*, pp. 651–752.

Mexico environmental considerations were part of the arguments invoked by the parties to the controversy: Tecmed argued that the Environmental Protection Agency's decision to refuse renewal of the permit mandating the closure of the landfill amounted to an indirect expropriation of Tecmed's investment.[54]

As the NAFTA tribunal asserted in *Methanex*

> non-discriminatory regulation for a public purpose, which is enacted in accordance with due process and, which affects, inter alios, a foreign investor or investment is not deemed expropriatory and compensable unless specific commitments had been given by the regulating government to the then putative foreign investor.[55]

This, in particular, is controversial since otherwise these measures would constitute expropriation in the different variations.[56] It has still not been settled how arbitral tribunals address regulatory interference on environmental grounds.[57] While the Methanex case has had far-reaching implications, looking at the NAFTA case law as a whole, there are several cases in which expropriation was determined by the arbitral tribunals.[58] The bottom line is that there is no clear-cut, 'a priori' solution. For instance, a pending case before a NAFTA tribunal (the Lone Pine arbitration) deals with the revocation of the company's right to mine for oil and gas under the St Laurence River, affected by the Government of Quebec's fracking moratorium.[59] In the company's view, this revocation was 'arbitrary, capricious, and illegal (…) without due process, without compensation, and with no recognizable public purpose'.[60]

Another aspect concerns procedural transparency and right to information in environmental matters.[61] Procedural transparency is crucial in informing the

---

54 Tecnicas Medioambientales Tecmed S.A. v. United Mexican States, ICSID Case No. AR-B(AF)/00/2 (*Tecmed v Mexico*), paras. 95–96, available at https://cf.iisd.net/itn/2018/10/18/tecmed-v-mexico/ accessed 1 April 2020.

55 Methanex, at 1456, available at https://www.italaw.com/cases/683 accessed 1 April 2020.

56 M. Paparinskis, 'Regulatory Expropriation and Sustainable Development' (July 10, 2010), in M.W. Gehring, M.C. Cordonnier-Segger, and A. Newcombe (eds), *Sustainable Development in International Investment Law*, Kluwer Law International, available at SSRN: http://ssrn.com/abstract=1698192 accessed 1 April 2020.

57 Sornarajah, *The International Law on Foreign Investment* (3rd edn Cambridge University Press 2013), p. 110.

58 A. Álvarez Jiménez, 'The Methanex Final Award. An Analysis from the Perspectives of Environmental Regulatory Authorities and Foreign Investors' (2006) *Journal of International Arbitration*, p. 427.

59 Lone Pine Resources Inc. v. The Government of Canada, ICSID Case No. UNCT/15/2, available at http://www.italaw.com/cases/1606#sthash.N21Ep9gk.dpuf accessed 1 April 2020.

60 Lone Pine Resources Inc v. The Government of Canada, Notice of Arbitration, 6 September 2013, para 11.

61 T. Weiler, 'Good Faith and Regulatory Transparency: The Story of Metalclad V. Mexico', in *International Investment Law and Arbitration. Leading Cases from The Icsid, Nafta, Bilateral Treaties and Customary International Law*, USA 2004, 701.

public if a dispute concerning public interests exists and its content (allegations, state's wrongdoings, affected interests, etc.).[62] At the international level, the right to access to information in environmental matters has been recognised in Principle 10 of the Rio Declaration on Environment and Development, which affirms that every individual must have access to information, the opportunity to participate in decision-making and access to redress and remedy.[63] The principle encompasses the action plan under the Declaration that underlines the need for access to information on an international level to achieve sustainable development.[64]

In Europe, the right has been further developed by the Aarhus Convention (on Access to Information, Public Participation in Decision-making and Access to Justice in Environmental Matters), in force since 2001.[65] Freedom of information as a human right is embodied in different international instruments, such as Article 10 of the European Convention on Human Rights.[66] The ECHR has given rise to an interesting case law on access to information based on compliance with Articles 6, 8 and 10: *López Ostra v Spain* (1994), Guerra v Italy (1998), Fadeyeva v Russia (2005) and Hardy v UK (2012). Also, specifically concerning foreign investment, in *Reyes v. Chile* before the Inter-American Court of Human Rights, the petitioners alleged that the State had violated the principle of free access to state-held information when the Chilean Committee on Foreign Investment failed to release information about a deforestation project the petitioners wanted to evaluate.[67] The I. A. Court upheld the claim on the basis of Article 13 of the American Convention on Human Rights, which embodies the right to 'seek, receive and impart' information as 'a requisite for the very exercise of democracy'.[68]

While it is out of question that investment agreements may give rise to environmental and sustainable development issues, the emergence of an autonomous right to transparency in international investment law is still questionable. The

62 Joachim Delaney and Daniel Barstow Magraw, 'Procedural Transparency', in Peter Muchlinski, et al. (eds), *The Oxford Handbook of International Investment Law* (2008), p. 731.

63 The Access to Information, Public Participation in Decision-making and Access to Justice in Environmental Matters (Aarhus Convention), adopted on June 25, 1998, in Aarhus, Denmark, and entering into force on October 30, 2001. The Convention constitutes the first internationally binding mechanism for access to information and public participation in environmental matters. It was negotiated between countries of the United Nations Economic Commission for Europe (UNECE) but is open to all States.

64 Rio Declaration, Principle 1, A/CONF.151/26 (Vol. I), available at https://www.un.org/en/development/desa/population/migration/generalassembly/docs/globalcompact/A_CONF.151_26_Vol.I_Declaration.pdf accessed 1 April 2020.

65 Aarhus Convention (on Access to Information, Public Participation in Decision-making and Access to Justice in Environmental Matters), Article 2.3.

66 In addition, the EU has adopted the Directive 2003/4/EC on public access to environmental information.

67 See *Reyes v. Chile*, Case 12.108, Inter-Am. C.H.R., Report No. 60/03, OEAISer.UV/II. 118, doc. 70, rev. 2,159 (2003).

68 Ibid.

ultimate power to determine whether documents are made public is in the hands of the arbitral tribunal and the parties.

Over the past ten years, there has been deep concern about procedural transparency and accommodating public interest in investment-State arbitration. Consequently, transparency rules have been adopted in ISDS. Provisions range from publishing certain documents relating to the arbitration procedure to allowing amicus curiae submissions. The 2006 ICSID arbitration rules contain a specific provision regarding amicus curiae briefs,[69] legally recognizing the right to make such submissions, apart from specific information that should be disclosed.[70]

Previous ICSID case law provides good ground for reflection on the relationships between environmental protection and international investment law. In *Bi-water Gauff v. Tanzania* and *Vivendi v. Argentina*, the arbitral tribunal just transcribed parts of the amicus curiae submission.[71] The possibility to submit amicus curiae briefs does not imply the petitioners' right to access to documents submitted by either party. ICSID tribunals have reacted in similar ways in this regard. In *Biwater Gauff v. Tanzania*, the tribunal did not grant the petitioner's request to access additional information, including documents containing the claims of the parties.[72] Two main reasons were put forward by the tribunal. First, it did not authorize the disclosure of information, based on a strict interpretation of ICSID rules. Second, it rejected the petition, arguing that the dispute was a 'very public and widely reported dispute' and that the information that gave rise to the amici's request to intervene was sufficient to make further submissions. In a similar vein, the arbitral tribunal in Suez Vivendi granted permission to file an amicus curiae brief but denied access to the parties' submissions.

In order to address these issues, international investment agreements include more sophisticated provisions (not to lower environmental standards, to adhere to specific MEAs and to reinforce international cooperation in environmental matters) with a separate dispute settlement procedure or chapter to deal with environmental issues. Public interest litigation and the right to regulate for environmental reasons continue to develop case law and jurisprudential rules addressing conflicts between these two diverse areas of law. An emerging law-making and case law has resulted from Bilateral Investment Agreements to megaregional and multilateral agreements.

69 ICSID Arbitration Rules, at Rule 37(2).

70 K. Tienhaara, 'Third-Party Participation in Investment-Environment Disputes: Recent Developments' (2007) 16(2) *RECIEL*, pp. 230–242.

71 Both the Biwater and the Vivendi tribunals order groups of NGOs to submit a single amicus curiae brief. See Biwater No. 5, providing that the five NGOs, from Tanzania and the U.S., submit a single amicus curiae submission. See also Vivendi, requiring the five NGOs, from Argentina and the U.S., to file a single amicus curiae brief.

72 *Biwater Gauff (Tanzania) Ltd. v. United Republic of Tanzania*, Procedural Order No. 5, 2 February 2007, available at https://www.italaw.com/cases/157 accessed 1 April 2020.

PERENCO ECUADOR LTD V REPUBLIC OF ECUADOR, ICSID CASE NO. ARB/08/6, INTERIM DECISION ON THE ENVIRONMENTAL COUNTERCLAIM, 11 AUGUST 2015

A Introduction

34. Ecuador presented the environmental counterclaim on the basis that its experts had determined the existence of an "environmental catastrophe" in the two oil blocks situated in the country's Amazonian rainforest that had been worked by the consortium under Perenco's operatorship. Ecuador viewed this as an extremely serious matter deserving the most careful consideration by the Tribunal. On this point, the Tribunal cannot but agree. Proper environmental stewardship has assumed great importance in today's world. The Tribunal agrees that if a legal relationship between an investor and the State permits the filing of a claim by the State for environmental damage caused by the investor's activities and such a claim is substantiated, the State is entitled to full reparation in accordance with the requirements of the applicable law.

35. The Tribunal further recognises that a State has wide latitude under international law to prescribe and adjust its environmental laws, standards and policies in response to changing views and a deeper understanding of the risks posed by various activities, including those of extractive industries such as oilfields. All of this is beyond any serious dispute and the Tribunal enters into this phase of the proceeding mindful of the fundamental imperatives of the protection of the environment in Ecuador.

(…)

Conclusion on Perenco's Environmental Management Practices in Blocks 7 and 21

447. In sum, the Tribunal considers that Perenco's claims of strong environmental law compliance are not made out. While the Tribunal is not prepared to find that Perenco consistently sought to conceal instances of contamination, there is some evidence that it was less than forthcoming in some instances. The 2010 memorandum's comment on the Payamino 2–8 contamination that the "State will probably assume that we are hiding many more [environmental] damages and will scrutinize the operations area in search for more damages and it will probably find them" is very troubling. This evidence, combined with the company's failure to document the environmental condition of the two Blocks at the time of the acquisition of its interests, its failure to conduct the statutorily required audits in 2004, its use of outdated environmental documents during the

(Continued)

course of the operations, its failure to obtain necessary licenses, the increase in the incidence of nonconformities detected in the 2006 and 2008 audits, and Mr. Puente's unchallenged testimony as to the approach taken in the 2008 Block 7 audit do not paint a picture of a responsible environmental steward.

Source:https://www.italaw.com/sites/default/files/case-documents/italaw6315.pdf

5 Energy, renewable energy and environmental protection

The synergies between international energy law and IEL have gone through various stages. Traditionally, their mutual interactions have been, to an extent, related to the fulfilment of environmental obligations on the international sphere. The body of international legislation referring to traditional energy sources contains some elements pertaining to that relationship. Clearly, the shift in the relationship between the two fields has been closely linked to developments in the climate change regime. Moving away from fossil fuels and increasing shares in the production of renewable energy have changed the dynamics. Certainly, the international legal regime for renewable energy sector has brought about a new model for the relationship between international energy law and IEL: namely, under the climate change regime.

To meet their obligations and achieve the set targets, governments promote renewable energy technologies to reduce greenhouse gases (GHG) emissions and increase the production of green energy. Relevant technological development has fostered a new legal framework. However, implementing measures may be interfering with national trade law and WTO provisions. This may lead to conflicts between the domestic renewable energy support (incentives) and the basic principles of the world trading regime. Here, the legal debate arises as to the appropriateness of State measures used for incentivizing renewable energy development and their deployment, as they may be in contradiction with basic trade law principles. These conflicts have led to an emergence of trade-related disputes in different international law fora – namely, in the WTO system, particularly the wind and solar energy sectors – due to the persistence of protectionist practices.

The full deployment of renewable energies, particularly in the solar and wind sectors, requires government subsidies. On the one hand, only a few countries are willing to subsidize an industry that relies primarily on imported technology. On the other hand, these support measures are often classed as actionable subsidies under international trade law. The prevalence of protectionist policies in the wind and solar industries have given rise to different trade conflicts. Another crucial point for this analysis regards the previously alluded 'environmental exception', as mentioned in the literature examining conflicts between trade and the environment which has blossomed over the past decades.[73]

Renewable energy law cases pose the question of the controversial relations between environmental protection and trade liberalisation.[74] Although there are some analogies, renewable energy-related cases before WTO panels are different. Unlike other 'environmental' exceptions under Article XX GATT they present two distinctive features: the indirect nature of the environmental benefit alluded to (an indirect relationship between the measure adopted and the goal of protection of the environment) and the scope of WTO provisions that may be affected by the measures in question. Another controversial issue regards the eligibility of the measures to support the production of renewable energy, as they may be in contradiction with the Agreement on Subsidies and Countervailing (ASCM) or fall outside the scope of the GATT Article XX exceptions.[75]

Thus, the applicability of the environmental exception to renewable energy support measures is arguable. States have found it difficult to justify the use of certain subsidies or industrial policies under GATT Article XX to foster the development and deployment of renewable energy. States are faced with the need to prove a complex and indirect link between, on the one hand, renewable energy technology and health, and, on the other hand, the necessity in the adoption of the measures to reduce the reliance on fossil fuels and prevent climate change.

To illustrate, in 2013, in the dispute 'Canada - Certain Measures Affecting the Renewable Energy Generation Sector' the Appellate Body (AB) decided on the compatibility of measures regarding the renewable energy sector brought by Japan and the EU against Canada. For the first time, a WTO panel and the AB, the highest WTO body, were confronted with the application of renewable measures.

In the dispute, Japan and the EU alleged that the 2009 Ontario FIT program was in violation of different provisions of the WTO legal framework.[76] Specifically, they claimed that the Ontario program violated provisions on national treatment under GATT III (4 and TRIMs 2.1), amounting to a prohibited subsidy under article 3.1(b) of the ASCM due to the LCRs included in the FIT program.

Even though these rulings threw some light on the interpretation of WTO rules on trade, investment measures and subsidies concerning sustainable energy, several obstacles were present. One of the main difficulties faced by both the WTO Panel and the AB regarded the qualification of the measure as an

73 Alan Boyle and James Harrison, 'Judicial Settlement of International Environmental Disputes: Current Problems' (2013) 4(2) *Journal of International Dispute Settlement*, pp. 245–276.
74 WTO, Appellate Body Report, *United States –Import Prohibition of Certain Shrimp and Shrimp Products* WT/DS58/AB/R (12 October 1998).
75 At least in accordance with recent Appellate Body decisions in ongoing disputes.
76 Appellate Body. (2013). Canada - Certain Measures Affecting the Renewable Energy Generation Sector. Appellate Body Report WT/DS412/AB/R / WT/DS426/AB/R, adopted 6 May 2013.

actionable subsidy. The panel and AB followed a two-stage test to determine the compatibility of a supporting measure with WTO law regulating subsidies. The following questions were posed: (1) Does the measure constitute a financial contribution? (2) Does the measure grant a benefit? (3) Is the measure only applicable to specific cases? The analysis goes on to determine whether the actionable subsidy has caused adverse effects to the interests of another WTO member. In principle, an actionable subsidy is not in violation of WTO law per se. This is only the case if the subsidy has adverse effects. The final ruling included a dissent between the members of the panel regarding the choice of the wholesale market benchmark for a FIT Without LCR. The dissenting opinion was in disagreement regarding the benchmark used to determine compatibility with WTO law.

In *Canada - Renewable Energy*, the AB ruled that local content requirements (LCRs) were unacceptable.[77] Finally, the AB found that Ontario's FIT program was in violation of its national treatment obligation under the TRIMs and GATT agreement because of its LCRs. In sum, LCRs attached to an FIT are illegal under GATT and TRIMs, as found by the panel and confirmed by the AB. Nevertheless the status of FITs within the WTO subsidy agreement remained unanswered. In other words, what would be the implications of FITs without local content requirements taking the wholesale electricity market as a benchmark?[78]

After the first case, the WTO had to deal with other similar issues: in particular, if a feed-in tariff constitutes a subsidy issue, as discussed in more detail below. In November 2012, China requested consultations with the EU on Italian and Greek FITs containing LCRs (see below and Table 2). In February 2013, the United States requested consultations with India regarding incentive programs with LCRs relating to solar cells and solar modules, which according to the complainant were in violation GATT, TRIMs and ASCM.

The AB intended to avoid deciding on the matter of whether or not an FIT constitutes a subsidy. In its reasoning on market creation, it benchmarked different markets to determine the existence of a subsidy. The conclusion reached does not solve all the problems caused by renewable energy trade where it affects the WTO regime.

These same issues resurfaced in WTO adjudication, which demonstrates the intricacies of the relationship between different areas of international law. Clearly, within WTO dispute settlement, the AB is constrained by the subject matter of the disputes and procedural aspects involved in the particular controversy. WTO members are then called to provide clarity on the appropriate policy measures to encourage the renewable energy sector in the transition to a green economy,

---

77　Jan-Christoph Kuntze, and Tom Moerenhout, Local Content Requirement 2013. Local Content Requirements and the Renewable Energy Industry – A Good Match? Geneva: ICTSD, available at http://ictsd.org/i/publications/165193/?view=details accessed 17 April 2020.

78　In particular, how the panel would qualify the measure in terms of financial contribution, benefit and specificity. According to the latest update available on the case, the respondent notified the implementation of the measures on 5 June 2014.

evaluating the need for additional rules to be adopted in the future. Emerging countries have proven to be active in the renewable energy adjudication within WTO, bringing in their own stances on the matter.

The Committee on Trade and Environment has a broad portfolio which enables it to discuss the relationship between trade and sustainable development. Although there has been a debate about renewable energy support measures, the compatibility of renewable support measures and WTO law should be further discussed by other committees, such as[79] the Committee on Subsidies and Countervailing Measures[80] and the Trade Policy Review Body.[81]

In overcoming fragmentation, a different approach integrating the various elements in the equation is necessary. Determining what constitutes a subsidy from a WTO law perspective would eliminate or reduce uncertainty for both investors in renewables and governments designing their renewable energy policies.

DS456: INDIA—CERTAIN MEASURES RELATING TO SOLAR CELLS AND SOLAR MODULES

5.3.5 Conclusion

5.150. We have found above that, in determining whether a responding party has identified a rule that falls within the scope of "laws or regulations" under Article XX(d) of the GATT 1994, a panel should evaluate and give due consideration to all the characteristics of the relevant instrument(s) and should avoid focusing exclusively or unduly on any single characteristic. In particular, it may be relevant for a panel to consider, among others: (i) the degree of normativity of the instrument and the extent to which the instrument operates to set out a rule of conduct or course of action that is to be observed within the domestic legal system of a Member; (ii) the degree of specificity of the relevant rule; (iii) whether the rule is legally enforceable, including, e.g. before a court of law; (iv) whether the rule has been adopted or recognized by a competent authority possessing the necessary powers under the domestic legal system of a Member; (v) the form and title given to any instrument or instruments containing the rule under the domestic legal system of a Member; and (vi) the penalties or sanctions that may accompany the relevant rule. In some cases, such as those involving a specific, legally enforceable rule under a single provision of a domestic legislative act, determining whether a respondent has identified "laws or regulations" within the meaning of Article XX(d) may be

(Continued)

---

79 Ibid.
80 WTO members notify this Committee of the adoption of subsidy programs.
81 This body undertakes trade policy reviews of members, which could address renewable energy-related trade aspects.

a relatively straightforward exercise. In other cases, however, the assessment may be more complex. Importantly, this assessment must always be carried out on a case-by-case basis, in light of the specific characteristics and features of the instruments at issue, the rule alleged to exist, and the domestic legal system of the Member concerned.

5.151. We recall that India has not demonstrated that the passages and provisions of the domestic instruments it identified, when read together, set out the obligation "to ensure ecologically sustainable growth while addressing India's energy security challenge, and ensuring compliance with its obligations relating to climate change", as alleged by India. We have also concluded that the Panel did not err in finding that India did not demonstrate that the international instruments it had identified fall within the scope of "laws or regulations" under Article XX(d) in the present dispute. Consequently, we uphold the Panel's finding, in paragraph 7.333 of its Report, that India has not demonstrated that the DCR measures are measures "to secure compliance with laws or regulations which are not inconsistent with the provisions of [the GATT 1994]", and the Panel's ultimate finding, in paragraph 8.2.b of its Report, that the DCR measures are not justified under Article XX(d) of the GATT 1994.

Source: http://www.wto.org/english/tratop_e/dispu_e/
cases_e/ds456_e.htm

6 International human rights and international environmental law compliance: harnessing human rights and compliance with IEL

Intrinsically, International Human Rights Law (IHRL) and IEL are interlinked. The 1972 Stockholm Declaration ushered in a new era in the protection of environmental rights, recognizing the right 'to freedom, equality and adequate conditions of life, in an environment of a quality that permits a life of dignity and well-being'.[82] Principle 10 operated as the driver for legislative change in IEL and national legal systems. Nonetheless, progress was made in IEL, including the reception and full implementation of environmental democracy rights.[83] This was particularly true in some regions, such as LAC, where the enjoyment of environmental access rights has been hindered due to multiple factors.[84] In Latin America and the Caribbean, the protection of environmental rights is

---

82 'Declaration of the UN Conference on the Human Environment' UN Doc A/Conf.48/14 (5 June 1972) 11 ILM 1416.
83 See n 1. See also the work and reports published by the UN Special Representative on Human Rights and the Environment, available at https://www.ohchr.org/en/Issues/environment/SRenvironment/Pages/SRenvironmentIndex.aspx accessed 1 April 2020.
84 ECLAC, 'Observatory on Principle 10', available at http://observatoriop10.cepal.org/es accessed 1 April 2020.

multi-layered and takes place at different levels (national, regional and international).[85] Environmental access rights were examined in the 2018 Advisory Opinion of the Inter-American Court of Human Rights.[86]

A question posed here is whether there is a self-standing right to a healthy environment. Several obstacles to the access to a healthy environment have been linked to fundamental human rights such as the right to life and even cultural rights.

In terms of the (implicit or explicit) right to a healthy environment, the relationships between IEL and IHRL have been present since the beginning of IEL: Issues related to the protection of human health were considered one of the central aspects in its evolution. At the same time, the right to a healthy environment has become a necessary element for the enjoyment of human rights, as evidenced by, *inter alia*, the 1972 Stockholm Declaration of the United Nations Conference on the Human Environment (hereinafter 'the Stockholm Declaration'), the 1982 World Charter for Nature and the 1992 Rio Declaration on Environment and Development (hereinafter 'the Rio Declaration').

The last four decades have witnessed a change in perceptions of the relationship between environmental protection and the safeguard of human rights.[87] Since 1970 environmental protection has been on the international agenda, including the link with human rights, as demonstrated in Principle 1 of the Stockholm Declaration, which recognises 'the fundamental right to freedom, equality and adequate conditions of life, in an environment of a quality that permits a life of dignity and well-being'.[88] In addition, the Brundtland Report (1987) defined the basis for sustainable development, taking into consideration the protection of human rights.[89]

From the IHRL standpoint, the conception of human rights as universal, indivisible and interdependent[90] led to a shift in the protection of access to a healthy environment as one of the so-called third generation rights. In turn, the concept of sustainable development has helped to strengthen the interactions between the IHRL and IEL,[91] reflected specially in the Millennium

85 James May and Erin Daly, *Global Environmental Constitutionalism* (Cambridge University Press 2016), p. 4.

86 Inter-American Court of Human Rights, Advisory Opinion OC 13/17 15 November 2017, available at https://www.corteidh.or.cr/docs/opiniones/seriea_23_ing.pdf accessed 1 April 2020.

87 Edith Brown Weiss, 'The Evolution of International Environmental Law' (2011) 54 *Japanese Yearbook of International Law*, pp. 1–27.

88 Declaration of the United Nations Conference on the Human Environment (1972), World Charter for Nature (1982) and the Rio Declaration on Environment and Development (1992). Edith Brown Weiss, 'In Fairness to Future Generations and Sustainable Development' (1992) 8(1) *American University International Law Review*, pp. 19–26.

89 Report of the World Commission on Environment and Development: "Our Common Future", Document A/42/427 August 4, 1987.

90 World Conference on Human Rights, 14–25 June, 1993. Vienna Declaration and Programme of Action.

91 See Belen Olmos Giupponi, (ed), *Medio ambiente, cambio climático y derechos humanos* (DIKE, Bogotá/San José 2011), pp. 93–116.

Development Goals (2000) and the Johannesburg Declaration on Sustainable Development (2002). These instruments have accentuated the need to guarantee the protection of the environment while pursuing the achievement of economic development.

The interrelation between these various international protection regimes can be observed in both international jurisprudence and State practice. From the perspective of IHRL, considerations about the recognition of a self-standing right to the environment have been formulated by human rights protection bodies as well as by international human rights tribunals established in various regions. In this regard, two models can be identified: one for the indirect recognition of environmental rights (followed by the European Convention on Human Rights and Fundamental Freedoms) and one for the direct recognition of environmental rights, embodied by the Inter-American and African Human Rights System, respectively.[92]

As a result, it can be said that the interrelation between IEL and IHRL is manifested through various norms of regional human rights law in the Inter-American context that provide for a recognition of the right to a healthy environment.[93]

The international legal landscape of environmental access rights has changed significantly since the 1990s. Over the last several years, there has been a growing trend in IEL towards the conclusion of treaties embodying environmental access rights.[94] In Europe, the Convention on Access to Information, Public Participation in Decision-making and Access to Justice in Environmental Matters (Aarhus Convention) enshrined the three core environmental access rights with a specific scope and a regional focus.[95] Some MEAs also embody environmental access rights such as public participation: the Convention of Biological Diversity (CBD),[96] the UN Framework Convention on Climate Change (UNFCCC)[97] and the Minamata Convention,[98] among others.

Outside the IEL realm, the implementation of environmental access rights has been advanced through public interest litigation before regional human

---

92 Malgosia Fitzmaurice, 'Environmental Degradation', in D. Moeckli and S. Sivakumaran (eds), *International Human Rights Law* (2 edn Oxford University Press 2014), pp. 590–609.

93 Request for Advisory Opinion to the Inter-American Court of Human Rights, p. 46. See also OAS Resolution 56/09.

94 J. Viñuales, 'The Rio Declaration on Environment and Development: Preliminary Study', in J Viñuales, (ed), *The Rio Declaration on Environment and Development: A Commentary* (Oxford University Press 2015), pp. 1, 32; J. Ebbesson, 'Principle 10' in Viñuales, ibid., 287.

95 Convention on Access to Information, Public Participation in Decision-Making and Access to Justice in Environmental Matters (adopted 25 June 1998, entered into force 30 October 2001) 2161 UNTS 447 (Aarhus Convention).

96 Convention on Biological Diversity (adopted 5 June 1992, entered into force 29 December 1993) 1760 UNTS 79 art 14.

97 United Nations Framework Convention on Climate Change (adopted 29 May 1992, entered into force 21 March 1994) 1771 UNTS 107.

98 Minamata Convention on Mercury (adopted 10 October 2013; entered into force 16 August 2017) 55 ILM 582.

rights courts.[99] Principle 10-related issues have been discussed in various manners and with regional differences. In Europe, the European Court of Human Rights (ECtHR) has chiefly relied on the principle to protect the right to a private and family life in line with Article 8 of the European Convention of Human Rights and the freedom of expression, as enshrined in Article 10 in relation to access to environmental information.[100]

In addressing the implementation of environmental access rights vis-à-vis IHRL, environmental law scholars draw the distinction between the former as 'procedural rights'[101] and the latter as 'substantive rights'.[102] Although the distinction may be useful to dissect and analyse the panoply of rights from a theoretical standpoint, in their implementation both types of rights are interrelated and interdependent.

Environmental law scholars have argued in favour of access to environmental information as a fundamental part of the right to an adequate environment as a human right enshrined in national legal systems (namely, in national constitutions).[103] In this vein, scholars have underlined the idea that evolution towards the recognition of environmental access rights (particularly access to environmental information) has been hailed by the enactment of progressive national legislation.[104] In sum, the emphasis has been on the interface between IHRL and IEL as two different but interrelated fields with areas of convergence, as evidenced by international and regional legal instruments and case law.[105]

99 Christian Schall, 'Public Interest Litigation Concerning Environmental Matters before Human Rights' (2008) 20 *Journal of Environmental Law*, p. 417.
100 See, e.g., *Guerra and Others v Italy* App No 14967/89 (ECtHR, 19 February 1998) para 60; *McGinley and Egan v United Kingdom* App No 21825/93 and 23414/94 (ECtHR, 9 July 1998) para 101; *Taşkin and others v Turkey* App No 46117/99 (ECtHR, 10 November 2004) para 119; and *Roche v United Kingdom* App No 32555/96 (ECtHR, 19 October 2005) para 162.
101 May and Daly (n 85) at 77.
102 See Jutta Brunnée, 'Procedure and Substance in International Environmental Law: Confused at a Higher Level?' (2016) 5 *ESIL Reflection*, p. 1; and Brigitte Peters, 'Unpacking the Diversity of Procedural Environmental Rights: The European Convention on Human Rights and the Aarhus Convention' (2018) 30 *Journal of Environmental Law*, p. 1.
103 Agustina Herrera Espinoza, Paloma Moreno Ovando and Reyna Escobedo Fernández, 'El Acceso a la Información Ambiental' (2013) 29 *Cuestiones Constitucionales*, p. 219; F. Ramírez Parada, 'Acceso a la Información Ambiental' (2011) 38 *Revista Chilena de Derecho*, p. 311; L Orellana Bautista, 'El Derecho de Acceso a la Información Pública Ambiental', available at https://www.oefa.gob.pe/?wpfb_dl=9535; Organization of American States, 'Marco Conceptual del Derecho Ambiental, Programa Interamericano de Capacitación Judicial sobre el Estado de Derecho Ambiental (2016), available at http://www.oas.org/es/sedi/dsd/publicaciones/judicial-modulo_ii.pdf accessed 1 April 2020.
104 Ludwig Krämer, 'Transnational Access to Environmental Information' (2012) 1(1) *Transnational Environmental Law*, pp. 95–104.
105 Amedeo Postiglione, 'Human Rights and the Environment' (2010) 14(4) *The International Journal of Human Rights*, pp. 524–541.

UNEP Training Manual on International Environmental Law

United Nations Environment Programme (2006). UNEP Training Manual on International Environmental Law.

Compliance means the fulfilment by the contracting parties of their obligations under a multilateral environmental agreement and any amendments to the multilateral environmental agreement. Compliance means the state of conformity with obligations, imposed by a State, its competent authorities and agencies on the regulated community, whether directly or through conditions and requirements in permits, licences and authorizations, in implementing multilateral environmental agreements.

UNEP (2002): Compliance with and enforcement of multilateral environmental agreements. UNEP Governing Council Decision, adopted October 2002 in Nairobi.

These guidelines were adopted in February 2002 by UNEP Governing Council decision SSVII/4 for the purpose of enhancing compliance with, and enforcement of environmental law, and are referred to as Guidelines for Compliance with and Enforcement of Multilateral Environmental Agreements.

Source: https://wedocs.unep.org/bitstream/handle/
20.500.11822/20599/UNEP_Training_Manual_Int_
Env_Law.pdf?sequence=1&isAllowed=y

Bibliography

Álvarez Jiménez, A, 'The Methanex Final Award. An Analysis from the Perspectives of Environmental Regulatory Authorities and Foreign Investors' (2006) 23(5) *Journal of International Arbitration*, p. 427.

Bartels, L, 'The Chapeau of the General Exceptions in the WTO GATT and GATS Agreements: A Reconstruction' (2015) 109 *American Journal of International Law*, p. 95, available at SSRN: https://ssrn.com/abstract=2557971 or http://dx.doi.org/10.2139/ssrn.2557971 accessed 1 April 2020.

Birnie, P, Boyle, A, and Redgwell, C, *International Law and the Environment* (3rd edn Oxford University Press 2009), p. 115.

Bowman, M, Davies, Peter, and Redgwell, Catherine, *Lyster's International Wildlife Law* (2nd edn Cambridge University Press 2010).

Boyle, A and Harrison, J, 'Judicial Settlement of International Environmental Disputes: Current Problems' (2013) 4(2) *Journal of International Dispute Settlement*, pp. 245–276.

Brown Weiss, E, 'In Fairness to Future Generations and Sustainable Development' (1992) 8(1) *American University International Law Review*, pp. 19–26.

Brown Weiss, E, 'The Evolution of International Environmental Law' (2011) 54 *Japanese Yearbook of International Law*, pp. 1–27.

Brunnée, J, 'Procedure and Substance in International Environmental Law: Confused at a Higher Level?' (2016) 5 *ESIL Reflection*, p. 1; and B Peters, 'Unpacking the Diversity of Procedural Environmental Rights: The European Convention on Human Rights and the Aarhus Convention' (2018) 30 *Journal of Environmental Law*, p. 1.

Carter Morgan, J III, 'Fragmentation of International Environmental Law and the Synergy: A Problem and a 21st Century Model Solution' (2017) 18 *Vermont Journal of Environmental Law*, p. 133.

Charnovitz, S, "The WTO's Environmental Progress" (2007) 10(3) *JIEL*, pp. 685–706.

CITES, Appendices I, II and III. CITES, Howe CITES Works, available at https://www.cites.org/eng/disc/how.php accessed 1 April 2020.

Condon, BJ, 'Treaty Structure and Public Interest Regulation in International Economic Law' (2014) 17(2) *Journal of International Economic Law*, 333.

Condon, B and Sinha, T, *The Role of Climate Change in Global Economic Governance* (OUP 2013); Tim Stephens, *International Courts and Environmental Protection* (CUP 2009); Sophie Thoyer and Benoit Martimort-Asso, *Participation for Sustainability in Trade* (Ashgate – Global Environmental Governance Series 2007); Timothy Swanson and Sam Johnston, *Global Environmental Problems and International Environmental Agreements-The Economics of International Institution Building* (Edward Elgar 1999) and Jochem Wiers, *Trade and Environment in the EC and the WTO* (Europa Law Publishing 2003).

Dupuy, PM and Viñuales, J, *International Environmental Law* (CUP 2015), pp. 394–395.

Dupuy, PM and Viñuales, J, 'Intellectual Property Rights and the Environment', in PM Dupuy and J Viñuales, *International Environmental Law* (Oxford University Press 2015), pp. 403–413. Claudio Chiarolla, 'Intellectual Property from a Global Environmental Law Perspective: Lessons from Patent Disclosure Requirements for Genetic Resources and Traditional Knowledge' (2019) 8(3) *Transnational Environmental Law*, pp. 503–521.

ECLAC, 'Observatory on Principle 10', available at http://observatoriop10.cepal.org/es accessed 1 April 2020.

European Court of Human Rights, Guerra and Others v Italy App No 14967/89 (ECtHR, 19 February 1998) para 60; McGinley and Egan v United Kingdom App No 21825/93 and 23414/94 (ECtHR, 9 July 1998) para 101; Taşkin and others v Turkey App No 46117/99 (ECtHR, 10 November 2004) para 119; and Roche v United Kingdom App No 32555/96 (ECtHR, 19 October 2005) para 162.

Fitzmaurice, M, 'Environmental Degradation', in D Moeckli and S Sivakumaran (eds), *International Human Rights Law* (2nd edn Oxford University Press 2014), pp. 590–609.

Gantz, DA, 'Global Trade Issues in the New Millennium: Potential Conflicts between Investors Rights and Environmental Regulation under Nafta's Chapter XI' (2001) *George Washington International Law Review*.

GATT, Article XX.

Gehring, MW and Cordonier Segger, Mc, Precaution in World Trade Law: The Precautionary Principle and Its Implications for the World Trade Organization, available at https://www.cisdl.org/wp-content/uploads/2018/05/Precaution-in-World-Trade-Law-2003.pdf accessed 1 April 2020.

Gentile, D, 'International Trade and the Environment: What Is the Role of the WTO?' (2009) 19(1) *FELW*, pp. 195–230;

Gruszczynski, LA, 'EC – Seal Products Case: Public Morality Meets the World Trade Court' (2014) 3(1–2) *Polish Review of International and European Law*, pp. 101–119, available at https://ssrn.com/abstract=3098942 accessed 1 April 2020.

Herrera Espinoza, A, Moreno Ovando, P, and Escobedo Fernández, R, 'El Acceso a la Información Ambiental' (2013) 29 *Cuestiones Constitucionales* p. 219; Ramírez Parada, F, 'Acceso a la Información Ambiental' (2011) 38 *Revista Chilena de Derecho*, p. 311; Orellana Bautista, L, 'El Derecho de Acceso a la Información Pública Ambiental', available at https://www.oefa.gob.pe/?wpfb_dl=9535; Organization of American States, 'Marco Conceptual del Derecho Ambiental, Programa Interamericano de Capacitación Judicial sobre el Estado de Derecho Ambiental (2016), available at http://www.oas.org/es/sedi/dsd/publicaciones/judicial-modulo_ii.pdf accessed 1 April 2020.

Inter-American Court of Human Rights, Advisory Opinion OC 13/17 15 November 2017, available at https://www.corteidh.or.cr/docs/opiniones/seriea_23_ing.pdf accessed 1 April 2020.

Inter-American Court of Human Rights, Request for Advisory Opinion to the Inter-American Court of Human Rights, p. 46. See also OAS Resolution 56/09.

Krämer, L, 'Transnational Access to Environmental Information' (2012) 1(1) *Transnational Environmental Law*, pp. 95–104.

Kuntze, Jan-Christoph and Moerenhout, Tom, Local Content Requirement 2013. Local Content Requirements and the Renewable Energy Industry – A Good Match? Geneva: ICTSD, available from http://ictsd.org/i/publications/165193/?view=details accessed 17 April 2020.

Lixinski, L, *Intangible Cultural Heritage in International Law* (Oxford University Press 2013).

Loritz, DR, 'Corporate Predators Attack Environmental Regulations: It's Time to Arbitrate Claims Filed under NAFTA's Chapter 11' (2000) 533 *Loyola of Los Angeles International & Comparative Law Review*, p. 533.

Magraw, J, 'Procedural Delaney and D. Barstow Transparency', in Peter Muchlinski, et al. (eds), *International Investment Law* (Oxford University Press 2008), p. 731.

Marlles, JR 'Public Purpose, Private Losses: Regulatory Expropriation and Environmental Regulation in International Investment Law' (2007) 16 *Journal of Transnational Law and Policy*, p. 275.

May, J and Daly, E, *Global Environmental Constitutionalism* (Cambridge University Press 2016), p. 4.

Neumayer, E, *Greening Trade and Investment: Environmental Protection without Protectionism* (Earthscan 2001).

Neumayer, E, 'Pollution Havens: An Analysis of Policy Options for Dealing with an Elusive Phenomenon' (2001) 10(2) *Journal of Environment & Development*, pp. 147–177.

OECD, Cost-Benefit Analysis and the Environment: Further Developments and Policy Use, OECD Publishing, (2018 Paris), available at https://doi.org/10.1787/9789264085169-en.

Olmos Giupponi, Belen, (ed), *Medio ambiente, cambio climático y derechos humanos* (DIKE, Bogotá/San José2011), pp. 93–116.

Paparinskis, M, 'Regulatory Expropriation and Sustainable Development' (July 10, 2010), in MW Gehring, MC Cordonnier-Segger, and A Newcombe (eds), *Sustainable Development in International Investment Law*, Kluwer Law International, available at SSRN: http://ssrn.com/abstract=1698192 accessed 1 April 2020.

Pavoni, R, 'Mutual Supportiveness as a Principle of Interpretation and Law-Making: A Watershed for the 'WTO-and-Competing-Regimes' Debate?' (2010) 3 *European Journal of International Law*, pp. 649, 654–655.

Postiglione, A, 'Human Rights and the Environment' (2010) 14(4) *The International Journal of Human Rights*, pp. 524–541.

Rao, 'Facing Arbitration for Environmental Regulation' (2005) 5(1) *Sustainable Development Law & Policy*, p. 66.

Rogers, L, 'Intangible Cultural Heritage and International Environmental Law: The Cultural Dimension of Environmental Protection' (2017) 29(3) *Historic Environment*, pp. 30–43.

Schall, C, 'Public Interest Litigation Concerning Environmental Matters before Human Rights' (2008) 20 *Journal of Environmental Law*, p. 417.

Tienhaara, K, 'Third-Party Participation in Investment-Environment Disputes: Recent Developments' (2007) 16(2) *RECIEL*, pp. 230–242.

Tienhaara, K, *The Expropriation of Environmental Governance* (Cambridge University Press 2009).

Tienhaara, K, Regulatory Chill and the Threat of Arbitration: A View from Political Science (October 28, 2010). Evolution in Investment Treaty Law and Arbitration, Chester Brown, Kate Miles, eds., Cambridge University Press, 2011, available at SSRN: http://ssrn.com/abstract=2065706 accessed 1 April 2020.

UNECE, Convention on Access to Information, Public Participation in Decision-Making and Access to Justice in Environmental Matters (adopted 25 June 1998, entered into force 30 October 2001) 2161 UNTS 447 (Aarhus Convention).

United Nations, Convention on Biological Diversity (adopted 5 June 1992, entered into force 29 December 1993) 1760 UNTS 79 art 14.

United Nations, Minamata Convention on Mercury (adopted 10 October 2013; entered into force 16 August 2017) 55 ILM 582.

United Nations, 'Declaration of the UN Conference on the Human Environment' UN Doc A/Conf.48/14 (5 June 1972) 11 ILM 1416.

United Nations, Declaration of the United Nations Conference on the Human Environment (1972), World Charter for Nature (1982) and the Rio Declaration on Environment and Development (1992).

United Nations, United Nations Framework Convention on Climate Change (adopted 29 May 1992, entered into force 21 March 1994) 1771 UNTS 107.

United Nations, UN Special Representative on Human Rights and the Environment, available at https://www.ohchr.org/en/Issues/environment/SRenvironment/Pages/SRenvironmentIndex.aspx accessed 1 April 2020.

United Nations, Report of the World Commission on Environment and Development: 'Our Common Future', Document A/42/427 August 4, 1987.

United States — Import Prohibition of Certain Shrimp and Shrimp Products- WTO case Nos. 58 (and 61). Ruling adopted on 6 November 1998.

United States — Restrictions on Imports of Tuna, the 'Tuna-dolphin' Case, Ruling Not Adopted, Circulated on 3 September 1991. Case brought by Mexico et al. United States — Restrictions on Imports of Tuna, "son of tuna-dolphin", ruling not adopted, circulated on 16 June 1994.

Van den Bossche, P and Zdouc, Werner, *The Law and Policy of the World Trade Organization: Text, Cases and Materials* (4th edn Cambridge University Press 2017).

Viñuales, J, 'The Rise and Fall of Sustainable Development', 22(1) *Review of European Community and International Environmental Law* (2013), p. 1.

Viñuales, J, 'The Rio Declaration on Environment and Development: Preliminary Study' in J Viñuales, (ed), The Rio Declaration on Environment and Development: A Commentary (Oxford University Press 2015), pp. 1, 32; J Ebbesson, 'Principle 10' in Viñuales, ibid., 287.

Viñuales, J, 'Sustainable Development', in L Rajamani and J Peel (eds), *The Oxford Handbook of International Environmental Law* (2nd edn Oxford University Press 2019), available at https://www.ceenrg.landecon.cam.ac.uk/working-paper-files/wp20 accessed 1 March 2020.

Weiler, T, 'Good Faith and Regulatory Transparency: The Story of Metalclad V. Mexico', in International Investment Law and Arbitration. Leading Cases from The Icsid, Nafta, Bilateral Treaties and Customary International Law, USA 2004, 701.

Weinstein, M and Charnovitz, S, The Greening of the WTO' (2001) 80(6) *Foreign Affairs*, pp. 147–156.

World Conference on Human Rights, 14–25 June, 1993. Vienna Declaration and Programme of Action.

WTO, Appellate Body (2013). Canada – Certain Measures Affecting the Renewable Energy Generation Sector. Appellate Body Report WT/DS412/AB/R / WT/DS426/AB/R, adopted 6 May 2013.

WTO, 'The Committee on Trade and Environment' (World Trade Organization 2019), available at https://www.wto.org/english/tratop_e/envir_e/wrk_committee_e.htm accessed 1 March 2020.

WTO, "Early Years: Emerging Environment Debate in GATT/WTO"(World Trade Organization 2019), available at https://www.wto.org/english/tratop_e/envir_e/hist1_e.htm accessed 1 March 2020; Will Martin and L. Alan Winters, The Uruguay Round Widening and Deepening the World Trading System (The World Bank 1995), p. 2.

WTO, Dispute Settlement: Dispute DS332. Brazil – Measures Affecting Imports of Retreaded Tyres, available at http://www.wto.org/english/tratop_e/dispu_e/cases_e/ds332_e.htm accessed 10 January 2015.

WTO, DS332: Brazil-Measures Affecting Imports of Retreaded Tyres, available at https://www.wto.org/english/tratop_e/dispu_e/cases_e/ds332_e.htm accessed 1 April 2020.

WTO, Dispute Settlement. DS400: European Communities — Measures Prohibiting the Importation and Marketing of Seal Products, available at https://www.wto.org/english/tratop_e/dispu_e/cases_e/ds400_e.htm accessed 1 April 2020.

WTO, 1994 Marrakesh Agreement Establishing the World Trade Organisation. Done at Marrakesh on 15 April 1994. Entry into force: 1 January 1995, available at https://www.wto.org/english/docs_e/legal_e/04-wto_e.htm accessed 1 April 2020.

WTO, Subjects Treated under the Doha Development Agenda, available at https://www.wto.org/english/tratop_e/dda_e/dohasubjects_e.htm accessed 1 April 2020.

WTO, Sustainable Development, available at https://www.wto.org/english/tratop_e/envir_e/sust_dev_e.htm accessed 1 April 2020.

WTO, Sustainable Development, available at https://www.wto.org/english/tratop_e/envir_e/sust_dev_e.htm accessed 1 March 2020.

WTO, Technical Barriers to Trade (TBT) Agreement was adopted on, available at https://www.wto.org/english/tratop_e/tbt_e/tbt_e.htm#:~:text=The%20Technical%20Barriers%20to%20Trade, create%20unnecessary%20obstacles%20to%20trade accessed 1 April 2020.

WTO, The Doha Round, available at https://www.wto.org/english/tratop_e/dda_e/dda_e.htm accessed 1 March 2020.

WTO, *United States –Import Prohibition of Certain Shrimp and Shrimp Products* WT/DS58/AB/R (12 October 1998), available at https://www.wto.org/english/tratop_e/dispu_e/cases_e/ds58_e.htm accessed 1 March 2020.

6 Non-compliance and international environmental dispute resolution

1 Introduction

International dispute settlement as a formal, decentralised, consensual and eminently judicial or quasi-judicial system offers limited possibilities when dealing with non-compliance. Contrary to this view, international environmental law (IEL) processes are less formal, and even if they are de-centralised there is a certain concentration of processes around MEAs. Even though the system still presents several shortcomings, it has developed towards more sophisticated mechanisms.

Usually, IEL has been subject to criticism due to the absence of adequate enforcement methods. Partly in response to this, various mechanisms have been instituted in IEL to determine the extent to which States comply with their commitments. Customary norms in IEL provide for traditional mechanisms under the SR regime, as previously discussed. Under MEAs, several tools and mechanisms have been set up to monitor State behaviour and determine if there is compliance with the norms.

Often underlined as a shortcoming of the international legal system, the lack of a centralised judicial or quasi-judicial system in IEL has resulted in several separate compliance scattered regimes structured around the respective MEAS. Various proposals endorsing the creation of an international environmental court have been discussed; however, none of them have come to fruition. A certain evolution is observed in MEAs' compliance systems, which have been incorporating improved compliance and non-compliance mechanisms. At present, IEL is taking stock of the practice gained in cases dealing with non-compliance in different judicial and non-judicial settings.

Outside formal international channels, communities affected by environmental damage and degradation have set up parallel informal mechanisms and forums as they are often precluded from participating in these formal international forums due to a lack of appropriate legal standing. Hence, bottom-up transnational environmental law litigation has emerged, giving rise to a growing area of informal environmental conflict resolution (IECR). This denotes a broader conception of the various channels and avenues that can be drawn upon to solve an environmental conflict.

Against this backdrop, this chapter aims to scrutinize the various non-compliance processes, including those which have emerged parallel to traditional environmental dispute settlement methods. It seeks to contribute to IEL scholarship by examining examples of international dispute settlement and transnational environmental conflict resolution. This entails addressing certain fundamental questions about the nature and effectiveness of mechanisms and the consideration of IECR as an emerging area in IEL.[1]

2 Non-compliance with international environmental law: ways to deal with it

Non-compliance defines a situation in which IEL norms have not been completely fulfilled, or adequate implementation measures have not been taken by the addressees of the norms (in most of the cases, States). Each MEA establishes institutional arrangements to adequately monitor the implementation of norms and guarantee compliance with IEL.[2]

Assessing compliance and non-compliance with a particular MEA requires a better grasp and understanding of the specific legal framework set up by the MEA. Rather than merely examining the formal obligations imposed on the States, one needs to look beyond the norms to identify the different aspects influencing compliance with IEL norms. The evolution observed in this field shows a shift from the traditional and formal mechanisms used in monitoring compliance to more collaborative solutions.

Sometimes, compliance with IEL is articulated through mechanisms fostering 'partnership solutions' (those which require the collaboration or consent of concerned Party States) comprising reporting obligations, inspections, monitoring, assistance and a certain level compliance control. Their main goal is to avoid non-compliance, addressing different levels of state inability to conform to Treaty obligations. Non-confrontational mechanisms could be classified into different categories: compliance control, compliance assistance and ad-hoc or 'tailored' mechanisms.

Compliance control mechanisms encompass a wide range of methods to guarantee compliance with treaty obligations. These mechanisms can be set up in an institutionalised and formalised manner to monitor the compliance of Treaty Parties. These mechanisms are instituted under the Treaty in question (or set up by a decision made by the main decision-making institution) which creates international bodies tasked with the function to check compliance.

---

1 Malgosia Fitzmaurice, 'International Protection of the Environment' (2001) 293 *RCADI*, pp. 9–488. N. Craik, 'Recalcitrant Reality and Chosen Ideals: The Public Function of Dispute Settlement in International Environmental Law' (1998) 10(2) *Georgetown International Environmental Law Review*, pp. 551–580.
2 Robin R. Churchill and Geir Ulfstein, 'Autonomous Institutional Arrangements in Multilateral Environmental Agreements: A Little-Noticed Phenomenon in International Law' (2000) 94(4) *The American Journal of International Law*, pp. 623–659.

Although not all compliance control mechanisms entail the imposition of formal sanctions, a transparency dimension related to access to information brings about more legitimacy while putting pressure on non-compliant parties. Transparency is key in this regard, a way of stating relevant facts for the implementation of treaty provisions. This generates a sort of a disciplinary effect for Treaty Parties as this objective statement of facts leads to the visibilisation of non-compliance. Transparency may also help parties to achieve better compliance levels by adopting appropriate measures.

Closely conversant to the issue of transparency, some MEAs may provide for inspections as means to corroborate compliance or to determine non-compliance with treaty obligations. Inspections take place through in-situ visits to ensure either that implementing activities are conducted or that the right conditions are in place. It must be noted, however, that there is still resistance to this type of mechanism in IEL. This appears to be linked to the intervention in domestic affairs implied by inspections. Some MEAs (such as CITES) involve NGOs in the performance of those inspections. Under its legal framework, Treaty Parties have accorded Trade Records Analysis of Flora and Fauna in Commerce (TRAFFIC), together with the CITES Secretariat, to carry out inspections within the Treaty Parties' territory.[3]

Ad-hoc non-compliance procedures have the primary aim of addressing the lack of compliance with specific treaty obligations and can be triggered by any event that falls within the category of non-compliance. Like implementation review procedures, NCPs are applied more or less systematically to deal with cases of non-compliance. Under some MEAs, as in the case of the Montreal Protocol, the Climate Change Convention and the Desertification Convention, Treaty Parties, the Secretariat and the concerned State have been entitled to trigger the procedure. NGOs may request that a Treaty Party or the Secretariat start such a procedure. Other MEAs foresee the involvement of NGOs, which are on occasion admitted as observers and able to exercise the right to participate in the Compliance Committees with different rights under each legal framework. In the framework of the Aarhus Convention and the Alpine Convention, NGOs are also granted a limited right to set the NCP in motion.

In terms of the second category, assistance mechanisms seek to help States build capacity in order to guarantee compliance with treaty commitments. The goal of these mechanisms is to offer alternatives to the State in order to make up for the lack of preparation and appropriate resources by reinforcing specific competences and supporting Treaty Parties' institutions. This is the case with financial and technical assistance. A growing trend in IEL consists of granting funding and financial assistance to level the playing field in terms of technical capacities to enable developing and less-developed countries to advance implementation. In turn, developed State and donors can contribute with financial

---

3 See *Memorandum of Understanding between TRAFFIC and CITES*, available at https://cites.org/sites/default/files/common/disc/sec/CITES-TRAFFIC.pdf accessed 1 April 2020.

assistance. Specific environmental funds are tailored and instituted under specific MEAs (like the Ramsar Convention) or international treaties with a bearing on environmental protection, such as the 1972 World Heritage Convention.

Under each MEA the obligations of Treaty Parties vary considerably, which is also reflected in the type of control they can exercise. Some treaties only provide a formal control of implementation, whereas in others (particularly the Montreal Protocol and the new generation of MEAs) compliance control is foreseen in a broader sense.

Different dispute settlement mechanisms are triggered in the event of non-compliance. Usually, formal dispute resolution mechanisms are used in serious events of non-compliance. There are also in-between solutions, as offered by some MEAs, i.e. partly formal solutions. Many MEAs provide for negotiation as an initial step or phase to deal with non-compliance. If the negotiations fail, other mechanisms become available. Some MEAs prefer more diplomatic/pragmatic approaches to formal and restrictive mechanisms to use in dealing with cases of non-compliance. This is the case with performance review information; financial tools or mechanisms; and, in general, non-compliance response measures. NCPs are analysed in the next section of this chapter. In addition to the formal and traditional international dispute settlement mechanisms, less formal mechanisms have also emerged in IEL incorporating elements of alternative dispute resolution and offering distinctive solutions to deal with environmental conflicts.

Overall, a move towards conflict prevention and non-compliance avoidance is observed, and various preventative techniques are deployed to either diffuse conflict surrounding compliance with IEL or to avert non-compliance, both of which are becoming more widespread in international environmental treaties.

3 Non-compliance procedures (NCPs)

NCPs have become the most relied-upon form of monitoring the fulfilment of environmental obligations under MEAs. This implies shifting the focus away from the traditional ex-post intervention based on attaching negative consequences to the infringement of an environmental norm. Overall, NCPs contribute to the implementation of environmental treaties through the provision of financial or technical assistance and the imposition of sanctions aimed at guaranteeing an acceptable level of compliance with the MEAs. Several environmental treaties establish a body tasked with ensuring compliance and that similar mechanisms are instituted under regimes created by environmental treaties.[4]

Usually, non-compliance procedures are set up by legally binding IEL norms: either treaty provisions or legally binding decisions passed by main treaty bodies.[5]

---

4 See, for instance, the Basel Convention on the Control of Transboundary Movements of Hazardous Wastes and their Disposal 1989, art 19.

5 UNEP Division of Environmental Law and Conventions, Compliance Mechanism under Selected Multilateral Environmental Agreements (UNEP 2007), available at http://hdl.handle.net/20.500.11822/7507 accessed 1 March 2020.

On some occasions, soft-law norms also come under scrutiny under NCPs. The mushrooming of NCPs under MEAs reveals different types of mechanisms. Formal NCPs can take different shapes in order to deal with non-compliance problems under the respective treaties, though they operate in a similar fashion in practice.[6]

Some MEAs may refer to non-compliance amounting to the breach and non-application of treaty provisions. In assessing whether international actors have or have not fulfilled their international environmental obligations, one must look at the wording of the treaty but also at its object and purpose.[7] However, the NCPs remit do not cover failure to take effective measures to achieve treaty objectives, i.e. the adoption of measures would suffice. This narrow concept of non-compliance is questionable as it does not reflect the effectiveness of the regime in question.[8]

With regard to the nature of the NCPs, they function more as an alternative dispute resolution method or dispute avoidance processes.[9] Literature in the field has underlined the idea that the ultimate purpose of these procedures is to ensure a satisfactory level of compliance with treaty obligations.[10] NCPs seem to operate more on a consensual basis than other compliance mechanisms. The underlying technique in all these mechanisms is international conciliation, guided by the principles of global environmental responsibility, as laid down in different international legal instruments.[11]

Compliance procedures vary from treaty to treaty, but they share some common features.[12] First, they are usually based on multilateral treaties. Second, in principle, there is no need for the respondent State's consent before the process can be initiated. Third, there is no requirement for a specific standing before making a complaint, and they base their effectiveness on the principle of inter-state cooperation.[13]

Considered a legal innovation when its NCP was introduced under the Montreal Protocol (MP), NCPs have been widely disseminated and incorporated in other MEAs.[14] In this regard, the MP constitutes an authentic game-changer

---

6 Thomas Gehring, 'International Environmental Regimes: Dynamic Sectoral Legal Systems', 1 *YBIEL*, p. 35.

7 Simon Marsden, 'Non-Compliance Procedures' (2017) 28 *Yearbook of International Environmental Law*, pp. 111–115, available at https://doi.org/10.1093/yiel/yvy025 accessed 1 March 2020.

8 David G. Victor, Karl Raustiala, and Eugene Skolnikoff (eds), *Implementation and Effectiveness of International Environmental Commitments* (MIT Press 1998), pp. 6–8.

9 Patricia Birnie, Alan Boyle, and Catherine Redgwell, *International Law and the Environment* (3rd edn Oxford University Press 2009), p. 243.

10 Tullio Treves, *Non-Compliance Procedures and Mechanisms and the Effectiveness of International Environmental Agreements* (TMC Asser Press 2009).

11 Boyle, p. 128.

12 See, for instance, compliance procedures established under the 1992 OSPAR Convention, Article 23; 2000 Protocol on Biosafety, Article 34; 2001 POPS Convention, Article 10; 2003 Protocol on Pollutant Release and Transfer Registers, Article 22.

13 Birnie, Boyle, and Redgwell (n 9) at 246.

14 UNEP, Key Achievements of the Montreal Protocol to Date (1987–2012), available at https://ozone.unep.org/sites/default/files/Key_achievements_of_the_Montreal_Protocol_2012.pdf accessed 1 March 2020.

and a 'role model' for other MEAs which have adopted similar systems.[15] Across MEAs, some cases are cited as 'success stories' to analyse compliance with IEL. In line with the features already mentioned, the MP comprises a non-confrontational procedure aimed at preventing environmental damage.[16] Indeed, the system instituted therein seeks to induce compliance with IEL norms by not singling out the concerned State as a culprit.[17] Rather the opposite, the State in question may provide explanations about the lack of compliance to reduce it to the minimum or to bring its behaviour in line with treaty commitments.

The underlying goal is to prevent or mitigate environmental damage that might arise because of non-compliance. Ultimately, NCPs rely on the international law principle of good faith.[18] Whereas the utility/relevance of NCPs on paper lies on legal principles, in practice their effectiveness seems to depend upon two main factors: the number of contracting parties which have accepted the mechanism (not opting out) and the array of responses available to the parties in the event of non-compliance.

NCPs are rooted (explicitly or implicitly) in treaty provisions, which are in most cases developed by decisions adopted by treaty bodies, such as the Conference of the Parties or the Meetings of the Parties (as in the case of Aarhus). In terms of the binding nature of NCPs, some of them have been established without any specific treaty provision, as in the cases of CITES or the Basel Convention, but have then been regulated through secondary law, i.e. decisions adopted by the treaty bodies. The type of norms regulating a specific NCP mechanisms has an impact on its binding character and, therefore, the compelling effect of the decisions adopted as a consequence. The binding character may reside in the wording of the treaty expressly providing for it or in the consensus element (i.e. if States decide to amend the treaty to confer that character). Sometimes, treaty provisions opt towards attributing the mechanisms with a merely consultative and optional nature, as in the case of the Aarhus Committee.[19] More controversial are cases in which the treaties remain silent, in which case the powers attributed to the treaty bodies come into play as if they were allowed to adopt formally binding non-compliance decisions.[20] Clearly, this does not mean that non-binding compliance decisions adopted by NCPs carry no normative power as some of them are considered authoritative and must be followed by the States.

---

15 Martti Koskenniemi, 'Breach of Treaty or Non-Compliance? Reflections on the Enforcement of the Montreal Protocol' (1992) 3(1) *Yearbook of International Environmental Law*, pp. 123–162, available at https://doi.org/10.1093/yiel/3.1.123 accessed 1 March 2020.

16 Pierre-Marie Dupuy and Jorge E. Viñuales, *International Environmental Law* (Cambridge University Press 2015), pp. 284–285.

17 Ibid.

18 The principle is of customary nature, being set out in Article 26 of the Vienna Convention on the Law of the Treaties in terms of pacta sunt servanda ('agreements must be kept').

19 A. Andruseveich, T. Alge, and C. Konrad (eds), *Case Law of the Aarhus Convention Compliance Committee* (2004–2014), available at https://www.unece.org/fileadmin/DAM/env/pp/compliance/CC_Publication/ACCC_Case_Law_3rd_edition_eng.pdf accessed 1 March 2020.

20 See the discussion in Dupuy and Viñuales (n 16) at 287.

Somehow, the force of the decision depends upon State consent expressed in one way or the other to support the work of the Conference of the Parties (COP) or the Conference of the Parties serving as the meeting of the Parties (CMP).[21]

The membership of NCP bodies becomes relevant for the assessment of the effectiveness and neutrality of the various mechanisms, particularly in terms of what concerns the composition, the way in which the members are appointed and the nature of their function (if they represent a State party or are considered 'independent experts'). International practice shows that NC organs are often composed by State representatives selected by treaty bodies based on different criteria, such as equal geographical representation, as in the case of the Espoo Convention and the LRTAP Convention. Independent experts are appointed under the Aarhus Convention who serve in a personal capacity, pro bono, and are experts in the field. A mixed system is observed in other environmental treaties, like the Compliance Committee under the Kyoto Protocol, which consists of 20 experts who act in an independent capacity based on technical expertise and geographical representation, holding plenary sessions as a 'facilitative branch' or as 'an enforcement branch'.

With regard to who sets the NCP process in motion, the options are self-triggering,[22] other States, treaty bodies or authorised third-parties.[23] Self-triggering has been hailed because of the non-confrontational nature of NCPs; however, it only covers certain treaty provisions concerning financial and/or technical assistance rather than provisions dealing with substantive obligations.[24] The specific treaty may provide for the possibility that another State party can rely on the mechanism without invoking direct harm when non-compliance affects global commons and the general interest, such as with regard to the protection of the ozone layer, climate conditions or biodiversity when endangered species are affected. Whenever non-compliance does not affects general State interest or the global common, only those States directly affected are entitled to set the mechanisms in motion.[25]

A more centralised system comes into play when the treaty monitoring body is tasked with setting the NCP off, calling on States to fulfil the substantive or procedural obligations assumed under the treaty. This procedure presents itself as more advantageous than the others since it is managed by a neutral body which has an overview of the procedure and can act as an intermediary between the different interests at stake, also incorporating the view of third parties, such as sectors of the civil society.

21 Jutta Brunée, 'COPing with Consent: Law-making under Multilateral Environmental Agreements' (2002) 15(1) *Leiden Journal of International Law*, pp. 1–52.

22 Monreal NCP; Basel; Ramsar; CITES; Kyoto; Cartagena; Aarhus.

23 Malgosia Fitzmaurice, 'Non-Compliance Procedures and the Law of Treaties' (2009) in Tullio Treves et al. (eds), *Non-Compliance Procedures and Mechanisms and the Effectiveness of International Environmental Agreements* (Springer 2009), pp. 453–481.

24 Dupuy and Viñuales (n 16) at 289.

25 Basel Convention, para. 9 (b); Cartagena Protocol, para. IV.1(b).

Precisely, these third parties which can be 'the public' or representatives of the civil society may be authorised by the treaty to forward non-compliance queries to the treaty body. A clear example of this is the Aarhus Convention, which represents a singular case as it opened the possibility of referring communications to the Compliance Committee. As the extensive practice of the ACCC shows, many cases are referred by non-governmental organisations, which have a general interest fostering environmental democracy and transparency. What it is decisive is the type of mechanism – more technical or politically oriented – an aspect which has been extensively addressed in the literature to underline the need for neutrality and to avoid distortions caused by the political issues.[26]

Throughout the non-compliance process, the main question concerns the effectiveness of the mechanisms. The key aspect in this regard is the type of measures taken by NCPs. Although the binding character of the decisions adopted remained disputed, the plethora of decisions can range from facilitative measures, such as determining the need for financial assistance (a milder approach to the issue), to more stringent measures, such as the imposition of sanctions which denote a more formal stance to non-compliance. For instance, the International Whaling Commission (IWC) represents an interesting example of a progressive use of NCPs tools. IWC Infractions Sub-Committee Member States are bound by Art. IX (1) of the IWC Convention to ensure compliance.

In a taxonomy of the NCPs, various systems can be identified. In Table 6.1, various NCP mechanisms established under MEAs are compared following the most relevant categories for the analysis.

4 Environmental dispute resolution

The settlement of international environmental disputes is still scattered and de-centralised, i.e. it takes place before various fora.[27] The appropriateness of judicial dispute settlement to deal with environmental controversies has been question. Scholars have argued that, due to the features of IEL law, rather than adversarial systems of judicial enforcement it is less confrontational and more managerial approaches that would improve compliance.[28] In what follows, different means for the settlement of international environmental disputes will be examined.

26 Gunther Handl, 'Compliance Control Mechanisms and International Environmental Obligations' (1997) 5 *Tulane Journal of International and Comparative Law*, pp. 29–49.

27 Cesare P.R. Romano, 'International Dispute Settlement', in Daniel Bodansky, Jutta Brunnée, and Ellen Hey (eds), *The Oxford Handbook of International Environmental Law* (OUP 2008).

28 Joost Pauwelyn, 6. 'Judicial Mechanisms: Is There a Need for a World Environment Court?', in W. Bradnee Chambers and Jessica F. Green (eds), *Reforming International Environmental Governance: From Institutional Limits to Innovative Reforms* (UN University 2005). See, also, Joost Pauwelyn and Rebecca J Hamilton, 'Exit from International Tribunals' (2018) 9(4) *Journal of International Dispute Settlement*, December, pp. 679–690.

Table 6.1 Comparison between different NCP mechanisms

MEA	CITES Convention on the International Trade of Endangered Species of Wild Fauna & Flora	Kyoto Protocol	Montreal Protocol	Aarhus Convention	Cartagena Protocol
Type of NCP	Mechanism Created in the Treaty CITES This broad participation, combined with the ability of CITES to recommend effective sanctions, including trade suspensions, make it one of the most effective MEAs	Explicitly Instituted in the treaty Independent Experts	Explicitly Instituted in the treaty State representatives	Explicitly Instituted in the treaty Independent Experts	Explicitly Instituted in the treaty
Compliance obligations and procedure	Article VIII (1): 'The Parties shall take appropriate measures to enforce the provisions of the present Convention and to prohibit trade in specimens in violation thereof'.	Annex I (Annex I Party)	Annex IV: Non-compliance procedure Annex III: Non-compliance procedure	MOP in October 2002 the Meeting adopted a decision on review of compliance (Decision I/7)	Article 29, paragraph 5 Article 34 MOP – Decision BS-I/7

(*Continued*)

MEA	CITES Convention on the International Trade of Endangered Species of Wild Fauna & Flora	Kyoto Protocol	Montreal Protocol	Aarhus Convention	Cartagena Protocol
Compliance Mechanism	Committee Broad membership Standing Committee and not the Conference of the Parties decides on individual non-compliance measures Although the CoP can review a particular case, its role is often to direct and oversee the general handling of compliance.	Compliance Committee Made up of two branches: a facilitative branch and an enforcement branch.	Non-Compliance Mechanism Multilateral Fund	Compliance Committee Independent experts	Compliance Committee Independent experts Regional representation
Triggering of the procedure	Triggered treaty organ by States	State concerned and others	Treaty organ and others (all)	State concerned and others (including NGOs)	State concerned and others (injured)
Expected Results Assistance Request for information, warning and sanctions	Effective sanctions, including trade suspensions, make it one of the most effective MEAs	Assistance, request for information warnings and sanctions	Assistance, request for information warnings and sanctions	Assistance, request for information warnings and sanctions	Advice or assistance, request to develop a compliance action plan, measures in the case of repeated non-compliance

Source: Author's own elaboration.

Formal methods available to the parties to an international environmental conflict (art 33 UN Charter), are of judicial and non-judicial nature (diplomatic), this latter offering the benefits of flexibility, cheapness, privacy and freedom to determine the details of the proceedings.[29] International environmental conflict resolution departs from traditional law-making and dispute settlement, directing attention towards the transnational character of the actors, processes (law-making and decision-making) and outputs instead. Referring to a wide range of areas, international law scholars identify the category of international rule-making, coining the term 'informal international lawmaking' (known as IN- LAW).[30]

As regards judicial review or quasi-judicial proceedings, older MEAs do not provide for specific dispute settlement mechanisms, whereas more recent MEAs generally contain dispute settlement clauses. These clauses (such as Article 20 Basel Convention, Article 11 Vienna Convention and Article 14 UNFCC) usu-ally stipulate that disputes should first be settled by negotiation or mediation. Failing to settle the dispute by these means, it may be brought before the ICJ or an arbitration body upon the condition that the Parties have accepted the compulsory obligation to submit disputes to these bodies. In some cases, these mechanisms work even short of the State's consent and collaboration.

In recent years, the term 'conflict resolution' has prevailed over 'dispute settlement', which evokes a more formal institutionalization. International environmental conflict resolution alludes to mechanisms set outside formal gov-ernmental channels and structured around claims from civil society. IECR en-compasses wide-ranging mechanisms.

The starting point for this approach is the conceptualisation of environmen-tal conflicts. While there is no commonly accepted definition of these, there have been some attempts to define them in the literature. Some scholars de-fine them as a subset of controversies involving not only conflicts over access and management of natural resources but also those which cover a combination of issues, such as health, race and ethnicity, economic development and gov-ernance, and multiple jurisdictions and levels thereof.[31] Other scholars allude to disputes involving the use of natural resources or the choice of appropriate standards for environmental protection,[32] or international conflicts caused by environmental problems.[33] For the purpose of this chapter, this definition will be borne in mind; the term 'informal environmental adjudication' will also be used interchangeably.

---

29 Birnie, Boyle, and Redgwell (n 9).

30 Ibid.

31 T.P. D'Estree, E.F. Dukes, and J. Navarrete-Romero, 'Environmental Conflict and Its Resolu-tion', in R.B. Bechtel and A. Churchman (eds), *Handbook of Environmental Psychology* (Wiley 2002).

32 L. Susskind and A. Weinstein, 'Towards a Theory of Environmental Dispute Resolution' (1980) 9 *BC Environmental Affairs Law Review*, pp. 311, 312, available at http://lawdigitalcommons. bc.edu/ealr/vol9/iss2/4 accessed 10 March 2019.

33 Cesare Romano, *The Peaceful Settlement of International Environmental Disputes: A Pragmatic Approach* (International Environmental Law and Policy Series, Vol 56 2000), p. 4.

IECR is consubstantial to cross-border cooperation between various actors, including the participation of public and private actors and/or international organizations. The IECR fora are characterised by their informality rather than the fact that they occur in a traditional international organization. In terms of actors, there is also a certain level of informality: IECR happens between actors other than traditional public actors (such as regulators or environmental agencies), and it is not based on a formal treaty or other traditional source of international law.[34] This framing provides a fertile ground for the conceptualization of IECR as a phenomenon which takes places outside formal governmental and state channels, comprising a wide range of actors and leading to the creation of specific norms.

Through IECR, parties to an environmental dispute resort to mechanisms that transcend the courtroom, going beyond institutionalized state channels and introducing other fora. In terms of the outcome of the process, IECR decisions do not constitute binding national or international law as such. The extent to which and manner in which formal channels take into consideration outputs stemming from these informal processes is still a matter of scholarly debate. This would be equivalent to 'informal justice system', drawing the distinction between state-administered formal justice systems and non-state administered informal justice systems.[35] IECR emphasizes the global nature of IEL in a move away from the traditional state-centred mechanisms.[36] Transnational IECR mechanisms are placed in the grey zone between law and non-law in terms of the resolution of the conflicts; the question that emerges is how to appropriately gauge the elements present in IECR to facilitate access to justice and settle a dispute.

First, there is the question of the role of IECR within the overall institutional justice architecture. Recent years have witnessed a proliferation of environmental courts and tribunals which conceivably furthers access to environmental justice, yet IECR and transnational law-making have become more significant.[37] These new specialized environmental courts and tribunals require a new theoretical model capable of explaining and accommodating environmental adjudication.[38] Why is it still necessary to resort to transnational conflict resolution processes? The answer is that, despite the possibility to submit claims before a growing

---

34 Joost Pauwelyn, 'Informal International Lawmaking: Framing the Concept', in Pauwelyn, Wessel and Wouters (n 7) pp. 13–34, at 22.

35 Ewa Wojkowska, *Doing Justice: How Informal Justice Systems Can Contribute* (United Nations 2006), available at https://www.un.org/ruleoflaw/blog/document/doing-justice-how-informal-justice-systems-can-contribute/ accessed 1 April 2020.

36 Malgosia Fitzmaurice and Catherine Redgwell, 'Environmental Non-compliance Procedures and International Law' (2000) 31 *NYIL*, pp. 35–65.

37 D.C. Smith, 'Environmental Courts and Tribunals: Changing Environmental and Natural Resources Law Around the Globe' (2018) 36(2) *Journal of Energy & Natural Resources Law*, pp. 137–140.

38 C. Warnock, 'Reconceptualising Specialist Environment Courts and Tribunals' (2017) 37(3) *Legal Studies*, pp. 391–417.

number of environmental courts and tribunals, their jurisdiction is still confined to territorial borders.[39] While there have been initiatives to create an International Environmental Court and other multi-national environmental adjudication bodies, they have not received significant support from States.[40]

Finally, the organisation of IECR processes raises certain controversial issues. Often, IECR proceedings involve citizens acting as a 'private attorney general': namely, bringing a claim into the public interest. One of the controversial issues posed is whether it is appropriate for private individuals to claim to know and represent the public interest in such settings.

There is an ever-growing body of legal scholarship on environmental conflict resolution; however, interdisciplinary approaches are less common. Although a great deal of attention has been devoted to analysing the resolution of environmental conflicts through formal methods, few studies have emphasized the transnational law elements. Informality plays a significant role in the conceptualization of this type of conflict resolution, being the predominant sphere in which it takes place. Against this backdrop, the chapter fills a gap in the literature of transnational environmental law, contributing to reflections about the various manner in which environmental conflicts are settled.

a The actors

Traditionally, in the face of non-compliance with IEL norms, States have been endowed with the power to bring the controversy before international bodies. Progressively, the lists of actors involved in international environmental settlement have expanded to comprise non-state actors.[41]

In principle, any party to a specific international environmental treaty or the treaty secretariat can kick-start a dispute resolution procedure for non-compliance. Wherever the treaty provisions allow for this, NGOs and members of the public may also put forward a complaint, submit a report or provide information to the body in charge of administering compliance with the treaty.

b The procedures

Although, in many cases, MEAs include the possibility to settle the dispute before an international judicial body, this is considered the last resort. Before adjudicating a particular dispute, treaties may indicate that the parties should attempt to resolve the dispute through other methods. In particular, mediation

39 R.J. Lazarus, 'Pursuing 'Environmental Justice: The Distributional Effects of Environmental Protection' (1992) 87 *Northwestern University Law Review*, p. 787.

40 O.W. Pedersen, 'An International Environmental Court and International Legalism' (2012) 24(3) *Journal of Environmental Law*, pp. 547–558.

41 Philippe Sands, 'International Environmental Litigation and Its Future' (1999) 32 *University of Richmond Law Review*, p. 1619, available at http://scholarship.richmond.edu/lawreview/vol32/iss5/7 accessed 1 April 2020.

and conciliation are considered steps that come before adjudicating a dispute. Mediation implies the assistance of a third party who acts as a mediator. The parties to the dispute retain control throughout the process. Other resolution methods include conciliation, enquiry and fact-finding. Parties may seek a non-formalised role for a third party. The resort to these various mechanisms can be foreseen in a staggered way.

Enquiry predominantly focusses on the determinations of facts, whereas conciliation may involve findings both of law and of fact. Again, party control remains paramount as State parties in the first instance are not legally required to follow any of the findings of these bodies. Arbitration constitutes another means of dispute settlement involving the intervention of a third party which can settle the dispute by issuing a legally binding decision. Early IEL cases have been settled through arbitration.

c Legal systems and values: fragmentation and international environmental law

Questions that are often posed in the context of international environmental dispute settlement concern the issue about fragmentation in IEL. Equally pertinent for the discussion of IEL dispute settlement is the questions of fairness, which, in turn, relates to the notion of environmental justice.

In terms of environmental justice, some of the claims on the international level revolve around injustice in the distribution of costs, including environmental risks; this prevents affected individuals and communities from bringing a matter before national courts.[42] Amongst other limitations in addressing crucial environmental problems, the traditional conflict resolution system is mainly bilateral and state-centred, offering few possibilities for the participation of non-state actors. Non-state actors face constraints as they are often precluded from instituting proceedings in IEL. IECR mechanisms grant non-state actors greater access to justice, responding to stakeholders' demands for equality before the law and during the proceedings. IECR processes seek to protect specific human rights and to enhance access to environmental justice.

5 International courts and tribunals

The settlement of international environmental disputes before international courts and tribunals is characterised as scattered and fragmented. It relies on the evolution of the system and the competence allocated to each international body. Generally, judicial and non-judicial mechanisms are used as a last resort when other diplomatic and non-judicial mechanisms fail to reach a solution to environmental disputes.

---

42 R.J. Lazarus, 'Fairness in Environmental Law' (1997) 27(3) *Environmental Law*, pp. 705–739, 711 and 713.

Not all international courts and tribunals have entertained jurisdiction in environmental disputes. After a long while, the International Court of Justice began to decide cases involving compliance with IEL. The ICJ, exercising its authority in the interpretation of the sources, has spelled out the features of compliance with IEL: namely, customary international law.[43]

The framework of the international environmental governance system is based on MEAs and a network of soft-law instruments. The role of international courts and tribunals (ICTs) is crucial in the IEL compliance system. More specifically, ICTs have so far increased the effectiveness of international environmental governance. Due to the lack of a specific International Environmental Court (IEC), the resolution of IEL disputes takes place before different bodies. The need for an IEC has been long discussed in IEL scholarship.

In the landscape of IEL compliance, judicial and arbitral proceedings constitute the traditionally predominant dispute-settlement mechanisms.[44] Turning to the role that some ICTs have played in international environmental governance through the lenses of IEL compliance, the emphasis is on the International Court of Justice (ICJ) and the dispute-settlement mechanisms under the Law of the Sea Convention. The International Tribunal for the Law of the Sea (ITLOS) is particularly important for the protection of the marine environment and global environmental issues. Other uses of dispute-settlement procedures outside of these forums can be found in the realm of the World Trade Organization (WTO). In the WTO framework, both the panels and the Appellate Body have decided various cases involving the protection of the environment, as has been extensively discussed in another chapter of this book.

Overall, the ICJ forum has only recently been used for the resolution of IEL disputes. The general competence of the ICJ covers those cases in which the application of IEL is at stake, relating to the implementation of treaty provisions or customary international law norms. The IEL framework applicable to the settlement of disputes before international law bodies comprises international and transnational law principles. Various principles of substantive and procedural character emanate from the Rio Declaration, such as the preventive and precautionary principles that guide the interpretation of IEL norms.[45] The preventative and precautionary principles are particularly relevant to assessing due diligence on the part of actors involved in the environmental field and inform

---

43 Jean d'Aspremont, 'The International Court of Justice as the Master of the Sources' (February 5, 2020). Carlos Espósito and Kate Parlett (eds), *The Cambridge Companion to the International Court of Justice* (Cambridge University Press 2021), available at SSRN: https://ssrn.com/abstract=3532329 or http://dx.doi.org/10.2139/ssrn.3532329 accessed 1 April 2020.

44 Monica Feria-Tinta and Simon Milnes, 'The Rise of Environmental Law in International Dispute Resolutions' (2018) *Yearbook of International Environmental Law*, pp. 1–18.

45 Also, we can identify principles of cooperation (N°s 7, 9, 12, 14 y 27); responsibility for environmental harm (N° 13); common but differentiated responsibilities (N° 7); polluter pays (N° 16); and certain human rights, such as healthy and productive life in harmony with nature (N° 1).

the duty to carry out an environmental impact assessment ('EIA').[46] Principles are relied upon by the ICJ to ascertain obligations under IEL, as argued by the ICJ in *Pulp Mills on the Uruguay River* and the cases between Costa Rica and Nicaragua.[47]

IEL cases before the ICJ include the application of some general customary rules, such as permanent sovereignty over natural resources, the principle of prevention of transboundary harm and the obligation to carry out EIAs in certain cases.[48] Those who defend the precautionary principle as a customary rule [49] circumscribe it as a fourth standard of this nature, placing the principle as a foundational rule of IEL, or a rule of interpretation of other norms or guidelines, by the which all States are bound, except persistent objector.[50] No Court so far has ruled that the precautionary principle has the character of the customary rule of international law, but they have not wished to assert that it does not either. International courts may be receptive to the precautionary principle without having to determine whether it is a mandatory rule in international law.[51]

However, a set of individual opinions can be identified that could crystallize into a majority opinion,[52] which defends the customary nature of the principle. Some key concepts relating to the precautionary principle include its relationship to the environmental standard of proof; its role as a principle of interpretation of conventional norms; and its link with the duty of due diligence and, consequently, with the principle of prevention.

---

46 Other procedural rights contained in the Rio Declaration are notification in case of emergency (N° 18); notification and consultation in case of risk of environmental transboundary effects (N° 19); peaceful settlement of disputes (N° 26); and the environmental democracy, which comprises rights of participation, access to environmental information and access to environmental justice (N° 10).

47 International Court of Justice, Pulp Mills on the River Uruguay (Argentina v. Uruguay), Judgment of 20 April 2010 https://www.icj-cij.org/files/case-related/135/135-20100420-JUD-01-00-EN.pdf 1 April 2020 accessed 1 April 2020. Certain Activities Carried Out by Nicaragua in the Border Area (Costa Rica v. Nicaragua) Proceedings joined with Construction of a Road in Costa Rica along the San Juan River (Nicaragua v. Costa Rica) on 17 April 2013, available at https://www.icj-cij.org/en/case/150 accessed 1 April 2020.

48 ICJ, *Pulp Mills on the River Uruguay* (Argentina v. Uruguay), Judgment of 20 April 2010, par. 203 y ss.

49 See, among others, O. Mcintyre and T. Mosedale, 'The Precautionary Principle as a Norm of Customary International Law' (1997) 9(2) *Journal of Environmental Law*, p. 221; J. Cameron and J. Abouchar, (1991): 'The Precautionary Principle: A Fundamental Principle of Law and Policy for the Protection of Global Environment' (1991) 14(1) *Boston College International and Comparative Law Review*, p. 19 y ss.

50 See Ole Pedersen, 'From Abundance to Indeterminacy: The Precautionary Principle and Its Two Camps of Custom' (2014) 3(2) *Transnational Environmental Law*, p. 323.

51 Caroline Foster, 'Adjudication, Arbitration and the Turn to Public Law 'Standards of Review': Putting the Precautionary Principle in the Crucible' (2012) 3(3) *Journal of International Dispute Settlement*, p. 534.

52 Philippe Sands, (2002), 'Los Tribunales Internacionales y el Principio de Precaución', in AA.VV. *La precaución, de Rio a Johannesburgo. Actas de la Mesa Redonda de la Geneva Environment Network* (Geneva Environment Network, 2002), p. 36.

In this way, the precautionary principle has been addressed, especially in cases before the ICJ and the ITLOS. The issue has also been debated within the WTO Dispute Settlement System in food security.[53] However, both the Appellate Body and a Panel have noted that '[s]ince the legal status of the precautionary principle remains unsettled [...], we consider that prudence suggests that we not attempt to resolve this complex issue, particularly if it is not necessary to do so'.[54]

Regarding the ICJ, in the *Gabcíkovo – Nagymaros* case, Hungary argued that the obligation not to cause harm in the territory of another State had evolved towards an *erga omnes* obligation to prevent harm, in accordance with the precautionary principle.[55] Although in this case, the discussion was about the implications of the precautionary measures for the project, other very relevant considerations were made therein.[56] In the *Pulp Mills* case, the question was whether jurisdiction over the interpretation and application of an international treaty included the obligations of the parties under the provisions of other international treaties and general international law as well as the role they would have in a particular case. In this regard, the ICJ argued that the precautionary principle could be a relevant element for the interpretation and application of the Uruguay River Statute without indicating the extent to which it would be applicable in the case as well as its justification.

Finally, in the case of the Pulp Mills on the River Uruguay, Judge Greenwood provided a different view regarding the application of the precautionary principle. In effect, he pointed out that the nature of environmental conflicts affects not the burden of proof but rather the standard of proof.[57] He added that the application of a high standard of environmental testing may have an effect of rendering it almost impossible to meet the burden of proof of environmental damage in terms such that the actual effect attributable to principle 15 of the Rio Declaration is to lower the standard of proof for whoever has to prove the risk or environmental damage.[58]

---

53 See, among others, Caroline Foster, 'Precaution, Scientific Development and Scientific Uncertainty under the WTO Agreement on Sanitary and Phytosanitary Measures' (2009) 18(1) *Review of European, Comparative & International Environmental Law*, p. 50.

54 See *European Communities – Measures Concerning Meat and Meat Products (Hormones)* (WT/DS26/AB/R y WT/DS48/AB/R), Report of the Appellate Body of January 16th, 1998; *European Communities – Measures Affecting the Approval and Marketing of Biotech Products* (WT/DS291/R, WT/DS292/R y WT/DS293/R), report of the *panel* of September 29th, 2006, paragraph 7.89.

55 ICJ, *Gabcikovo/Nagymaros Project* (Hungary v Slovakia), Decision of 25th September 1997, para. 97.

56 ICJ, *Gabcikovo/Nagymaros Project* (Hungary v Slovakia), Decision of 25th September 1997, para. 113.

57 ICJ, *Pulp Mills on the River Uruguay* (Argentina v. Uruguay), Judgment, I.C.J. Reports 2010, Separate Opinion of Judge Greenwood, para. 26.

58 Birnie, Boyle and Redgwell (n 9) at 154 and 157.

Except in the case of the ICJ – which is a Court of general jurisdiction[59] – the absence of an international tribunal linked to environmental treaties obliges a court to address conflicts of this nature from the point of view of the treaty to be interpreted and applied by the respective Court. For example, in the cases of the ITLOS, environmental conflicts must be formulated from the perspective of the United Nations Convention on the Law of the Sea (hereinafter 'UN-CLOS'), whereas in the case of the WTO Dispute Settlement Mechanism, the notion of 'covered agreements' provided in the Dispute Settlement Understanding applies. Also, it must be added that there are few international environmental treaties that provide resources for jurisdictional means of dispute settlement.

Thus, invocation of the precautionary principle has been made in certain cases depending on the treaty – when it is part of the framework of jurisdiction of the court – or as a customary rule of general international law, when its application is intended to justify beyond the treaty or when an attempt is made to interpret the provision of a treaty taking into account 'any relevant rule of international law applicable between the parties'.[60]

Interstate environmental disputes originated in non-compliance with IEL may also be settled by resorting to arbitration. Some environmental disputes fall within the competence of international arbitration courts, such as the Permanent Court of Arbitration (PCA), which has dealt with legal disputes that have arisen under a variety of treaties, some of them of a multilateral nature, such as the 1992 OSPAR Convention, the 1982 UN Convention on the Law of the Sea, the 1960 Indus Waters Treaty and the 1976 Rhine Chlorides Convention.[61] Other interstate environmental disputes brought before the PCA have arisen under bilateral treaties and ad-hoc arbitration agreements. In other draft agreements, resorting to the PCA is included among dispute settlement options, such as in the Draft International Covenant on Environment and Development.[62] It is worth noting that this is a model agreement developed by NGOs to facilitate treaty negotiations in the environmental sector. In those cases administered by the PCA, it acts as the appointing authority and the forum for the arbitration of disputes arising from a number of environmental treaties.

A good example of this can be found in the *Indus Water Kishenganga* case (*Pakistan v. India*) of the Permanent Court of Arbitration, relating to a project of a hydroelectric plant on the *Kishenganga/Neelum River*.[63] Pakistan argued that, among other obligations, India should apply a precautionary approach to its

---

59 As well as the case of arbitration Courts in environmental cases.

60 Vienna Convention on the Law of Treaties, Artícle 31.3.c).

61 Permanent Court of Arbitration, available at https://pca-cpa.org/en/services/arbitration-services/environmental-dispute-resolution/ accessed 1 April 2020.

62 IUCN, Draft International Covenant on Environment and Development. Fifth Edition: Updated Text, 2017, available at https://sustainabledevelopment.un.org/index.php?page=view& type=400&nr=2443 accessed 1 April 2020.

63 In possible contradiction of a bilateral agreement signed in 1960, concerning the use of the waters of the *Indus System of Rivers*, within which is situated the *Kishenganga/Neelum*.

activities on the containment dam.[64] India's response was twofold: (1) to discuss its character as a customary rule because a number of important countries had strongly discussed this customary nature and (2) because it is not applicable to the case due to its different possible meanings.[65]

The arbitrators did not pronounced in the partial award or in the final award on this issue. However, they noted that

> the Court does not consider it appropriate, and certainly not necessary, for it to adopt a precautionary approach and assumes the role of policymaker in determining the balance between acceptable environmental change and other priorities, or to permit environmental considerations to override the balance of other rights and obligations expressly identified in the Treaty.[66]

Thus, the State in which the project or activity is carried out has a wide margin of appreciation in relation to the application of the precautionary principle. An additional question to be considered is whether the protection of the right to live in a healthy environment can lead to the obligation of the State to act under the precautionary principle in the face of a project or activity in which there is uncertainty of serious or irreversible damage to the environment, which at the same time affects this fundamental right.

In the context of non-compliance-related litigation in IEL, there is an emerging case law concerning the concept of due diligence echoed in the responsibility of the State and accountability of non-state actors vis-à-vis an obligation of conduct. In the case of environmental damage, State and non-state actions should be examined in order to prevent damage.

The concept of due diligence takes into consideration the idea that, jointly with the powers in its territory, international actors possess a corresponding obligation to protect other actors by adopting all appropriate measures and prevent environmental damage. In terms of States, this means that they have the obligation to safeguard the security of other States as well as the people under its jurisdiction. The content of the obligation to act with due diligence has been used in different fields, ranging from International Human Rights Law (IHRL)[67] to Law of the Sea[68] and IEL.[69] In the field of IEL, the obligation of due diligence

---

64 Permanent Court of Arbitration, *The Indus Waters Kishenganga Arbitration* (Pakistan v. India), Partial Award of 18 February 2013, para. 223.

65 Ibid., para. 227.

66 Ibid., para. 112.

67 IACHR, *Velásquez Rodríguez v. Honduras*, decision of July 29th, 1988, para. 172, *Godínez Cruz v. Honduras*, decision of January 20th, 1989, para. 182, among others.

68 ITLOS, *Responsibilities and Obligations of States Sponsoring Persons and Entities with Respect to Activities in the Area* (Request for Advisory Opinion submitted to the Seabed Disputes Chamber), February 1st, 2011, para. 117.

69 In this sense, it can be seen in the contributions of the ILA Study Group on Due Diligence, especially the 2014 (Washington) and 2016 (Johannesburg) reports, both available at http://www.ila-hq.org/en/study-groups/index.cfm/cid/1045 accessed 1 April 2020.

has a specific meaning, and it implies preventing and progressively achieving the protection of the environment on the international level.[70] It also corresponds to the obligation to take measures in line with the duty of due diligence to prevent environmental damage.[71]

In order to comply with the duty of due diligence from the IEL perspective, following the jurisprudence of the ITLOS on responsibilities of the State sponsoring the prospecting or exploration of the seabed beyond its jurisdiction, it can be argued that the duty of due diligence also involves the direct obligation to conduct an EIA in certain cases – reflecting the preventive principle – as well as adopting a precautionary approach when deciding on operating authorizations for specific projects, works or activities.[72]

In addition, and following the reasoning of the ICJ in the Pulp Mills case, the preventive principle has its origins in the duty of due diligence.[73] Moreover, the preventive dimension of environmental protection has increasingly been understood as a duty of due diligence, regardless of whether the activities are capable of causing transboundary harm or are purely domestic activities.[74] Further, it added that, in order to comply with the obligation of due diligence to prevent transboundary environmental damage, a State must determine if there is a significant risk of transboundary harm, which may trigger the requirement to conduct an EIA, prior to carrying out an activity that has the potential to adversely affect the environment of another State.[75]

States must ensure that activities carried out within its jurisdiction and under its control do not cause damage to the environment of other States, or areas outside the national jurisdiction (Principle No. 2 of the Rio Declaration), recognized by the ICJ as part of the *corpus* of international law relating to the environment.[76] Upon this basis, environmental legislation has been developed, especially in the field of environmental management instruments, such as environmental impact assessments in the case of projects that are capable of having a significant impact on environment.

70 Rumiana Yotova, 'The Principles of Due Diligence and Prevention in International Environmental Law' (2016) 75(3) *The Cambridge Law Journal*, pp. 445–448.
71 Certain Activities Carried out by Nicaragua in the Border Area (Costa Rica v Nicaragua) and Construction of a Road in Costa Rica along the San Juan River (Nicaragua v Costa Rica), ICJ Reports 2015. These are the latest in a line of cases raising key principles of international environmental law before the ICJ, following Pulp Mills (2010), Aerial Herbicide Spraying (2013) and Whaling in the Antarctic (2014).
72 Ibid., para. 122.
73 ICJ, *Pulp Mills on the River Uruguay* (Argentina v. Uruguay), Judgment of 20 April 2010.
74 Jorge E. Viñuales, 'The Rio Declaration on Environment and Development. Preliminary Study' (2015), in Jorge E. Viñuales (ed), *The Rio Declaration on Environment and Development: A Commentary* (Oxford University Press 2015), p. 23.
75 ICJ, *Certain Activities Carried out by Nicaragua in the Border Area (Costa Rica V. Nicaragua) Construction of a Road in Costa Rica along the San Juan River (Nicaragua V. Costa Rica).* Decision of 16 December, 2015, para. 104.
76 ICJ, *Legality of the Threat or Use of Nuclear Weapons*, Advisory Opinion of 8 July 1996, para. 29; *Pulp Mills on the River Uruguay* (Argentina v. Uruguay), Judgment of 20 April 2010, para. 101.

In the case of ITLOS, its jurisdiction is more restricted than that of the ICJ insofar as it is competent to hear disputes submitted to it under the UNCLOS or other agreements conferring jurisdiction.[77] In turn, in order to settle the disputes, it must resort to UNCLOS 'and to the other norms of international law that are not incompatible with it'.[78] Thus, ITLOS has been requested on some occasions to order preventive measures invoking the precautionary principle. ITLOS has referred to the precautionary principle when it has been requested to provide advisory opinions.[79] In those cases, the analysis of the precautionary principle was based on texts expressed in specific agreements.

In the case of provisional measures, the first case concerned the conservation of *Southern Bluefish Tuna*, filed by Australia and New Zealand. In this case, the Court, was asked to order the Parties to act consistently with the precautionary principle in fishing for bluefish tuna while the substance of the matter was settled.[80] The second was in the *MOX Plant* case, in which Ireland requested the Tribunal, *inter alia*, to suspend the authorization of the MOX Plant, arguing that the United Kingdom must prove that discharges and other consequences of the operation of the MOX Plant would not cause damage to the environment, based on the precautionary principle. From a procedural point of view –according to the Irish argument – the precautionary principle can inform the assessment of the urgency of the provisional measures to be taken in connection with the operation of the MOX Plant.[81] Finally, in the case of the *Strait of Johor*, Malaysia argued that Singapore had violated several rules of UNCLOS, in addition to the precautionary principle, 'which under international law must be a direct party in the application and implementation of those obligations'.[82]

Consequently, one of the issues to be determined by ITLOS was to what extent the precautionary principle informs the sense of urgency that must exist to justify the imposition of provisional measures under the rules of the UNCLOS. In this regard, in *Southern Bluefish Tuna*, ITLOS argued that the parties should 'act with "prudence and caution" to ensure that effective conservation measures are taken to prevent serious harm to the stock of southern bluefin tuna'.[83] It also stated that there was no scientific certainty as to the measures to be taken for the conservation of that species, nor was there any agreement on the effect of the

---

77 Article 21 of the Statute of ITLOS.
78 Article 293 UNCLOS.
79 ITLOS, *Responsibilities and Obligations of States Sponsoring Persons and Entities with Respect to Activities in the Area*, Advisory Opinion of February 1st, 2011; ITLOS, *Request for an Advisory Opinion Submitted by the Sub-Regional Fisheries Commission* (SRFC), Advisory Opinion, 2 April 2015.
80 ITLOS, *Southern Bluefish Tuna Cases*, Provisional Measures, Order of 27 August 1999, paras. 31.3 and 32.3.
81 ITLOS, *MOX Plant Case*, Provisional Measures, Order of 3 December 2001, para. 71.
82 ITLOS, *Case Concerning Land Reclamation by Singapore in and Around the Straits of Johor*, Provisional Measures, Order of 8 October 2003, para. 74.
83 ITLOS, *Southern Bluefish Tuna Cases*, Provisional Measures, Order of 27 August 1999, para. 77.

conservation measures.[84] Moreover, although the Court could not make a conclusive assessment of the evidence submitted, it suggested that the provisional
measures should be adopted as a matter of urgency to preserve the rights of the
parties and avoid further deterioration of the bluefin tuna stock.[85] In this sense,
although ITLOS avoided using the words 'principle' or 'approach', the reference
to the lack of scientific certainty as a main element of the decision makes it possible to point out that this was a case in which ITLOS came close to applying
that principle, as has been recognized in several opinions in that case as well as
in the *MOX Plant* case and in the Advisory Opinion on *Activities in the Area*,
as discussed below.[86]

In the *MOX Plant* case, ITLOS reiterated that 'prudence and caution' require the parties to cooperate by exchanging information regarding the risks
and effects of the operation of the MOX Plant, developing mechanisms for risk
management.[87] In the case of the *Strait of Johor*, ITLOS reiterated that 'prudence and caution' require Malaysia and Singapore to establish mechanisms to
exchange information, assess the risks and effects of land reclamation, and develop mechanisms for risk management.[88] It can be argued, therefore, that the
requirement of urgency for provisional measures is implicit when it is held that
the protection of the rights of the parties or the marine environment is needed
by the precautionary principle/approach.[89]

Although in the first two cases, Australia, New Zealand and Ireland, respectively, have argued that the precautionary principle is a customary rule of general
international law, ITLOS has been extremely cautious in its analysis. However,
the recognition of the duty to cooperate in relation to the marine environment
in the *MOX Plant* and *Strait of Johor* cases is closely connected with the precautionary principle.[90]

In the Advisory Opinion on the *Activities in the Area*, ITLOS analysed the
duty of due diligence, identifying certain direct obligations, such as that (1) to
assist the Authority in the control that must be exercised over activities in the
area; (2) to apply a precautionary approach; (3) to apply the best environmental

84 ITLOS, *Southern Bluefish Tuna Cases*, Provisional Measures, Order of 27 August 1999,
para. 79.

85 ITLOS, *Southern Bluefish Tuna Cases*, Provisional Measures, Order of 27 August 1999,
para. 80.

86 ITLOS, *Responsibilities and Obligations of States Sponsoring Persons and Entities with Respect to
Activities in the Area* (Request for Advisory Opinion submitted to the Seabed Disputes Chamber), February 1st, 2011, para. 132.

87 ITLOS, *MOX Plant Case*, Provisional Measures, Order of 3 December 2001, paras. 82 to 84.

88 ITLOS, *Case Concerning Land Reclamation by Singapore in and Around the Straits of Johor*,
Provisional Measures, Order of 8 October 2003, para. 99.

89 B. Kwiatkowska, 'The *Ireland v United Kingdom* (Mox Plant) Case: Applying the Doctrine
of Treaty Parallelism' (2003) 18(1) *The International Journal of Marine and Coastal Law*,
p. 40.

90 F. Orrego, 'The International Tribunal of the Law of the Sea and Provisional Measures: Settled
Issues and Pending Problems' (2007) 22(3) *The International Journal of Marine and Coastal
Law*, p. 458.

practices; (4) to adopt measures in order to ensure the adoption of guarantees in the event of an emergency order by the Authority, aimed at the protection of the marine environment; (5) to ensure the availability of resources to compensate for damages caused by pollution, and (6) to develop an environmental impact assessment.[91]

In the case of the precautionary principle, both the regulation of polymetallic nodules of sulphides – relevant to the analysis of the case – contain specific provisions concerning the application of the precautionary principle in terms of Principle 15 of the Rio Declaration so that this provision becomes binding on the sponsoring States of activities in the Area in terms such that the implementation of the precautionary approach in the way it is defined in those regulations is one of its obligations.[92] However, ITLOS addressed two outstanding issues from the previous finding. The first is that the regulations on sulphides and polymetallic nodules are limited to the processes of prospecting and exploration but not exploitation. In this way, the question of whether there is an obligation to implement the precautionary principle in the latter aspect remains open. The second issue lies in the fact that Principle 15 of the Rio Declaration provides for the precautionary approach 'in line with the capacities' of States, thereby introducing differences in their application according to the degree of development.

In response to these questions, ITLOS recognized that the precautionary principle is an integral part of the due diligence of the sponsoring States and therefore applies even outside the scope of the regulations for sulphides and polymetallic nodules. Also, it is applied in those cases where the scientific evidence concerning the scope and negative impacts of the activity in question is insufficient, but there are plausible indications of potential risks.[93] The Court added that the precautionary approach had been incorporated into a growing number of treaties and other instruments under the terms of Principle 15 of the Rio Declaration and therefore believed that it had begun a trend towards making this approach a customary rule of international law.[94]

Another dimension of the precautionary principle lies in its role as an element of normative interpretation. In general, it is not complex to explain precaution as a general principle of law which may not necessarily be created to be a legal

---

91 ITLOS, *Responsibilities and Obligations of States Sponsoring Persons and Entities with Respect to Activities in the Area* (Request for Advisory Opinion submitted to the Seabed Disputes Chamber), February 1st, 2011, paras. 121 and 122.

92 ITLOS, *Responsibilities and Obligations of States Sponsoring Persons and Entities with Respect to Activities in the Area* (Request for Advisory Opinion submitted to the Seabed Disputes Chamber), February 1st, 2011, para. 127.

93 ITLOS, *Responsibilities and Obligations of States Sponsoring Persons and Entities with Respect to Activities in the Area* (Request for Advisory Opinion submitted to the Seabed Disputes Chamber), February 1st, 2011, para. 131.

94 ITLOS, *Responsibilities and Obligations of States Sponsoring Persons and Entities with Respect to Activities in the Area* (Request for Advisory Opinion submitted to the Seabed Disputes Chamber), February 1st, 2011, para. 135.

rule but may have a relevant influence on the interpretation, application and development of other rules of law in the same way as other environmental principles, such as sustainable development.[95] In this regard, and in accordance with international jurisprudence, the precautionary principle can serve as an element of interpretation of other rules of the legal system, both at the level of treaties and at the level of internal rules. Thus, in the Case of the *Pulp Mills* on the River Uruguay, the ICJ pointed out that the precautionary principle may serve to interpret the Statute of 1975.[96]

In general, the decision-making process on the precautionary principle makes it possible to identify a set of measures, which in some cases have to do with administrative decisions and in others can be applied by judges in environmental disputes. Thus, these measures usually manifest: (1) a possible obligation for policymakers to assume the worst of scenarios when evaluating the measures to be adopted for the development of a project or activity, (2) require such projects to adopt the best available technologies and measures, (3) the obligation for anyone intending to develop an economic activity to prove that such activity will not result in environmental damage or (4) prohibit any activity or project.

As can be seen, alternatives 1 and 2 are typically policy-kind decisions, often covered by the principle of institutional balance at the domestic level or by the doctrine of margin of appreciation in international law. However, measures 3 and 4 may be adopted by judicial decision.

In sum, from the standpoint of international dispute settlement, a number of non-compliance cases relating to IEL have arisen before the ITLOS, the Permanent Court of Arbitration and the ICJ. An important aspect to be highlighted concerns separate opinions which feature nuances concerning compliance. To illustrate in the ITLOS, Judge Rüdiger Wolfrum acknowledged that the precautionary principle has the effect of changing the burden of proof. Thus, it was pointed out that, in the event that there is an interest in doing or continuing an activity, one must prove that said activity is not going to result in damage.[97] In the same vein, Judge Gavan Griffith referred to the obligations of the OSPAR Convention in his dissenting opinion referring to the arbitral award made by the Permanent Court of Arbitration.[98]

95 A. Boyle, 'The Environmental Jurisprudence of the International Tribunal of the Law of the Sea' (2007) 22(3) *The International Journal of Marine and Coastal Law*, p. 375.

96 ICJ, *Pulp Mills on the River Uruguay (Argentina v. Uruguay)*, Judgment, I.C.J. Reports 2010, para. 164.

97 ITLOS, *MOX Plant Case*, Provisional Measures, Order of 3 December 2001, Separate Opinion of Judge Wolfrum.

98 Permanent Court of Arbitration, *Dispute Concerning Access to Information under Article 9 of the OSPAR Convention* (Ireland v. United Kingdom), Final Award, 2 July 2003, Dissenting Opinion of /Gavan Griffith QC, para. 72.

INTERNATIONAL TRIBUNAL FOR THE LAW OF THE SEA (ITLOS)

Advisory Opinion of 1 February 2011

Responsibilities and obligations of States sponsoring persons and entities with respect to activities in the Area

The content of "due diligence" obligations may not easily be described in precise terms. Among the factors that make such a description difficult is the fact that "due diligence" is a variable concept. It may change over time as measures considered sufficiently diligent at a certain moment may become not diligent enough in light, for instance, of new scientific or technological knowledge. It may also change in relation to the risks involved in the activity.

Source: https://www.itlos.org/cases/list-of-cases/case-no-17/

---

6 Human rights courts and regional mechanisms

It has long been discussed whether regional human rights courts have the specific competence to adjudicate about environmental issues. Human rights courts and bodies have dealt with environmental claims in the framework of IHRL. Clearly, the question that arises here is whether IEL compliance can be dealt with by human rights courts and regional mechanisms. While they may offer the possibility to safeguard environmental access rights, the extent to which non-compliance with IEL is addressed is always related to the protection of human rights. Moreover, many of the available human rights instruments did not initially include environmental protection within their scope. After the first cases, matters and protection developed incrementally.

In the Strasbourg system, the wording of the European Convention does not explicitly address the protection of environmental rights. Nonetheless, the European Court of Human Rights (ECtHR) case law has greatly contributed to the 'greening' of human rights protection based on the interpretation of Articles 2, 8 and 10 of the European Convention on Human Rights (ECHR). In turn, the American Convention on Human Rights (ACHR) mandates that States respect the rights and freedoms enshrined therein, incorporating only in Article 26 the commitment to guaranteeing the progressive development of economic, social and cultural rights.

In Europe, leading cases have heralded a new era in the protection of the environment, opening another channel to deal with non-compliance with environmental law. Amongst the cases that have arisen under Article 8 of the ECHR, the first relevant to environmental protection was *Lopez Ostra v Spain*, in which the court upheld a complaint against the government's failure to deal with pollution originating in smells, noise and fumes from a waste-treatment plant located in the vicinity of the applicant's home. The environmental damage interfered with the applicant's private life in violation of Article 8 as the authorities had not struck a fair balance between the interests at stake. In *Guerra and others v Italy* the focus was placed on the right to information concerning a chemical factory producing fertiliser which has caused several accidents and poisoning in the city. The Court took the view that there had been a violation of Article 8 because of the delay in providing information to the applicants which was necessary to perform a risk assessment. Other cases, like *Budayeva and Others v Russia*, referring to a mudslide where people died, unveiled the interconnections between lack of compliance with environmental law and violation of human rights in a causal relation. In its conclusions, the Court determined that the Russian Federation had violated Article 2 by failing to implement land-planning and emergency relief policies in a hazardous area where there was a foreseeable risk to lives. Later cases have further delimited the scope of the protection granted under the ECHR. In *Hatton and Others v United Kingdom* (2003) and *Kyrtatos v Greece* (2003), the Court emphasised the necessary link between human rights and environmental damage. *Kyrtatos v Greece* concerned the challenging of a government's decision to demolish buildings that supposedly affected protected species. The First Section of the ECtHR determined that no violation of Article 8 had been proven as the applicants were not able to demonstrate that the damage to the birds and other protected species directly infringed their private or family life rights.

Turning now to the ACHR, similarly, its text does not contain any explicit references to sustainable development or environmental protection. However, there is an intrinsic relationship between Articles 1.1, 4.1 and 5.1, and the right to a healthy environment. The Protocol to the Convention on Economic, Social and Cultural Rights (also known as the 'Protocol of San Salvador') of 17 November 1988 includes the so-called rights of solidarity – the right to health, food and a healthy environment, among others.[99] It also requires States to take into account the progressive nature of such rights.

In view of this, both human rights bodies of the Inter-American System, the Inter-American Court of Human Rights and the Inter-American Commission on Human Rights, have begun to recognize the protection of new generations of human rights, including a healthy and ecologically balanced environment in parallel with the recognition and protection of the rights of indigenous peoples.[100]

In light of specific cases, the Commission and the Court have gradually taken on the protection of the right to a healthy environment. This evolution has been possible through a systematic and evolving interpretation of the norms making

---

99 Thus, in para. 11, it states that '(1). Everyone has the right to live in a healthy environment and to have basic public services. (2). State Parties shall promote protection, preservation and improvement of the environment'.

100 Moreover, the Inter-American Commission of Human Rights extended the Rapporteurship on Economic, Social and Cultural Rights to environmental Rights, see https://www.oas.org/en/iachr/desc/ accessed 1 April 2020.

up the legal framework, considering both individual and collective rights, in particular those of indigenous communities and peoples.

In *Kawas Fernández v. Honduras* the Court indicated that the protection of the environment falls within the safeguard of human rights. In this case, it determined the violation of the freedom of association of a group of environmentalists aimed at protecting natural resources.[101] Moreover, the progressive protection of the human right to the environment in the ISHR has gained importance in the case of indigenous peoples. In this case, as well as in others decided by the Court, the responsibility of the State not to guarantee the right to indigenous property was established. Indeed in *Kawas*, the Court compared the universal, indivisible and interdependent character of human rights to the link between civil and political rights; economic; social and cultural rights; and solidarity rights, including the right to environment.[102] In the case of the Indigenous Peoples of *Mashco Piro, Yora and Amahuaca*, the Commission granted provisional measures to guarantee their life and personal integrity, and to eradicate activities of illegal logging in their legally protected territory since they were exposed to risk of extinction.[103]

Moreover, in a number of cases, both the Court and the Commission have issued measures aimed at protecting the environmental rights of indigenous communities or persons from NGOs dedicated to environmental protection and training and counselling indigenous and peasant communities that have been persecuted and threatened, as in *Yatama v Nicaragua* (2005),[104] *Marco Arana Mirtha Vásquez and others v Peru*[105] and *Teodoro Cabrera García and Rodolfo Montiel Flores v Mexico*.[106]

The obligation to carry out an EIA is also based on international human rights law, as referred to in *Saramaka v. Suriname*. In this decision, the Court reiterated that the State had an obligation to consult with the Saramaka people in accordance with their customs and traditions, guaranteeing their right to be effectively consulted on legislative, administrative or other measures as well as the obligation to carry out previous studies of social and environmental impact and any restriction on property rights, particularly development or investment plans that affect them. In particular, the Court required previous studies of social and environmental impact in order to obtain objective measures of impact on land and people, and knowledge about environmental and health risks.[107]

101 IACHR, *Kawas Fernández v. Honduras*, Decision of April 3, 2009.
102 Ibid.
103 IACHR, 22 March 2007.
104 In this case, the Court recognizes the right of political participation and the judicial protection of the members of indigenous and ethics communities of the Caribbean coast, organised in defense of the historical rights of the indigenous peoples and their territories, in order to establish and protect their cultural identity, customs and autonomous organization.
105 IACHR, 23 April 2007. These people were part of an organisation dedicated to the environment, technical and legal assistance, and were threatened by pro-mining people.
106 Petitioners were dedicated to the protection of environmental and human rights and were objects of assaults and violations of their associative rights. That was the reason why the Commission suited on June 24th, 2009.
107 IACHR, *Pueblo Saramaka v. Surinam*, Decision of November 28th, 2007 and August 12th, 2008.

INTER-AMERICAN COURT OF HUMAN RIGHTS

Advisory Opinion OC-23/17

... the Court found that, to respect and ensure the rights to life and personal integrity: a. States are obligated to prevent significant environmental damages within and outside their territory. b. To comply with this obligation of prevention, States must regulate, supervise and monitor the activities under their jurisdiction that could cause significant damage to the environment; carry out environmental impact assessments when there is a risk of significant damage to the environment; prepare contingency plans in order to establish safety measures and procedures to minimize the possibility of major environmental disasters, and mitigate any significant environmental damage that could have occurred, even when this happened despite preventive actions by the State. c. States must act in keeping with the precautionary principle to protect the rights to life and to personal integrity in the event of possible serious and irreversible damage to the environment, even in the absence of scientific certainty. d. States are obligated to cooperate, in good faith, to protect against environmental damage. e. To comply with the obligation of cooperation, when States become aware that an activity planned under their jurisdiction could generate a risk of significant transboundary damage and in cases of environmental emergencies, they must notify other States that could be affected, as well as consult and negotiate in good faith with the States potentially affected by significant transboundary damage. f. States have the obligation to ensure the right of access to information recognized in Article 13 of the American Convention in relation to possible damage to the environment. g. States have the obligation to ensure the right to public participation of the persons subject to their jurisdiction, as established in Article 23(1)(a) of the Convention, in the decision-making process and in the issuing of policies that may affect the environment. h. States have the obligation to ensure access to justice, regarding the state obligations for the protection of the environment previously indicated in this Opinion.

Source: Advisory Opinion (OC-23/17) – Inter-American Court of Human Rights. On 7 February 2018, available at https://www. corteidh.or.cr/docs/opiniones/seriea_23_ing.pdf

INTER-AMERICAN COURT OF HUMAN RIGHTS

Comunidad Mayagna (Sumo) Awas Tingni v. Nicaragua

146. The terms of an international human rights treaty have an autonomous meaning, so that they cannot be equated with the meaning attributed to

them in domestic law. In addition, such human rights treaties are living instruments whose interpretation has to be adapted to the evolution of the times, and in particular to the current living conditions.

147. In turn, Article 29.b of the Convention provides that no provision may be interpreted as 'limiting the enjoyment and exercise of any right or freedom which may be recognized under the laws of any of the State parties or in accordance with another convention to which one of these States is a party'.

148. Through an evolutionary interpretation of the international instruments for the protection of human rights, taking into account the applicable rules of interpretation and, in accordance with Article 29.b of the Convention –which prohibits a restrictive interpretation of rights-, this Court considers that Article 21 of the Convention protects the right to property in a sense that includes, among others, the rights of members of indigenous communities within the framework of communal property, which is also recognized in the Political Constitution of Nicaragua.

Source: IACHR, *Comunidad Mayagna (Sumo) Awas Tingni v. Nicaragua*, Decision of August 31st, 2001 (Free translation).

On a regional level, the EU has developed through a progressive incorporation of specific environmental protection provisions and the case law of the Court of Justice.[108] EU environment policy is based on Articles 11 and 191–193 of the Treaty on the Functioning of the European Union. Under Article 191, combating climate change is an explicit objective of EU environmental policy. Sustainable development is an overarching objective for the EU, which is committed to a 'high level of protection and improvement of the quality of the environment' (Article 3 of the Treaty on European Union).[109]

The EU and national governments have set clear objectives to guide European environment policy until 2020 and beyond, with expectations of where to be by 2050, thanks to the support of dedicated research programmes, legislation and funding.

Protect, conserve and enhance the EU's natural capital; turn the EU into a resource-efficient, green, and competitive low-carbon economy; and safeguard EU citizens from environment-related pressures and risks to health and well-being. To enable it to properly fulfil its task, the Court has been given clearly defined jurisdiction, which it exercises on references for preliminary rulings and in various categories of proceedings (actions for failure to fulfil obligations; actions for

---

108 Francis Jacobs, 'The Role of the European Court of Justice in the Protection of the Environment' (2006) 18(2) *Journal of Environmental Law*, pp. 185–205.

109 Suzanne Kingston, Veerle Heyvaert and Aleksandra Čavoški, *EU Environmental Law* (Cambridge University Press 2017). Maria Lee, *EU Environmental Law, Governance and Decision-Making* (Bloomsbury 2014).

annulment; actions for failure to act, appeals, reviews). As regards the interpretation and application of Community environmental law, the Court's rulings mainly come from actions for failure to fulfil obligations (Articles 226–228 of the EC Treaty) or from references for preliminary rulings (Article 234 of the EC Treaty).

Judgment of the Court of 2 August 1993

Commission of the European Communities v Kingdom of Spain

Conservation of wild birds - Special protection areas

Case C-355/90

1   Articles 3 and 4 of Directive 79/409 on the conservation of wild birds require Member States to preserve, maintain and re-establish the habitats of the said birds as such, because of their ecological value. The obligations on Member States under those articles exist even before any reduction is observed in the number of birds or any risk of a protected species becoming extinct has materialized.

2   In implementing Directive 79/409 on the conservation of wild birds, Member States are not authorized to invoke, at their option, grounds of derogation based on taking other interests into account. With respect, more specifically, to the obligation to take special conservation measures for certain species under Article 4 of the directive, such grounds must, in order to be acceptable, correspond to a general interest which is superior to the general interest represented by the ecological objective of the directive. In particular, the interests referred to in Article 2 of the directive, namely economic and recreational requirements, do not enter into consideration, as that provision does not constitute an autonomous derogation from the general system of protection established by the directive.

3   In choosing the territories which are most suitable for classification as special protection areas pursuant to Article 4(1) of Directive 79/409 on the conservation of wild birds, Member States have a certain discretion which is limited by the fact that the classification of those areas is subject to certain ornithological criteria determined by the directive, such as the presence of birds listed in Annex I to the directive, on the one hand, and the designation of a habitat as a wetland area, on the other.

4   However, Member States do not have the same discretion under Article 4(4) of the directive to modify or reduce the extent of such areas.

Source: https://eur-lex.europa.eu/legal-content/EN/
ALL/?uri=CELEX%3A61990CJ0355

EUROPEAN COURT OF HUMAN RIGHTS

Kyrtatos v Greece (2003)

The applicants challenged the Government's failure to demolish buildings where the permits to build on a swamp had been ruled unlawful by the Greek Court. The First Section held that there was no violation of Article 8, as the applicants had not shown how damage to the birds and other protected species directly affected their private or family life rights.

Para 52: "Neither Art. 8 nor any of the other Articles of the Convention are specifically designed to provide general protection of the environment as such; to that effect, 6 other international instruments and domestic legislation are more pertinent in dealing with this particular aspect."

Source: https://hudoc.echr.coe.int/fre#{%22itemid%22:
[%22001–61099%22]} 40 EHRR 16

EUROPEAN COURT OF HUMAN RIGHTS

Grand Chamber

Hatton and Others v United Kingdom (2003)

4. The Court's assessment

96. Article 8 protects the individual's right to respect for his or her private and family life, home and correspondence. There is no explicit right in the Convention to a clean and quiet environment, but where an individual is directly and seriously affected by noise or other pollution, an issue may arise under Article 8. Thus, in Powell and Rayner v. the United Kingdom, (judgment of 21 February 1990, Series A no. 172, § 40), where the applicants had complained about disturbance from daytime aircraft noise, the Court held that Article 8 was relevant, since "the quality of [each] applicant's private life and the scope for enjoying the amenities of his home [had] been adversely affected by the noise generated by aircraft using Heathrow Airport". Similarly, in the López Ostra v. Spain judgment of 9 December 1994, Series A no. 303-C, § 51, the Court held that Article 8 could include a right to protection from severe environmental pollution, since such a problem might "affect individuals' well-being and prevent them from enjoying their homes in such a way as to affect their private and family life adversely, without, however, seriously endangering their health". In Guerra v. Italy (judgment of 19 February 1998, Reports of Judgments and Decisions 1998-I), which, like López Ostra, concerned environmental pollution, the Court observed that "[the] direct effect of

(Continued)

the toxic emissions on the applicants' right to respect for their private and family life means that Article 8 is applicable" (§ 57).

97. At the same time, the Court re-iterates the fundamentally subsidiary role of the Convention. The national authorities have direct democratic legitimation and are, as the Court has held on many occasions, in principle better placed than an international court to evaluate local needs and conditions (see, for example, the Handyside v. the United Kingdom judgment of 7 December 1976, Series A no. 24, § 48). In matters of general policy, on which opinions within a democratic society may reasonably differ widely, the role of the domestic policy maker should be given special weight (see James and Others v. the United Kingdom, judgment of 21 February 1986, Series A no. 98, p. 32, § 46, where the Court found it natural that the margin of appreciation "available to the legislature in implementing social and economic policies should be a wide one").

98. Article 8 may apply in environmental cases whether the pollution is directly caused by the State or whether State responsibility arises from the failure properly to regulate private industry. Whether the case is analysed in terms of a positive duty on the State to take reasonable and appropriate measures to secure the applicants' rights under paragraph 1 of Article 8 or in terms of an interference by a public authority to be justified in accordance with paragraph 2, the applicable principles are broadly similar. In both contexts regard must be had to the fair balance that has to be struck between the competing interests of the individual and of the community as a whole; and in both contexts the State enjoys a certain margin of appreciation in determining the steps to be taken to ensure compliance with the Convention. Furthermore, even in relation to the positive obligations flowing from the first paragraph of Article 8, in striking the required balance the aims mentioned in the second paragraph may be of a certain relevance (see the above-mentioned Powell and Rayner judgment, § 41 and the above-mentioned López Ostra judgment, § 51).

99. The Court considers that in a case such as the present, involving State decisions affecting environmental issues, there are two aspects to the inquiry that may be carried out by the Court. First, the Court may assess the substantive merits of the Government's decision, to ensure that it is compatible with Article 8. Secondly, it may scrutinise the decision-making process to ensure that due weight has been accorded to the interests of the individual.

100. In relation to the substantive aspect, the Court has held that the State must be allowed a wide margin of appreciation. In Powell and Rayner, for example, it asserted that it was "certainly not for the Commission or the Court to substitute for the assessment of the national authorities any other assessment of what might be the best policy in this difficult social and technical sphere", namely the regulation of excessive aircraft

noise and the means of redress to be provided to the individual within the domestic legal system. The Court continued that "this is an area where the Contracting States are to be recognised as enjoying a wide margin of appreciation" (op. cit., § 44).

101. In other cases involving environmental issues, for example planning cases, the Court has also held that the State must be allowed a wide margin of appreciation. The Court explained the reasons for this approach in Buckley v. the United Kingdom, where the applicant complained that she had been denied planning permission to install a residential caravan on land that she owned (judgment of 25 September 1996, Reports of Judgments and Decisions 1996-IV, §§ 74–77):

"As is well established in the Court's case-law, it is for the national authorities to make the initial assessment of the 'necessity' for an interference, as regards both the legislative framework and the particular measure of implementation.... Although a margin of appreciation is thereby left to the national authorities, their decision remains subject to review by the Court for conformity with the requirements of the Convention. The scope of this margin of appreciation is not identical in each case but will vary according to the context.... Relevant factors include the nature of the Convention right in issue, its importance for the individual and the nature of the activities concerned.

The Court has already had occasion to note that town and country planning schemes involve the exercise of discretionary judgment in the implementation of policies adopted in the interest of the community.... It is not for the Court to substitute its own view of what would be the best policy in the planning sphere or the most appropriate individual measure in planning cases.... By reason of their direct and continuous contact with the vital forces of their countries, the national authorities are in principle better placed than an international court to evaluate local needs and conditions. In so far as the exercise of discretion involving a multitude of local factors is inherent in the choice and implementation of planning policies, the national authorities in principle enjoy a wide margin of appreciation.

The Court cannot ignore, however, that in the instant case the interests of the community are to be balanced against the applicant's right to respect for her 'home', a right which is pertinent to her and her children's personal security and well-being.... The importance of that right for the applicant and her family must also be taken into account in determining the scope of the margin of appreciation allowed to the respondent State. Whenever discretion capable of interfering with the enjoyment of a Convention right such as the one in issue in the present case is conferred on national authorities, the procedural safeguards available to the individual will be especially material in determining whether the respondent State has, when fixing the regulatory framework, remained within its margin of

(Continued)

appreciation. Indeed, it is settled case-law that, whilst Article 8 contains no explicit procedural requirements, the decision-making process leading to measures of interference must be fair and such as to afford due respect to the interests safeguarded to the individual by Article 8....

The Court's task is to determine, on the basis of the above principles, whether the reasons relied on to justify the interference in question are relevant and sufficient under Article 8 § 2."

102. The Court has recognised that, where Government policy in the form of criminal laws interferes with a particularly intimate aspect of an individual's private life, the margin of appreciation left to the Government will be reduced in scope (Dudgeon v. the United Kingdom, judgment of 22 October 1981, Series A no. 45, p. 21, § 52).

103. The Court is thus faced with conflicting views as to the margin of appreciation to be applied: on the one hand, the Government claim to a wide margin on the ground that the case concerns matters of general policy, and, on the other hand, the applicants' claim that where the ability to sleep is affected, the margin is narrow because of the "intimate" nature of the right protected. This conflict of views on the margin of appreciation can be reconciled only by reference to the context of a particular case.

Source: 34 EHRR 1, https://hudoc.echr.coe.int/fre#{%22ite mid%22:[%22001–61188%22]}

EUROPEAN UNION

Order of the General Court (Second Chamber)

8 May 2019

(Action for annulment and damages — Environment — Greenhouse gas emissions — 2030 climate and energy package — Directive (EU) 2018/410 — Regulation (EU) 2018/842 — Regulation (EU) 2018/841 — Lack of individual concern — Inadmissibility)

In Case T-330/18,

Armando Carvalho, residing in Santa Comba Dão (Portugal), and the other applicants whose names are set out in the annex, (1) represented by G. Winter, Professor, R. Verheyen, lawyer, and H. Leith, Barrister,

applicants,

v

European Parliament, represented by L. Darie and A. Tamás, acting as Agents, and

Council of the European Union, represented by M. Moore and M. Simm, acting as Agents,

defendants,

APPLICATION under Article 263 TFEU seeking, first, annulment in part of Directive (EU) 2018/410 of the European Parliament and of the Council of 14 March 2018 amending Directive 2003/87/EC to enhance cost-effective emission reductions and low-carbon investments, and Decision (EU) 2015/1814 (OJ 2018 L 76, p. 3), in particular Article 1 thereof, Regulation (EU) 2018/842 of the European Parliament and of the Council of 30 May 2018 on binding annual greenhouse gas emission reductions by Member States from 2021 to 2030 contributing to climate action to meet commitments under the Paris Agreement and amending Regulation (EU) No 525/2013 (OJ 2018 L 156, p. 26), in particular Article 4(2) thereof and Annex I thereto, and Regulation (EU) 2018/841 of the European Parliament and of the Council of 30 May 2018 on the inclusion of greenhouse gas emissions and removals from land use, land use change and forestry in the 2030 climate and energy framework, and amending Regulation (EU) No 525/2013 and Decision No 529/2013/EU (OJ 2018 L 156, p. 1), in particular Article 4 thereof, and, second, compensation under Articles 268 and 340 TFEU in the form of an injunction for the damage that the applicants claim to have suffered.

Source: http://curia.europa.eu/juris/document/document.jsf?
text=&docid=214164&pageIndex=0&doclang=EN&
mode=lst&dir=&occ=first&part=1&cid=4417306

Bibliography

Birnie, P, Boyle, A, and Redgwell, C, *International Law and the Environment* (3rd edn Oxford University Press 2009).

Boyle, A., 'The Environmental Jurisprudence of the International Tribunal of the Law of the Sea' (2007) 22(3) *The International Journal of Marine and Coastal Law*, p. 375.

Cameron, J and Abouchar, J, 'The Precautionary Principle: A Fundamental Principle of Law and Policy for the Protection of Global Environment' (1991) 14(1) *Boston College International and Comparative Law Review*, p. 19.

Craik, N, 'Recalcitrant Reality and Chosen Ideals: The Public Function of Dispute Settlement in International Environmental Law' (1998) 10(2) *Georgetown International Environmental Law Review*, pp. 551–580.

d'Aspremont, J, 'The International Court of Justice as the Master of the Sources (February 5, 2020)', in Carlos Espósito and Kate Parlett (eds), *The Cambridge Companion to the International Court of Justice* (Cambridge University Press 2021), available at SSRN: https://ssrn.com/abstract=3532329 or http://dx.doi.org/10.2139/ssrn.3532329 accessed 1 April 2020.

D'Estree, TP, Dukes, EF, and Navarrete-Romero, J, 'Environmental Conflict and Its Resolution', in RB Bechtel and A Churchman (eds), *Handbook of Environmental Psychology* (Wiley 2002), pp. 589–606.

European Communities – Measures Concerning Meat and Meat Products (Hormones) (WT/DS26/AB/R y WT/DS48/AB/R), Report of the Appellate Body of January 16th, 1998; European Communities – Measures Affecting the Approval and Marketing of Biotech Products (WT/DS291/R, WT/DS292/R y WT/DS293/R), report of the panel of September 29th, 2006, paragraph 7.89.

Feria-Tinta, M, and Milnes, S, 'The Rise of Environmental Law in International Dispute Resolution: The Inter-American Court of Human Rights Issues a Landmark Advisory Opinion on the Environment and Human Rights' (2018) 27 *Yearbook of International Environmental Law*, pp. 1–18.

Fitzmaurice, MA, 'International Protection of the Environment' (2001) 293 *RCADI*, pp. 9–488.

Fitzmaurice, MA and Redgwell, C, 'Environmental Non-compliance Procedures and International Law' (2000) 31 *NYIL*, pp. 35–65.

Foster, C, 'Precaution, Scientific Development and Scientific Uncertainty under the WTO Agreement on Sanitary and Phytosanitary Measures' (2009) 18(1) *Review of European, Comparative & International Environmental Law*, p. 50.

Foster, C, 'Adjudication, Arbitration and the Turn to Public Law 'Standards of Review': Putting the Precautionary Principle in the Crucible' (2012) 3(3) *Journal of International Dispute Settlement*, p. 534.

IACHR, *Kawas Fernández v. Honduras*, Decision of April 3, 2009.

IACHR, *Pueblo Saramaka v. Surinam*, Decision of November 28th, 2007 and August 12th, 2008.

IACHR, *Velásquez Rodríguez v. Honduras*, Decision of July 29th, 1988, para. 172, Godínez Cruz v. Honduras, Decision of January 20th, 1989, para. 182.

ICJ, *Certain Activities Carried out by Nicaragua in the Border Area (Costa Rica V. Nicaragua)* Construction of a Road in Costa Rica along the San Juan River (Nicaragua V. Costa Rica). Decision of 16 December, 2015, para. 104.

ICJ, *Gabcikovo/Nagymaros Project (Hungary v Slovakia)*, Decision of 25th September 1997, para. 97.

ICJ, *Gabcikovo/Nagymaros Project (Hungary v Slovakia)*, Decision of 25th September 1997, para. 113.

ICJ, Legality of the Threat or Use of Nuclear Weapons, Advisory Opinion of 8 July 1996, para. 29; *Pulp Mills on the River Uruguay (Argentina v. Uruguay)*, Judgment of 20 April 2010, para. 101.

ICJ, *Pulp Mills on the River Uruguay (Argentina v. Uruguay)*, Judgment, I.C.J. Reports 2010, Separate Opinion of Judge Greenwood, para. 26.

ICJ, *Pulp Mills on the River Uruguay (Argentina v. Uruguay)*, Judgment of 20 April 2010.

International Court of Justice, *Pulp Mills on the River Uruguay (Argentina v. Uruguay)*, Judgment of 20 April 2010.

ITLOS, *Case Concerning Land Reclamation by Singapore in and Around the Straits of Johor*, Provisional Measures, Order of 8 October 2003, para. 74.

ITLOS, *Case Concerning Land Reclamation by Singapore in and Around the Straits of Johor*, Provisional Measures, Order of 8 October 2003, para. 99.

ITLOS, *MOX Plant Case, Provisional Measures*, Order of 3 December 2001.

ITLOS, *MOX Plant Case*, Provisional Measures, Order of 3 December 2001, Separate Opinion of Judge Wolfrum.

ITLOS, *Responsibilities and Obligations of States Sponsoring Persons and Entities with Respect to Activities in the Area* (Request for Advisory Opinion submitted to the Seabed Disputes Chamber), February 1st, 2011, para. 117.

ITLOS, *Responsibilities and Obligations of States Sponsoring Persons and Entities with Respect to Activities in the Area*, Advisory Opinion of February 1st, 2011; ITLOS, Request for an Advisory Opinion submitted by the Sub-Regional Fisheries Commission (SRFC), Advisory Opinion, 2 April 2015.

ITLOS, *Responsibilities and Obligations of States Sponsoring Persons and Entities with Respect to Activities in the Area* (Request for Advisory Opinion submitted to the Seabed Disputes Chamber), February 1st, 2011, para. 132.

ITLOS, *Southern Bluefish Tuna Cases*, Provisional Measures, Order of 27 August 1999, paras. 31.3 and 32.3.

IUCN, *Draft International Covenant on Environment and Development*. Fifth Edition: Updated Text, 2017, available at https://sustainabledevelopment.un.org/index.php?page=view&type=400&nr=2443 accessed 1 April 2020.

Jacobs, F, 'The Role of the European Court of Justice in the Protection of the Environment' (2006) 18(2) *Journal of Environmental Law*, pp. 185–205.

Kingston, S, Heyvaert, V, and Čavoški, A, *EU Environmental Law* (Cambridge University Press 2017).

Kwiatkowska, B, 'The Ireland v United Kingdom (MOX Plant) Case: Applying the Doctrine of Treaty Parallelism' (2003) 18(1) *The International Journal of Marine and Coastal Law*, p. 40.

Lazarus, RJ, 'Fairness in Environmental Law' (1997) 27(3) *Environmental Law*, pp. 705–739, 711 and 713.

Lazarus, RJ, 'Pursuing 'Environmental Justice': The Distributional Effects of Environmental Protection' (1992–1993) 87 *Northwestern University Law Review*, p. 787.

Lee, M, *EU Environmental Law, Governance and Decision-Making* (Bloomsbury 2014).

Mcintyre, O and Mosedale, T, 'The Precautionary Principle as a Norm of Customary International Law'(1997) 9(2) *Journal of Environmental Law*, p. 221.

Orrego, F, 'The International Tribunal of the Law of the Sea and Provisional Measures: Settled Issues and Pending Problems' (2007) 22(3) *The International Journal of Marine and Coastal Law*, p. 458.

Pauwelyn, J, 'Informal International Lawmaking: Framing the Concept', in Pauwelyn, Wessel & Wouters, *Informal International Lawmaking* (Oxford University Press 2012) pp. 13–34, at 22.

Pedersen, O. 'From Abundance to Indeterminacy: The Precautionary Principle and its Two Camps of Custom' (2014) 3(2) *Transnational Environmental Law*, p. 323 y ss.

Pedersen, OW, 'An International Environmental Court and International Legalism' (2012) 24(3) *Journal of Environmental Law*, pp. 547–558.

Permanent Court of Arbitration, available at https://pca-cpa.org/en/services/arbitration-services/environmental-dispute-resolution/ accessed 1 April 2020.

Permanent Court of Arbitration, Dispute Concerning Access to Information under Article 9 of the OSPAR Convention (Ireland v. United Kingdom), Final Award, 2 July 2003, Dissenting Opinion of /Gavan Griffith QC, para. 72.

Permanent Court of Arbitration, The Indus Waters Kishenganga Arbitration (Pakistan v. India), Partial Award of 18 February 2013, para. 223.

Romano, C, *The Peaceful Settlement of International Environmental Disputes: A Pragmatic Approach* (International Environmental Law and Policy Series, Vol. 56, Kluwer Law International 2000), p. 4.

Sands, P, 'International Environmental Litigation and Its Future' (1999) 32 *University of Richmond Law Review*, p. 1619, available at http://scholarship.richmond.edu/lawreview/vol32/iss5/7 accessed 1 April 2020.

Sands, P, "Los Tribunales Internacionales y el Principio de Precaución", in UNEP La precaución, de Rio a Johannesburgo. *Actas de la Mesa Redonda de la Geneva Environment Network* (UNEP 2002). http://onubib.uv.es/browserecord.php?-action=browse&-recid=71335.

Smith, DC, 'Environmental Courts and Tribunals: Changing Environmental and Natural Resources Law Around the Globe' (2018) 36(2) *Journal of Energy & Natural Resources Law*, pp. 137–140.

Susskind, L and Weinstein, A, 'Towards a Theory of Environmental Dispute Resolution' (1980) 9 *BC Environmental Affairs Law Review*, pp. 311, 312, available at http://lawdigitalcommons.bc.edu/ealr/vol9/iss2/4 accessed 10 March 2019.

Viñuales, Jorge E, 'The Rio Declaration on Environment and Development. Preliminary Study', in Jorge E. Viñuales (ed), *The Rio Declaration on Environment and Development: A Commentary* (Oxford University Press 2015), p. 23.

Warnock, C, 'Reconceptualising Specialist Environment Courts and Tribunals' (2017) 37(3) *Legal Studies*, pp. 391–417.

Wojkowska, E, *Doing Justice: How Informal Justice Systems Can Contribute* (UN 2006).

Yotova, R, 'The Principles of Due Diligence and Prevention in International Environmental Law' (2016) 75(3) *The Cambridge Law Journal*, pp. 445–448.

7 Private sector involvement and civil society participation in international environmental law compliance

1 Introduction

In this chapter, two emerging trends in international environmental law (IEL) are studied: private sector involvement in compliance and the participation of civil society in mechanisms ensuring IEL compliance. The purpose is two-fold: to enquire on developments in the observance of IEL by the private sector and to investigate the latest changes in the participation of civil society organisations in IEL. It was a long-held assumption that compliance with the relevant IEL was a matter for states, but the shifting features of compliance demonstrate new patterns in relation to IEL. Alongside requirements imposed on States to ensure compliance with norms, private sector involvement is progressively gaining momentum. This trend can be observed in the climate change regime and, more broadly, in the legal framework of the Law of the Sea with respect to the responsibilities and obligations of states sponsoring persons and entities which undertake activities in the Area.[1]

Whereas the engagement of the private sector in the process of implementing international and national environmental law norms is a growing trend, there are still unclarified issues. The participation of civil society organisations in IEL compliance can take different forms depending on each MEA.

Initially, they did not play a significant role in IEL, but they have incrementally developed functions in treaty making and monitoring compliance with IEL; they can also set in motion procedures or court actions (in the field of international human rights law) to enforce compliance with environmental provisions. A significant barrier to their participation in IEL compliance is the lack of legal standing as the right to take action to enforce compliance with IEL provisions still lies with the States. Nevertheless, the increasing participation of the organised civil society through NGOs constitutes an invaluable help in addressing negative consequences stemming from non-compliance.

---

1 Lee Paddock, Du Qun, Louis J. Kotzé, David L. Markell, Kenneth J. Markowitz, and Durwood Zaelke (eds), *Compliance and Enforcement in Environmental Law: Toward More Effective* (Edward Elgar 2011).

2 Private sector involvement in IEL compliance

The definition of private sector which is borne in mind for this chapter alludes to an initiative which aims to engage the business community in efforts to support compliance with the environmental rule of law.[2] Although not set in stone, the concept of the private sector generally comprises 'for-profit, and commercial enterprises or businesses; business associations and coalitions (cross-industry, multi-issue groups; cross industry, issue-specific initiatives; industry-focussed initiative); including but not limited to corporate philanthropic foundations'.[3]

The private sector can play an array of different roles in law-making, standard-setting, compliance and accountability for environmental damage.[4] Specifically, for the purpose of this book the notion will be further narrowed down to place the emphasis on business. Multinational corporations (MNCs) have operated as the drivers for change in the area of private sector involvement. Some sectors are particularly crucial for involvement in IEL compliance, such as international investment law.[5] Some scholars have argued that the role of multinational companies in sustainable development have increased in light of the evolution of perceptions towards their environmental protection efforts.[6]

Gradually, the private sector has borne more responsibility to promote environmentally responsible conduct. International businesses play a key role in causing environmental harm but also in contributing global solutions. Composition, structure, aims and values are quite heterogeneous, and there is no one-size-fits-all approach to their function in IEL. Although States continue to be the direct addressees of IEL norms, businesses are also affected by environmental regulations and are active in standard-setting processes. As actors of IEL, they might be the driving forces in development and compliance with IEL.

Business actors intervene indirectly through national governments on the international scale. As in the case of NGOs, industry groups lobby to impose their positions. A growing trend is their participation in international forums. Like other non-state organisations, business groups that have recognised status can

---

2 United Nations – Global Compact, Business for the Rule of Law (B4ROL), available at https://www.unglobalcompact.org/library/1341 accessed 1 April 2020.

3 United Nations. 2009. Guidelines on Cooperation between the United Nations and the Private Sector, available at https://www.un.org/en/ethics/assets/pdfs/Guidelines-on-Cooperation-with-the-Business-Sector.pdf accessed 1 March 2020.

4 On standard-setting and transnational regulation, see Veerle Heyvaert, *Transnational Environmental Regulation and Governance: Purpose, Strategies and Principles* (Cambridge University Press 2018).

5 Benjamin J. Richardson, *Socially Responsible Investment Law: Regulating the Unseen Polluters* (Oxford University Press 2008).

6 Sandrine Maljean-Dubois and Vanessa Richard, 'The Applicability of International Environmental Law to Private Enterprises', in Pierre-Marie Dupuy and Jorge E. Viñuales (eds), *Harnessing Foreign Investment to Promote Environmental Protection: Incentives and Safeguards* (Cambridge University Press 2013), pp. 69–96.

participate at intergovernmental conferences and meetings. In addition, business can act independently from States in IEL through the adoption of their own norms and standards in specific sectors.

Collaboration with business actors in the implementation and compliance with IEL may prompt a behavioural change. Certification processes assist States in checking compliance with IEL in sectors such as forestry. Similarly, private business engage in the measurement, reporting and verification of emissions reductions under the climate change regime.

The lines that separate the private sphere from the public sphere are, at the moment, blurred. In terms of IEL law-making, industry and business groups partake in the negotiations, sometimes providing key expertise. The private sector plays an important role in standard-setting under different regimes, such as the International Organization for Standardization.[7] Self-regulation is an attempt to address environmental problems from a business standpoint by adopting soft-law rules. Private initiatives such as the Equator Initiative illustrate the role of the private sector in environmental protection. The initiative involves private sector business, along with local communities and indigenous peoples, to achieve agreements in the areas of nature-based solutions and sustainable development.[8] Equally important is engagement with the Forest Stewardship Council, which contributes to the implementation of standards in codification processes and at different stages of the supply chain.[9] This leads to other manners of international environmental governance with a transnational imprint.

Whether soft-law norms have the ability to steer IEL towards a more responsible business conduct model is contentious.[10] Whilst IEL's main goal is to bring more private sector stakeholders on board, a legal and policy environment defining roles and responsibilities, and transparent processes for this involvement are necessary. Along with increased inter-state cooperation, private sector involvement is pivotal for IEL compliance. No State can effectively combat global warming without considering private sector involvement. State can impose restrictions upon GHG emissions and engage in reforestation, but if the private

---

7 Naomi Roht-Arriaza, '"Soft Law" in a "Hybrid" Organization: The International Organization for Standardization', in Dinah Shelton (ed), *Commitment and Compliance: The Role of Non-binding Norms in the International Legal System* (Oxford University Press 2007), p. 263.

8 The main aim of the Equator Initiative is to bring 'together the United Nations, governments, civil society, businesses and grassroots organizations to recognize and advance local sustainable development solutions for people, nature and resilient communities', available at https://www.equatorinitiative.org/ accessed 1 March 2020.

9 The Forest Stewardship Council (FSC) is a non-profit organisation which promotes an environmentally, socially and economically sustainable management of the world's forests. Available at https://fsc.org/en/about-us accessed 1 March 2020.

10 Dinah Shelton, 'Chapter 5. The Environment and Natural Resources, Part II Perspectives on Compliance with Non-binding Norms', in Dinah Shelton (ed), *Commitment and Compliance: The Role of Non-binding Norms in the International Legal System* (Oxford University Press 2007).

sector does not play along all efforts in prevention, adaptation and mitigation will be fruitless.

In advancing reform, IEL needs to adjust to the circumstances and to the pace of the developments. This implies a certain responsiveness of IEL as a system of law in all its functions. Frameworks, such as corporate social responsibility in international law, have also proved to be controversial. Initially considered self-regulation at its best, corporate social responsibility has gradually shifted from being a merely ethical approach to becoming a legal approach in the form of soft law. However, its capacity to foster a real alternative to dealing with environmentally harmful investment practices is still limited. One way to go is to improve the governance of the Multinational Corporations (MNC) and Responsible Business Conduct (RBC), outlining some priority areas for action. A more effective legal approach would be to apply the due diligence principle to this area, advocating for more international responsibility of MNC. The reform of the international legal system in this area can take a different turn by incorporating elements from the systems to evolve to a mixed or hybrid system.

The practice of international organisations in the field of economic cooperation, such as the OECD, has pioneered the raising of the standards and progress to a more coherent; consistent; and, perhaps, stringent focus on environmental protection.[11]

In the area of green growth, certain emerging approaches by States put too much emphasis on the development of a more sustainable approach that incorporates IEL. A market systems approach to this issue incorporates the development of value chains and places the emphasis on markets for environmental products and services. The intervention of private sector actors might also prove problematic. Amongst other questions raised, there is environmental governance and its role in developing States. As non-state actors, MNCs have increased their participation in compliance. The system should ideally progress to a more balanced participation of different actors, not only States.

Take, for instance, the question of climate change. Clearly, States should incorporate private sector efforts, such as the Clean Development Mechanism. Are States ecological/environmental guardians or custodians? In the face of climate change, States should act and react; unilateral actions are condemned to be ineffective. The dimensions and characteristics of the environmental problem make a coordinated response necessary.

Greening business comes at an economic cost (payment of taxes' investment in greener technology), yet the consequences of inaction are far less onerous on business. The severe impacts of climate change may complete alter (or even destroy) the sources for the production of raw material. Fair trade practices

11 OECD, *Private Sector Engagement to Address – Climate Change and Promote Green Growth* (OECD Private Sector Peer Learning Policy Brief 4), available at https://www.oecd.org/dac/peer-reviews/Policy-Brief-4-Private-Sector-Engagement-to-Address-Climate-Change-and-Promote-Green-Growth.pdf accessed 1 March 2020.

incentivising compliance and quality assurance of processes attempt to engage the other side of the equation: consumers. Green-washing without real commitment to compliance does not produce the desired effect.[12] Many companies for their own good seek to introduce sustainable practices through complying with IEL. Biodiversity and benefit sharing agreements is an area in which more initiatives involving the private sector have taken place under REDD+ ("Reducing Emissions from Deforestation and forest Degradation").

From a different stance, more environmental regulations applicable to private sector may operate as environmental constraints. States still enjoy a certain amount of leeway in order to make policies and adopt measures in this area seeking to secure their international economic influence. The undesired effect of strict environmental legislation on trade and investment may make businesses move to States, where they can increase their market shares. Tempting as this sounds, the idea of a level playing in international/transnational environmental regulation is far from a reality and requires a precise engineering of the system, contemplating many different interests.

States' unilateral action is no longer conceivable, and all attempts to address global environmental problems by just adopting a top-down and inter-state approach may be ineffective. Actions and regulations should be taken at a level adequate to achieve the safeguarding of the environment as the ultimate goal. Co-operation with the private sector is necessary to secure effective compliance with IEL. Ideally, environmental aims should guide the activities of relevant actors in the private sector.

Initiatives such as the Global Compact rely on a set of principles on human rights, labour, the environment and anti-corruption rooted in intergovernmental agreements.[13] Global Compact is a voluntary initiative based on CEO commitments to implement universal sustainability principles supporting United Nations (UN) Sustainable Development Goals (SDGs).

In terms of regulation and soft-law instruments, businesses have collaborated with States in the adoption of non-binding regulations, setting sector-standards standards through non-binding norms, such as International Code of Conduct on the Distribution and Use of Pesticides adopted by the FAO.[14] In the same vein, the Bonn Guidelines on Access to Genetic Resources deal with obligations not only for States but also for commercial users in bioprospecting.[15] Soft IEL

---

12 Neil Gunningham, R.A. Kagan and D. Thornton, *Shades of Green-Business, Regulation, and Environment* (Stanford University Press 2003).

13 Global Compact, About us, available at https://www.unglobalcompact.org/about accessed 1 April 2020.

14 Food and Agriculture Organization of the United Nations Rome, International Code of Conduct on the Distribution and Use of Pesticides (2003), Adopted by the Hundred and Twenty-third Session of the FAO Council in November 2002, available at http://www.fao.org/3/y4544e/y4544e02.htm#bm2.1 accessed 1 April 2020.

15 CBD Secretariat, Bonn Guidelines on Access to Genetic Resources and Fair and Equitable Sharing of the Benefits Arising out of their Utilization, available at https://www.cbd.int/doc/publications/cbd-bonn-gdls-en.pdf accessed 1 April 2020.

norms set forth specific commitments, sometimes acknowledged as direct obligations for businesses, as in the framework of the World Summit on Sustainable Development.[16] Traditionally, there has been an avoidance of the wording of environmental obligations for businesses in IEL which has been overcome through an international recognition, first of corporate accountability, broadly understood to have progressed onto corporate responsibility.

Private sector involvement requires an appropriate legal and policy framework with the definition of roles and responsibilities, incorporating transparency into processes, leading to the award of contracts. The legal framework includes environment protection as designed in IEL and enforced by the government, strengthening the regulatory functions to ensure that private sector participation respects environmental norms.

The role of the private sector in IEL compliance, although not yet clearly regulated and still controversial, has grown into an area for development. There is a sore need to strike the right balance between private businesses interests and environmental protection, with the States acting as ecological guardians. Without a proper legal framework, the 'greenness' of these initiatives will be no more than empty words.

FAO

International Code of Conduct on the Distribution and Use of Pesticides

2003

Article 1. Objectives of the Code

1.1 The objectives of this Code are to establish voluntary standards of conduct for all public and private entities engaged in or associated with the distribution and use of pesticides, particularly where there is inadequate or no national legislation to regulate pesticides.

1.2 The Code is designed for use within the context of national legislation as a basis whereby government authorities, pesticide manufacturers, those engaged in trade and any citizens concerned may judge whether their proposed actions and the actions of others constitute acceptable practices.

1.3 The Code describes the shared responsibility of many sectors of society to work together so that the benefits to be derived from the necessary and acceptable use of pesticides are achieved without significant

---

16 Elisa Morgera, 'From Stockholm to Johannesburg: From Corporate Responsibility to Corporate Accountability for the Global Protection of the Environment?' (2004) 13 *Review of European Community & International Environmental Law*, pp. 214–222.

adverse effects on human health or the environment. To this end, all references in this Code to a government or governments shall be deemed to apply equally to regional groupings of governments for matters falling within their areas of competence.

1.4 The Code addresses the need for a cooperative effort between governments of pesticide exporting and importing countries to promote practices that minimize potential health and environmental risks associated with pesticides, while ensuring their effective use.

1.5 The entities which are addressed by this Code include international organizations, governments of exporting and importing countries, pesticide industry, application equipment industry, traders, food industry, users, and public-sector organizations such as environmental groups, consumer groups and trade unions.

1.6 The Code recognizes that training at all appropriate levels is an essential requirement in implementing and observing its provisions. Therefore, governments, pesticide industry, users of pesticides, international organizations, non-governmental organizations (NGOs) and other parties concerned should give high priority to training activities related to each Article of the Code.

1.7 The standards of conduct set forth in this Code:

1.7.1 encourage responsible and generally accepted trade practices;

1.7.2 assist countries which have not yet established regulatory controls on the quality and suitability of pesticide products needed in that country to promote the judicious and efficient use of such products and address the potential risks associated with their use;

1.7.3 promote practices which reduce risks in the handling of pesticides, including minimizing adverse effects on humans and the environment and preventing accidental poisoning resulting from improper handling;

1.7.4 ensure that pesticides are used effectively and efficiently for the improvement of agricultural production and of human, animal and plant health;

1.7.5 adopt the "life-cycle" concept to address all major aspects related to the development, regulation, production, management, packaging, labelling, distribution, handling, application, use and control, including post registration activities and disposal of all types of pesticides, including used pesticide containers;

1.7.6 are designed to promote Integrated Pest Management (IPM) (including integrated vector management for public health pests);

(*Continued*)

1.7.7 include reference to participation in information exchange and international agreements identified in Annex 1, in particular the *Rotterdam Convention on the Prior Informed Consent Procedure for Certain Hazardous Chemicals and Pesticides in International Trade.*

Source: http://www.fao.org/3/y4544e/
y4544e02.htm#bm2.1

UNITED NATIONS GUIDELINES

Partnerships with the Business Sector

b In considering such collaborations and partnerships, the UN will seek to engage with Business Sector entities that:

   i demonstrate responsible citizenship by supporting the core values of the UN and its causes as reflected in the Charter and other relevant conventions and treaties;

   ii demonstrate a commitment to meeting or exceeding the principles of the UN Global Compact by translating them into operational corporate practice within their sphere of influence including and not limited to policies, codes of conduct, management, monitoring and reporting systems.

c The UN will not engage with Business Sector entities that are complicit in human rights abuses, tolerate forced or compulsory labour or the use of child labour 5, are involved in the sale or manufacture of anti-personnel landmines or cluster bombs, or that otherwise do not meet relevant obligations or responsibilities required by the United Nations.

d The UN will not engage with Business Sector entities violating sanctions established by the UN Security Council.

e The UN should not partner with Business Sector entities that systematically fail to demonstrate commitment to meeting the principles of the UN Global Compact. However, the UN may consider collaboration specifically intended to address this failure of commitment.

10 UN entities may establish additional eligibility and exclusionary criteria for screening companies appropriate to their specific mission and advocacy role.

11 Partner selection will be subject to due diligence processes established by the UN entity considering the partnership. UN entities are encouraged to consult with each other as part of the due diligence process. UN entities reserve the right to choose their partners on a case-by-case basis and to undertake research in support of such decisions.

Source: https://www.unglobalcompact.org/library/3431

Pulp Mills on the River Uruguay (Argentina v. Uruguay), ICJ, Judgment of 20 April 2010

Due diligence

(...)

185. In the view of the Court, the purpose of Article 36 of the 1975 Statute is to prevent any transboundary pollution liable to change the ecological balance of the river by co-ordinating, through CARU, the adoption of the necessary measures. It thus imposes an obligation on both States to take positive steps to avoid changes in the ecological balance. These steps consist not only in the adoption of a regulatory framework, as has been done by the Parties through CARU, but also in the observance as well as enforcement by both Parties of the measures adopted.

187. The Court considers that the obligation laid down in Article 36 is addressed to both Parties and prescribes the specific conduct of co-ordinating the necessary measures through the Commission to avoid changes to the ecological balance. An obligation to adopt regulatory or administrative measures either individually or jointly and to enforce them is an obligation of conduct. Both Parties are therefore called upon, under Article 36, to exercise due diligence in acting through the Commission for the necessary measures to preserve the ecological balance of the river. 188. This vigilance and prevention is all the more important in the preservation of the ecological balance, since the negative impact of human activities on the waters of the river may affect other components of the ecosystem of the watercourse such as its flora, fauna, and soil. The obligation to co-ordinate, through the Commission, the adoption of the necessary measures, as well as their enforcement and observance, assumes, in this context, a central role in the overall system of protection of the River Uruguay established by the 1975 Statute. It is therefore of crucial importance that the Parties respect this obligation.

(...)

197. Thirdly, the obligation to "preserve the aquatic environment, and in particular to prevent pollution by prescribing appropriate rules and measures" is an obligation to act with due diligence in respect of all activities which take place under the jurisdiction and control of each party. It is an obligation which entails not only the adoption of appropriate rules and measures, but also a certain level of vigilance in their enforcement and the exercise of administrative control applicable to public and private operators, such as the monitoring of activities undertaken by such operators, to safeguard the rights of the other party. The responsibility of a party to the 1975 Statute would therefore be engaged if it was shown that it had failed to act diligently and thus take all appropriate measures to enforce its relevant regulations on a public or private operator under its jurisdiction. The obligation of due diligence under Article 41 (a) in the adoption and

(*Continued*)

enforcement of appropriate rules and measures is further reinforced by the requirement that such rules and measures must be "in accordance with applicable international agreements" and "in keeping, where relevant, with the guidelines and recommendations of international technical bodies". This requirement has the advantage of ensuring that the rules and measures adopted by the parties both have to conform to applicable international agreements and to take account of internationally agreed technical standards.

Source: https://www.icj-cij.org/en/case/135/judgments

3 Civil society participation in environmental compliance

Recent years have witnessed an increase in the role and participation of global civil society in agenda-setting, international law-making and environmental governance in IEL.[17] This trend towards broadening the participation of the civil society in the various processes articulated under MEAs has been referred to as the 'democratisation' of IEL.[18]

Environmental diplomacy has borne its fruits in some areas of IEL, such as climate change, biodiversity and international water law.[19] When it comes to law-making, the horizontal structure of IEL is reflected in the classification and definition of norms in the contemporary context, which includes NGO practices in the global legal arena, leading to the adoption of legal norms.[20] The notion of 'public interest' applicable under different international environmental regimes serves as the common denominator for participation in different processes. As Bodansky indicates, the sources of influence consist in expertise, representation of interests and financial support.[21]

The proliferation of treaty regimes and negotiations of new international legal instruments has facilitated the participation of civil society organisations in IEL. Vital points in this evolution have been environmental conferences and the ensuing environmental declarations, such as the Stockholm Conference and Declaration and the 1982 Rio Summit, and the 2012 Rio Plus

---

17 Barbara Woodward, 'Global Civil Society and International Law in Global Governance: Some Contemporary Issues' (2006) 8(2) *International Community Law Review*, pp 247–355.

18 Fred L. Morrison and Rüdiger Wolfrum (ed), *International, Regional, and National Environmental Law* (Kluwer Law International 2000).

19 Beatriz Barreiro Carril and Belen Olmos Giupponi, *La participación de la Sociedad Civil en los procesos de integración en Iberomérica* (Dykinson 2011).

20 Barbara Woodward, 'Global Civil Society in International Lawmaking and Global Governance, Theory and Practice' (Brill 2010) 2 *Queen Mary Studies in International Law*, pp. 105–149.

21 Daniel Bodansky, *The Art and Craft of International Environmental Law* (Harvard University Press 2010), pp. 126, 127.

Summit. Specifically, Principle 10 of the Rio Declaration called attention to public participation becoming a catalyst for participation, which has since then been introduced as a goal in many MEAs. The focal point in the organisation of multilateral conferences has shifted to a more participatory scheme, as demonstrated by the UN Commission on Sustainable Development's trajectory.[22] NGOs have contributed to the various outputs emanating from these Conferences, bringing forward specific proposals for the implementation of IEL norms.

Steady progress in participation has been observed over the last several decades, which have witnessed how civil society organisations have developed their own alternative agendas. This participation is referred to, in different manners, as 'civil society engagement" or "public participation'. Participation takes a variety of forms, ranging from the role of observers to the possibility of bringing allegations of non-compliance against party States, differently termed under MEAs (for instance, under Aarhus these claims are called 'communications').

Intergenerational equity cuts across all these issues permeating environmental activism. Activism and effective participation in treaty-making and compliance, however, are not necessarily correlated. NGOs have increased their participation in Treaty conferences, contributing their own stance in these fora.[23] Extinction rebellion has become prominent in the realm of climate change, backing the 'wide-ranging policy changes needed to transition to net zero greenhouse gas emissions and halt the extinction of species' without a formal channel to harness participation[24]

Formal and informal mechanisms that channel the participation of civil society have proliferated in IEL. In terms of the formal or institutionalised participation of the civil society, there has been a growing trend to include mechanisms in MEAs, namely based on the recognition by governments that access to information, participation and justice in environmental issues foster environmental protection and sustainable development.

The participation of civil society brings about questions on the legitimacy of the different actors conforming this group in IEL, particularly, in terms of the validity of the representation of the NGOs in the field of compliance and implementation in the context of IEL. The particular role of NGOs in appropriately representing main interests in the process of assuring compliance varies across the different MEAs.

For the purpose of this book, the focus will be placed on participation in mechanisms or processes that monitor implementation and compliance with

22 United Nations, *Commission on Sustainable Development (CSD)*, available at https://sustainabledevelopment.un.org/csd.html accessed 1 April 2020.

23 Peter Bombay, 'The Role of NGOs in Shaping Community Positions in International Environmental Fora', (2001) 10 *Review of European Community & International Environmental Law*, pp. 163–167.

24 Extinction Rebellion, 'Our Demands', available at https://rebellion.earth/the-truth/demands/ accessed 1 April 2020.

environmental treaties. Each MEA institutes the respective environmental treaty body, such as under the Aarhus Convention, the Water Convention, the Protocol on Water and Health, and the Basel Convention.[25] The extent of participation depends upon the wording of the MEA and the practice of the compliance committee.

In the progress and enforcement of international law, NGOs have steadily consolidated a role in law-making and compliance over the last several decades.[26] Considerable differences, similarities and best practices with regard to civil society participation in compliance are observed. However, there are still several gaps in procedure and philosophy among the Compliance Committees. Different slants are presented under international environmental treaties.

NGOs embody the institutionalised participation of civil society in IEL, being referred to in several IEL instruments.[27] While the role of NGOs has remained pivotal in IEL, few MEAs contain specific routes and mechanisms to channel their participation in compliance procedures.[28] In the domain of compliance with IEL, NGOs have been defined as organisations independent from States and governments with a specific and identifiable non-profit goal, which have a certain stability in terms of trajectory and institutional set-up.[29] There is no specific typology or final classification of NGOs based on the aim that they are able to perform research activities or political activities ('activism', 'pressure groups'), contributing through established channels to the development of compliance with IEL, or display their activities outside institutionalised channels and formal procedures (by demonstrating or protesting). Based on the geographical scope, NGOs can act at a regional, national or international level. Finally, in terms of the administrative and governance structure with an incidence on legitimacy, NGOs can be more centralised or operate in a decentralised way. The question of the funding is relevant for neutrality and guarantees of a non-partisan intervention.

Understanding the role of NGOs, and its evolution from a peripheral function to a central role in IEL compliance, implies to examine their functions

---

25 UNDP, *Promoting Sustainable Development through More Effective Civil Society Participation in Environmental Governance. A Selection of Country Case Studies from the EU-NGOs Project*, available at https://ec.europa.eu/environment/international_issues/pdf/EU_NGOs_publication_20161219.pdf accessed 1 April 2020.

26 Farhana Yamin, 'NGOs and International Environmental Law: A Critical Evaluation of their Roles and Responsibilities' (2001) 10 *RECIEL*, p. 149; Bombay (n 23) at 163.

27 Such as Article 71 UN-Charta, Chapter 27 of Agenda 21, article 7 para. 6 UNFCC.

28 See the overview in Philippe Sands, Jacqueline Peel, Adriana Fabra, and Ruth MacKenzie, *Principles of International Environmental Law* (3rd edn CUP 2012), p. 112; Patricia Birnie, Alan Boyle, and Catherine Redgwell, *International Law and the Environment* (3rd edn Oxford University Press 2009), p. 66.

29 Astrid Epiney, 'The Role of NGOs in the Process of Ensuring Compliance with MEAs', in Ulrich Beyerlin, Peter-Tobias Stoll, and Rüdiger Wolfrum (eds), *Ensuring Compliance with Multilateral Environmental Agreements: Academic Analysis and Views from Practice* (Brill 2006), pp. 319–352.

guaranteeing, advancing and monitoring implementation and application of MEAs as well as their participation in mechanisms of judicial or quasi-judicial control. Largely, the NGOs' functions in compliance control and enforcement of MEAs is related to the general approach to compliance and the mechanisms that are provided for in the relevant MEAs.

Drawing on Epiney's work, NGOs' compliance-related functions in IEL can be categorised as:

a Involvement in non-confrontational mechanisms

NGOs take part in non-confrontational mechanisms devoted to compliance assistance and compliance control. They participate in assistance mechanisms aimed at enhancing Treaty Parties' competences and their institutions to ensure IEL compliance. NGOs are generally involved through institutional channels or financial support. To illustrate, NGOs are involved in debt-for-Nature Swaps where they acquire a part of the debts from a developing State that commits to adopting certain environmental protection measures.[30] An example of this are National Environmental Funds, which are used to mobilize resources for local financial mechanisms that attempt to collect the funds to finance certain local measures at an international level. These measures include capacity- and institution-building, where IEA allocate competences to NGOs to achieve the objectives of the treaty or agreement.[31] These tasks can even be of scientific nature.[32] In addition, NGOs can contribute informally to tasks performed by international organisations.

As regards compliance control mechanisms that operate in an institutionalised and formalised way to monitor the compliance of Treaty Parties with treaty commitments, the international bodies created by the respective treaty guide these mechanisms setting rules for participation. NGOs, have become increasingly involved in the framework of implementation and review mechanisms (under which reporting obligations for States, monitoring and/or inspections are provided) instituted under the new generation of MEAs in different fields of IEL, such as biodiversity and climate change.

Evidently, the role and the involvement of the NGOs varies under the MEAs; sometimes they are expressly formulated, and other times, formulation is more

---

30 Jeremy Heep, 'From Private to Public: Giving Effect to the "Debt" Component of Debt for Nature Swaps' (1994) 37 *GYIL*, p. 422; M. Bothe and P.H. Sand (eds), *Environmental Policy. From Regulation to Economic Instruments* (Brill 2003), p. 417. 'Environmental Policy: From Regulation to Economic Instruments', in *The Centre for Studies and Research in International Law and International Relations.* Consulted online on 09 October 2020, available at http://dx.doi.org/10.1163/1875-8096_pplcdu_ej.9780792335559.3-873 accessed 1 April 2020.

31 See article 5 Antarctic Seals Convention, article 8 World Heritage Convention, article 8 Ramsar Convention.

32 See, for instance, article 5, Antarctic Seals Convention.

implicit.[33] NGOs can also partake in compliance in an independent and informal manner by informing the international bodies about facts and problems. Up to a certain extent, the information provided by NGOs adds to verification tasks performed by treaty bodies, often supplementing the information given by the States and displayed in their reports.

Compliance monitoring can take place through a continuous collection of data about environmental quality and human activities, which have an impact on the environment. Reporting systems usually restrict State obligations to activities that fall into Treaty obligations. Significant NGOs such as the International Union for Conservation of Nature (IUCN) and World Wide Fund for Nature (WWF) have performed a relevant role in shaping IEL.

Sometimes, participation is restricted to representative NGOs, such as IUCN, TRAFFIC ("Trade Records Analysis of Flora and Fauna in Commerce") and WWF, which are active in wildlife conservation and protection of biodiversity, due to the scale required in terms of costs and the specific scientific expertise demanded under the treaty. Whereas the participation of NGOs in reporting systems is not always explicitly recognised, in other cases the participation in monitoring systems may be laid down in MEAs, as in the Washington Convention.

In other compliance mechanisms, such as inspection, the intervention of NGOs is rather infrequent; a small number of MEAs grant a role to NGOs during these inspections. Participation in inspections is more common in biodiversity and nature conservation, as in the case of the CITES.[34] Under CITES Strategic vision, a role in inspection was allocated to TRAFFIC (coordinated by the CITES Secretariat) to carry out inspections in the territories of Treaty Parties. CITES also foresees cooperation on enforcement through the International Consortium on Combating Wildlife Crime.[35]

Within ad-hoc Non-Compliance Procedures that provide for this system (such as the Montreal Protocol, the Climate Change Convention or the Desertification Convention), only Treaty Parties, the Secretariat or the concerned State are authorised to set the process in motion. NGOs fulfil a less relevant role, being able to ask for the triggering of the compliance procedure. Other MEAs contemplate the possibility that NGOs participate in the procedure as observers, being, sometimes, granted the right to participate in the Compliance Committees or equivalent treaty bodies. There is a wide range of possibilities under this type of mechanism as regulations under the various legal frameworks differ. For instance, in the Aarhus Convention and the Alpine Convention, NGOs possess restricted rights to activate the Non-Compliance Procedure.

33 Cesare Pitea, 'NGOs in Non-Compliance Mechanisms under Multilateral Environmental Agreements: From Tolerance to Recognition?', in Tullio Treves et al. (eds), *Civil Society, International Courts and Compliance Bodies* (T.M.C. Asser Press 2004), p. 205.

34 CITES, Cooperation and partnerships, available at https://www.cites.org/eng/disc/coop.php accessed 1 April 2020.

35 Resolution Conf. 18.3 on CITES Strategic Vision, pp. 2021–2030.

b Participation in mechanisms of confrontational nature (quasi-judicial control or mechanisms of compliance (and enforcement) to determine state responsibility)

NGOS may also intervene in the adoption of measures that would force States to comply through judicial and quasi-judicial mechanisms.[36] However, their role in the field of traditional state responsibility or application of inter-state measures, such as in the realm of WTO cases also involving environmental protection, is quite limited.[37]

The participation of NGOs in international environmental dispute settlements presents many nuances.[38] The role of NGOs before the ICJ is limited as they do not have direct access. Notwithstanding, they may submit observations or engage in lobbying.[39] Other international tribunals, such as the International Tribunal for the Law of the Sea, confer legal standing to States, international actors and certain private organisations. It is worth noting that the United Nations Convention on the Law of the Sea (UNCLOS) and the Statute of the International Tribunal for the Law of the Sea only refer to organisations that directly undertake research or exploitation of the seabed, leaving out other organisations.[40] Yet the Parties to conclude an agreement by providing that other organisations have access to the International Tribunal for the Law of the Sea.[41]

Before the WTO bodies, NGOs can submit amicus curiae briefs before the Appellate Body pursuant to article 13 (1) DSU. NGOs have put forward analysis about environmental protection that contains the observations of interested individuals, mainly organisations under Article XX of GATT, such as in the *Retreaded Tyres*[42] and *Shrimps-Turtle* cases.[43]

---

36 Ulrich Beyerlin, 'The Role of NGOs in International Environmental Litigation' (2001) 61 *ZaöRV*, p. 357.

37 Axel Bree, *Harmonization of the Dispute Settlement Mechanisms of the Multilateral Environmental Agreements and the World Trade Agreements* (Schmidt 2003).

38 Alan Boyle, 'Proliferation of International Jurisdiction and Its Implications for the Court', in D.W. Bowett et al. (eds), *The International Court of Justice: Process, Practice and Procedure* (British Institute of International and Comparative Law 1997), pp. 124–125.

39 Article 34 (2) and 66 (2) of the statute of the ICJ could at least be interpreted in the sense that the Court may admit its observations of NGOs. D. Shelton, 'The Participation of Nongovernmental Organizations in International Judicial Proceedings' (1994) 88 *AJIL*, p. 611.

40 Arts 87,153 (2) (b), article 37 of the Statue. Yoshifumi Tanaka, *The Peaceful Settlement of International Disputes* (Cambridge University Press 2018), pp. 131, 164.

41 Tanaka (n 40) at 229, 243. T.A. Mensah, 'Dispute Settlement Regime of the United Nations Convention on the Law of the Sea', in *Max Planck Yearbook of United Nations Law*, vol. 2 (1998), p. 307. Alan Boyle, 'Dispute Settlement and the Law of the Sea Convention: Problems of Fragmentation and Jurisdiction' (1997) 46 *ICLQ*, pp. 37, 53.

42 CIEL, Amicus Curiae Brief to the Appellate Body in Brazil – Measures Affecting Imports of Retreaded Tyres (October 2007), available at https://www.ciel.org/wp-content/uploads/2015/05/Brazil_Tires_Amicus_3Jul06.pdf 1 April 2020.

43 WTO, Participation in Dispute Settlement Proceedings, 9.3 Amicus Curiae Submissions, Appellate Body Report, US — Shrimp, paras. 105–108. WTO, Appellate Body Report, United States-Import Prohibition of Certain Shrimp and Shrimp Products, WT/DS58/AB/R, adopted 6 November 1998, DSR 1998:VII, 2755.

NGOs can participate in other proceedings, such as arbitration tribunals in-stituted to settled a specific dispute, as in the *Rainbow Warrior* case, or more institutionalised tribunals as the International Centre for the Settlement of In-vestment Disputes (ICSID) tribunals, including the possibility for NGOs to sub-mit amicus curiae files.

c Ad-hoc participation in compliance

NGOs can participate through mechanisms beyond the confrontational/ non-confrontational in terms of forcing States' obligations to conform to Treaty obligations or forcing States to take measures compensating for Non-Compliance with treaty commitments or those referring not to a particular MEA but to gen-eral conditions that facilitate compliance with MEAs. This would be a case of access to environmental information on the part of NGOs or intervention in the protection of human rights.[44]

The function of NGOs in compliance with IEL has considerably increased; however, there is still a democratic deficit under some MEAs when it comes to compliance with IEL obligations.[45] Further consolidating and formally enact-ing the role of NGOs in compliance assistance and control would require an enhanced role of non-state actors in the international legal system. Scholars have argued for a stronger involvement of NGOs in the enforcement process through the incorporation of independent knowledge, recognition of organisations which pursue (exclusively or at least mainly) an environmental protection goal, improvement of compliance and enforcement by the participation of national or regional NGOs and increasing the transparency of compliance and enforcement procedures.[46] This would entail the formulation of proposals based on a careful examination of existing mechanisms, followed by the introduction of reforms to compliance mechanisms across MEAs and a reinforcing of the general role of NGOs. To illustrate NGOs' role, it is worth taking a look at some enforcement and compliance mechanisms under MEAs in the following sections.

Establishing the International Consortium on Combating Wildlife Crime

We, the Secretary-General of the Convention on International Trade in Endangered Species of Wild Fauna and Flora (CITES), the Secretary Gen-eral of ICPO-INTERPOL, the Executive Director of the United Nations

---

44 Ibid. See, as well, M. Bothe, 'The Evaluation of Enforcement Mechanisms in International Envi-ronmental Law', in R. Wolfrum (ed), *Enforcing Environmental Standards: Economic Mechanisms as Viable Means?* (Springer 1996), pp. 13–38.

45 Michael Faure and Peter De Smedt (eds), *Environmental Enforcement Networks: Concepts, Imple-mentation and Effectiveness* (Edward Elgar 2015).

46 Epiney (n 29).

Office on Drugs and Crime (UNODC), the President of the World Bank, and the Secretary General of the Customs Cooperation Council (known as the World Customs Organization (WCO));

NOTING that the member States and Parties of CITES, ICPO-INTERPOL, UNODC, World Bank and WCO have expressed a desire that the agencies liaise together more closely;

HEREBY agree, within the context of their respective responsibilities, capabilities, and priorities to: highlight within their institutions the importance of the fight against wildlife crimes and other related violations and promote ICCWC among governments of States, through inter alia, relevant international fora; work collaboratively to support national law enforcement agencies, and regional wildlife law enforcement agreements, bodies and networks in responding to transnational wildlife crimes through, inter alia, the provision of our available expertise and resources, and to raise awareness of wildlife crimes and other related violations in the wider law enforcement community; assist countries in reviewing their current responses to wildlife crimes and related violations, facilitate national multi-agency interaction and cooperation, and encourage effective responses throughout the justice system; develop a joint work program that will include joint activities in the fields of capacity building, operational support and coordination of transnational interdiction efforts; disseminate existing, and jointly develop new, capacity building materials and tools to enhance the knowledge and skills of national agencies in combating wildlife crime and related violations; undertake research into the causes, nature, scale and value of wildlife crime and related violations and propose innovative ways to prevent and discourage such crime and related violations, for example, through the provision of socioeconomic incentives which encourage local communities to use natural resources in a lawful and sustainable manner and to participate in related monitoring and control efforts; assist in promoting best practice in the fields of natural resource conservation and management; and where appropriate, seek donor support to enable the provision of such services in the form of joint projects and programmes.

We further agree that our agencies, when collaborating together, will work under the title, the 'International Consortium on Combating Wildlife Crime'.

Source: https://cites.org/sites/default/files/i/iccwc/mou_0.pdf

4 A bottom-up approach to compliance in IEL

Transnational actors add up multi-layered normative forms of compliance in addition to those established in the treaties, including memoranda of understandings, informal gentlemen's agreements, pacts and codes of conduct. IEL does not always offer the appropriate institutional setting to accommodate these proposals stemming from civil society or business. Sometimes, these alternative approaches are not a matter of a deliberate or reflective choice[47] but a solution that is articulated as a response by communities to an environmental problem or challenge.[48] MEA provisions operate as 'enablers' for these bottom-up approaches to operate.[49]

The nature of IEL law-making processes may enable bottom-up compliance mechanisms or participatory processes. The existence of multiple rule-generating communities rather than a predictable and centralized process foster a bottom-up approach to compliance. Some MEAs offer interesting insights into non-traditional manners of compliance, which have taken root. Although law-making and compliance continue to be mostly state-centring in IEL, there are increasingly new spaces to articulate a bottom-up approach to compliance.

Against this backdrop, it is worth mentioning the role of IUCN as a bottom-up approach to compliance. Although compliance with the relevant sector of IEL is a matter for the respective State, NGOs also participate in this bottom-up approach. As different sets of problems require different IEL responses, not all stakeholders are equipped with the appropriate skills to address them from a bottom-up standpoint.

Scholars have frequently noted that, in international law, there are some specific cases of MEAs that fit into the category of bottom-up approach to compliance. Bottom-up approaches incorporate the participation of different stakeholders, such as businesses, NGOs and local communities. Two examples are worth mentioning here: the United Nations Convention to Combat Desertification (UNCCD) from the 1990s and the Paris Agreement, adopted in 2015 with the caveat that in the climate change regime the mechanisms are not yet fully in place.

The United Nations Convention to Combat Desertification (UNCCD) is often cited as an example of a bottom-up approach. Concluded with the aim to find global responses to desertification, the UNCCD provides for the adoption of strategies and plans to prevent soil degradation individually and regionally, promoting the restoration of degraded lands. One of the salient features of the UNCCD is the option for a bottom-up approach to engage communities in the definition of solutions for specific desertification problems.[50] Because of the nature of the problem at hand (stopping desertification requires the cooperation of local communities), the UNCCD guarantees the far-reaching participation of NGOs.

---

47 Janet K. Levit, 'Bottom-Up International Lawmaking: Reflections on the New Haven School of International Law' (2007) 32 *The Yale Journal of International Law*, p. 125.

48 Alon Tal and Jessica Cohen, 'Bringing "Top-down" to "Bottom-up": A New Role for Environmental Legislation in Combating Desertification' (2007) 31 *Harvard Environmental Law Review*.

49 Mor Mitrani, 'Global Civil Society and International Society: Compete or Complete? Alternatives: Global, Local, Political' (2013) 38(2) *Alternatives: Global, Local, Political*, pp. 172–188.

50 Kyle W. Danish, 'International Environmental Law and the "Bottom-Up" Approach: A Review of the Desertification Convention' (1995) 3(1) *Indiana Journal of Global Legal Studies*, Article 9.

Under the UNCCD model, NGOs should be consulted during the planning of projects. As a result, the projects should be defined and coordinated with the local population.[51] The Convention determines that NGOs shall liaise with the local population. In addition, it views NGOs as experts able to provide opinions while developing strategies to combat desertification.[52] Although treaty Parties are under the obligation to involve NGOs, States enjoy a certain amount of leeway to fulfil obligations at their own discretion.

Traditionally, the international climate change regime has been considered an example of a bottom-up approach to compliance as MNCs operating in Kyoto signatory States are bound to fulfil Kyoto-related obligations, such as emission targets, taxes and regulatory standards.[53] Under the implementation of the Kyoto Protocol (KP), different non-state actors have come together. As part of the process, NGOs have gathered information on environmental practices, closely working with trade associations, intergovernmental organizations and investment funds to incentivize corporations to decrease greenhouse gas emissions. Governmental divisions, such as provinces and states, have, in turn, passed legislation for incentives towards the reduction of greenhouse gas emissions, fostering a transparent reporting system in the area of climate change. These various interactions have led to the creation of a market for emissions rights, with monitoring for corporations that have engaged in climate change-related practices, to reduce the build-up of greenhouse gases. This market was created by allowing members to trade emissions credits and agreeing on overall reductions in emissions levels.

Article 15 of the 2015 Paris Agreement creates a new compliance mechanism.[54] Pursuant to the Decision of the Conference of the Parties to the UNFCCC adopting the Paris Agreement the mechanism would consist of 12 persons 'with recognized competence in relevant scientific, technical, socioeconomic or legal fields'.[55] The mechanism aims 'to facilitate implementation of and promote compliance with the provisions of this Agreement'.[56]

5 Institutionalised mechanisms for the participation of the global civil society in IEL compliance

The burgeoning compliance literature in IEL has looked into how law shapes the behaviour of the various actors participating in the implementation process.

---

51 Article 19 (1) (a), (3) UNCCD.

52 Article 10 (2) (f) UNCCD.

53 Levit (n 47), at 402 and 403.

54 Annalisa Savaresi and Francesco Sindico, 'The Role of Law in a Bottom-up International Climate Governance Architecture: Early Reflections on the Paris Agreement' (2016) QIL-QDI, available at http://www.qil-qdi.org/role-law-bottom-international-climate-governance-architecture-early-reflections-paris-agreement/ accessed 1 April 2020.

55 Levit (n 47).

56 Alexander Zahar, 'A Bottom-Up Compliance Mechanism for the Paris Agreement' (2017) 1(1) *Chinese Journal of Environmental Law*, available at SSRN: https://ssrn.com/abstract=2912560

This has spurred debate about more participatory models for the management of compliance and the impact of the global civil society on compliance.

Special mention must be made of the institutionalised participation of global civil society in negotiations of IEL treaties and the monitoring of compliance with IEL.[57] This sometimes implies re-thinking international structures and international governance to allow more participation.

Civil society organisations have access to participation through international organisations that perform a role in global environmental law.[58] Collective actions and citizens' groups, particularly those operating in specific sub-fields of IEL, actively scrutinise the implementation of IEL norms, pushing the boundaries of IEL to counteract a perceived move away from democracy.

Traditionally, these organisations had been involved in international human rights law processes, widening their participation in environmental protection. The linkages to international human rights law continue to be evident in areas such as environmental access rights.[59] Principle 10 provided fertile ground for the development of access to environmental information, public participation and justice in environmental matters. Human rights law has nurtured a broader global trend towards environmental rights, enhancing NGOs' role in compliance with IEL.

In the section below, the different modes of participation, articulated under multilateral and regional treaties, are further explored.

a Multilateral forums

The participation of civil society organisations in international multilateral fora mainly takes place through committees created to manage the implementation of a particular treaty, the conferences of the parties organised under MEAs and subsidiary bodies established as the main organ of a specific treaty. Multilateral fora refer not only to those of an inter-governmental nature but also to non-formal settings organised by the civil society, such as meetings to discuss compliance-related aspects.[60]

Less formal participation takes place within multilateral meetings around specific topics and sectors of IEL, which often take place in parallel to COPs or intergovernmental meetings. A different question, though, attempts to determine to what extent these fora accurately reflect the practices and preferences

---

57 Laura Pedraza-Farina, 'Conceptions of Civil Society in International Law-making and Implementation: A Theoretical Framework' (2013) 34 *The Michigan Journal of International Law*, p. 605.

58 Michelle M. Betsill and Elisabeth Corell (eds), *NGO Diplomacy: The Influence of Nongovernmental Organizations in International Environmental Negotiations* (MIT Press 2008).

59 Martine Beijerman, 'Conceptual Confusions in Debating the Role of NGOs for the Democratic Legitimacy of International Law' (2018) 9(2) *Transnational Legal Theory*, pp. 147–173.

60 The Center for International Environmental Law (CIEL), for instance, is often convening meetings with representatives of Compliance Mechanisms to discuss aspects related to the increased participation of civil society.

of the groups represented, which brings us back to the question of legitimacy. Another relevant aspect concerns the role of these mechanisms and institutions as determinants of compliance. An essential element of compliance analysis is how stakeholders respond and react to changes. Ultimately, the question that is posed is how the various NGOs' contributions can be appropriately harnessed.

This strengthens the call for a re-examination of the traditional international law categories in compliance and may help guide the discipline to more inclusive schemes, widening the participation of the various components of IEL. In furtherance of a new system, the current mechanism would benefit from a centralised organisation that could coordinate the activities. Those who call for more participation from civil society organisations are aware of the difficulties in implementing these views.

Lacking a centralised and proper international environmental organisation, environmental protection at the universal level falls under the remit of UNEP and UNDP. NGOs partake in a wide range of compliance activities, including capacity building, either by expressly being engaged to do so by international organisations or entities, or by acting independently and deploying their own resources. Participation materialises through the COPs and other mechanisms established by MEAs, such as the Basel Convention, the UN-FCCC, the Convention on Biological Diversity (CBD), the Convention on Desertification and the Stockholm Convention. Under these MEAs, these institutions provide a space for participation by hosting regular meetings, creating opportunities to take part in other mechanisms. Typically, these imply participation in the respective complaint systems. COP decisions have further clarified the contents and scope of the specific treaty obligations, developing the provisions and setting up specific mechanisms through the adoption of specific procedural rules.

Insightful analysis into different types of participation under different MEAs' mechanisms provides a clear landscape of participation in practice. The cases below demonstrate a representation of the participation of the NGOs.

Under the Montreal Protocol, NGOs have played a vital role in the process by participating in governmental lobbying and raising public awareness of ozone depletion. NGOs have also endorsed the reliance on environmentally friendly alternatives to CFC substances. In their interaction with institutionalised mechanism, NGOs undertook a significant role in formal meetings. For example, they actively participated in the Second Meeting of the Parties in London 1990, influencing the draft provisions of the Montreal Protocol.[61] In the negotiations leading to the adoption of the Vienna Convention, NGOs enjoyed an enhanced participation.[62]

---

61 Non-Governmental Organizations' Efforts to Protect Stratospheric Ozone, available at http://lup.lub.lu.se/luur/download?func=downloadFile&recordOId=4448289&fileOId=4467239 1 April 2020.

62 A. Gillespie, *Climate Change, Ozone Depletion and Air Pollution XIV. Non-Governmental Organizations* (Brill 2006), pp. 263–268.

The Basel Convention presents another significant example of the participation of the NGOs in implementation and compliance.[63] The Implementation and Compliance Committee (BCICC) offers a certain degree of participation to NGOs; however, it does not fulfil all the standards of transparency regarding the compliance mechanisms reviewed. This is mainly because public communications are not accepted, and, as a rule, proceedings are closed to the public, except when the parties agree otherwise, and findings are not published online. NGOs have put forward the shortcomings of the compliance mechanisms of the BCICC.[64] An effective participation under the BC could project positive spillover effects in the negotiations for Compliance Committee under Rotterdam and the Stockholm Conventions, which are still ongoing.[65]

b Regional organisations and forums

Regional organisations have taken action to enforce compliance with treaty provisions, incorporating the views of organisations of the global civil society. In Europe, under the auspices of the UNECE various regional treaties concluded have addressed specific environmental law problems.

The Aarhus Convention Compliance Committee (ACCC) is considered a successful mechanism for the participation of civil society, as one of the most transparent and inclusive compliance mechanisms. It was created at the first Aarhus Meeting of the Parties (MoP) in 2002, and it is composed of nine independent experts. Public participation in the activities of the Committee has developed over several years of practice; it accepts communications directly from the public, welcoming civil society participation in the review process and ensuring transparency in the compliance system with the publication of its findings and communications online. The importance of the ACCC is reflected in the number of communications received from the public.[66]

Other compliance mechanisms initially established under the UNECE, which were then opened for accession to all UN Member States, are the Protocol on Water and Health and the Water Convention. Following in the footsteps of the Protocol on Water and Health Compliance Committee (PWHCC), it accepts

---

63　Basel Convention on the Control of Transboundary Movements of Hazardous Wastes and Their Disposal, available at http://www.basel.int/ 1 April 2020.

64　CIEL, 'Strengthening Civil Society Participation in Environmental Treaty Compliance' (March 2018), available at https://www.ciel.org/civil-society-participation-environmental-treaty-compliance/ accessed 1 April 2020.

65　CIEL, 'Toxics Triple COP Parties Press "Pause" on Compliance Mechanism' (June 2017), available at https://www.ciel.org/toxics-triple-cop-parties-press-pause-compliance-mechanism/ accessed 1 April 2020.

66　Aarhus Convention Compliance Committee, Case Law of the Aarhus Convention Compliance Committee (2004–2014), available at https://www.unece.org/fileadmin/DAM/env/pp/compliance/CC_Publication/ACCC_Case_Law_3rd_edition_eng.pdf accessed 1 April 2020. To give an example, during the first 15 years of the Committee's existence, the body has heard nearly 150 communications as well as Party submissions and requests for action from the MoP.

communications from members of the public and publishes its files and complaints online. The level of participation at the PWHCC is less than under the Aarhus mechanism, as demonstrated by the few communications submitted by the public.[67] Another regional environmental treaty, the Convention on the Protection and Use of Transboundary Watercourses and International Lakes (Water Convention), foresees the establishment of the Water Convention Implementation Committee (WCIC), set up in 2012, which offers an even more restricted participatory role to civil society organizations and members of the public than its counterparts.[68] Although the Committee accepts submissions of information from the public, it does not receive communications or pledges. Only Parties or the WCIC itself are allowed to set a review of implementation and compliance in motion. The role of NGOs is limited to providing the WCIC with the information needed to activate its own compliance review. If the Committee decide to act on the submission, then information-providing NGOs are invited to seat at the table of the proceedings.

In the Americas, the participation of NGOs has had a limited scope under the San Salvador Protocol. NGOs can submit complaints to the Inter-American Commission of Human Rights in the regional human rights system.[69] The Organisation of American States (OAS) offers a forum for strengthening the environmental rule of law, increasing the role performed by civil society organisations in compliance with regional environmental law. Certain progress may be achieved by the adoption of the Regional Agreement on Access to Information, Public Participation and Justice in Environmental Matters in Latin America and the Caribbean (Escazu Agreement), the negotiation of which process was started by NGOs that maintain a steady active participation during the negotiation and adoption of the different provisions.[70] The RAEAR stipulates that the first COP must create a Compliance Committee and enact specific procedural rules which will define the contours of the participation of organisations of the civil society in compliance.

Considering the role of NGOs in other regions, the revised African Convention on the Conservation of Nature and Natural Resources (2017) does not specifically provide for non-governmental participation in compliance.[71] As seen

---

67 Since it was set up in 2007 the Committee has only published a few communications between the public and Committee initiatives.

68 The Water Convention's was opened to global participation in 2016; Chad and Senegal acceded, and other States have started accession processes.

69 Additional Protocol to the American Convention on Human Rights in the area of Economic, Social and Cultural Rights, available at https://www.oas.org/juridico/english/treaties/a-52.html accessed 1 April 2020.

70 Regional Agreement on Access to Information, Public Participation and Justice in Environmental Matters in Latin America and the Caribbean signed in March 2018 and open to signature and ratification in September 2018, available at https://www.cepal.org/en/escazuagreement accessed 1 April 2020.

71 Date of last signature: 4 February 2019. Available at https://au.int/en/treaties/african-convention-conservation-nature-and-natural-resources-revised-version accessed 1 April 2020. Signatures and ratifications, available at https://au.int/sites/default/files/treaties/7782-sl-revised_african_convention_on_the_conservation_of_nature_and_natural_resources.pdf accessed 1 April 2020.

in other regions, the specific provisions on participation are usually decided by the COPs or MOPs, as in this case. In the African sphere, very active NGOs like the Environmental Compliance Institute (ECI), a not-for-profit NGO, have a significant role in compliance with IEL.

In Asia, in the framework of ASEAN two specific environmental treaties have been concluded: the ASEAN Agreement on Transboundary Haze Pollution and the Agreement on the Establishment of the ASEAN Centre for Biodiversity.[72] There is an effervescent scenario for NGOs operated in the region.[73] Under the first treaty, there is no specific mention of the participation of the regional civil society, but it foresees the COP and the Secretariat, which may incorporate the input from civil society groups. In turn, the Agreement on the Establishment of the ASEAN Centre for Biodiversity, in its article 2, foresees that the Centre will facilitate cooperation and coordination among the members of ASEAN, and with relevant national governments, regional and international agreements, on the conservation and sustainable use of biological diversity and the fair and equitable sharing of the benefits of its use.[74]

With the universalisation of regional environmental treaties, UNECE has extended the geographical influence of the treaties concluded under its auspices by spreading good practice in access and participation to other regions.

THE AFRICAN COMMISSION ON HUMAN AND PEOPLES' RIGHTS (AFRICAN COMMISSION)

51st Ordinary Session held from 18 April to 2 May 2012

Banjul, The Gambia

Considering its mandate to promote human and peoples' rights in Africa under the African Charter on Human and Peoples' Rights (the African Charter);

Recalling Articles 20, 21 and 24 of the African Charter as elaborated by the 2011 Tunis Reporting Guidelines and the 2010 Nairobi Implementation Guidelines on Economic, Social and Cultural Rights, particularly in protecting the rights of peoples to pursue their social and economic

---

72 Association of Southeast Asian Nations, ASEAN Cooperation on Environment, https:// environment.asean.org/agreements/ 1 April 2020. ASEAN Agreement on Transboundary Haze Pollution (2002), available at http://environment.asean.org/wp-content/uploads/2015/06/ASEANAgreementonTransboundaryHazePollution.pdf accessed 1 April 2020.

73 JoAnn Fagot Aviel, 'Placing Human Rights and Environmental Issues on ASEAN's Agenda: The Role of Non-governmental Organizations' (2000) 8(20 *Asian Journal of Political Science*, pp. 17–34.

74 Agreement on the Establishment of the ASEAN Centre for Biodiversity (2005), available at http://environment.asean.org/wp-content/uploads/2015/07/Agreement-on-the-Establishment-of-ACB.pdf accessed 1 April 2020.

development in terms of policies they have freely chosen; to freely dispose of their natural resources in the exclusive interest of the people; and to generally satisfactory environment;

Noting the interdependence between human rights and development;

Recalling Principle 2 of the 1992 Rio Declaration on Environment and Development establishing State sovereignty over natural resources, read with Principle 1 providing that "human beings are at the centre of concerns for sustainable development. They are entitled to a healthy and productive life in harmony with nature" and Principle 22 providing that "local communities have a vital role in environmental management and development and, as a result, their identity, culture and interests must be protected";

Noting that there has recently been rapid progress in the definition of minimum international standards with respect to natural resources required to maintain life itself, in particular the recent recognition of the human right to food and the human right to water and sanitation;

Observing that current natural resources governance is gravely hampered by ill-planned development, misappropriation of land, corruption, bad governance and prevailing insecurities, amongst others;

Mindful of the disproportionate impact of human rights abuses upon the rural communities in Africa that continue to struggle to assert their customary rights of access and control of various resources, including land, minerals, forestry and fishing;

Proposals and abstracts

Calls upon States Parties to

   i Reaffirm that, in accordance with the Rio Declaration and African Charter principle of State sovereignty over natural resources, the State has the main responsibility for ensuring natural resources stewardship with, and for the interest of, the population and must fulfill its mission in conformity with international human rights law and standards;

  ii Confirm that all necessary measures must be taken by the State to ensure participation, including the free, prior and informed consent of communities, in decision making related to natural resources governance;

 iii Recommit themselves to vigorously fighting corruption at all levels of decision making by strengthening and enforcing criminalization of corruption, decisively ending impunity and ensuring asset recovery and repatriation for illicitly expatriated capital;

 iv Ensure that respect for human rights in all matters of natural resources exploration, extraction, toxic waste management, development, management and governance, in international cooperation, investment agreements and trade regulation prevails, and in particular:

(*Continued*)

Establish a clear legal framework for sustainable development as it impacts on natural resources, in particular water, that would make the realization of human rights a prerequisite for sustainability;

Strengthen regional efforts, such as the 2009 ECOWAS Directive on Mining and the African Commission's Working Group on Extractive Industries and Human Rights, to promote natural resources legislation that respect human rights of all and require transparent, maximum and effective community participation in a) decision-making about, b) prioritization and scale of, and c) benefits from any development on their land or other resources, or that affects them in any substantial way;

Set up independent monitoring and accountability mechanisms that ensure that human rights are justiciable and extractive industries and investors legally accountable in the country hosting their activities and in the country of legal domicile;

Ensure independent social and human rights impact assessments that guarantee free prior informed consent; effective remedies; fair compensation; women, indigenous and customary people's rights; environmental impact assessments; impact on community existence including livelihoods, local governance structures and culture, and ensuring public participation; protection of the individuals in the informal sector; and economic, cultural and social rights.

Done in Banjul, The Gambia, 2 May 2012

Source: African Commission https://www.achpr.org/sessions/resolutions?id=243#:~:text=The%20African%20Commission%20on%20Human, Rights%20(the%20African%20Charter)%3B

Bibliography

ASEAN, Agreement on the Establishment of the ASEAN Centre for Biodiversity (2005), available at http://environment.asean.org/wp-content/uploads/2015/07/Agreement-on-the-Establishment-of-ACB.pdf accessed 1 April 2020.

Association of Southeast Asian Nations, ASEAN Cooperation on Environment, https://environment.asean.org/agreements/ 1 April 2020. ASEAN Agreement on Transboundary Haze Pollution (2002), available at http://environment.asean.org/wp-content/uploads/2015/06/ASEANAgreementonTransboundaryHazePollution.pdf accessed 1 April 2020.

Barreiro Carril, B and Olmos Giupponi, B, *La participación de la Sociedad Civil en los procesos de integración en Iberomérica* (Dykinson 2011).

Beijerman, M, 'Conceptual Confusions in Debating the Role of NGOs for the Democratic Legitimacy of International Law' (2018) 9(2) *Transnational Legal Theory*, pp. 147–173.

Betsill, M and Corell, E, (eds), *NGO Diplomacy: The Influence of Nongovernmental Organizations in International Environmental Negotiations* (MIT Press, 2008).

Beyerlin, U, 'The Role of NGOs in International Environmental Litigation' (2001) 61 *ZaöRV*, p. 357.

Bodansky, D, *The Art and Craft of International Environmental Law* (Harvard University Press 2010), pp. 126, 127.

Bombay, P, 'The Role of NGOs in Shaping Community Positions in International Environmental Fora', (2001) 10 *Review of European Community & International Environmental Law*, pp. 163–167.

Bothe, M, 'The Evaluation of Enforcement Mechanisms in International Environmental Law', in R. Wolfrum (ed), *Enforcing Environmental Standards: Economic Mechanisms as Viable Means?* (Springer 1996), pp. 13–38.

Boyle, A, 'Proliferation of International Jurisdiction and Its Implications for the Court', in D.W Bowett et al. (eds), *The International Court of Justice: Process, Practice and Procedure* (British Institute of International and Comparative Law 1997), pp. 124–125.

Bree, A, *Harmonization of the Dispute Settlement Mechanisms of the Multilateral Environmental Agreements and the World Trade Agreements* (Schmidt 2003).

CBD Secretariat, Bonn Guidelines on Access to Genetic Resources and Fair and Equitable Sharing of the Benefits Arising Out of Their Utilization, available at https://www.cbd.int/doc/publications/cbd-bonn-gdls-en.pdf accessed 1 April 2020.

CIEL, Amicus Curiae Brief to the Appellate Body in Brazil – Measures Affecting Imports of Retreaded Tyres (October 2007), available at https://www.ciel.org/wp-content/uploads/2015/05/Brazil_Tires_Amicus_3Jul06.pdf 1 April 2020.

CIEL, 'Strengthening Civil Society Participation in Environmental Treaty Compliance' (March 2018), available at https://www.ciel.org/civil-society-participation-environmental-treaty-compliance/ accessed 1 April 2020.

CIEL, 'Toxics Triple COP Parties Press "Pause" on Compliance Mechanism' (June 2017), available at https://www.ciel.org/toxics-triple-cop-parties-press-pause-compliance-mechanism/ accessed 1 April 2020.

CITES, Cooperation and Partnerships, available at https://www.cites.org/eng/disc/coop.php accessed 1 April 2020.

Danish, KW, 'International Environmental Law and the "Bottom-Up" Approach: A Review of the Desertification Convention' (1995) 3(1) *Indiana Journal of Global Legal Studies*, Article 9, pp. 133–176.

Epiney, A, 'The Role of NGOs in the Process of Ensuring Compliance with MEAs', in Ulrich Beyerlin, Peter-Tobias Stoll, Rüdiger Wolfrum (eds), *Ensuring Compliance with Multilateral Environmental Agreements: Academic Analysis and Views from Practice* (Brill 2006), pp. 319–352.

Extinction Rebellion, 'Our Demands', available at https://rebellion.earth/the-truth/demands/ accessed 1 April 2020.

Fagot Aviel, JoAnn, 'Placing Human Rights and Environmental Issues on ASEAN's Agenda: The Role of Non-governmental Organizations' (2000) 8(20) *Asian Journal of Political Science*, pp. 17–34.

Faure, M and De Smedt, Peter, (eds), *Environmental Enforcement Networks: Concepts, Implementation and Effectiveness* (Edward Elgar 2015).

Food and Agriculture Organization of the United Nations Rome, International Code of Conduct on the Distribution and Use of Pesticides (2003), Adopted by the Hundred and Twenty-third Session of the FAO Council in November 2002, available at http://www.fao.org/3/y4544e/y4544e02.htm#bm2.1 accessed 1 April 2020.

Gillespie, A, *Climate Change, Ozone Depletion and Air Pollution XIV*. Non-Governmental Organizations (Brill 2006), pp. 263–268.

Gunningham, N, Kagan, RA, and Thornton, D, *Shades of Green-Business, Regulation, and Environment* (Stanford University Press 2003).

Heep, J, 'From Private to Public: Giving Effect to the "Debt" Component of Debt for Nature Swaps' (1994) 37 *GYIL*, p. 422; in M. Bothe and P. H. Sand (eds), *Environmental Policy. From Regulation to Economic Instruments* (Brill 2003), p. 417. 'Environmental Policy: From Regulation to Economic Instruments', in The Centre for Studies and Research in International Law and International Relations. Consulted online on 09 October 2020, available at http://dx.doi.org/10.1163/1875–8096_pplcdu_ej.9780792335559.3–873 accessed 1 April 2020.

Heyvaert, V, *Transnational Environmental Regulation and Governance: Purpose, Strategies and Principles* (Cambridge University Press 2018).

IASHR, Additional Protocol to the American Convention on Human Rights in the Area of Economic, Social and Cultural Rights, available at https://www.oas.org/juridico/english/treaties/a-52.html accessed 1 April 2020.

Levit, J, 'Bottom-Up International Lawmaking: Reflections on the New Haven School of International Law' (2007) 32 *The Yale Journal of International Law*, p. 125.

Maljean-Dubois, S and Richard, Vanessa, 'The Applicability of International Environmental Law to Private Enterprises', in Pierre-Marie Dupuy and Jorge E. Viñuales (eds), *Harnessing Foreign Investment to Promote Environmental Protection: Incentives and Safeguards* (Cambridge University Press 2013), pp. 69–96.

Mensah, TA, 'Dispute Settlement Regime of the United Nations Convention on the Law of the Sea', in *Max Planck Yearbook of United Nations Law*, vol. 2 (1998), p. 307. Alan Boyle, 'Dispute Settlement and the Law of the Sea Convention: Problems of Fragmentation and Jurisdiction' (1997) 46 *ICLQ*, pp. 37, 53.

Mitrani, M, 'Global Civil Society and International Society: Compete or Complete? Alternatives: Global, Local, Political' (2013) 38(2) *Alternatives: Global, Local, Political*, pp. 172–188.

Morgera, E, 'From Stockholm to Johannesburg: From Corporate Responsibility to Corporate Accountability for the Global Protection of the Environment?' (2004) 13 *Review of European Community & International Environmental Law*, pp. 214–222.

Morrison, FL, and Wolfrum, Rüdiger, (ed), *International, Regional, and National Environmental Law* (Kluwer Law International 2000).

OECD, Private Sector Engagement to Address – Climate Change and Promote Green Growth (OECD Private Sector Peer Learning Policy Brief 4), available at https://www.oecd.org/dac/peer-reviews/Policy-Brief-4-Private-Sector-Engagement-to-Address-Climate-Change-and-Promote-Green-Growth.pdf accessed 1 March 2020.

Paddock, Lee, Du, Qun, Kotzé, Louis J, Markell, David L, Markowitz, Kenneth J, and Zaelke, Durwood, (eds), *Compliance and Enforcement in Environmental Law: Toward More Effective* (Edward Elgar 2011).

Pedraza-Farina, L, 'Conceptions of Civil Society in International Law-making and Implementation: A Theoretical Framework' (2013) 34 *The Michigan Journal of International Law*, p. 605.

Pitea, C, 'NGOs in Non-Compliance Mechanisms under Multilateral Environmental Agreements: From Tolerance to Recognition?', in Tullio Treves et al. (eds), *Civil Society, International Courts and Compliance Bodies* (T.M.C. Asser Press 2004), p. 205.

Richardson, BJ, *Socially Responsible Investment Law: Regulating the Unseen Polluters* (Oxford University Press 2008).

Roht-Arriaza, N. "'Soft Law" in a "Hybrid" Organization: The International Organization for Standardization', in Dinah Shelton (ed), *Commitment and Compliance: The Role of Non-binding Norms in the International Legal System* (Oxford University Press 2007), p. 263.

Sands, P, Peel, J, Fabra, A, and MacKenzie, R, *Principles of International Environmental Law* (3rd edn CUP 2012), p. 112; Patricia Birnie, Alan Boyle, and Catherine Redgwell, *International Law and the Environment* (3rd edn Oxford University Press 2009), p. 66.

Savaresi, A and Sindico, F, 'The Role of Law in a Bottom-up International Climate Governance Architecture: Early Reflections on the Paris Agreement' (2016) QIL-QDI, available at http://www.qil-qdi.org/role-law-bottom-international-climate-governance-architecture-early-reflections-paris-agreement/ accessed 1 April 2020.

Shelton, D, 'Law, Non-Law and the Problem of "Soft Law"', in Dinah Shelton (ed), *Commitment and Compliance: The Role of Non-binding Norms in the International Legal System* (Oxford University Press 2007), pp. 1–18.

Tal, A and Cohen, J, 'Bringing "Top-down" to "Bottom-up": A New Role for Environmental Legislation in Combating Desertification' (2007) 31 *Harvard Environmental Law Review*, pp. 163–217.

Tanaka, Y, *The Peaceful Settlement of International Disputes* (Cambridge University Press 2018), pp. 131, 164.

UNDP, Promoting Sustainable Development through More Effective Civil Society Participation in Environmental Governance. A Selection of Country Case Studies from the EU-NGOs Project, available at https://ec.europa.eu/environment/international_issues/pdf/EU_NGOs_publication_20161219.pdf accessed 1 April 2020.

UNECE, Aarhus Convention Compliance Committee, Case Law of the Aarhus Convention Compliance Committee (2004–2014), available at https://www.unece.org/fileadmin/DAM/env/pp/compliance/CC_Publication/ACCC_Case_Law_3rd_edition_eng.pdf accessed 1 April 2020.

UNECLAC, Regional Agreement on Access to Information, Public Participation and Justice in Environmental Matters in Latin America and the Caribbean signed in March 2018 and open to signature and ratification in September 2018, available at https://www.cepal.org/en/escazuagreement accessed 1 April 2020.

United Nations, Basel Convention on the Control of Transboundary Movements of Hazardous Wastes and Their Disposal, available at http://www.basel.int/ 1 April 2020.

United Nations, Commission on Sustainable Development (CSD), available at https://sustainabledevelopment.un.org/csd.html accessed 1 April 2020.

United Nations, Global Compact, About us, available at https://www.unglobalcompact.org/about accessed 1 April 2020.

United Nations – Global Compact, Business for the Rule of Law (B4ROL), available at https://www.unglobalcompact.org/library/1341 accessed 1 April 2020.

United Nations. 2009. Guidelines on Cooperation between the United Nations and the Private Sector, available at https://www.un.org/en/ethics/assets/pdfs/Guidelines-on-Cooperation-with-the-Business-Sector.pdf accessed 1 March 2020.

Woodward, B, 'Global Civil Society and International Law in Global Governance: Some Contemporary Issues' (2006) 8(2) *International Community Law Review*, pp. 247–355.

Woodward, B, 'Global Civil Society in International Lawmaking and Global Governance, Theory and Practice', (2010) 2 *Queen Mary Studies in International Law*, pp. 105–149.

WTO, Participation in Dispute Settlement Proceedings, 9.3 Amicus Curiae Submissions, Appellate Body Report, US — Shrimp, paras. 105–108. WTO, Appellate Body Report, United States-Import Prohibition of Certain Shrimp and Shrimp Products, WT/DS58/AB/R, adopted 6 November 1998, DSR 1998:VII, 2755.

Yamin, F, 'NGOs and International Environmental Law: A Critical Evaluation of Their Roles and Responsibilities' (2001) 10 *RECIEL*, p. 149.

Zahar, A, 'A Bottom-Up Compliance Mechanism for the Paris Agreement' (2017) 1(1) *Chinese Journal of Environmental Law*, available at SSRN: https://ssrn.com/abstract=2912560.

Part 3
Case studies

8 Climate change

Assessing innovation in compliance and private sector involvement

1 Introduction

In this chapter, compliance with IEL is analysed in light of the legal regime created under the Framework Convention on Climate Change, the Kyoto Protocol and the Paris Agreement. In examining compliance, the analysis also comprises the Montreal Protocol on Substances that Deplete the Ozone Layer. The system has been structured around the 1992 United Nations Framework Convention on Climate Change, the 1997 Kyoto Protocol and the 2015 Paris Agreement, together making up several compliance decisions adopted at the COPs and by the specific Non-Compliance Mechanism (NCM).

International climate change law (ICCL) has revealed new approaches to compliance. In their path to becoming carbon-neutral States are facing significant challenges to implement international climate change norms. First, States are adopting measures on the reduction of greenhouse gas emissions based on the introduction of market mechanisms that involve the private sector. Second, there is an emerging 'climate change litigation' before national courts and international tribunals (closely linked to access to environmental justice) featuring claims regarding companies' liability and state responsibility for climate change. Both features are object of in-depth analysis in this chapter.

Compliance with international climate change norms has led to new implementation obligations as well as socio-economic co-benefits for governments and the private sector, such as cost savings, income diversification, capacity building and job creation. There are also some ecological co-benefits. Indicators of implementation include emissions reduction and the adoption of incentive mechanisms to minimise the impact of climate change.[1]

With regard to the type of implementation system, one observes a sort of metamorphosis of compliance under the international climate change regime. A new

---

1 See Yamide Dagnet, Nathan Cogswell, Eliza Northrop, Joe Thwaites, Cynthia Elliott, Kelly Levin, Niklas Höhne, Neil Bird, Amy Kirbyshire, Sebastian Oberthür, Marcelo Rocha, and Pedro Barata, *Setting the Paris Agreement in Motion: Key Requirements for the Implementing Guidelines* (World Resources Institute August 2018), available at https://www.wri.org/publication/pact-implementing-guidelines accessed 1 April 2020.

generation of compliance mechanisms started with the Montreal Protocol (MP), which projected its influence beyond ozone depletion being rolled out to other areas, such as atmospheric pollution. The MP foresaw a new system of implementation, comprising regulation of trade, compliance facilitation elements and management of non-compliance through a novel non-compliance procedure.[2] The United Nations Framework Convention on Climate Change (UNFCCC) represented another turning point in addressing greenhouse gases and introducing the principles to set up a system to progressively curb the emissions, differentiating and allocating responsibilities and commitments to States. The Kyoto Protocol operationalized the commitments assumed under the UNFCCC by imposing specific obligations on industrialized countries and economies. In this evolution, the Paris Agreement (PA) introduced an updated version of the commitments.[3]

Climate change law, as a novel sector of law, presents certain distinctive features. The first is its transnational character, which is consubstantial to the trans-boundary effects of climatic phenomena. However, there are problems in defining a correct approach to climate change issues. Notably, due to the existence of diverse legal systems a one-size-fits-all solution seems untenable. To illustrate, it suffices to mention the differences between common and civil law systems when it comes to environmental law. Although the differences are blurred in some sectors of environmental law, differences persist.

Second, one must underline the multilevel governance of global climate change and the role of sub-national, national, international and regional dimensions of CCL. Gradually, regional organisations have taken up functions and obligations in the climate change regime, such as the European Union (EU). The latter is a peculiar case as the EU shares competences with Member States in environmental matters, and international treaties are thus incorporated into EU law, the EU being actively involved in the UNFCCC negotiations. Other regional organisations, such as the Central American Integration System (SICA), are also moving toward a more active role, even though on a more modest scale. SICA Member States coordinated their positions before the Conference of the Parties (COP 21). The existence of more coordination often has the effect that international norms are interpreted by domestic courts according to specific guidelines and following specific priorities. Specifically, concerning the application and interpretation of climate change law this entails, on the one hand, that there is a sort of intermediary (the community or regional law level) which may increase the complexity; on the other hand, the existence of common guidelines dictated by regional bodies may foster a harmonious interpretation of the norms.

2 Bryan A. Green, 'Lessons from the Montreal Protocol: Guidance for the Next International Climate Change Agreement' (2009) 39(1) *Environmental Law*, pp. 253–283.
3 IISD, Paris Agreement Implementation Guidelines: How Do We Get There? (IISD 2018), available at http://sdg.iisd.org/commentary/policy-briefs/paris-agreement-implementation-guidelines-how-do-we-get-there/ accessed 1 April 2020.

Third, closely linked to the question of multilevel governance, there is private sector involvement in environmental compliance.[4] Particularly, this is an emergent trend in certain climate change-related areas, such as trading of emissions rights and projects registered under the Clean Development Mechanism. To provide another example, the United Nations Programme on Reducing Emissions from Deforestation and Forest Degradation (or UN-REDD Programme) offers a framework for collaborative alliances between the private sector and governments. Whereas the engagement of the private sector in the process of implementing international and national environmental law norms is a growing trend, there are still unclarified issues.

Fourth, as regards the sources of international climate change law, international environmental law (IEL) principles are shaping the manner in which national judges interpret environmental law. Inter-generational equity and the precautionary principle play a significant role in climate change litigation before domestic courts.[5] Specifically, in the climate change regime the principle of common but differentiated responsibilities adds a solidarity dimension to the norms. Also, the precautionary principle constitutes the cornerstone in the application of norms and settlement of disputes. This is particularly true in climate change litigation as the scientific evidence available may be uncertain. Bodansky, Brunee and Rajamani cite other relevant principles arising out of the no-harm rule in the context of trans-boundary pollution (harm prevention and due diligence, procedural obligations and prevention and precaution).[6]

Altogether, these features are bringing new challenges to climate justice as they imply the adoption of a new approach, different from the mind-set of the national judge, who is more used to settling other kind of disputes (such as land or strictly environmental law disputes). In order to tackle the new challenges posed by climate change litigation it is crucial to build upon previous experience.

2 Legal framework for compliance with international climate change law: the evolution of the compliance mechanisms

The sector of atmospheric pollution in IEL has elicited a great deal of scholarly debate, particularly in terms guaranteeing compliance with norms by using ad-hoc mechanisms. Normative design in this sector has followed the imprint of other 'framework' conventions geared to reach consensus amongst States.[7]

4 Belen Olmos Giupponi, 'Assessing Climate Change MRV Initiatives in Latin America: Bridging Theory and Practice', in *INECE Report* (Rotterdam University Press 2016).
5 Rosemary Lyster and Eric Coonan, 'The Precautionary Principle: A Thrill Ride on the Roller Coaster of Energy and Climate Law' (2009)18(1) *RECIEL*, p. 38.
6 Daniel Bodansky, Jutta Brunnée and Lavanya Rajamani, *International Climate Change Law* (Oxford University Press 2016), pp. 40–43.
7 David Freestone, 'The United Nations Framework Convention on Climate Change – The Basis for the Climate Change Regime', in Cinnamon Piñon Carlarne, Kevin R. Gray, and Richard Tarasofsky (eds), *The Oxford Handbook of International Climate Change Law* (OUP 2016).

Standards set by treaty committees are based on evidence of the harmful effects of climate change and compliance.

Following in the footsteps of the LRTAP, the normative design of the climate change regime included this type of international treaty.[8] The idea behind this was to have a legal umbrella which would facilitate the negotiations in order to set specific legal commitments and targets, enabling States to achieve progress in the field by adjusting them to different stages of the negotiations. With this purpose in mind, the 1992 United Nations Framework Convention opened a new period in the fight against atmospheric pollution, introducing new principles that regulate compliance activities, such as common but differentiated responsibilities.[9]

The combination of different strands in the regulation and implementation of ICCL has given rise to an ad-hoc system. Compliance with ICCL is multi-layered and in continuous evolution (a progress that has been stalled sometimes). Under the UNFCCC there is a scientific strand, along with other legal and political strands that have shaped this evolving system. Reliance on scientific data provided by the Intergovernmental Panel on Climate Change (IPCC) influences the whole compliance system, also known as the scientific pillar. To this end, the IPCC's main function is to provide support to other treaty bodies in the various areas of the compliance.[10] This strand is interlinked with the other two areas: the political and legal dimensions. Ultimately, the legal strand is a result of the deep interactions occurring in the other two strands (scientific and political).

Noticeably, the nature and dimensions of the problem posed by accelerated climate change requires tailor-made solutions. The environmental issue consists of the protection of the atmosphere as a global common threatened by human-made emissions of greenhouse gases (GHGs), which include not only carbon dioxide but also methane, nitrogen oxides and some Chlorofluorocarbons (CFCs) and Hydrochlorofluorocarbons (HCFCs), leading to an accumulation of gasses and energy, provoking human-induced global warming. The main source of this global warming is fossil fuel-related process, together with other agricultural processes that release some of these GHGs into the atmosphere.

As a starting point, the UNFCCC set out the main principles that govern the ICCL system: intergenerational equity (Article 3.1), common but differentiated responsibilities (Article 3.1) and the precautionary principle (Article 3.3). The manner in which the UNFCCC has set up the distinction between different groups of countries is correlated to the lists included in Annex I and Annex II.

---

8 Anna Huggins, *Multilateral Environmental Agreements and Compliance: The Benefits of Administrative Procedures* (Routledge 2018).

9 Zerrin Savaşan, *Paris Climate Agreement: A Deal for Better Compliance? Learned from the Compliance Mechanisms of the Kyoto and Montreal Protocols* (Springer 2019).

10 Navraj Singh Ghaleigh, 'Science and Climate Change Law – The Role of the IPCC in International Decision-Making', in Kevin R. Gray, Richard Tarasofsky, and Cinnamon Carlarne (eds), *The Oxford Handbook of International Climate Change Law* (Oxford University Press 2016).

This framework determined legally and in practice differential treatment for the two groups of States. Certainly, Article 4 contemplates different groups of obligations for the parties. First, those applicable to all parties in terms of emissions reduction (Article 4.1), gathering and communication of information (Article 12.1). Second, commitments for developed States and States undergoing a transition to a market economy ('Parties included in Annex I') are spelled out as follows: reduction of emissions (Article 4.2) and flexibilities for countries in transition, and communication of supplementary information undertaken only by developed States (Article 4.3, 4 and 12.3) ('Parties included in Annex II'). Third, there is cooperation and assistance obligations from developed States and the emissions reduction obligations of developing States (Article 4.7). The different categories were built upon the principle of common but differentiated responsibilities, which has completely permeated the institutional set-up. Risking polarisation in terms of compliance, the divide between the two groups has been discussed and revisited to reflect changes in the commitments assumed by States.

At the heart of the compliance, the system relies on the IPCC, tasked with the mission of examining scientific evidence on the subject, assessing it and drafting reports summarising the main findings along with recommendations to the Secretariat. The assessment reports outline the scientific basis, impacts, adaptation and vulnerability and mitigation measures, together with the 'summary for policymakers', considered guidelines that need to be endorsed by the representatives of State Parties to the IPCC.[11] The various reports that the IPCC has issued have informed the content of climate change policies, though they remain cautious about the role of human activities in contributing to climate change.[12]

The architecture of the international climate change legal system entails legal, economic and political elements. The UNFCC created a COP (Article 7), a Secretariat (Article 8) and the subsidiary bodies: a scientific body (Article 9) and an implementation body (Article 10). Unlike other Secretariats under MEAs, under the UNFCCC, the Secretariat displays a more significant role. The Secretariat is in charge of the follow-up of the commitments. Innovation was harnessed through the introduction of market-based mechanisms and other novel tools with the aim of progressively increasing the participation of the private sector in compliance. For instance, Article 11 establishes a financial mechanism which developed into the 'Green Climate Fund'; established in 2010, it has the objective of assisting developing countries in reducing their greenhouse gas emissions, enhancing their ability to counteract climate change's negative impact, and will

---

11 Appendix A to the Principles Governing IPCC Work, Procedures for the Preparation, Review, Acceptance, Adoption, Approval and Publication of IPCC Reports. Adopted at the Fifteenth Session (San Jose, 15–18 April 1999) amended at the Twentieth Session. (Paris, 19–21 February 2003), Twenty-first Session (Vienna, 3 and 6–7 November 2003), and Twenty-Ninth Session (Geneva, 31 August–4 September 2008).

12 AR6 Climate Change 2021: Impacts, Adaptation and Vulnerability, The Working Group II contribution to the Sixth Assessment Report (*forthcoming*).

have a significant role in the context of the Paris Agreement and keeping the global temperature below two degrees C.[13]

The Compliance Committee of the Kyoto Protocol is made up of two branches: a facilitative branch[14] and an enforcement branch.[15] In turn, the enforcement branch is 'responsible for determining whether a Party included in Annex I (Annex I Party) is not in compliance with its emissions targets, the methodological and reporting requirements for greenhouse gas inventories, and the eligibility requirements under the mechanisms'.[16]

The 1997 KP spelled out the obligations and provided more detailed commitments, which have evolved into leading commitments in the field of international regulation in air pollution. However, the choice of the legal tools to control greenhouse gas emissions, although adequate on paper, is difficult to implement, as demonstrated by the lengthy ratification process and states' positions vis-à-vis the commitments. Building an effective international regime to solve climate change-related problems proves difficult as they are deeply entangled with other areas of law, and the causes and effects are rooted in economic activities. Differential state engagement (from committed to reluctant states) remained a problem throughout the implementation of the Kyoto Protocol. Whereas the European Union and its members, along with other industrialised countries, decided to lead the implementation, other parties, like the United States and emerging countries, positioned themselves against hard commitments. A further group of States stayed 'on the fence'. States leading by example have sanctioned specific systems and legal frameworks, such as the ad-hoc Emissions Trading System (ETS).

In terms of the legacy of the KP, it encompassed a new regulatory approach that remained relevant for a period, namely, from its entry into force until the 2011 Durban Conference.[17] The KP followed the traditional type of framework treaty, as per Article 17 of the UNFCCC; the ratification technique set out in Article 25(1) determined to a long ratification period. According to Article 25(1), the KP had to be ratified by at least 55 states parties to the Convention, including representation from a number of Annex I that accounted for total carbon dioxide emission in the baseline year 1990, representing 55%.[18] Another les-

---

13 Green Climate Fund, About GCF, available at https://www.greenclimate.fund/about accessed 1 April 2020.

14 Kyoto Protocol Compliance Committee, Facilitative Branch, available at https://cop23.unfccc.int/process/bodies/constituted-bodies/compliance-committee-cc/facilitative-branch

15 Kyoto Protocol Compliance Committee, Facilitative Branch, available at https://unfccc.int/compliance-committee-bodies-page accessed 1 April 2020.

16 Kyoto Protocol Compliance Committee, An Introduction to the Kyoto Protocol Compliance Mechanism, available at https://unfccc.int/process/the-kyoto-protocol/compliance-under-the-kyoto-protocol/introduction

17 The 2011 Durban Conference witnessed the split between the States which rejected the assumptions of new commitments, such as Canada, Russia and Japan.

18 Joanna Depledge, *Tracing the Origins of the Kyoto Protocol: An Article-By-Article Textual History*, Technical paper FCCC/TP/2000/2, UNFCCC (2000), available at https://unfccc.int/resource/docs/tp/tp0200.pdf accessed 1 March 2020.

son to be learned from its application concerns the lack of flexibility. Emerging economies which would increase emissions during the period were not bound to comply with any specific targets or quantified obligations. Under the KP the regime had a clear focus on the obligations of Annex I States, excluding others (Article 3(1) and Annex B), and this was embodied in the mandate '[n]ot to introduce any new commitments for Parties not included in Annex I'.[19] This specific set-in-stone provision and negotiating guideline hinder any possibility to adjust the commitments, so the KP became outdated over time. Such a clause may add a significant hurdle to compliance without allowing for periodical up-dates of the legal commitments, leaving States with high emission levels (like emerging countries and the US as the 'big elephant in the room') off the hook.

The decade under the KP can be called the 'decade of building up' of the system, complemented by the adoption of various accords and additional agreements, such as the 'Copenhagen Accord' and the 'Cancun Agreements'.[20] Under the KP, the main obligation laid down was to curb GHG identified in Annex A of the Protocol from regulation, taking as year base 1990 except for emissions of certain gases. Emission reduction targets were numerically expressed in order to be fulfilled during a specific commitment period.

The KP brought in innovation by incorporating market mechanisms, further developing the strategy of the Montreal Protocol, adding mechanisms that are more sophisticated based on the idea of trading of emission rights in an ad-hoc institutional structure, which provides for the transfer of emissions allowance from one user (State or private party authorised to do so) to another. These emissions rights are measured in units, 'assigned amount units' (or AAUs) and the 'emission reduction units' (or 'ERU'), which are set out in Annex B for listed countries. The emission market facilitates the transactions between those States that are interested in selling the excess and those States which are willing to buy the emission rights.[21]

Considered a game-changer, the 2015 Paris Agreement paved the way for a new understanding of climate change obligations as all contracting States were supposed to submit their nationally determined contributions (NDCs).[22] In a

19 Berlin mandate, para. II.2.(b).
20 Copenhagen Accord, Decision 2/CP.15, 30 March 2010, DOC. FCCC/CP/2009/11/Add.1. The 'Cancun Agreements', available at https://unfccc.int/process/conferences/pastconferences/cancun-climate-change-conference-november-2010/statements-and-resources/Agreements accessed 1 April 2020.
21 Sander Simonetti and Rutger de Witt Wijnen (2009-10-01), 'International Emissions Trading and Green Investment Schemes', in David Freestone and Charlotte Streck, *Legal Aspects of Carbon Trading: Kyoto, Copenhagen, and beyond* (Oxford University Press 2009). Retrieved 11 May. 2020, from https://www.oxfordscholarship.com/view/10.1093/acprof:oso/9780199565931.001.0001/acprof-9780199565931-chapter-7 accessed 1 April 2020.
22 UN Climate Change, *Nationally Determined Contributions (NDCs)*, available at https://unfccc.int/process-and-meetings/the-paris-agreement/the-paris-agreement/nationally-determined-contributions-ndcs#:~:text=Nationally%20determined%20contributions%20(NDCs)%20are,the%20impacts%20of%20climate%20change accessed 1 April 2020.

compare and contrast exercise, the PA represents an evolution of the previous system with a different strategy and variable flexibility in terms of the commitments. When fully implemented, the Committee established to facilitate implementation and promote compliance under the PA will operate under the decision governing its activities.[23] It remains to be seen if the Committee will enable compliance of all States in light of the NDCs submitted. Its launch is dependent on the election of its members. With regard to the nature of the Paris Agreement, scholars have emphasised the sui generis nature of the Agreement which integrates elements of a diverse legal nature (including soft-law norms) and core provisions.[24]

Differentiation within the compliance system in terms of developing and developed countries has been attenuated by the introduction of the NDCs. Decisions adopted to date only provide for flexibility in terms of procedural deadlines for Parties in view of their domestic capabilities. Nevertheless, developing countries, as a category, are subject to the flexibility provided for in Article 13. Similarly, as a group of countries they are still entitled to financial assistance in order to co-fund their participation in the activities of the Committee. The triggering of the procedures is another important piece of the new system. A distinctive note is the agreement between the Parties about the Committee's mandate to start non-compliance procedures on its own initiative in certain cases and, in the event of serious and persistent failure, to comply with the transparency guidelines, with the agreement of the Parties.[25]

The strategy followed in the Paris Agreement attempted to reach broad consensus, leaving future details to be determined once the treaty came into force. As a result, the ratification of the Paris Agreement is one of the fastest MEAs. Article 17 of the Kyoto Protocol provided for reliance on emission trading schemes.

The Compliance Committee will be established to scrutinise environmental policy and law, investigate complaints and take enforcement action against public authorities, if necessary, to uphold environmental standards. The Rulebook confirms that the PACC's powers will cover all climate change legislation and hold governments to account on their respective commitments to reach emissions reductions by the target dates. According to the UNFCCC, this ambition will be supported by championing efficiency-based solutions, helping to demonstrate a commitment to tackle climate change.

---

23 Article 15, paragraphs 1 and 2, of the Paris Agreement. Further detail was included in decision 1/CP.21 paragraphs 102 and 103.
24 Daniel Bodansky, The Paris Climate Change Agreement: A New Hope? (2016) 110(2) *American Journal of International Law*, pp. 288–319. Daniel Bodansky and Jutta Brunnée, and Lavanya Rajamani, *Introduction to International Climate Change Law* (Oxford University Press 2017).
25 20/CMA.1 Modalities and procedures for the effective operation of the committee to facilitate implementation and promote compliance referred to in Article 15, paragraph 2, of the Paris Agreement, available at https://unfccc.int/sites/default/files/resource/CMA2018_03a02E.pdf, accessed 1 April 2020.

3 Measures on the reduction of greenhouse gas emissions with private sector involvement

Under the international climate change regime, three different systems were introduced to address the increase of GHG emissions and the problem of human-induced global warming: the clean development mechanism, the emission trading system and a reporting system.[26] By private sector in this specific case, we understand both the industry and the non-profit sector, represented by non-governmental organisations (NGOs).[27]

In the functioning of the climate change regime, the progressive use of market-based mechanisms is seen as another innovation to deal with compliance or prevent non-compliance. Market-based mechanisms had been introduced and relied upon in other areas of IEL, but notably they have been tapped into under the international climate change regime. The trading of emissions has been based on international climate change law. The use of market-based mechanisms in the system aims at improving the level of implementation to efficiently limit and reduce greenhouse gasses emissions. The system put into practice by the KP considered clean air as a commodity, making it one of the tradable commons. However, KP failed to remain attuned to changing situations as the fluctuations of the emission market did not contribute a great deal to the stability of the model.

Article 15 of the Paris Agreement does not regulate the new compliance mechanisms in detail but instead outlines in two sub-articles its configuration for the whole agreement. Details about the compliance mechanism are further elucidated in the Rulebook of the Paris Agreement, mainly drawn up in the Conference of the Parties (COP) 24, covering aspects such as mitigation, adaptation, loss and damage, indigenous people's platform and transparency, and the register of nationally determined contributions.[28]

The initial idea behind the cap-and-trade system was the allocation of pollution quotas amongst main emitters and the creation of a market for emissions rights. Clearly, a system as such cannot resolve the problem and requires a mechanism to guarantee compliance. In practice, the emerging market created on the basis of the allocation of emissions rights, leading to the sale of the unused credits (excess). The effectiveness of the system rests on market forces, and this caused some disruptions in practice due to the low price of carbon. The system heavily relies on the incentives; therefore, as in the case of the CO_2 European emission allowances price, the drop of the price of CO_2 decreased encouragement to comply with curbing the emissions.

26 D. Freestone and C. Streck, *Legal Aspects of Carbon trading* (Oxford University Press 2009).

27 Cathrin Zengerling, *Greening International Jurisprudence: Environmental NGOs before International Courts, Tribunals, and Compliance Committees* (Brill/Nijhoff 2013).

28 Katowice Rulebook, Adopted at the COP24 held in Katowice, Poland, available at https://cop24.gov.pl/news/news-details/news/the-katowice-rulebook-main-principles-of-the-document/ accessed 1 March 2020.

The reduction of greenhouse emissions in developing countries has taken different forms. Multiple initiatives in the agricultural sector have focussed on curbing emissions and dealing with the adaptation and mitigation challenges posed by climate change. Few solutions, however, have addressed the needs of producers and local communities. In Costa Rica, initiatives implemented in the coffee sector have emphasised the participation of small coffee producers and local communities.

Targeting specific GHGs (emissions of nitrous oxide, CO_2 and methane), initiatives like carbon neutral coffee or coffee nationally appropriate mitigation actions (NAMA) have been launched. This has led to emissions reductions concerning the use of fertilisers, increasing awareness about the release of gases into water and air. By creating a new labelling system, coffee producers have benefited from access to markets.

The advantages presented by other market-based mechanisms, such as ecological services, have also contributed to a new paradigm of re-distribution of benefits. The PA has introduced new legal bases for private sector involvement in ICCL by integrating specific provisions to channel non-governmental participation.

Against this background, from a conceptual standpoint social justice in the context of climate change should take into consideration the following aspects: transparency, including the participation of sectors involved; the achievement of the Sustainable Development Goals; and access to environmental information and environmental justice.

Market mechanisms prove to work well in conjunction with other ancillary provisions that complete the system adopted at the COPs.[29] These mechanism are rooted in the UNFCCC, which serves as the ground to build on the experience and improve mechanisms such as REDD-Plus, which has been updated on several occasions.

The ICCL system was based on the creation of market-based mechanisms, calling on States to set a limit, or cap, on greenhouse gas emissions, thereby introducing emissions rights. If States or private parties that have been allocated emissions rights reduce emissions below their cap, they can trade the equivalent excess in emissions rights (measured in tonnes of CO_2). On the other hand, States and companies that fall short of their target may acquire these rights on the market. Putting a tag on emissions can bring numerous benefits. At the same time, emissions trading raises some crucial issues, such as measurement (i.e. how to ensure that each unit equates a true one-tonne reduction). In addition, the system needs to guarantee that each unit is used only once through the adoption of clear rules and transparency.[30]

---

29 See, for instance, Green Climate Fund, Cancun Agreements (Decision1/CP.16); In decision 9/CP.19 the COP decided to establish the Lima REDD+ Information Hub on the REDD+ Web Platform as a means to publish information on the results of REDD+ activities and corresponding results-based payments and the Work Programme on Results-based Finance to Progress the Full Implementation of the Activities Referred to in Decision 1/CP.16, para. 70.

30 UNFCCC, What Are Market and Non-Market Mechanisms?, available at https://unfccc.int/topics/what-are-market-and-non-market-mechanisms accessed 1 March 2020.

PARIS AGREEMENT

2015

Article 2

1   This Agreement, in enhancing the implementation of the Convention, including its objective, aims to strengthen the global response to the threat of climate change, in the context of sustainable development and efforts to eradicate poverty, including by:

    a   Holding the increase in the global average temperature to well below 2°C above pre-industrial levels and pursuing efforts to limit the temperature increase to 1.5°C above pre-industrial levels, recognizing that this would significantly reduce the risks and impacts of climate change;

    b   Increasing the ability to adapt to the adverse impacts of climate change and foster climate resilience and low greenhouse gas emissions development, in a manner that does not threaten food production; and

    c   Making finance flows consistent with a pathway towards low greenhouse gas emissions and climate-resilient development.

2   This Agreement will be implemented to reflect equity and the principle of common but differentiated responsibilities and respective capabilities, in the light of different national circumstances.

Article 3

As nationally determined contributions to the global response to climate change, all Parties are to undertake and communicate ambitious efforts as defined in Articles 4, 7, 9, 10, 11 and 13 with the view to achieving the purpose of this Agreement as set out in Article 2. The efforts of all Parties will represent a progression over time, while recognizing the need to support developing for the effective implementation of this Agreement.

Article 4

1   In order to achieve the long-term temperature goal set out in Article 2, Parties aim to reach global peaking of greenhouse gas emissions as soon as possible, recognizing that peaking will take longer for developing country Parties, and to undertake rapid reductions thereafter in accordance with best available science, so as to achieve a balance between anthropogenic emissions by sources and removals by sinks of greenhouse gases in the second half of this century, on the basis of equity, and in the context of sustainable development and efforts to eradicate poverty.

(*Continued*)

Article 6

1   Parties recognize that some Parties choose to pursue voluntary cooperation in the implementation of their nationally determined contributions to allow for higher ambition in their mitigation and adaptation actions and to promote sustainable development and environmental integrity.

2   Parties shall, where engaging on a voluntary basis in cooperative approaches that involve the use of internationally transferred mitigation outcomes towards nationally determined contributions, promote sustainable development and ensure environmental integrity and transparency, including in governance, and shall apply robust accounting to ensure, inter alia, the avoidance of double counting, consistent with guidance adopted by the Conference of the Parties serving as the meeting of the Parties to this Agreement.

3   The use of internationally transferred mitigation outcomes to achieve nationally determined contributions under this Agreement shall be voluntary and authorized by participating Parties.

4   A mechanism to contribute to the mitigation of greenhouse gas emissions and support sustainable development is hereby established under the authority and guidance of the Conference of the Parties serving as the meeting of the Parties to this Agreement for use by Parties on a voluntary basis. It shall be supervised by a body designated by the Conference of the Parties serving as the meeting of the Parties to this Agreement, and shall aim:

   a   To promote the mitigation of greenhouse gas emissions while fostering sustainable development;

   b   To incentivize and facilitate participation in the mitigation of greenhouse gas emissions by public and private entities authorized by a Party;

   c   To contribute to the reduction of emission levels in the host Party, which will benefit from mitigation activities resulting in emission reductions that can also be used by another Party to fulfil its nationally determined contribution; and

   d   To deliver an overall mitigation in global emissions.

Article 7

1   Parties hereby establish the global goal on adaptation of enhancing adaptive capacity, strengthening resilience and reducing vulnerability to climate change, with a view to contributing to sustainable development and ensuring an adequate adaptation response in the context of the temperature goal referred to in Article 2.

2 Parties recognize that adaptation is a global challenge faced by all with local, subnational, national, regional and international dimensions, and that it is a key component of and makes a contribution to the long-term global response to climate change to protect people, livelihoods and ecosystems, taking into account the urgent and immediate needs of those developing country Parties that are particularly vulnerable to the adverse effects of climate change.

3 The adaptation efforts of developing country Parties shall be recognized, in accordance with the modalities to be adopted by the Conference of the Parties serving as the meeting of the Parties to this Agreement at its first session.

4 Parties recognize that the current need for adaptation is significant and that greater levels of mitigation can reduce the need for additional adaptation efforts, and that greater adaptation needs can involve greater adaptation costs.

5 Parties acknowledge that adaptation action should follow a country-driven, gender-responsive, participatory and fully transparent approach, taking into consideration vulnerable groups, communities and ecosystems, and should be based on and guided by the best available science and, as appropriate, traditional knowledge, knowledge of indigenous peoples and local knowledge systems, with a view to integrating adaptation into relevant socioeconomic and environmental policies and actions, where appropriate.

6 Parties recognize the importance of support for and international cooperation on adaptation efforts and the importance of taking into account the needs of developing country Parties, especially those that are particularly vulnerable to the adverse effects of climate change.

7 Parties should strengthen their cooperation on enhancing action on adaptation, taking into account the Cancun Adaptation Framework, including with regard to:

a Sharing information, good practices, experiences and lessons learned, including, as appropriate, as these relate to science, planning, policies and implementation in relation to adaptation actions;

b Strengthening institutional arrangements, including those under the Convention that serve this Agreement, to support the synthesis of relevant information and knowledge, and the provision of technical support and guidance to Parties;

c Strengthening scientific knowledge on climate, including research, systematic observation of the climate system and early warning systems, in a manner that informs climate services and supports decision-making;

(Continued)

  d Assisting developing country Parties in identifying effective adaptation practices, adaptation needs, priorities, support provided and received for adaptation actions and efforts, and challenges and gaps, in a manner consistent with encouraging good practices; and

  e Improving the effectiveness and durability of adaptation actions.

8 United Nations specialized organizations and agencies are encouraged to support the efforts of Parties to implement the actions referred to in paragraph 7 of this chapter, taking into account the provisions of paragraph 5 of this chapter.

9 Each Party shall, as appropriate, engage in adaptation planning processes and the implementation of actions, including the development or enhancement of relevant plans, policies and/or contributions, which may include:

  a The implementation of adaptation actions, undertakings and/or efforts;

  b The process to formulate and implement national adaptation plans;

  c The assessment of climate change impacts and vulnerability, with a view to formulating nationally determined prioritized actions, taking into account vulnerable people, places and ecosystems;

  d Monitoring and evaluating and learning from adaptation plans, policies, programmes and actions; and

  e Building the resilience of socioeconomic and ecological systems, including through economic diversification and sustainable management of natural resources.

10 Each Party should, as appropriate, submit and update periodically an adaptation communication, which may include its priorities, implementation and support needs, plans and actions, without creating any additional burden for developing country Parties.

11 The adaptation communication referred to in paragraph 10 of this chapter shall be, as appropriate, submitted and updated periodically, as a component of or in conjunction with other communications or documents, including a national adaptation plan, a nationally determined contribution as referred to in Article 4, paragraph 2, and/or a national communication.

12 The adaptation communications referred to in paragraph 10 of this chapter shall be recorded in a public registry maintained by the secretariat.

13 Continuous and enhanced international support shall be provided to developing country Parties for the implementation of paragraphs 7, 9, 10 and 11 of this chapter, in accordance with the provisions of Articles 9, 10 and 11.

14 The global stocktake referred to in Article 14 shall, inter alia:

    a   Recognize adaptation efforts of developing country Parties;

    b   Enhance the implementation of adaptation action taking into account the adaptation communication referred to in paragraph 10 of this chapter;

    c   Review the adequacy and effectiveness of adaptation and support provided for adaptation; and

    d   Review the overall progress made in achieving the global goal on adaptation referred to in paragraph 1 of this chapter.

Article 8

1 Parties recognize the importance of averting, minimizing and addressing loss and damage associated with the adverse effects of climate change, including extreme weather events and slow onset events, and the role of sustainable development in reducing the risk of loss and damage.

2 The Warsaw International Mechanism for Loss and Damage associated with Climate Change Impacts shall be subject to the authority and guidance of the Conference of the Parties serving as the meeting of the Parties to this Agreement and may be enhanced and strengthened, as determined by the Conference of the Parties serving as the meeting of the Parties to this Agreement.

3 Parties should enhance understanding, action and support, including through the Warsaw International Mechanism, as appropriate, on a cooperative and facilitative basis with respect to loss and damage associated with the adverse effects of climate change.

Article 9

1 Developed country Parties shall provide financial resources to assist developing country Parties with respect to both mitigation and adaptation in continuation of their existing obligations under the Convention.

2 Other Parties are encouraged to provide or continue to provide such support voluntarily.

3 As part of a global effort, developed country Parties should continue to take the lead in mobilizing climate finance from a wide variety of sources, instruments and channels, noting the significant role of public funds, through a variety of actions, including supporting country-driven strategies, and taking into account the needs and priorities of developing country Parties. Such mobilization of climate finance should represent a progression beyond previous efforts.

(*Continued*)

Article 14

1   The Conference of the Parties serving as the meeting of the Parties to this Agreement shall periodically take stock of the implementation of this Agreement to assess the collective progress towards achieving the purpose of this Agreement and its long-term goals (referred to as the "global stocktake"). It shall do so in a comprehensive and facilitative manner, considering mitigation, adaptation and the means of implementation and support, and in the light of equity and the best available science.

2   The Conference of the Parties serving as the meeting of the Parties to this Agreement shall undertake its first global stocktake in 2023 and every five years thereafter unless otherwise decided by the Conference of the Parties serving as the meeting of the Parties to this Agreement.

3   The outcome of the global stocktake shall inform Parties in updating and enhancing, in a nationally determined manner, their actions and support in accordance with the relevant provisions of this Agreement, as well as in enhancing international cooperation for climate action.

Article 15

1   A mechanism to facilitate implementation of and promote compliance with the provisions of this Agreement is hereby established.

2   The mechanism referred to in paragraph 1 of this chapter shall consist of a committee that shall be expert-based and facilitative in nature and function in a manner that is transparent, non-adversarial and non-punitive. The committee shall pay particular attention to the respective national capabilities and circumstances of Parties.

3   The committee shall operate under the modalities and procedures adopted by the Conference of the Parties serving as the meeting of the Parties to this Agreement at its first session and report annually to the Conference of the Parties serving as the meeting of the Parties to this Agreement.

Source: https://unfccc.int/process-and-meetings/
the-paris-agreement/the-paris-agreement

4 The emerging 'climate change litigation' before national courts and international tribunals: effective de-centralising compliance control?

Due to the complexities and interdisciplinary nature of the international climate change legal framework, its effects on domestic legal systems are considerable. National courts are faced with manifold questions, such as determining causation of environmental harm originating in climate change and adopting appropriate reparations. In the absence of a comprehensive international legal framework for climate change litigation (CCL), the legal scenario is fragmented as it comprises a wide range of international and domestic law provisions.

This is closely linked to access to environmental justice, featuring claims regarding companies' liability and state responsibility for climate change proposing alternative compliance methods and alternative means of achieving compliance.

Notably, the implementation of obligations under the climate change regime within the national sphere constitutes a legal conundrum and involves different government levels. Non-compliance with the norms of the international climate legal system (broadly defined) has led to emerging litigation in several developing countries. This inobservance may be directly related to the cap on CO_2 emissions or may consist of difficulties arising out of the implementation of specific provisions (such as the production of diesel cars), the prevention of a potential environmental harm or the reparation of actual environmental damage.

Interestingly, complaints are submitted in the event of natural disasters or the threat of environmental harm. At this point, it is also worth noticing that there are a strain of cases in which the protection of human rights granted in national constitutions and international human rights treaties is invoked as the main cause of action.[31] Remarkably, the protection of the right to life and the right to a healthy environment are frequently argued to be the foundation of the claims. CCL does not operate in a vacuum, and, therefore, the interplay with other areas of international law is not infrequent.

At the outset, an important distinction relates to the difference between climate change litigation and climate justice. This distinction is not minor, particularly in the developing world. Whereas climate change litigation encompasses all the different procedural avenues to address climate change-related environmental damage, climate justice refers to the outcome of the process, i.e. to achieve a fair outcome.

This type of litigation raises questions for the current debate and the future development of climate change law as a discipline. In this spirit, the emergence of a transnational climate change legal regime from a bottom-up approach, includes climate change litigation cases across various regions and countries.

The UNFCCC has given rise to a complex legal system (with the Kyoto Protocol and the Paris Agreement as the central legal instruments) that must, in turn, be incorporated into national legal orders.[32] In addition, the body of decisions emanating from the COPs also have (direct or indirect effect) on domestic law.[33]

---

31 Atieno Mboya, 'Human Rights and the Global Climate Change Regime' (2018) 58 *Natural Resources Journal*, pp. 51–74.

32 The Kyoto Protocol was adopted in Kyoto, Japan, on 11 December 1997 and entered into force on 16 February 2005. This international legal framework includes other relevant international agreements, such as the 1987 Montreal Protocol on Substances that Deplete the Ozone Layer.

33 During COP22, held in 2016 in Marrakech, further modifications were introduced to the current legal framework in order to implement the Paris Agreement, such as the adoption of the Partnership for Global Climate Action.

Climate change litigation has resulted in a new legal scenario in which the national judge is called to adjudicate complex cases involving the application of specific international law or international law-driven provisions, sometimes being faced with a legal lacuna or loophole. The resilience of the national legal systems (as regards their domestic environmental law) to provide an adequate response is tested. To make matters even more complex, common law and civil law systems operating in national spheres respond differently to the legal challenges posed by climate change. Even if legal scholars have tried to bridge them, taking a comparative law perspective to find a solution, one must remain cautious and bear in mind the differences between both systems. To illustrate, in common law jurisdiction, if a court finds that specific emissions by a company are contributing to climate change, under tort law, the court is called to determine whether the company has a duty of care to the claimant, grounding its analysis in previous case law. Civil law systems are statutory and rely on a compilation of legal provisions (civil or agrarian codes), which often precludes the possibility of going beyond the textual interpretation of the law.

CCL brings several challenges to national law and justice that mainly concern the sources of law and the role of the judges when resolving climate change-related disputes. One of the main challenges regarding CCL is that the frame for analysing climate change claims consists of an emerging and relatively new legal subject. Prior to scrutinising those challenges, it is useful to refer to the foundation of CCL and to the concept of climate justice, and to then address the specific features of climate change law and the current legal landscape of CCL.

For the purposes of this chapter, climate change litigation is understood as any legal action (rooted in public, human rights or criminal law) which is brought before the courts or quasi-judicial bodies (such as governmental Commissions) concerning the effects of climate change. Although the definition may seem clear, it is quite complex to demarcate what constitutes climate change litigation as there are several implications, and it is difficult to trace the various actions (personal choices, commercial and industrial activities) that cumulatively result in climate change. Ultimately, every single action has a carbon footprint. In order to circumscribe the scope of the analysis, CCL is understood as covering only disputes in which climate change argument is unambiguously included as part of the claimant's or defendant's case.

Climate justice stems from environmental justice, a term coined in sociology by Bullard, encompassing several principles which guarantee to 'be based on mutual respect and justice for all peoples, free from any form of discrimination or bias'.[34] Notably, the inequality dimension constitutes an essential element of it.

34 Robert D. Bullard, 'Environmental Justice for All', Environmental Justice: An Interview with Robert Bullard Earth First! Journal, July 1999, http://www.ejnet.org/ej/bullard.html See also, First National People of Color Environmental Leadership Summit held on October 24–27, 1991, in Environmental Justice Principles, available at http://www.ejnet.org/ej/principles.pdf accessed 1 April 2020.

In turn, climate justice is defined by reference to human rights as access to justice to

> safeguarding the rights of the most vulnerable people and sharing the burdens and benefits of climate change and its impacts equitably and fairly. Climate justice is informed by science, responds to science and acknowledges the need for equitable stewardship of the world's resources.[35]

Hence, the protection of human rights underpins the notion of climate justice through the various principles deemed the tenets. According to the Mary Robinson Foundation, a series of principles/obligations should be observed by states. These are, namely, to: respect and protect human rights; support the right to development; share benefits and burdens equitably; ensure that decisions on climate change are participatory, transparent and accountable; highlight gender equality and equity; harness the transformative power of education for climate stewardship; and use effective partnerships to secure climate justice.[36]

This distinctive stance was observed in COP 21, where the environmental justice movement called for the adoption of a 'Mother Earth approach'. A shift in the conception of climate justice under the Paris Agreement (PA) can be observed as the preamble notes

> the importance of ensuring the integrity of all ecosystems, including oceans, and the protection of biodiversity, recognized by some cultures as Mother Earth, and noting the importance for some of the concept of "climate justice", when taking action to address climate change.[37]

Equally, the PA acknowledges vulnerabilities in facing climate change and sticks to the principle of common but differentiated responsibilities, which is related to equity in sharing the burden of negative climate effects.

Commitments arising from the Paris Agreement have been deemed by some scholars to be flexible in-between the political and legal spheres.[38] As regards the terms and the legal components of the agreement, much of its content is difficult to fit into the frame of hard law in light of the Vienna Convention on the Law of the Treaties (VCLT). Whereas many provisions in the text do not create any binding obligations, others create a cascade of treaty obligations. The PA presents a combination of hard- and soft-law norms. For instance, a 'hard-law approach' is

35 Mary Robinson Foundation, Climate Justice Principles, available at http://www.mrfcj.org/wp-content/uploads/2015/09/Principles-of-Climate-Justice.pdf accessed 1 April 2020.

36 Ibid.

37 Reportedly, the origin of the inclusion of climate justice and mother earth in the PA responds to a request by ALBA countries in charge of drafting the preamble.

38 Anne-Marie Slaughter, 'The Paris Approach to Global Governance', Project Syndicate, 28 December 2015, available at https://scholar.princeton.edu/sites/default/files/slaughter/files/projectsyndicate12.28.2015.pdf accessed 1 April 2020.

taken in art 2, which states the objective of limiting emissions; art 1 reflects the commitment to achieve a balance between anthropogenic emissions; and other key obligations are found in art 4. In turn, NDCs imposing specific emissions-reduction commitments are binding upon all the states. However, when it comes to NDCs, particularly of developing states, the language is not equivalent to duties. It conveys the idea of progressive improvement and not backsliding, rather than strongly emphasising states' obligations. For developed countries the duty is more specific with emissions targets, as established in art 14. In terms of finance and the obligation to provide financial resources for mitigation and adaptation as a primary obligation, the language is of duty. The accompanying decision is more specific. Adaptation is formulated in more pre-emptive terms in art 7. The language of duties is also present in the provisions governing transparency, with the aim of creating an enhanced transparency framework. In sum, the PA laid the groundwork for the development of a robust and comprehensive accountability framework, a unique compromise in which international obligations may progress.

As already indicated, the climate change regime intersects with other regimes, and much attention has been devoted to the interplay with international human rights law.[39] Interaction with other regulatory regimes that complement climate change law should not be overlooked, though. By way of illustration, the International Law Commission (ILC)'s work on international liability for injurious consequences arising out of acts not prohibited by international law contributes the legal principles of due diligence and strict liability as the standards to be applied to adjudicate the CCL cases.[40]

In an alternative (and, sometimes, complementary) view of climate justice, the term 'climate fairness' has been proposed. Climate fairness comprises substantive and procedural strands, and is rooted in IEL principles: sustainable development, access rights and intra and inter-generational equity. It reflects the idea of 'common but differentiated responsibilities' and emphasises the fact that all states must contribute to emissions reduction.[41]

As regards the characteristics of climate change litigation (CCL), complex jurisdictional issues arise from the nature of climate change, understood as a global, trans-boundary environmental crisis.[42]

---

39 Office of the United Nations High Commissioner for Human Rights, *Report on the relationship between climate change and human rights* (A/HRC/10/61).

40 United Nations, A/CN.4/471 Survey on liability regimes relevant to the topic International liability for injurious consequences arising out of acts not prohibited by international law: Study prepared by the Secretariat, 1995, vol. II(1), available at https://legal.un.org/ilc/documentation/english/a_cn4_471.pdf accessed 1 March 2020.

41 Jorge E. Viñuales, 'Balancing Effectiveness and Fairness in the Redesign of the Climate Change Regime' (2011) 24(1) *Leiden Journal of International Law*, pp. 223, 251–252.

42 Climate change litigation, tort law approaches from a common law perspective. Climate Change: A New Realm of Tort Litigation, and How to Recover When the Litigation Heats Up, Santa Clara Law Review, Vol. 51, Issue 1 (2011), pp. 265–229, 251 *Santa Clara Law Review* 265 (2011). Daniel A. Farber, 'Apportioning Climate Change Costs' (2008) 26(1) *UCLA Journal of Environmental Law and Policy*, pp. 21–54.

As regards the jurisdictional issues that arise, these concern the claimants, the defendants/those responsible for the damages and the main aim and the content of the claims.

First, the claimants cover the affected individuals and groups in both developed and developing countries. In developing states, the claimants are likely to be the most vulnerable people: those with no or fewer prior contributions to global greenhouse gas emissions. In terms of CCL, the main question regards legal standing to lodge climate change-related claims. Affected individuals and groups may bring climate change-related claims to different legal sectors (administrative/public, criminal, civil and human rights law). Legal standing is determined by each set of applicable norms. Non-governmental organisations are also at the forefront of CCL. The case of *Urgenda* sets an interesting precedent in this regard as it deals with the legal standing of environmental groups to question the fulfilment of the state's obligations.[43] The admissibility of the petitions depends on the specific context and the norms applicable to the case.

Second, in terms of the defendants/those responsible for the damages, the most contentious issue is the accountability of private persons. Even though in international law States are responsible for curbing greenhouse gas emissions, companies are involved in most pollutant activities. The jurisdictional question at issue concerns the possibility for the judges of those nation-states to exercise extra-territorial jurisdiction over private defendants such as multinational companies, particularly if their main headquarters or seat of business is located in a country outside the court's jurisdiction. The UN's Guiding Principles on Business and Human Rights currently represents the main legal instrument calling on companies to respect human rights and engage in environmental protection.[44] The Principles apply to all of the activities of the corporations, covering the impacts of business throughout different operations, wherever they take place.[45]

The case of *Greenpeace Southeast Asia* unveils the complexities of CCL as it involves various companies coming before the Supreme Court of the Philippines. The contentious issue regarded the Commission's jurisdiction over the respondents, which were active in different countries. In fairness, the responsibility of businesses to respect human rights should be made effective, in particular when they carry out activities with far-reaching implications beyond the seat of business or when they breach, cause or are involved directly or indirectly in activities that infringe upon human rights and cause environmental harm.

---

43 Roger Cox, *A Climate Change Litigation Precedent Urgenda Foundation v the State of The Netherlands*, CIGI Papers N 79 – November 2015, available at https://www.cigionline.org/sites/default/files/cigi_paper_79.pdf.

44 United Nations Human Rights Council, Resolution Adopted by the Human Rights Council: 17/4 Human Rights and Transnational Corporations and Other Business Enterprises, Seventeenth Session, July 06.

45 United Nations, Guiding Principles at 2, principles 11–12 at 13–14.

As regards the content of the different claims, CCL has taken place in a variety of areas of law deeply connected to climate change (CC). In fact, the subject matter of the litigation is diverse: there are claims arising in public/administrative law, civil law, criminal law and human rights. Another controversial aspect is the possibility of submitting cross-boundary claims from affected individuals or groups who have allegedly suffered environmental damages as a result of the operations of multi-national corporations.[46] The United Kingdom's jurisdiction offers an interesting case in this regard: in *Bodo Community & Ors v Shell Development Company of Nigeria*, the UK Supreme Court confirmed its jurisdiction over a Nigerian subsidiary of a UK domiciled parent.[47] In another case, the High Court exercised jurisdiction over Vedanta Resources, a company with its main seat of business in London, concerning a claim brought by Zambian applicants affected by its subsidiary's copper mining operations.[48]

Clearly, the emerging CCL has brought major jurisdictional challenges as the claims span from complaints against governments to those involving multinational corporations. Challenges posed by climate change litigation are related to its multilevel nature at the subnational, national and transnational levels. Climate justice attempts to meet those challenges.

From a theoretical standpoint, there is the question of the scope of climate justice: whether it is understood along the lines of a narrower idea of justice as representing just legal obligations or embodies climate justice in the widest possible sense that fulfils legitimate expectations aiming at a fair outcome.

Compliance with CC law takes place at different levels. Administrative decisions in accordance with the UNFCCC regime must be adopted by each contracting party. In terms of checks and balances, the responsibility to implement the commitments falls upon the executive, not the courts. Whilst States have taken up the obligation to inform about progress in this regard, the attainment of national commitments needs to be supported by courts. It is their responsibility to monitor the government's response in light of the Principles of environmental law. Accordingly, courts must ensure compliance by interpreting the law.

Drawing on existing case law, there are different aspects that have particular significance in CCL. As observed in both developing and developed states, no serious challenges are posed to the scientific consensus on CC. Judges must solve the cases according to evidence provided by the IPCC and resolve the cases by weighing the evidence as in *Massachusetts v EPA*, decided by the US Supreme Court under the Clean Air Act.[49] In the face of unchallenged evidence that global warming causes severe environmental damages, the Supreme Court upheld the EPA's powers to regulate on emissions reduction. The arguments

---

46 Environmental Law Alliance Worldwide, *Holding Corporations Accountable for Damaging the Climate* (2014).

47 *Bodo Community v Shell Petroleum Development Co of Nigeria Ltd* [2014] EWHC 1973 (TCC).

48 *Lungowe v Vedanta* [2016] EWHC 975 (TCC).

49 U.S. Supreme Court, *Massachusetts v. Environmental Protection Agency*, 549 U.S. 497 (2007).

brought up the issues of causation and reversibility of climate change to finally uphold the responsibility of the EPA under the Clean Air Act.

Another issue concerns CCL remedies that courts are granting and the suitability of the court in dealing with CCL. Ultimately, this will (up to a certain extent) depend on the approach to international law (dualist or monist systems). A difference may also be appreciated between the major and minor courts (hierarchy), and the role of the court. Sands has clearly underlined the role of international courts in nurturing these roots in domestic law when addressing the issue of the rule of law and CCL.[50]

Various Principles that are at the heart of environmental litigation are revealed to be crucial for CCL, such as the Roman law Principle of *res communis*, applicable to international environmental litigation. The ideas of environmental trusteeship and enforceable norms reverberate in expressions contained in different rulings. For instance, in the *Dam Case* before the International Court of Justice, Judge Weeramantry delineated the contours of the obligations as follows:

> We have entered an era of international law in which international law serves not only the interests of individual States, but looks beyond them and their parochial concerns to the greater interests of humanity and planetary welfare ... When we enter the arena of obligations which operate erga omnes rather than inter partes, rules based on individual fairness and procedural compliance may be inadequate ... International environmental law will need to proceed beyond weighing the rights and obligations of parties within a closed compartment of individual State self-interest, unrelated to the global concerns of humanity as a whole.[51]

Among the various climate change cases, the case of *Urgenda* represents that which is most directly related to climate change. In addition, there are other cases in which climate change is mentioned as the main cause of environmental damage.[52] Interestingly, courts in developing countries have started adjudicating climate change claims, invoking the protection of human rights. In order to uphold human rights in the context of climate change, the Supreme Court of the Philippines referred to basic rights that pre-date any constitutional rights.[53] South Asian courts have referred to the right to live in a healthy environment. In a case concerning air pollution in Delhi as long ago as 1990, the Indian Supreme Court articulated environmental protection around the safeguarding of

---

50 Philippe Sands, 'Climate Change and the Rule of Law: Adjudicating the Future in International Law' (2016) 28(1) *Journal of Environmental Law*, p. 19.

51 International Court of Justice, *Gabcikovo-Nagymaros Project (Hungary v Slovakia)*, Judgment, 1. C. J. Reports 1997, para. 118.

52 *Urgenda decision* (Urgenda Foundation v the State of the Netherlands, C/09/456689/HA ZA 13-1396, Judgment of 24 June 2015). This decision has been appealed by the government.

53 Supreme Court (Philippines), *Case International Service for the Acquisition of Agri-Biotech Applications (SAAA), Inc. v. Greenpeace Southeast Asia I-SEA*.

fundamental rights. China is an interesting example of how compliance by the executive is complemented by the actions of the courts. Environmental resources adjudication tribunals have upheld jurisdiction over natural resources, emissions reductions in climate change and emissions and energy cases.[54] Pakistan and Bangladesh have taken similar approaches.

Perhaps the best example comes from the High Court of Lahore in the case brought by Mr Leghari, a farmer who questioned climate change effects and climate change policies, and in which the judges agreed that nothing had been done on the ground.[55] It was decided that the court should take a direct interest in supervising. The court ordered the establishment of a CC commission. Although there was a national climate change policy and a detailed adaptation and mitigation programme, the court observed a lack of effective implementation. The claimant was representing the main interests.

Courts have the judicial review powers necessary to monitor these decisions, focussing and drawing on previous groundwork in environmental case law concerning water, marine areas and energy. In other words, courts need to adapt legal Principles to address the challenges domestically, which requires the cooperation of all the relevant parties.

In a broader approach to CCL and looking outside the domestic jurisdiction, it is also interesting to see how the previous experiences feed back into other common law jurisdictions, suspending injunctions by courts. Also, other trends make it possible to postulate that arbitration could constitute a viable legal avenue for CCL. For instance, the IBA's report signposted arbitration amongst the various possible procedural channels to achieve climate justice.[56]

Some focal points of interest stemming from the practice of domestic tribunals can be identified:

-   *Legal standing:* A broad legal standing in CCL remains controversial in the present context. Proponents have been given a boost more recently in the case of *Juliana v Oregon*, which came before the US district court with a claim promoted by Earth Guardians.[57] Claimants challenged the federal government with regard to the reduction of emissions. Amongst other arguments, claimants alluded to the right to a climate system and to the public trust doctrine. The government's argument of lack of standing was initially rejected.
-   *Evidence and procedure:* Courts and judges face the challenge of understanding and relying on climate science, but the lack of full scientific certainty should not be an obstacle for claimants. In this regard, the precautionary

54 There are 5,000 around the country.
55 *Ashgar Leghari v. Federation of Pakistan*, Lahore High Court, Pakistan, 4 September 2015 Case No: W.P. No. 25501/2015.
56 International Bar Association (IBA), *Achieving Justice and Human Rights in an Era of Climate Justice* (2014).
57 District Court for the District of Oregon, *Juliana v. U.S.* (2015). For an update on the current situation see https://www.ourchildrenstrust.org/us/federal-lawsuit/.

Principle may constitute a helpful tool. It may provide assistance to judges in order to examine petitions when serious environmental risks are posed by climate change, even if the harm is uncertain, as has been established in some comparative law cases.[58] The key question is whether the scientific evidence could be conclusive to demonstrate that certain human activities are rapidly impacting on climate events, as observed in previous and pending cases which may have significant implications for climate change litigation.[59]

- *Causation:* Closely related to the previous jurisdictional question, there is the necessary link between the lack of compliance and the harmful activities. In *Urgenda* the judges asserted human-generated climate change as beyond dispute, requesting that the Dutch government strengthen its plans to cut emissions. In the case of climate change, a court may need to assert that the defendant has contributed to the harm in a manner that can be traced back and be quantifiable with reasonable certainty. This is often referred to as the causation hurdle.

- *Remedies:* Claimants affected by climate change may seek remedies that they consider appropriate to protect not only their lives and rights but also their livelihoods and their specific ecosystem.[60] Climate change victims may request a range of remedies from the courts, including declaratory orders, compensatory damages or injunctions. The relief courts may grant depends on the particular circumstances of the case and the norms applicable. In some cases, petitioners may want to request a mitigation action to reduce climate change-related harmful activities, as in the case of heavily pollutant sectors, especially those concerned with the extraction and use of fossil fuels, the main source of greenhouse gas emissions. Another possible measure that may be sought may consist in achieving greater transparency on the part of companies to disclose more information about their activities, enabling a more consistent monitoring of compliance with national and international climate, environmental and human rights laws.

A particularly controversial aspect of climate change litigation relates to the division of powers between the different branches of the government and the system of checks and balances. Essentially, the judiciary must be careful when exercising decision-making powers in climate change issues, bearing in mind that judges are not supposed to intervene in policymaking. In the United States this was precisely the main defendants' argument in climate change litigation. In some cases, some defendants have successfully argued that climate change litigation

---

58 Supreme Court of the Philippines, *Case International Service for the Acquisition of Agri-Biotech Applications (SAAA), Inc. v. Greenpeace Southeast AsiaI-SEA (Philippines)*.

59 James Thornton and Howard Covington, 'Climate Change before the Court', Carbon Brief, available at https://www.carbonbrief.org/guest-post-climate-change-before-the-court.

60 There is an interesting debate regarding the anthropocentric approach to climate change and the granting of specific protection for nature or ecosystems in themselves. Unfortunately, space precludes the possibility of discussing these issues in depth.

raises non-justiciable political questions.[61] In contrast, in a case recently decided in the US a federal judge took a different view, acknowledging that the complexity of climate change litigation should not impede the submission of claims, particularly in those cases where fundamental rights are at stake.[62]

JUDGMENT OF THE COURT (SIXTH CHAMBER) OF 8 SEPTEMBER 2016

E.ON Kraftwerke GmbH v Bundesrepublik Deutschland

Request for a preliminary ruling from the Verwaltungsgericht Berlin

Reference for a preliminary ruling — Environment — Greenhouse gas emission allowance trading scheme within the European Union — Directive 2003/87/EC — Harmonised free allocation of emission allowances — Decision 2011/278/EU — Change to the allocation — Article 24(1) — Obligation of the operator of the installation to provide information — Scope

Case C-461/15

(...)

34 In the system of allocation of emission allowances, the Member States, as noted in paragraph 26 above, are to calculate for each year, on the basis of the information collected pursuant to Article 7 of Decision 2011/278, the number of emission allowances allocated free of charge to each incumbent installation on their territory. It is therefore for the competent authorities of the Member States alone to assess, on the basis of the information collected from the operators, whether that information is such as to have an impact on the determination of the number of allowances allocated.

35 Moreover, neither from Directive 2003/87, in particular Article 7, nor from Decision 2011/278 does it appear that the EU legislature intended to allow operators to choose the information they have to submit pursuant to those provisions according to the impact it is thought to have on the allocation of emission allowances.

36 It may be seen from the provisions of Article 24 of that decision that they aim to take account of changes to the operation of installations, in order for the Member States, in a first stage, to determine the number of emission allowances allocated free of charge to each incumbent installation on their territory and for the Commission, in a second stage, to

---

61 *American Electric Power Co, Inc., et al v Connecticut*, 206 F Supp 2d 265 (SDNY, 2005). It must be noted, however, that the argument was upheld by the District Court of New York but was not the main ground for the rejection of the petitioner's claims.

62 *Kelsey Cascadia Rose Juliana, et al v the United States of America*, No. 6:15-cv-01517-TC, 8 April 2016.

determine the final total annual amount of emission allowances allocated free of charge.

37 In that context, as recalled in paragraph 27 above, the Member States must ensure that the data collected from the operators and used for allocation purposes is complete and consistent and presents the highest achievable accuracy. It is therefore for the Member States to determine themselves what relevant information for the competent authorities must be collected from the operators.

(...)

40 In the light of the above considerations, the answer to the questions referred for a preliminary ruling is that Article 24(1) of Decision 2011/278 must be interpreted as not precluding a Member State from requiring undertakings which, being subject to the greenhouse gas emission allowance trading obligation within the EU, receive a free allocation of those allowances to provide information relating to all planned or effective changes to the capacity, activity level and operation of an installation, without limiting that requirement solely to information relating to changes that would affect the allocation.

Source: https://eur-lex.europa.eu/legal-content/EN/
TXT/?uri=CELEX%3A62015CJ0461

5 The future of compliance with international climate change law: the way forward

Gaps in compliance with the ICCL and the lack of effectiveness of norms have been made evident. Although compliance mechanisms established by the treaties represent progress they are not sufficient to ensure compliance with duties laid down in different ICCL instruments. In light of the evidence of monitoring, there are several gaps in the implementation of the norms, such as specific implementation rules.

The supplementary Bangkok Climate Change talks made uneven progress on the guidelines that will help States to implement the Paris Climate Change Agreement. Implementation guidelines are necessary to adopt transparent and practical climate action worldwide. By having a look at compliance records, independent monitoring for compliance and an enforcement mechanism for non-compliance are key to ensuring an effective implementation of ICCL. The past decade for ICCL showed a transition into a new model, designed to address challenges imposed by the system faced with several compliance pressures. The Kyoto Compliance Committee took a pragmatic approach by carrying out initial compliance reports as a way to deal with non-compliance and led to the adoption of measures to remedy this.

Decisions adopted address compliance and strive to go beyond regulatory compliance, pushing beyond mere regulatory compliance by offering economic incentives exceeding mere regulatory compliance, thereby attaining a higher degree of effectiveness. Compliance with ICCL, monitored through the Committees and the Secretariat has given rise to a continuous international practice subject to volatile negotiations under the COP. Commitments under the Paris Agreement related to environmental protection and compliance with limits or requirements to curbing the emissions fall within the monitoring powers of the Committee. Some lessons can be learned from the Kyoto Protocol period as it acted as the prelude or preparation for the PA. In this regard, the main aspect on compliance related to less-differentiated obligation on States and the identification of the factors to be relied upon to secure compliance with ICCL.

The conceptual underpinnings and recent developments in climate change litigation indicate the emergence of a de-centralised conflict resolution system which brings several challenges to environmental and climate justice.

The different meanings of compliance and multiple ways and mechanisms of enhancing the fulfilment of obligations under IEL have become evident under the PA. The effectiveness of the PA system is linked to the compliance period and commitments set out in the different instruments. Private sector involvement should also be factored in. A variety of practices may lead to diverging compliance costs across the private sector. Finally, the Paris Agreement poses new questions concerning compliance. It also provides a new framework to analyse national compliance with international environmental treaties. Despite growing pains experienced by the system as a whole, as previously noted, ICCL system represents a case of success to guarantee continuity of compliance.

ENFORCEMENT BRANCH OF THE COMPLIANCE COMMITTEE

CC-2007-1-13/Greece/EB

13 November 2008

Decision under Paragraph 2 of Section X

Party concerned: Greece

In accordance with the Procedures and mechanisms relating to compliance contained in the annex to decision 27/CMP.1 and adopted under Article 18 of the Kyoto Protocol and pursuant to the Rules of procedure of the Compliance Committee, the enforcement branch adopts the following decision:

BACKGROUND

1   On 17 April 2008, the enforcement branch adopted the final decision (document CC-2007-1-8/Greece/EB) that gave effect to the consequences contained in paragraph 18 of the preliminary finding of the branch as confirmed by and annexed to the final decision.

According to subparagraph (c) of this paragraph, Greece is not eligible to participate in the mechanisms under Articles 6, 12 and 17 of the Protocol pending the resolution of the question of implementation.

2   On 7 October 2008, the enforcement branch adopted a decision on the review and assessment of the plan submitted by Greece under paragraph 2 of section XV2 (documentCC-2007-1-9/Greece/EB) and requested Greece to submit, as early as possible, a revised plan (document CC-2007-1-10/Greece/EB).

3   Following an in-country review, the annual review report entitled "Report of the individual review of the greenhouse gas inventories of Greece submitted in 2007 and 2008 was published on 17 October 2008 (document FCCC/ARR/2008/GRC; hereinafter referred to as review report).

4   On 20 October 2008, the secretariat forwarded the review report to the Compliance Committee, including the members and alternate members of the enforcement branch, in accordance with paragraph 3 of section VI.

5   On 27 October 2008, Greece submitted a revised plan under paragraph 2 of section XV in response to the request of the enforcement branch referred to in paragraph 2 above (document CC-2007-1-11/ Greece/EB).

(…)

REASONS AND CONCLUSIONS

7   The expert review team (ERT) concluded that the national system of Greece is performing its required functions, as set out in the annex to decision 19/CMP.1. The ERT further concluded that the institutional, legal and procedural arrangements of the new national system are fully operational, and that Greece has the capacity, including relevant arrangements for the technical competence of staff within the national system, to plan, prepare and manage inventories and their timely submission to the secretariat. During the review, no questions of implementation were identified by the ERT.

8   The review report also confirmed that the ERT had in-depth discussion on all aspects of the national system with the relevant staff, and that the transfer of information and data from the institution with previous technical responsibility for the inventory preparation to the new team has been completed.

Source: https://unfccc.int/files/kyoto_protocol/
compliance/enforcement_branch/application/pdf/
cc-2007-1-13_greece_eb.pdf

Bibliography

Atieno, Mboya, 'Human Rights and the Global Climate Change Regime' (2018) 58(1) *Natural Resources Journal*, pp. 51–74. Accessed May 10, 2020, available at www.jstor.org/stable/26394775 accessed 1 April 2020.

Bodansky, D, Brunnée, J, and Rajamani, L, *International Climate Change Law* (Oxford University Press 2016), pp. 40–43.

Bodansky, D, The Paris Climate Change Agreement: A New Hope? (2016) 110(2) *American Journal of International Law*, pp. 288–319.

Bullard, RD, 'Environmental Justice for All', Environmental Justice: An Interview with Robert Bullard Earth First! Journal, July 1999, http://www.ejnet.org/ej/bullard.html See also, First National People of Color Environmental Leadership Summit held on October 24–27, 1991, in Environmental Justice Principles, available at http://www.ejnet.org/ej/principles.pdf accessed 1 April 2020.

Cox, R, *A Climate Change Litigation Precedent Urgenda Foundation v the State of The Netherlands*, CIGI Papers N 79 – November 2015, available at https://www.cigionline.org/sites/default/files/cigi_paper_79.pdf accessed 1 April 2020.

Dagnet, Yamide, Cogswell, Nathan, Northrop, Eliza, Thwaites, Joe, Elliott, Cynthia, Levin, Kelly, Höhne, Niklas, Bird, Neil, Kirbyshire, Amy, Oberthür, Sebastian, Rocha, Marcelo, and Barata, Pedro, *Setting the Paris Agreement in Motion: Key Requirements for the Implementing Guidelines* (World Resources Institute August 2018), available at https://www.wri.org/publication/pact-implementing-guidelines accessed 1 April 2020.

Depledge, J, *Tracing the Origins of the Kyoto Protocol: An Article-By-Article Textual History*, Technical paper FCCC/TP/2000/2, UNFCCC (2000), available at https://unfccc.int/resource/docs/tp/tp0200.pdf accessed 1 March 2020.

Freestone, D, and Streck, C, *Legal Aspects of Carbon Trading* (Oxford University Press 2009).

Freestone, D, 'The United Nations Framework Convention on Climate Change – The Basis for the Climate Change Regime', in Cinnamon Piñon Carlarne, Kevin R. Gray, and Richard Tarasofsky (eds), *The Oxford Handbook of International Climate Change Law* (Oxford University Press 2016), pp. 97–119.

Green, B, 'Lessons from the Montreal Protocol: Guidance for the Next International Climate Change Agreement' (2009) 39(1) *Lewis & Clark Environmental Law Review*, pp. 253–283.

Huggins, A, *Multilateral Environmental Agreements and Compliance: The Benefits of Administrative Procedures* (Routledge 2018).

IISD, *Paris Agreement Implementation Guidelines: How Do We Get There?* (IISD 2018), available at http://sdg.iisd.org/commentary/policy-briefs/paris-agreement-implementation-guidelines-how-do-we-get-there/ accessed 1 April 2020.

International Bar Association (IBA), *Achieving Justice and Human Rights in an Era of Climate Justice* (2014), available at https://www.ibanet.org/PresidentialTaskForceClimateChangeJustice2014Report.aspx accessed 1 April 2020.

International Court of Justice, *Gabcikovo-Nagymaros Project (Hungary v Slovakia)*, Judgment, 1. C. J. Reports 1997.

IPCC, Appendix A to the Principles Governing IPCC Work, Procedures for The Preparation, Review, Acceptance, Adoption, Approval and Publication of IPCC Reports. Adopted at the Fifteenth Session (San Jose, 15–18 April 1999) amended at the Twentieth Session. (Paris, 19–21 February 2003), Twenty-first Session (Vienna, 3 and 6–7 November 2003), and Twenty-Ninth Session (Geneva, 31 August – 4 September 2008).

Kyoto Protocol Compliance Committee, An Introduction to the Kyoto Protocol Compliance Mechanism, available at https://unfccc.int/process/the-kyoto-protocol/compliance-under-the-kyoto-protocol/introduction accessed 1 April 2020.

Kyoto Protocol Compliance Committee, Facilitative Branch, available at https://cop23.unfccc.int/process/bodies/constituted-bodies/compliance-committee-cc/facilitative-branch accessed 1 April 2020.

Kyoto Protocol Compliance Committee, Facilitative Branch, available at https://unfccc.int/compliance-committee-bodies-page accessed 1 April 2020.

Lyster, R, and Coonan, E, 'The Precautionary Principle: A Thrill Ride on the Roller Coaster of Energy and Climate Law' (2009) 18(1) *RECIEL*, p. 38.

Mary Robinson Foundation, *Climate Justice Principles*, available at http://www.mrfcj.org/wp-content/uploads/2015/09/Principles-of-Climate-Justice.pdf accessed 1 April 2020.

Office of the United Nations High Commissioner for Human Rights, *Report on the Relationship between Climate Change and Human Rights* (A/HRC/10/61).

Olmos Giupponi, B, 'Assessing Climate Change MRV Initiatives in Latin America: Bridging Theory and Practice', in *INECE Report* (Rotterdam University Press 2016).

Sands, P, 'Climate Change and the Rule of Law: Adjudicating the Future in International Law' (2016) 28(1) *Journal of Environmental Law*, p. 19.

Savaşan, Z, *Paris Climate Agreement: A Deal for Better Compliance? Learned from the Compliance Mechanisms of the Kyoto and Montreal Protocols* (Springer 2019).

Simonetti, S, and de Witt Wijnen, R, (2009-10-01), 'International Emissions Trading and Green Investment Schemes', in Legal Aspects of Carbon Trading: Kyoto, Copenhagen, and beyond (Oxford University Press). Retrieved 11 May. 2020, from https://www.oxfordscholarship.com/view/10.1093/acprof:oso/9780199565931.001.0001/acprof-9780199565931-chapter-7 accessed 1 April 2020.

Singh, NG, 'Science and Climate Change Law – The Role of the IPCC in International Decision-Making', in Kevin R. Gray, Richard Tarasofsky, and Cinnamon Carlarne (eds), *The Oxford Handbook of International Climate Change Law* (Oxford University Press 2016), pp. 55–71.

Slaughter, AM, 'The Paris Approach to Global Governance', Project Syndicate, 28 December 2015, available at https://scholar.princeton.edu/sites/default/files/slaughter/files/projectsyndicate12.28.2015.pdf accessed 1 April 2020.

Thornton, J, and Covington, H, 'Climate Change before the Court', Carbon Brief, available at https://www.carbonbrief.org/guest-post-climate-change-before-the-court accessed 1 April 2020.

UN Climate Change, Nationally Determined Contributions (NDCs), available at https://unfccc.int/process-and-meetings/the-paris-agreement/the-paris-agreement/nationally-determined-contributions-ndcs#:~:text=Nationally%20determined%20contributions%20(NDCs)%20are, the%20impacts%20of%20climate%20change accessed 1 April 2020.

UNFCCC, Katowice Rulebook, Adopted at the COP24 held in Katowice, Poland, available at https://cop24.gov.pl/news/news-details/news/the-katowice-rulebook-main-principles-of-the-document/ accessed 1 March 2020.

UNFCCC, What Are Market and Non-Market Mechanisms?, available at https://unfccc.int/topics/what-are-market-and-non-market-mechanisms accessed 1 March 2020.

United Nations, A/CN.4/471 Survey on Liability Regimes Relevant to the Topic International Liability for Injurious Consequences Arising Out of Acts Not Prohibited by International Law: Study Prepared by the Secretariat, 1995, vol. II(1), available at https://legal.un.org/ilc/documentation/english/a_cn4_471.pdf accessed 1 March 2020.

United Nations, Copenhagen Accord, Decision 2/CP.15, 30 March 2010, DOC. FCCC/CP/2009/11/Add.1. The 'Cancun Agreements', available at https://unfccc.int/process/conferences/pastconferences/cancun-climate-change-conference-november-2010/statements-and-resources/Agreements accessed 1 April 2020.

United Nations Human Rights Council, Resolution Adopted by the Human Rights Council: 17/4 Human Rights and Transnational Corporations and Other Business Enterprises, Seventeenth Session, July 06.

United States Court of Appeals for the Ninth Circuit, *Kelsey Cascadia – Rose Juliana, et al v the United States of America*, No. 6:15-cv-01517-TC, 8 April 2016.

Viñuales, JE, 'Balancing Effectiveness and Fairness in the Redesign of the Climate Change Regime' (2011) 24(1) *Leiden Journal of International Law*, pp. 223, at 251–252.

Zengerling, C, *Greening International Jurisprudence: Environmental NGOs before International Courts, Tribunals, and Compliance Committees* (Brill/Nijhoff 2013).

9 Biodiversity

A critical analysis of the effectiveness of compliance mechanisms under the Convention on Biological Diversity, the Cartagena Protocol on Biosafety, the Nagoya Protocol and CITES

1 Introduction

From an international environmental law (IEL) compliance perspective, there are several dimensions entrenched in the protection of biodiversity. First, the evolution of the international legal framework in this area has transitioned from initially regulating wildlife as a resource (allocating quotas and setting some cooperation principles) to the protection of wildlife. It has then become more focussed on the safeguard of biodiversity per se.[1] As a result, international law applicable in this area is diversified, presenting nuances when it comes to compliance. Biological diversity is understood and regulated from different angles in IEL. With that premise in mind, one can get a better grasp of the various compliance mechanisms available.

The starting points for IEL compliance in this particular field were the adoption of the 1973 Convention on International Trade in Endangered Species of Wild Fauna and Flora (CITES)[2] and the 'World Charter for Nature'.[3] CITES constitutes one of the oldest multilateral environmental agreements, introducing innovative means for compliance. The second instrument, adopted by the UN General Assembly, was meant to be an umbrella for the conservation of biodiversity. Although not successful (it was only passed as a non-binding instrument) the Charter heralded a new era, preceding other more sophisticated instruments, such as the various initiatives taken by the UNEP to adopt a framework convention that ultimately led to the drafting of the Convention on Biological Diversity (CBD), which was then adopted at the 1992 Rio Summit.[4]

---

1 Patricia Birnie, *International Regulation of Whaling: From Conservation of Whaling to Conservation of Whales and Regulation of Whale Watching* (Oceana Publications 1985). See, for instance, the first international treaties in the area: the Convention between the United States, Great Britain, Japan and Russia Providing for the Preservation and Protection of the Fur Seals and Sea Otters in the North Pacific Ocean (7th July 1911). *American Journal of International Law*, 5(S4), 267–274. M. Bowman, P. Davies, and C. Redgwell, *Lyster's International Wildlife Law* (Cambridge University Press 2010).

2 It has 155 states parties and has been in force since 1 July 1975.

3 UN General Assembly, World Charter for Nature, 28 October 1982, A/RES/37/7.

4 The Convention was drafted by the Intergovernmental Negotiating Committee which presented it to the Conference, The Convention's text was opened for signature on 5 June 1992 at the

The early approach to the matter of biodiversity protection emphasised trade and exploitation of natural resources, namely relating to fur seals, whaling and the protection of endangered species. Since then, IEL norms in the field have expanded to cover preservation of ecologically, culturally or aesthetically valuable sites and the question of genetic resources, benefit-sharing and genetically modified organisms. In terms of the specific environmental law problem addressed by the international legal instruments, it entails the protection of genetic diversity within each species, diversity between species and diversity of ecosystem within a region.[5] There is a wide-raging set of legal international instruments tackling different aspects of the multifaceted question of protection of biodiversity.[6]

2 Managing compliance with international biodiversity law (IBL)

IEL in this area is articulated around different pillars: protection of species, safeguarding of biodiversity and protection of sites. This particular structure translates into complex regulatory regimes, which incorporate a diversity of compliance techniques. Furthermore, when it comes to compliance with international biodiversity law there are clear interlinkages with other areas of IEL and international law, such as global animal law and international cultural heritage law.

In terms of the regulatory approaches to protecting biodiversity in international law, the first consisted in the management of biodiversity from a natural resources perspective. Under this approach, the central objective was to allocate quota and regulate economic activities.[7] The paradigmatic example of this is the Whaling Convention which then, through the implementation of moratorium, operated a shift towards a more protective approach. Evidently, in this case, the successful strategy consists in the moratorium shaping a new function of the Convention, turning it into an authentic conservation instrument.[8] Nevertheless, the controversy between commercial and the scientific purposes subsists,

---

United Nations Conference on Environment and Development (the Rio 'Earth Summit'). See, for instance, the 1979 Convention on the Conservation of Migratory Species of Wild Animals, which was adopted on 6th November 1979 and entered into force on 1 November 1983. Convention on Wetlands of International Importance, Especially as Waterfowl Habitat 1971; Convention on International Trade in Endangered Species 1973; Convention on the Conservation of Biological Diversity 1992 and Convention to Combat Desertification in those Countries Experiencing Serious Drought and/or Desertification, Particularly in Africa 1994.

5 L. Guruswamy, *International Environmental Law in a nutshell,* (Thomson Reuters 2012), p. 150.

6 Michael Bowman, Peter Davies and Edward Goodwin, *Research Handbook on Biodiversity and Law* (Edward Elgar Publishing 2016).

7 R. Rayfuse, 'Biological Resources' in D. Bodansky, J. Brunnée, and E. Hey (eds), *Oxford Handbook of International Environmental Law* (Oxford University Press 2007), pp. 362, 366, 360.

8 Patricia Birnie, Alan Boyle, and Catherine Redgwell, *International Law and the Environment* (3rd edn Oxford University Press 2009).

as evidenced by the ICJ Ruling.[9] Compliance is measured by the achievement of targets set for States regarding resources within the jurisdiction of one State or shared by different States. In this area, the function of IEL mainly consists in managing the exploitation of an endangered resource.[10] Legal techniques deployed in this regard include, amongst others, setting exploitation quotas (by species, region, or State, etc.), indicating the methods and technologies allowed for resource exploitation, setting specific periods and determining in which areas these activities will take place.[11] More recently, international legal instruments on biodiversity have encompassed preventative techniques by incorporating the requirement of environmental impact assessments across the field of biodiversity.[12]

Another preliminary question to be examined concerns the definitions used in IEL that, in turn, would lead to the choice of appropriate regulatory techniques and compliance mechanisms. IEL scholars point out the differences between 'site', 'habitat' and 'ecosystem' as the relevant categories to be considered in the regulation of biodiversity.[13] In the panoply of instruments regulating the field, 'natural site' in IEL is a predominant category, used to protect an area for its biodiversity and natural value, which is slightly different from the conceptualisation of 'site' (both natural and mixed) safeguarded under the World Heritage Convention, which factors in the cultural and human dimensions from a more anthropocentric perspective.[14] In turn, the term 'habitat' has a more general application, being used to preserve natural conditions necessary for certain species within a geographical area or for a particular sub-species within a determined geographical location.[15] An example of this generic protection type is the Ramsar Convention, which, for the inclusion of wetlands on the list, relies on a definition of the protected wetland with reference to 'ecology, botany, zoology, limnology or hydrology'.[16] Another category used is 'ecosystem', which is broader in scope and more holistic. It comprises not only the natural elements but also their respective interactions and their overall function as a whole.[17]

---

9 ICJ, *Whaling in the Antartic* (Australia v Japan), Judgment of 31 March 2014, available at https://www.icj-cij.org/en/case/148/judgments accessed 1 April 2020.

10 Pierre M. Dupuy and Jorge Viñuales, 'The Sources of International Environmental Law' in *International Environmental Law* (Cambridge University Press 2015), p. 160.

11 United Nations Environment Programme, *Law and National Biodiversity Strategies and Action Plans* (UNEP 2018).

12 Philippe Cullet and Sujith Koonan (eds), *Research Handbook on Law, Environment and the Global South* (Edward Elgar 2019).

13 Ben Boer, Chapter 20. Biodiversity Planning Law, UNEP, Ecolex, available at http://www2.ecolex.org/server2neu.php/libcat/docs/LI/MON-085693.pdf accessed 1 April 2020.

14 IUCN, available at https://www.iucn.org/theme/world-heritage/natural-sites accessed 1 April 2020.

15 Dupuy and Viñuales (n 10) at 160, 161.

16 Ramsar Convention, arts 1 and 2(2).

17 Vito De Lucia, 'Competing Narratives and Complex Genealogies: The Ecosystem Approach in International Environmental Law' (2015) 27(1) *Journal of Environmental Law*, pp. 91–117.

Different categorisations determine differential regulations, and there is a considerable overlap between the various regimes. The 'site' approach has been pervasively used under the WHC and EU Environmental law, with lists, classifications and actions to be taken when there is no correspondence with the criteria set. In turn, the habitats definition with a broad and a specific meaning has been included under several compliance mechanisms. Different legal techniques are used to protect the sites, translating in the creation of protected areas and 'buffer zones' under various MEAs (World Heritage Convention, the Man and the Biosphere regime, the Ramsar Convention, and the Convention on Migratory Species), creating a matrix with 'substantial overlaps, whereby individual sites can be listed under numerous regimes'.[18] The seemingly predominant approach is the ecosystem approach, used as a framework for environmental governance 'for the integrated management of and, water and living resources'.[19] Resources can be understood and defined in different manners as natural resources, biological resources, species and genetic resources.[20]

Trade-related measures draw on IEL and international trade law to harness the protection of biodiversity, using them to reduce the exploitation of species and resources, and prevent risks caused by the introduction of invasive species, which may hinder the ecological balance of the ecosystem. This can lead to restrictions on the export and/or import of specimens of selected species or specific measures adopted with regard to certain specimens, as contemplated in the periodical reports by the Committee on Trade and the Environment of the WTO.[21]

Although a bit generic, the classification of regulatory approaches into regulation and management of exploitation or harvest, protection of spaces

18 Alexander Gillespie, *Protected Areas and International Environmental Law* (Martinus Nijhoff Publishers 2007), p. 9. See, Chapter on Compliance at 231.

19 1 Decision V/6 'Ecosystem Approach' adopted by the Conference of the Parties to the Convention of Biological Diversity at its Fifth meeting, Nairobi, 15–26 May 2000, UNEP/COP/5/23.

20 Rayfuse (n 7).

21 WTO Matrix on Trade-Related Measures Pursuant to Selected Multilateral Environmental Agreements (MEAs), 9 Octubre 2017. Convention on International Trade in Endangered Species of Wild Fauna and Flora (CITES); Convention on the Conservation of Antarctic Marine Living Resources (CCAMLR); International Convention for the Conservation of Atlantic Tunas (ICCAT); United Nations Fish Stocks Agreement (UNFSA); Agreement on Port State Measures (PSMA); International Tropical Timber Agreement (ITTA); International Plant Protection Convention (IPPC); Convention on Biological Diversity (CBD); Nagoya Protocol on Access to Genetic Resources and the Fair and Equitable Sharing of Benefits Arising from their Utilization to the Convention on Biological Diversity; Cartagena Protocol on Biosafety to the Convention on Biological Diversity; Nagoya – Kuala Lumpur Supplementary Protocol on Liability and Redress to the Cartagena Protocol on Biosafety; Montreal Protocol and the Vienna Convention on Substances that Deplete the Ozone Layer; United Nations Framework Convention on Climate Change (UNFCCC); the Kyoto Protocol and the Paris Agreement; Basel Convention on the Control of Transboundary Movements of Hazardous Wastes and their Disposal; Rotterdam Convention on the Prior Informed Consent Procedure for Certain Hazardous Chemicals and Pesticides in International Trade; Stockholm Convention on Persistent Organic Pollutants; and Minamata Convention on Mercury.

and regulation of trade, offers an appropriate analytical framework to unpack the question of compliance under international biodiversity law.[22] Each regulatory approach corresponds to a different compliance mechanism and define measures that can be taken against States. With regard to the measures, various categorises have been proposed, such as the differentiation between measures regulating direct threats and those addressing indirect threats.[23] The distinction is theoretical, and, in some cases, there is not a clear-cut choice in favour of a particular regulatory approach but rather a combination of the different regulatory approaches and measures.[24] Often, there is a mix between the regulation of exploitation and trade along with protective measures, as shown by CITES or the CBD, regimes in which the protection of the resources/species intersect with the protection of the ecosystem.

According to this, the usual examples are those concerning the regulation of the exploitation and management of fisheries, governed by the UNCLOS and other related institutional frameworks, such as the Whaling Convention and the Northwest Atlantic Fisheries Organization (NAFO)[25] and the 1995 Straddling Fish Stock Agreement, correlative measures against illegal, unregulated and unreported fishing activities.[26] These regimes seek to regulate and, if necessary, prohibit the taking, hunting or killing of a particular species or group of species. They aim at restricting the direct use of species through hunting, fishing or collecting. Similarly, the harvest of genetic resources entails similar environmental compliance problems.[27]

Equally important is the consideration of biodiversity services and differential treatment in the compliance with IBL. Biodiversity services include the provision of services, regulating services and supporting services. Protection of biological diversity and resources encompasses services and the use of species and ecosystems. The CBD's scope is broad as it applies to an array of areas: terrestrial, marine and other aquatic biological diversity. Obligations on the contracting party relate to the various aspects of biodiversity within the domestic

---

22 Rayfuse (n 7) at 374. Dupuy and Viñuales (n 10) at 162.

23 Rayfuse (n 7) at 386–390.

24 Rayfuse (n 7) at 386; Dupuy and Viñuales (n 10) at 162.

25 Convention on Future Multilateral Cooperation on Northwest Atlantic Fisheries, adopted on 24 October 1978.

26 United Nations Convention on the Law of the Sea, 10 December 1982. It entered into force on 16 November 1994, in accordance with article 308(1).

27 M. Jeffrey, 'Bioprospecting: Access to Genetic Resources and Benefit Sharing under the Convention on Biodiversity and the Bonn Guidelines' (2002) 6 *Singapore Journal of International & Comparative Law*, p. 747 at 755. C. Hunter, 'Sustainable Bioprospecting: Using Private Contracts and International Legal Principles and Policies to Conserve Raw Materials' (1997) 25 *Boston College of Environmental Affairs Law Review*, p. 129 at 138. See, e.g., D. Leary, 'Bioprospecting and the Genetic Resources of Hydrothermal Vents on the High Seas: What Is the Existing Legal Position, Where Are We Heading and What Are Our Options?' (2004) 1 *MacQuarie Journal of International & Comparative Law*, p. 137; and D. Leary, 'Emerging Legal Regimes Regulating Bioprospecting for Thermophiles and Hyperthermophiles of Hydrothermal Vents' (2004) 6 *Marine Biotechnology*, p. 351.

jurisdiction. In terms of advancing biodiversity, States can extend the effect to areas within and beyond the national jurisdiction. Pursuant to article 4, each State should at least identify the different activities and monitor them. Being ratified by a significant number of States, the CBD is one of the universal MEAs. The aims of the CBD are twofold: it not only deals with conservation and the protection of endangered species but also sets out procedures aimed at the use of biological resources.

Under the CBD, the Subsidiary Body on Scientific, Technical and Technological Advice performs an advisory function in terms of compliance. The 2050 Vision, entitled 'Living in harmony with nature', [28] aims at '[m]ainstreaming biodiversity into national development plans as a principle and as a cross-cutting issue, which needs to be considered during implementation of the biodiversity framework'.[29] In the new strategy for a comprehensive and participatory post-2020 global process, several key sources of information are contemplated, with an emphasis on the contribution from the parties through several inputs and submissions, which depicts a more bottom-up process in the drafting of a compliance strategy in IBL.[30]

Since the focus of this book is compliance, three different regimes have been selected to exemplify its diverse aspects: CITES, Convention on Biological Diversity (CBD) and the Cartagena and Nagoya Protocols.

3 CITES (Convention on International Trade in Endangered Species of Wild Fauna and Flora). a. List technique. b. The permits system

CITES addresses the specific problem of the demand for endangered species of wild fauna and flora who are tradable or possess a commercial value, regulating the trade of wildlife species. It represents a successful case of a universal MEA, showing one of the largest records of ratifications.[31] It can be claimed that CITES has reached the goal set in the treaty on safeguarding endangered species, many of which have their habitats in developing countries (regarded as 'producers').

This success has led to a potential extension of the regime to other species not contemplated in other regimes. From a compliance standpoint, the main tool used by CITES has been the institution of trade restrictions through certain bureaucratic obstacles, preventing unregistered trade exchanges of allowed

---

28 Decision CBD/COP/DEC/14/34, 30 November 2018.
29 UNEP, *Towards the Vision 2050 on Biodiversity: Living in Harmony with Nature*, available at https://www.unenvironment.org/news-and-stories/story/towards-vision-2050-biodiversity-living-harmony-nature accessed 1 March 2020.
30 Conference of the Parties to the Convention on Biological Diversity (COP), Decision 14/34, Fourteenth meeting, Sharm-El-Sheikh, Egypt, 17–29 November 2018, available at https://www.cbd.int/doc/decisions/cop-14/cop-14-dec-34-en.pdf accessed 1 March 2020.
31 More than 175 States adhere to the treaty.

transactions in protected species. In relation to compliance, CITES shows a number of initiatives and regulatory techniques best exemplified by the 'list technique'.

This consist in the obligations taken under the treaty that apply to certain species and/or spaces which are normally listed in the appendix to the agreement. The list is not static and can be periodically updated to mirror the evolution and understanding of the circumstances surrounding the environmental problem. More complex models are also available, which imply the adoption of specific lists with obligations applicable to different species or spaces.

CITES sets up a Conference of the Parties (COP), which also monitors compliance. The institutional framework is completed by two treaty bodies created by the COP: a Plants Committee and an Animals Committee, whose memberships represent the main countries involved – namely, developing countries. The scope of the protection includes both plants and animals (alive or dead) as well as 'any readily recognizable part or derivative thereof', which applies to the trades of rhino horns or elephant tusks.[32]

One may argue that the effectiveness of this MEA resides in the simplification observed in terms of substantive duties imposed on States as there are but a few clear obligations. The main one is the establishment of a 'Management Authority' and a 'Scientific Authority'. This double-headed system is tasked with the administration of the permit system described below. Another substantive obligation, common to other MEAs, is the reporting system: each Party should submit annual reports to the Secretariat, accounting for the number and types of permits granted, and bi-annual reports about 'legislative, regulatory, and administrative measures taken to enforce the provisions of the Convention'.[33] The third substantive obligation consists in the duty of each party to follow the procedures concerning the documentation on the three appendices of protected species (the 'lists').

a List technique

CITES comprises three lists in Appendices I, II and III; however, the obligations relating to trade in specimens of the species listed in each of them are different. Appendix I refers to species subject to a prohibition of trade with some exceptions, including 'all species threatened by trade' (art. II(1)). In order to trade species included in Appendix I, a trader must obtain both an export and an import permit.

Species contained in Appendix II of CITES are those that may become threatened in the future without trade controls (art. II(2)). Appendix III covers species 'which any Party identifies as being subject to regulation within its jurisdiction for the purpose of preventing or restricting exportation' (art. II(3)).

---

32 CITES, art. I(b).
33 CITES, art. VIII. 7.

The species of Appendix II are at risk of becoming endangered if trade is not controlled. With regard to species listed in Appendix III, CITES establishes a system that fosters and facilitates the assistance of State parties in the implementation of the regulation.

The list technique has been used in other parts of IEL, such as with regard to the protection of natural areas or sites or cultural sites. In CITES, it includes assistance of other States parties in the implementation of the unilateral regulation. It also incorporates flexibility as the list modification system regulated in Articles XV and XVI provides for the possibility of issuing 'reservations' (Article XV(3), XVI(2) and XXIII). The institutional framework complements this technique, setting forth an implementation system, which is a core component of the regulation of trade with non-parties to CITES.

CITES provides for changes concerning the species comprised on the respective lists, including 'uplisting'. The amendment of Appendices I and II needs a two-thirds majority of parties present and voting at a meeting of the COP (art. XV). This mechanism has allowed for some flexibility being used dynamically to adjust to changing circumstances and granting more protection if needed. Up-listing has been relied upon quite frequently, such as in the case of the African elephant 'uplisted' to Appendix I in 1989 and the Cuvier's Gazelle, moved from Appendix III to Appendix I in 2007. Modifications to Appendix III operate in a simplified manner via any of the parties nominating a species as such (art XVI).

Moreover, in national court cases, the list system has been used to adjudicate controversies over illegal trade, which has reinforced compliance with the Convention.[34] One crucial aspect is how to manage the relations between State parties and third States concerning trade in endangered species, with some spillover effects due to their mutual interaction.

b The permits system

Under Appendix I, the importing State will issue an import permit only after its Scientific Authority advises that the import will not be 'detrimental to the survival of the species involved'.[35] The Scientific Authority should be satisfied about the suitability of the proposed recipient in the country of import (if it can suitably look after the specimen, if living).[36] The importing State's Management Authority must confirm the use of the specimen and that it is not 'for primarily commercial purpose'.[37] In turn, the exporting State may issue an export permit only after its Scientific Authority finds the exchange non-threatening to the

---

34 Indonesia's first court case involving CITES Appendix I listed Radiated Tortoise (2018), available at https://www.traffic.org/news/indonesias-first-court-case-involving-cites-appendix-i-listed-radiated-tortoise/ accessed 1 April 2020.

35 CITES, art. III. 3.

36 Ibid.

37 Ibid.

survival of that species.[38] Its Management Authority should (1) discover no violation of its domestic species protection laws; (2) believe that the transfer will minimize the risk of injury, damage to health or cruel treatment; and (3) confirm the previous granting of an import permit.[39] Under this Appendix, CITES prohibits the most harmful trade, establishing a complex record and paper trail for permissible exchanges.

Species included in Appendix II of CITES require an export permit, not an import permit. Permits under this Appendix follow the model of Appendix I, so the exporting party may award the permit upon its Scientific Authority determining that the exchange is non-threatening to the survival of the species. The Management Authority shall also determine that the specimen has both been legally obtained and is safely transferable (art. IV(2)). There is less involvement for the parties than under Appendix I; however, CITES still requires paper trail for all legal trade under Appendix II.

In order to trade in species on the Appendix III list, an export permit and a Certificate of Origin must be obtained. The export permit represents an exemption of the need of determination by exporting the State's Scientific Authority, requiring only the intervention of the Management Authority, certifying that no domestic laws were infringed in the capture of the specimen and that the transfer does not involve undue harm (art. V(2)). In addition, CITES mandates a Certificate of Origin for all trade under Appendix III and when the transaction involves parties that have not listed any species in Appendix III (art. V(3)).

c Assessing the effectivity of compliance with CITES

CITES represented a step forward and one in the right direction to protect endangered species. However, trade (both legal and illegal) in protected species has not stopped or diminished in the expected proportion. It is possible to put forward reservations against the listing of a species in Appendix I, II or III, or in any parts and derivatives of Appendix III. A reservation has the effect of avoiding the permit system with regard to that species, placing the objecting party as a non-party, in that it can freely trade with other non-parties.

Another aspect which generates implementation issues concerns the ability of parties to trade with non-party States (or an objecting party for a particular species), if the non-party issues 'comparable' documentation that 'substantially conforms' to CITES permits and certificates (art. X). This exposes trade to fraud by non-traders and non-parties.

The exemptions regime for listed species brings in more complexity. One of the main exceptions concerns specimens acquired within an owner's usual State of residence which are considered 'personal or household effects' and are generally not covered by CITES (art. VII(3)). Another exception consists of specimens

---

38 CITES, art. III (2).
39 CITES, art III.2

documented by an exporting State's Management Authority, as obtained before the species in question became listed (art. VII(2)). More significantly, CITES provides for yet another exception from restrictions species 'bred in captivity' if the trader gets a certificate of captive breeding from the State of export (art. VII(5)). The COP monitors this type of operations under Appendix I species globally, and has successfully called the Parties on to not receive certificates of captive breeding from unregistered facilities. Scientific exchanges are excluded from the regime, with the COP also overseeing a list of scientific institutions entitled to the exception for 'non-commercial loan, donation, or exchange between scientist or scientific institutions' (art. VII(6)).

The quota-allocation system species, operated by the COP, comprises species such as the leopard, some types of crocodilians and the cheetah, determining in some cases that trade within set limits will not be harmful to the survival of that species.[40] An example of this is the quota system applicable to the export of raw ivory.

Overall, the regime has performed well, with a good level of compliance, considering the scope and the resources available in the respective States. Illegal trade nevertheless remains a problem. One possible manner of reinforcing the system is to provide greater financial assistance from industrialized countries to developing parties in order to promote enforcement. The clearing house mechanism has fostered the sharing of good practice and provided parties with case studies which reinforce the application of the Convention at domestic level. Progressively, State parties are implementing the norms through effective measures.[41]

4 Involvement of private sector actors under the Convention on Biological Diversity (CBD)

Before delving into details about private sector involvement in IBL, it is worth referring to the functioning of the regime. The CBD recognizes sovereignty over genetic resources to States in whose territory they are situated, seeking to regulate access to (including the harvest of) genetic resources. The basis for this is the prior informed consent of the providing State, to be given on mutually agreed terms, which include the provision of a fair and equitable share of benefits resulting from their use by the exploiting State. The resources regulated under the CBD comprise all genetic resources, defined as genetic material of actual or potential value for humanity. The International Treaty on Plant Genetic Resources for Food and Agriculture (ITPGRFA) now governs access to plant genetic resources explicitly intended for food and agriculture.

---

40 CITES, Ninth meeting (1994) Res. 9.21.
41 See, for instance, CITES welcomes Belgian court judgement on illegal trade in birds of prey, available at https://www.cites.org/eng/cites_welcomes_Belgian_court_judgement_illegal_trade_birds_prey accessed 1 April 2020.

The main aim behind this regime is to guarantee the continued availability of these resources for humanity. Although States are assigned sovereignty over the resources, they shall facilitate access to them and not impose restrictions in breach of the CBD's objectives. Similarly, there is a time constraint as the allocation of sovereign rights is restricted to resources collected after the CBD entered into force (29 December 1993).

The private sector plays a relevant role in the protection and management of biodiversity. The notion of private sector in this case, comprises different stakeholders such as: indigenous peoples and local communities, subnational governments, cities and other local authorities, intergovernmental organizations, non-governmental organizations, women's groups, youth groups, the business and finance community, the scientific community, academia, faith-based organizations, representatives of sectors related to or dependent on biodiversity, citizens at large and other stakeholders.

In terms of public participation of stakeholders, their participation is encouraged and reinforced in the post-2020 global biodiversity framework. The processes are participatory, inclusive, gender responsive, transformative, comprehensive, catalytic, visible and knowledge-based, transparent, efficient, results-oriented, iterative and flexible. The 2050 Vision for Biodiversity reinforces the implementation of the 2030 Agenda for Sustainable Development. In turn, the Clearing-House Mechanism (CHM) contributes to the implementation of the Convention on Biological Diversity by promoting and facilitating scientific and technical cooperation.

The scope of application of the CBD is comprehensive, fostering harmonization across countries, aiming to protect determined species or groups of species as well as the biodiversity in a particular region. Its application, however, may lead to different issues. The FAO's contribution to the design of the compliance and implementation of the CBD should be noted.

There are some applicable principles upon which the regime is based, such as the Sustainable Development Principle as well as the idea of global commons and the protection of world heritage. The CBD places various obligations on States based on these principles. Sometimes commitments are formulated in a manner in which they are subject to conditions, like 'as far as possible' and 'as appropriate', which are attached to the obligations. This might lead to a differential approach between developed and developing State parties. In developing States, the main biodiversity holders lack of sufficient resources to implement the norms which might water down the legally binding nature of the treaty or lead to a shallow implementation of the treaty.

Overall, the CBD started a process of international consensus-building around the question of biodiversity and the conception of biodiversity. The CBD constitutes a unique international environmental regime with an almost universal membership, a science-based and comprehensive mandate, and sound international financial support for national implementation, with processes informed by scientific and technological advice, bringing together the public sector (governments), the private sector and local communities and in-digenous people.[42]

Amongst the various commitments allocated to States under the Convention, the parties should develop 'national strategies, plans or programmes for the conservation and sustainable use of biodiversity'. According to the CBD, art 6(a), goal-setting at the national level should be incorporated into other relevant national programs, in other relevant areas, such as forestry and agricultural planning (art. 6(b)). Each State must also carry out studies to identify the components of biodiversity, overseeing components which are in need of conservation and those offering 'the greatest potential for sustainable use' (art. 7 (a)–(b)).

Conservation obligations *in situ* entail the protection of biodiversity in its natural setting through the establishment of protected areas, the management of biological resources in these protected areas, the protection of ecosystems and the maintenance of viable species populations.[43] The CBD provides also for *ex situ* conservation and protection, including gene banks, captive breeding programs and zoos. Parties should undertake measures encouraging *ex situ* conservation by providing appropriate facilities and developing adequate spaces for species rehabilitation programmes.[44]

5 The Cartagena Protocol on Biosafety: compliance issues *ad intra* and *ad extra*

Tackling the issue of genetically modified organisms was the Cartagena Protocol on Biosafety (CPB), adopted as a supplementary agreement to the CBD covering living modified organisms (LMOs) resulting from modern biotechnology which may have adverse effects on biological diversity, also taking into account risks to human health.[45] Pursuant to Articles 8 (g.17) and 19 (3–4), the parties concluded the Cartagena Protocol on Biosafety (CPB) to the CBD to address the transboundary movement, transit, handling and use of LMOs (also known as genetically modified organisms or GMOs).[46] The Cartagena Protocol added another layer of protection, including minimising the impacts of biotechnology on the environment. The CPB expanded the main objective of the CBD, relating to 'the conservation of biodiversity, the sustainable use of its components and the fair and equitable sharing of the benefits arising out of the utilization of genetic resources'.[47] The protocol deals with the question of biotechnology and

---

42 Guruswamy (n 5) at 169.

43 CBD, Article 8.

44 CBD, Article 9.

45 CBD, The Cartagena Protocol on Biosafety – Introduction, available at https://bch.cbd.int/protocol accessed 1 April 2020.

46 Cartagena Protocol on Biosafety, adopted on 29 January 2000, art. 4. According to art. 37(1) the protocol entered into force on 11 September 2003, after the 50th instrument of ratification was deposited in 2003.

47 CBD, art. 1.

the adoption of adequate measures for the conservation of the environment and, at the same time, safeguarding of human health.

There is also a relevant teleological aspect, as mentioned in Article 19(3), which stipulates:

> The Parties shall consider the need for and modalities of a protocol setting out appropriate procedures, including, in particular, advance informed agreement, in the field of the safe transfer, handling and use of any living modified organism resulting from biotechnology that may have adverse effect on the conservation and sustainable use of biological diversity.[48]

The Conference of the Parties acts as well as the Conference for the Cartagena Protocol, deciding on compliance issues. Procedures and mechanisms on compliance under the Cartagena Protocol on Biosafety: The Intergovernmental Committee for the Cartagena Protocol on Biosafety[49] and the clearinghouse mechanism.[50]

The Cartagena Protocol provides for the Advance Informed Agreement (AIA) procedure, which places obligations on the exporters of GMOs. As a rule, a particular procedure should be followed, except in those cases in which is waived by the party of the import. For each procedure, the exporter State must provide a detailed, written description of the GMO to the importing State in advance of the first intentional transboundary shipment. In turn, the importing State must acknowledge receipt of the information within 90 days and then explicitly authorize the shipment within 270 days or state its reasons for rejecting it. Consent is not deemed implicit, so silence or the absence of a response is not equal to approval.

At the heart of this procedure lies the main goal to ensure that importing States have both the opportunity and the capacity to assess risks that may be associated with GMOs before agreeing to their import.[51] Interestingly, a number of GMOs are explicitly excluded from this procedure: GMOs in transit,[52] GMOs destined for contained use[53] and GMOs intended for direct use as food or feed, or for processing.[54] These exceptions can be further expanded by a decision of the Meeting of the Parties (MOP) to the Cartagena Protocol. This exclusion

---

48 CBD, art 19(3).
49 Cartagena Protocol on Biosafety, adopted in 2000 and entered into force in 2003; it currently has 170 Parties.
50 Kathryn Garforth, *Experience with the Compliance Procedures and Mechanisms of the Cartagena & Nagoya Protocols to the CBD*, Secretariat of the Convention on Biological Diversity, available at https://www.cms.int/sites/default/files/document/CPB-NP%20Protocols%20compliance_cbd.pdf accessed 1 April 2020.
51 CP, art. 7.
52 CP, art.6.
53 Ibid.
54 CP, art 7.2.

does not, however, imply that the import of these categories of GMOs should not be regulated by States.

Additional labelling requirements have been imposed by the COP. In this sense, labels must state that the shipment in question carries GMOs, identifying the organism and providing handling and storage requirements and a contact for further information.[55] Labelling requirements have turned out to be relevant under this regimen, and they may differ slightly depending upon whether the organism is intended for contained use or is to be intentionally introduced into the destination's environment. Further labelling requirements were imposed by the COP for GMOs' intended for use as food, feed or for processing.[56] The COPs serving as MOPs have introduced new requirements and further regulations on the use of GMOs and labelling requirements.

Compliance under the Cartagena Protocol is also facilitated through a Biosafety Clearing-House, which fosters the exchange of scientific, technical, environmental and legal information concerning GMOs, and assists parties in implementing their commitments.[57] The Guidelines for National participation in the Biosafety Clearing-House provide technical guidance to parties and other governments about the registration and submission of data to the Clearing-House.[58] The COP also looked into improving the efficiency of the Clearing-House mechanism.[59] COPs have tried to make the process available online and offline, including training for users in technological tools.[60] Information exchange to facilitate compliance becomes even more relevant with regard to GMOs intended for direct use as feed or food, or for processing; the CPB sets up a special procedure requiring States to exchange information at an early stage through the Biosafety Clearing-House. Accordingly, States must give notice to the Clearing-House of domestic authorizations of GMOs, making available copies of domestic laws and regulations concerning them.[61]

The approach taken to the issue aligns with the precautionary principle, following Principle 15 of the Rio Declaration. Based on this principle, States will decide whether or not to accept imports of GMOs on the basis of risk assessments, to be undertaken in a scientific manner following recognised risk

---

55 COP1, CBD, report of the First meeting of the Conference of the Parties serving as the Meeting of the Parties to the Protocol on Biosafety (2004).

56 COP3, March 2006, CBD Report of the Third meeting of the Conference of the Parties to the Convention on Biological Diversity serving as the Meeting of the Parties to the Cartagena Protocolo on Biosafety (2006), at 60–61.

57 CPB, art. 20 (1).

58 Biosafety COP-1 at 35–37.

59 Report of the Second Meeting of the Conference of the Parties to the Convention on Biological Diversity serving as the Meeting of the Parties to the Cartagena Protocol on Biosafey (2005), at 33–36.

60 Fifth Meeting of the Informal Advisory Committee of the Biosafety Clearing-House, 2009. UNEP/CBD/BS/BCH-IAC/5/2.

61 CPB, art. 11.

assessment techniques.[62] Wherever there is insufficient relevant scientific information, a State may decide to apply the precautionary approach and refuse the import of the GMO into its territory (art 10.6). In the assessments, the CP also recognises the right of the importing States to take into account socioeconomic considerations, like the value of biodiversity to its indigenous and local communities, in reaching a decision on the import of GMOs.[63]

The Cartagena Protocol focusses on international action, acknowledging that domestic measures are crucial to making its procedures effective. Civil society participation is also considered central for the operation of the regime. Parties to the protocol assume the commitment to promoting public awareness, ensuring public access to information and consulting the public in decisions concerning GMOs and biosafety. Similarly, parties should undertake national measures to prevent illegal shipments and accidental releases of GMOs, being obligated to notify affected or potentially affected States in the event that an unintentional release occurs. The COP set up a group tasked with developing rules and procedures for a liability and redress regime to deal with damages arising from transboundary GMO shipments; however, it took a while for a binding regime to be articulated.[64]

The Nagoya-Kuala Lumpur Protocol on Liability and Redress (in force since 2018),[65] another supplementary protocol under the umbrella of the CBD, allows countries to use their domestic law to seek redress under different liability (including civil liability) regimes against States.[66]

The Cartagena Protocol brings about the question of interactions with other areas or branches of international law, particularly with regard to international trade law regarding the commercialization of biotechnology and proliferation of GMOs in areas such as the pharmaceutical sector. Other close interrelations are with the WTO's Agreement on Sanitary and Phytosanitary Measures (1994, Annex 1A). Under this discipline, some scholars argue that free trade should prevail as a tool to advance SD. The controversial situation is given by decisions that ban GMOs as being potentially against free trade. Under the Sanitary and Phytosanitary Measures (SPS) Agreement, these decisions should be justified on principles of sound scientific knowledge based on scientific risk assessments.[67] The focus of the Cartagena Protocol is primarily environmental protection providing for exceptions to the free trade principle, allowing States to protect biosafety by banning GMOs on the basis of the precautionary principle in those

---

62 CPB, art. 15.

63 CPB, art. 26.1.

64 Biosafety COP-1, at 104–105.

65 https://www.cambridge.org/core/journals/international-legal-materials/article/nagoyakuala-lumpur-supplementary-protocol-on-liability-and-redress/23A125E4DD691400CD47C02E14 F761E2 accessed 1 April 2020.

66 The Supplementary Protocol aims to contribute to the conservation and sustainable use of biodiversity by providing international rules and procedures in the field of liability and redress relating to LMOs.

67 SPS Agreement, art 5.

cases in which strict scientific evidence is lacking. In terms of compliance and enforcement, any measure pertaining to these aspects will be comprised within the jurisdiction of the WTO Dispute settlement due to the absence of binding settlement procedures under the CBD and the CP. This is a quite controversial area at the intersection of both IEL and trade law.[68]

6 Benefit-sharing under the Nagoya Protocol

The Nagoya Protocol (NP) on Access to Genetic Resources and the Fair and Equitable Sharing of Benefits Arising from their Utilization to the Convention on Biological Diversity was adopted to complement the regime established under the umbrella of the CBD.[69] Its specific aim is to share the benefits arising from the utilization of genetic resources in a fair and equitable way. Therefore, the focus is on access and benefit-sharing (ABS). In terms of innovative compliance, the Nagoya Protocol[70] put forward a new system for compliance in this sector.[71]

There is no set definition of benefit-sharing, which 'is understood as encompassing multiple streams of benefits of local and global relevance that has as its beneficiaries a wider group than those actively or directly engaged in a specific activity triggering benefit sharing obligations'.[72]

Under the treaty, access and benefit-sharing covers important crops that together account for 80% of all human consumption (this comprises a pool of genetic resources accessible to everyone). States agree to make their genetic diversity and related information about the crops stored in their gene banks available to the rest upon the ratification of the Treaty through the Multilateral System (MLS).[73]

Article 34 of the Cartagena Protocol on Biosafety requires that the COP acting as the meeting of the Parties to the Protocol shall, at its first meeting, consider and approve cooperative procedures and institutional mechanisms to promote compliance with the provisions of the Protocol and address cases of non-compliance.

---

68 Kym Anderson and Chantal Pohl Nielsen, 'GMOs, the SPS Agreement and the WTO', in Anderson Kym, McRae Cheryl, and Wilson David (eds), *The Economics of Quarantine and the SPS Agreement* (University of Adelaide Press, 2001), pp. 305–331.

69 It entered into force on 12 October 2014, 90 days after the date of deposit of the 50th instrument of ratification.

70 Nagoya Protocol on Access and Benefit-sharing, adopted in 2010, entered into force in 2014, it currently has 85 Parties.

71 Elisa Morgera, Elsa Tsioumani, Matthias Buck, *Unravelling the Nagoya Protocol: A Commentary on the Nagoya Protocol on Biological Diversity* (Martinus Nijhoff Publishers 2014).

72 Elisa Morgera, 'An International Legal Concept of Fair and Equitable Benefit-sharing'" (SSRN, 2015; published in the *European Journal of International Law*).

73 FAO, International Treaty on Plant Genetic Resources for Food and Agriculture (2020) available at http://www.fao.org/plant-treaty/areas-of-work/the-multilateral-system/overview/en/ accessed 1 April 2020.

Access to genetic resources covered in the NP responds to the regulatory challenges, mainly in the area of food security.[74] Even if the NP represents progress, there are still some challenges when it comes to genetic resources. The first challenge is the legal status of the genetic resources, considered as common heritage of humankind or subject to sovereignty and ownership. The second challenge refers to the manner in which legal consequences are regulated (access, patentability or the right to replant). Finally, the third challenge is related to the different manners in which the status is defined.

As background to the adoption of the NP, different solutions were proposed. One of the possibilities was to extend the status of 'common heritage' to the derivative products of genetic resources, comprising plant varieties/variations developed by multinational companies. Another option was to subject genetic resources and plant varieties to a system of appropriation. Following in the footsteps of the CBD, the NP took that approach. The protocol also governs arrangements on access to genetic resources, further developing Article 15 of the CBD. The International Treaty on Plant Genetic Resources for Food and Agriculture (ITPGR) complements the Nagoya Protocol. The system lies on the sovereignty of the State where the resources are located to regulate access by granting or denying it. Access is thus subject not only to the consent of the State of origin of the genetic resources but also (where appropriate) to the 'indigenous and local communities' involved.[75] The sharing of the benefits arising from the use of the resources accessed depend on the arrangements with the State of origin or the communities concerned.[76] Benefit-sharing may consist of monetary rebates, licences to use intellectual property rights (IPRs) or co-ownership. The benefits are established on a case-by-case analysis. Although there is no formal specific legal instrument in this regard, some blueprint agreements setting a minimum content have been drafted to facilitate the process. There is a specific sub-regime applicable to plant genetic resources for food and agriculture: the 'Multilateral System of Access and Benefit Sharing', Annex to ITPGR, which mostly covers food destined for human consumption.[77] The system seeks to facilitate transactions on these resources by capping costs derived from the negotiation using a case-by-case analysis of access and benefit-sharing agreements.

The institutional mechanism under the NP comprises a Compliance Committee made up of 15 members (three per region) elected by the COP, serving as the meeting of the Parties to the Protocol (COP-MOP); members serve in their personal capacity. The Committee can conduct what are called 'cooperative procedures', which fosters the idea of cooperation to achieve compliance. The Committee shall receive, though the Secretariat, any submissions relating to compliance from (a) any Party with respect to itself or (b) any Party which is

---

74 J. Kloppenburg, 'Impeding Dispossession, Enabling Repossession: Biological Open Source and the Recovery of Seed Sovereignty' (2012) 10 *Journal of Agrarian Change*, p. 367.

75 Nagoya Protocol, Arts. 6(2) and 7.

76 CBD, Art. 15(5); Nagoya Protocol Article 6(1).

77 ITPGR, Article 10.

affected or likely to be affected with respect to another Party. The Committee also reviews general issues of compliance.

In 2010, the COP-MOP adopted a decision which expanded the scope of the intervention of the Committee, which may take certain measures if a Party fails to submit its national report, or information has been received through a national report or the Secretariat. These measures are adopted based on information from the Biosafety Clearing-House, showing that the Party concerned is faced with difficulties complying with its obligations under the Protocol.

The Committee has performed a supportive role based on experience from the first years of the Protocol, as shown in some particular cases.[78] As a regulatory umbrella, the CBD goal is two-fold: the conservation of biological diversity as such and the sustainable use of biological and genetic resources. Whereas the Cartagena Protocol covers risks associated with biotechnology, the NP goes further to regulate access to resources. The NP combines both types of objective conservation of biodiversity and the sustainable use of the resources. The object of the protection is 'genetic resources', which takes into consideration other elements also mentioned in the CBD, such as 'knowledge, innovation and practices of indigenous and local communities embodying traditional lifestyles relevant for the conservation and sustainable use of biological diversity'.[79] In line with this definition, the NP recognises the intrinsic connection between 'genetic resources' and 'traditional knowledge', as laid down in its Article 3. The NP safeguards 'traditional knowledge associated with genetic resources' in the areas of traditional medicine, agricultural practices and other practices concerning insects and personal care.[80]

There are different normative elements in the regime institute by the CBD; the obligations under the Convention and its protocols are monitored by a complex compliance system. In multilateral benefit-sharing mechanisms, their financial viability is another challenge: the Pandemic Influenza Preparedness (WHO PIP) Framework has put in place a system of mandatory contributions and current work under the International Treaty on Plant Genetic Resources for Food and Agriculture (ITPGRFA). In terms of information sharing as a form of non-monetary benefit-sharing, this generally relies on voluntary and decentralized initiatives both in multilateral and in bilateral systems. However, ongoing work under the ITPGRFA points towards a more institutionalized multilateral approach to information sharing. With regard to scientific cooperation and capacity building as forms of non-monetary benefit-sharing, there are several types

---

78 Elisa Morgera, *Study on Experiences Gained with the Development and Implementation of the Nagoya Protocol and Other Multilateral Mechanisms and the Potential Relevance of Ongoing Work Undertaken by Other Processes, Including Case Studies* ((2016) UNEP/CBD/A BS A10 EM/2016/ 2-22 December 2015.

79 NP, article 8 j.

80 Elisa Morgera and Elsa Tsioumani, 'Yesterday, Today, and Tomorrow: Looking Afresh at the Convention on Biological Diversity' (2010) 21(1) *Yearbook of International Environmental Law*, pp. 3–40.

contemplated in the more developed multilateral benefit-sharing systems (ISA, WHO and ITPGRFA).

The COP 2010 held in Nagoya devoted part of the work to the creation of structures to monitor compliance with the obligations of the Convention. The non-compliance procedure, together with other specific indicators, help to assess the development towards the fulfilment of the targets and goal set at the meetings.[81]

There is a wide participation in the process of compliance and enforcement through COPs, Governments, international agencies, research institutions, representatives of indigenous and local communities, and non-governmental organizations. All these entities are invited to submit case studies to the Executive Secretary on various thematic areas and cross-cutting issues, like access to and sharing of benefits resulting from the use of genetic resources.

Moreover, there are several interactions with other regimes, such as the International Treaty on Plant Genetic Resources for Food and Agriculture (ITPGRFA) already mentioned; the FAO regime on Genetic Resources for Food and Agriculture (CGRFA); the WHO; International fora on intellectual property rights (TRIPS, WIPO and UPOV); and the United Nations Convention on the Law of the Sea (UNCLOS).[82] The interrelation between regimes with close relations to the CBD/NP regime are the WHO's Pandemic Influenza Preparedness (PIP) Framework for the Sharing of Viruses and Access to Vaccines and Other Benefits, and the WTO Agreement.

Equally interesting to observe is the perception in ABS by the business sector and other non-state actors, agreements such as those in the Merck/InBio agreement, the Teff case and the Hoodia case.[83]

Further progress has been achieved with the signature of the world's first industry-wide benefit-sharing agreement reached in South Africa between the Khoikhoi and San, and the South African rooibos industry.[84] This is a ground-breaking agreement for a number of reasons. To start with, it is the first comprehensive agreement of this type concluded under the CBD. Second, despite being an agreement signed under the CBD it also includes a legal basis for restitution claims for traditional knowledge that date back to the 18th century, when they were given by Khoi and San ancestors to European settlers. This is the case as the CBD was only concluded in 1992 (and it cannot be applied retroactively), and rooibos tea has been in the public domain for around 150 years. Third, the activities comprised are related to trade rather than to bioprospecting, which is the specific activity captured under the CBD and the Nagoya Protocol.

---

81 Decision CP XI/3 'Monitoring Progress in Implementation of the Strategic Plan for Biodiversity 201–2020 and the Aichi Biodiversity Target' (advanced version).

82 C. Prip and K. Rosendal, *Access to Genetic Resources and Benefit-sharing from their Use (ABS) – State of Implementation and Research Gaps* (Fridtjof Nansens Institutt 2015).

83 Ibid.

84 D. Schroeder, R. Chennells, C. Louw, L. Snyders, and T. Hodges T (2020), 'The Rooibos Benefit Sharing Agreement–Breaking New Ground with Respect, Honesty, Fairness, and Care' (2020) 29(2) *Cambridge Quarterly of Healthcare Ethics*.

The key issue is the development and implementation of ABS agreements and how they draw upon previous agreements themselves and incorporate terms, recommendations, elements of the negotiations and approaches contained in documents that provide advice and guidance on the matter. The specificity of this case is that the NEMBA, the South African Biodiversity Act, has a broader scope than the CBD and the NP. Besides, the commercialization of rooibos is based on a shared transfer knowledge, a situation foreseen by the CBD and the National Environmental Management Biodiversity Act (NEMBA); therefore there is no time limit on the issue of restitution. NEMBA incorporates in its remit unchanged indigenous biological resources such as tea (when their use is based on indigenous TK) as long as there is commercial exploitation.[85]

Bioprospecting is an activity captured under the CBD, but some private sector companies operating in this area are only involved in biotrade. NEMBA defines bioprospecting as follows: 'any research on, or development or application of, indigenous biological resources for commercial or industrial exploitation' (...) 'including the utilisation ... of any information regarding any traditional uses of indigenous biological resources by indigenous communities'.[86] An NGO, Natural Justice provided legal support to the representatives of the indigenous communities (National Khoi & San Council) throughout the process.[87] Overall, in terms of benefit-sharing, the COP has functioned as the main compliance mechanisms, compiling good practice about access and benefit-sharing arrangements in specific sectors.[88]

MODEL ACCESS AND BENEFIT-SHARING AGREEMENT BETWEEN THE AUSTRALIAN GOVERNMENT AND ACCESS PARTY

14 Dispute Resolution

  14.1 No Legal Proceedings

    14.1.1 Subject to clause 14.2.2, both Parties agree not to commence any legal proceedings in respect of any dispute arising under this Deed, which cannot be resolved by informal discussion, until the procedure provided by this clause has been utilised.

---

85 Republic of South Africa, No. 10 of 2004: National Environmental Management: Biodiversity Act (2004), available at https://www.environment.gov.za/sites/default/files/legislations/nema_amendment_act10.pdf accessed 1 April 2020.

86 NEMBA, art 1 (1) (b).

87 Natural Justice, The Rooibos Access and Benefit Sharing Agreement, available at https://naturaljustice.org/the-rooibos-access-and-benefit-sharing-agreement/ accessed 1 April 2020.

88 For instance, at the seventh meeting of the COP, the Executive Secretary was requested to gather information and to carry out further analysis on a number of issues, including 'existing practices and trends with regard to commercial and other utilization of genetic resources and the generation of benefits' (Decision VII/19).

14.2 Dispute Resolution Procedure

14.2.1 Both Parties agree that any dispute arising during the course of this Deed is dealt with as follows:

a   the Party claiming that there is a dispute will send the other a written notice setting out the nature of the dispute;

b   the Parties will try to resolve the dispute though direct negotiation by persons who they have given authority to resolve the dispute;

c   the Parties have 20 Business Days from the receipt of the notice to reach a resolution or to agree that the dispute is to be submitted to mediation or some alternative dispute resolution procedure; and

d   if: A. there is no resolution of the dispute;

B   there is no agreement on submission of the dispute to mediation or some alternative dispute resolution procedure; or

C   there is a submission to mediation or some other form of alternative dispute resolution procedure, but there is no resolution within 20 Business Days of the submission, or such extended time as the Parties may agree in writing before the expiration of the 20 Business Days,

D   then, either Party may commence legal proceedings.

14.2.2 This clause does not apply to the following circumstances:

a   either Party commences legal proceedings for urgent interlocutory relief;

b   termination for default under clause 13; or

c   an authority of the Commonwealth, a State or Territory is investigating a breach or suspected breach of the law by the Access Party.

14.2.3 Despite the existence of a dispute, both Parties must (unless requested in writing by the other Party not to do so) continue to perform their respective obligations in accordance with this Deed.14.2.4. The operation of this clause survives the expiration or earlier termination of the Term of this Deed.

Source: https://www.wipo.int/tk/en/databases/contracts/
texts/australiaprovider.html#_Toc170201080

AGREEMENT ON ACCESS AND BENEFIT-SHARING FOR NON-COMMERCIAL RESEARCH

A Sector specific approach containing Model Clauses

4.4 Mutually Agreed Terms (MAT) The Mutually Agreed Terms are an agreement negotiated between the Provider and the User of the Genetic

(*Continued*)

Resources and/or holders of Traditional Knowledge associated to the Genetic Resources according to the national law of the country providing the resources. The MAT regulate conditions for the access to the Genetic Resources and to their associated Traditional Knowledge and the fair and equitable sharing of benefits that result from their use. They are adapted to the specific access situation.

4.5 Traditional Knowledge Option

4.5.1 Traditional Knowledge is the accumulated knowledge that is vital for the conservation and sustainable use of biological resources and/or which is of socioeconomic value, and which has been developed over the years in indigenous/local communities.

Option 4.5.2 Traditional Knowledge means "information or individual or collective practices of an indigenous or local community associated with the genetic heritage having real or potential value". The Mutually Agreed Terms can be contained in one document, or in a main document and ancillary agreements with specific stakeholder groups.

AGREEMENT

4.6 Prior Informed Consent (PIC)

Prior Informed Consent means the unilateral declaration of the Provider that he/she has been informed about the planned research and that he/she is willing to provide the required access to the Genetic Resource.

4.7 Product

Product means the result produced, obtained, extracted or derived from the Genetic Resource through research or research & development (R&D) activities, including data and information generated through analyses of the Genetic Resources.

4.8 Progeny

Progeny means unmodified offspring from the Genetic Resource.

4.9 Third Party

Third Party means any person or institution other than the Provider, the User and any collaborator under their control or supervision. A Third Party is not bound to the terms and conditions of this Agreement unless otherwise agreed with the User.

4.10 Unauthorized Person

Unauthorized Person means any person that came into possession of the Genetic Resources without the authorization of the User.

9. Benefit-Sharing

The benefits arising from the access and use of the Genetic Resources shall be shared fairly and equitably by the User, in accordance with the principles established in the CBD. Basic benefits to be shared include:
1. The offer to the Provider to include local researchers in the research

activities, if such interest exists. 2. In case of publications or oral presentation of the research results, full acknowledgement is to be given to the source of the Genetic Resource; 3. If TK associated to the Genetic Resources is involved, the research results published or presented orally will include full acknowledgement of the source of the Genetic Resources and the TK, if so required by the providers. 4. The Provider will receive a copy of all publications; 5. Research results will be communicated to involved stakeholders (e.g. communities, indigenous people) in an adequate manner and according to reasonable requirements of the Provider; 6. If applicable, share duplicate specimens with the repository in the Provider country in accordance with good scientific practice. In addition, the User agrees to share the following benefits: [Choose from the list of benefits appended to this Agreement; insert a detailed list of benefits here or in an annex]

18. Settlement of Disputes. The Parties agree to make attempts in good faith to negotiate the resolution of any disputes that may arise under this Agreement. If the Parties are not able to resolve a dispute within a period of [XX] months, such dispute shall be finally settled by an arbiter to be mutually agreed between the Parties.

Option 18.1

If the Parties are not able to resolve any dispute within a period of [XX] months, such dispute shall be resolved before the [XXXX] Court law as the only competent body for resolving disputes arising under this Agreement and in accordance with [XXX]. [Insert applicable Law; Jurisdiction]

Source: https://www.cbd.int/abs/doc/model-clauses/
noncommresearch-abs-agreement.pdf

Bibliography

Advisory Committee of the Biosafety Clearing-House, Fifth Meeting UNEP/CBD/BS/BCH-IAC/5/2 (2009).

Anderson, K and Nielsen, CP, 'GMOs, the SPS Agreement and the WTO', in A Kym, C McRae, and D Wilson (eds), *The Economics of Quarantine and the SPS Agreement* (University of Adelaide Press 2001), pp. 305–331.

Birnie, P, *International Regulation of Whaling: From Conservation of Whaling to Conservation of Whales and Regulation of Whale Watching* (Oceana Publications 1985).

Boer, B, Chapter 20. *Biodiversity Planning Law, UNEP, Ecolex,* available at http://www2.ecolex.org/server2neu.php/libcat/docs/LI/MON-085693.pdf accessed 1 April 2020.

Bowman, M, Davies, P, and Goodwin, E, *Research Handbook on Biodiversity and Law* (Edward Elgar Publishing 2016).

Bowman, M, Davies, P, and Redgwell, C, *Lyster's International Wildlife Law* (Cambridge University Press 2010).

CBD COP3, March 2006, CBD Report of the Third meeting of the Conference of the Parties to the Convention on Biological Diversity serving as the Meeting of the Parties to the Cartagena Protocolo on Biosafety (2006), at 60–61.

CBD Report of the Second Meeting of the Conference of the Parties to the Convention on Biological Diversity serving as the Meeting of the Parties to the Cartagena Protocol on Biosafey (2005), at 33–36.

CBD, The Cartagena Protocol on Biosafety – Introduction, available at https://bch.cbd. int/protocol accessed 1 April 2020.

Conference of the Parties to the Convention on Biological Diversity (COP), Decision 14/34, Fourteenth meeting, Sharm-El-Sheikh, Egypt, 17–29 November 2018, available at https://www.cbd.int/doc/decisions/cop-14/cop-14-dec-34-en.pdf accessed 1 March 2020.

Cullet, P and Koonan, S, (eds), *Research Handbook on Law, Environment and the Global South* (Edward Elgar 2019).

De Lucia, V, 'Competing Narratives and Complex Genealogies: The Ecosystem Approach in International Environmental Law' (2015) 27(1) *Journal of Environmental Law*, pp. 91–117.

FAO, *International Treaty on Plant Genetic Resources for Food and Agriculture* (2020) available at http://www.fao.org/plant-treaty/areas-of-work/the-multilateral-system/ overview/en/ accessed 1 April 2020.

Garforth, K, *Experience with the Compliance Procedures and Mechanisms of the Cartagena & Nagoya Protocols to the CBD*, Secretariat of the Convention on Biological Diversity, available at https://www.cms.int/sites/default/files/document/CPB-NP%20Protocols%20 compliance_cbd.pdf accessed 1 April 2020.

Gillespie, A, *Protected Areas and International Environmental Law* (Martinus Nijhoff Publishers 2007).

Guruswamy, L, *International Environmental Law in a nutshell* (Thomson Reuters 2012).

Hunter, C, 'Sustainable Bioprospecting: Using Private Contracts and International Legal Principles and Policies to Conserve Raw Materials' (1997) 25 *Boston College Environmental Affairs Law Review*, p. 129.

IUCN, available at https://www.iucn.org/theme/world-heritage/natural-sites accessed 1 April 2020.

Jeffrey, M, 'Bioprospecting: Access to Genetic Resources and Benefit Sharing under the Convention on Biodiversity and the Bonn Guidelines' (2002) 6 *Singapore Journal of International & Comparative Law*, p. 747.

Kloppenburg, J, 'Impeding Dispossession, Enabling Repossession: Biological Open Source and the Recovery of Seed Sovereignty' (2012) 10 *Journal of Agrarian Change*, p. 367.

Morgera, E, 'An International Legal Concept of Fair and Equitable Benefit-sharing' (2016) 27 (2) *European Journal of International Law*, pp. 353–383.

Morgera, E, Study on Experiences Gained with the Development and Implementation of the Nagoya Protocol and Other Multilateral Mechanisms and the Potential Relevance of Ongoing Work Undertaken by Other Processes, Including Case Studies (Montreal, Canada) (2016), UNEP/CBD/A BS A10 EM/2016/ 2–22 December 2015.

Morgera, E, and Tsioumani, E, 'Yesterday, Today, and Tomorrow: Looking Afresh at the Convention on Biological Diversity' (2010) 21(1) *Yearbook of International Environmental Law*, pp. 3–40.

Morgera, E, Tsioumani, E, and Buck, M, *Unravelling the Nagoya Protocol: A Commentary on the Nagoya Protocol on Biological Diversity* (Martinus Nijhoff Publishers 2014).

Prip, C and Rosendal, K, *Access to Genetic Resources and Benefit-sharing from their Use (ABS) – State of Implementation and Research Gaps* (Fridtjof Nansens Institutt, August 2015).

Rayfuse, R, 'Biological Resources' in D Bodansky, J Brunnée, and E Hey (eds), *Oxford Handbook of International Environmental Law* (Oxford University Press 2007), pp. 362, 366, 360.

Schroeder, D, Chennells, R, Louw, C, Snyders, L, and Hodges, T, 'The Rooibos Benefit Sharing Agreement–Breaking New Ground with Respect, Honesty, Fairness, and Care' (2020) 29(2) *Cambridge Quarterly of Healthcare Ethics*, pp. 285–301.

UN General Assembly, World Charter for Nature, 28 October 1982, A/RES/37/7.

UNEP, *Towards the Vision 2050 on Biodiversity: Living in Harmony with Nature*, available at https://www.unenvironment.org/news-and-stories/story/towards-vision-2050-biodiversity-living-harmony-nature accessed 1 March 2020.

United Nations, Cartagena Protocol on Biosafety, adopted on 29 January 2000, art. 4. According to art. 37(1) the protocol entered into force on 11 September 2003, after the 50th instrument of ratification was deposited in 2003.

United Nations, Convention on Future Multilateral Cooperation on Northwest Atlantic Fisheries, adopted on 24 October 1978.

United Nations Convention on the Law of the Sea, 10 December 1982.

United Nations, Decision CBD/COP/DEC/14/34, 30 November 2018.

United Nations, Decision CP XI/3 "Monitoring Progress in Implementation of the Strategic Plan for Biodiversity 201–2020 and the Aichi Biodiversity Target" (advanced version).

United Nations Environment Programme, Law and National Biodiversity Strategies and Action Plans (Nairobi, Kenya 2018).

United Nations, 1 Decision V/6 'Ecosystem Approach' adopted by the Conference of the Parties to the Convention of Biological Diversity at its Fifth meeting, Nairobi, 15–26 May 2000, UNEP/COP/5/23.

United Nations, Nagoya Protocol on Access and Benefit-sharing, adopted in 2010, entered into force in 2014, it currently has 85 Parties.

WTO, *Matrix on Trade-Related Measures Pursuant to Selected Multilateral Environmental Agreements* (WTO 2017), available at https://www.wto.org/english/tratop_e/envir_e/envir_matrix_e.htm accessed 1 April 2020.

10 Water resources

From a scattered compliance regime to a centralised compliance control

1 Introduction

International law regulating world's water resources has become a critical area in recent times due to several human and environmental threats to sustainability. International water law (IWL) as a legal system is characterised by a considerable dispersion as to the regulation of the various environmental problems and the different compliance mechanisms, on occasion testing the limits of compliance. Attempts to define IWL have referred to it as the 'law of the non-navigational uses of international watercourses', being mainly governed by the principle of equitable utilization and the principle of no significant harm.[1] However, this definition does not include other water bodies, such as transboundary aquifers, that are also an object of regulation in IWL. It is worth noting here the vast array of sources of IWL, ranging from declarations to bilateral treaties.[2] Hence, IWL encompasses international customary law as well as framework treaties with universal and regional scope of application, framework treaties and regional or binational water law treaties regulating specific water resources.[3]

Guaranteeing a fair and effective management of transboundary water resources is one of the most imperative contemporary challenges faced by States due to the pressures created by water scarcity, water stress of river basins and increasing levels of pollution.[4] With regard to surface waters, the world's more than two hundred international river basins host almost half the global population. Some States heavily rely on transboundary watercourses for at least some of their water needs, with many of them importing 'virtual water' from shared

---

1 Stockholm International Water Institute (SIWI), available at https://www.siwi.org/icwc-course-international-water-law/ accessed 1 March 2020.
2 FAO Legal Office, *Sources of International Water Law*, Development Law Service, FAO Legislative Study 65 1998.
3 Ute Mager, *International Water Law Global Developments and Regional Examples* (Jedermann-Verlag GmbH 2015).
4 The UN Millennium Development Goals Report indicates that more than 1.2 billion people in the world live under conditions of physical water scarcity, and another 1.6 billion people live in areas of economic/political water scarcity, where human, institutional and financial issues limit access to water.

river basins. In a future scenario of scarcity, underground sources represented by the aquifers hold the key to satisfying present and future needs. Furthermore, the impact of climate change on transboundary waters is increasing the level of uncertainty and environmental risks.[5]

In its varied sources, IWL reflects the same weaknesses observed in general international law. Different branches of IL converge in the protection of international water resources; these are mainly IEL but also, up to a certain extent, international heritage law and international human rights law.[6] Since water is considered a commodity from the perspective of public utilities, IWL also offer ramifications in international economic law (particularly, international investment law).[7] Another layer of regulation delves into access to water as an internationally protected right from the standpoint of individuals, groups and communities that claim to have equal access to water and sanitation.[8] The main topics in this sector have been the interaction with the international regime of pollution prevention and control as one of the main problems, and resource allocation in terms of compliance with IWL.[9]

De-centralisation of compliance and monitoring is another feature observed in IWL. Since there is no international institution with the definite power to enforce its rules, IWL relies on domestic law for its implementation.[10] States have entered into numerous subregional, regional and global water-related agreements, and endorsed the principles of IWL, leading to the creation of an extended network of international treaties providing for different ways to secure compliance with IWL. In spite of this, States seem not to fulfil their commitments, creating pockets of non-compliance in IWL which are often dealt with on a national level and only exceptionally at the international level.

This chapter first addresses the international governance of water, outlining the legal framework to set the background to the analysis of compliance in this legal sector. The chapter then examines state practice regarding compliance with IWL in a variety of ways. Taking into consideration the widespread State support for the United Nations Convention on the Law of the Non-Navigational Uses of

5 D. Ziganshina, 'International Water Law in Central Asia: Commitments, Compliance and beyond' (2009) 20(2/3) *Journal of Water Law*, pp. 96–107, available at http://www.lawtext. com/lawtextweb/default.jsp?PageID=2&PublicationID=8&pubSection=4#15 accessed 1 April 2020.

6 UNESCO, Hydro-diplomacy, Legal and Institutional Aspects of Water Resources Governance: From the International to the Domestic Perspective: Training Manual, Document code:SC-2016/ WS/20 (2016), available at https://unesdoc.unesco.org/ark:/48223/pf0000245262 accessed 1 April 2020.

7 Fabrizio Marrella, 'On the Changing Structure of International Investment Law: The Human Right to Water and ICSID Arbitration' (2010) 12 *International Community Law Review*, p. 335.

8 Philippe Cullet, *Water Law and Water Sector Reforms* (Oxford University Press 2009).

9 On water law, see, amongst others, William Howarth and Donald McGillivray, *Water Pollution and Water Quality Law* (Shaw & Sons 2001).

10 S. Burchi, *Domestic Water Laws for Effective Governance and for Compliance with International Commitments* (International Association for Water Law -AIDA- 2016).

International Watercourses ('UNWC' or 'International Watercourses Convention') in 1997, it turns to analyse compliance mechanisms set up in various international legal instruments, assessing the role they play.[11] Particularly, the focus is on those agreements of multilateral character, such as the previously alluded to UN Watercourses Convention. The adoption of this Convention constituted a major milestone in IWL as it introduced an overarching framework regulating the rights and duties of States sharing freshwater resources.[12]

Appropriately applied, IWL could play a preventative and restorative role, helping to address different climatic and environmental challenges. The chapter discusses the implications for IWL in light of the 1997 International Watercourses Convention (which entered into force in 2014), covering other recent developments. To illustrate the matter of compliance the chapter includes fragments of leading cases in the field and new cases, such as those brought before the International Court of Justice.[13] Finally, the chapter concludes with a reflection on the need for effective compliance mechanisms in IWL.

2 Water resources in international environmental law: dispersion of international norms and compliance

The use and management of shared water resources has been an area for cooperation in IEL. Traditionally, the utilisation of surface water and sweet water resources has been regulated through bilateral and regional treaties.[14] Specifically, river commissions are predecessors to a series of international norms regulating water resources and are often seen as laying the groundwork for the establishment of international organisations.[15]

Principles such as equitable and reasonable utilisation; the obligation not to cause significant harm; and principles of cooperation, information exchange, notification, consultation and peaceful settlement of disputes are all comprised in modern international memoranda, agreements and treaties. The function of the principles in IWL is to enhance effective transboundary water resources

---

11 UN, Convention on the Law of the Non-navigational Uses of International Watercourses 1997, available at https://legal.un.org/ilc/texts/instruments/english/conventions/8_3_1997.pdf accessed 1 April 2020.

12 The Convention was adopted on 21 May 1997 at the UN General Assembly.

13 International Court of Justice, *Pulp Mills on the River Uruguay* (Argentina v. Uruguay) Judgment of 20 April 2010 and *Certain Activities carried out by Nicaragua in the Border Area* Certain Activities Carried Out by Nicaragua in the Border Area (Costa Rica v. Nicaragua) Judgment of 16 December 2015.

14 FAO-Legal Office, Some General Conventions, Declarations, Resolutions and Decisions adopted by International Organizations, International Non-Governmental Institutions, International and Arbitral Tribunals, on International Water Resources – FAO Legislative Study 65 (Development Law Service 1998), available at https://www.peacepalacelibrary.nl/ebooks/files/w9549e00.pdf accessed 1 April 2020.

15 Sergei Vinogradov, Patricia Wouters and Patricia Jones, *Transforming Potential Conflict into Cooperation Potential: The Role of International Water Law* (UNESCO/IHP/WWAP 2003), available at https://unesdoc.unesco.org/ark:/48223/pf0000133258 accessed 1 April 2020.

management involving riparian States of shared watercourses, promoting sustainable development around the world. The principle of 'community of interest' was spelled out by the Permanent Court of International Justice in the following terms:

> [t]he community of interest in a navigable river becomes the basis of a common legal right, the essential features of which are the perfect equality of all riparian States in the use of the whole course of the river and the exclusion of any preferential privilege of any one riparian State in relation to the others.[16]

Notwithstanding, the various types of water resources regimes have received a scattered treatment in international law. There is not a single regime in IWL but different regimes applicable to different types of resources (groundwater, surface water, aquifers). Overall, there has been a shift from pollution control and water management to a focus on conservation of water resources. This considerable dispersion is, in turn, reflected in the compliance with IWL.

Access to water resources and conflicts resulting from the lack of access to water or water pollution have traditionally been well-researched areas in IEL. Long-lasting disputes and recent disputes relating to access to water resources have emphasised their relevance. Indeed, in the 2000s various legal controversies surrounding access to and conservation of water resources emerged in international litigation, with some cases being brought before the International Court of Justice.[17]

The legal status of water resources under international law varies according to the type of resources (surface or groundwater), the hydrological configuration and the regime adopted to regulate them, including groundwater and aquifers under the UN Draft Articles on the Law of Transboundary Aquifers and the UN International Watercourses Convention. From a natural resources perspective, various theories have emerged to underpin States' regulation, such as the theory of absolute territorial sovereignty and the theory of limited territorial sovereignty, balanced with the principle of equitable use and the no-harm principle.[18] Most freshwater sources are actually underground; geologically and hydrographically, groundwater interacts with surface water (international rivers). Therefore, for example, the pollution of surface water may have devastating consequences for groundwater. Polluting activities in groundwater or excessive withdrawal may also affect surface waters shared between two (or more) States.

16 PCIJ, River Oder Case (1929), File E. b. XX. Docket XVII. 2. Judgment No. 16, 10 September 1929, available at http://www.worldcourts.com/pcij/eng/decisions/1929.09.10_river_oder.htm accessed 1 April 2020.

17 ICJ, Pulp mills on the River Uruguay (Argentina v. Uruguay), Judgment of 20 April 2010, available at https://www.icj-cij.org/en/case/135/judgments accessed 1 April 2020.

18 Laurence Boisson de Chazournes, *Freshwater and International Law: The Interplay between Universal, Regional and Basin Perspectives* (UNESCO World Water Assessment Programme 2009).

IWL has evolved from including a predominant 'shared natural resources' slant to articulating other approaches based on sustainable management inspired by the sustainable development principle and human rights considerations.[19] Cases dating back to the period of the Permanent Court of International Justice, such as the previously mentioned dispute relating to the International Commission on the River Oder. In this case, the PCIJ stressed the relevance of the principle of equality of rights of States with a legitimate interest in the navigable use of a watercourse.[20]

Some States have led the way to more stringent legislation to protect water resources, like the European Union Member States, constructing the legal protection around directives, such as the Water Framework Directive (WFD), which provides for the management of water bodies based on river basins or catchments, involving the public in the management.[21] Although establishing common goals across the EU, the implementation of the WFD in each EU Member State has yielded different outcomes.[22]

Because of the reasons discussed above, compliance with IWL is difficult to secure in practice. In absence of a comprehensive and authoritative legal framework, various sets of rules apply in IWL, making the implementation of international law norms complicated. Several guidelines have been adopted to provide assistance to those involved in compliance and in international dispute settlement, and, more broadly, in international conflict resolution.[23]

Two UN Resolutions marked the starting point for the codification of the law of water resources in terms of ocean and freshwater resources: the Resolution 2570 (C) (XXV) (on law of the sea, the seabed and the ocean floor) and the other Resolution 2669 (XXV) (on international watercourses).[24] The trajectories of these resolutions differed significantly from each other in terms of the process

---

19 Several international legal instruments refer to the application of the sustainable development principle in IWL. See, for instance, UN CSD 2001, World Water Vision 2000, UN CSD 1998, Agenda 21 1992, Dublin Statement 1992.

20 Stephen C. McCaffrey, 'Case International Commission of the Oder', in Max Planck Encyclopedia of International Law [MPIL] (Oxford University Press 2007), available at https://opil.ouplaw.com/view/10.1093/law:epil/9780199231690/law-9780199231690-e1298 accessed 1 April 2020.

21 European Union, 'Introduction to the EU Water Framework Directive', available at https://ec.europa.eu/environment/water/water-framework/info/intro_en.htm, accessed 1 April 2020. Water Framework Directive, Cases concerning the infringement of the WFD have proliferated, see, for instance, Commission v Spain (Détérioration de l'espace naturel de Doñana) Case C-559/19.

22 Laurence Carvalho et al., 'Protecting and Restoring Europe's Waters: An Analysis of the Future Development Needs of the Water Framework Directive' (2019) 658 *Science of the Total Environment*, pp. 1228–1238.

23 Jerome Delli Priscoli and Aaron T. Wolf, *Managing and Transforming Water Conflicts* (Cambridge University Press 2010).

24 Muhammad Mizanur Rahaman, 'Principles of International Water Law: Creating Effective Transboundary Water Resources Management' (2009) 1(3) *International Journal of Sustainable Society*, pp. 207–233.

of codification and progressive development of IEL. As a result of the first one, the UNCLOS was adopted in 1982, whereas the Convention on the Law of the Non-Navigational Uses of International Watercourses was only concluded in 1997.[25]

Although some environmental provisions relating to the conservation of water resources are embodied in the law of the sea, the emphasis there is on pollution of the marine environment rather than on environmental compliance as such. The Convention on the Law of the Sea establishes a regimen that focusses on oceans but presents some significant commonalities with the law of international watercourses in terms of pollution control and conservation of resources. Both regimes are largely based on the rules and principles of customary international law created by consistent state practice.[26]

The dispersion of IWL is a pervasive feature which also influences compliance, with the exception of areas in which codification has operated, such as the non-navigational uses of international watercourses. Codification in terms of transboundary aquifers has led to the adoption of draft articles that, despite not being formally sanctioned as binding international law, reflect customary international law in this area, unveiling the intrinsic interconnections with other branches of international law, such as the law of cultural heritage. From a water management standpoint, initiatives like the Internationally Shared Aquifer Resources Management (ISARM), a joint initiative of UNESCO-IHP, UN/FAO and the International Association of Hydrogeologists (IAH), have contributed to a more comprehensive compliance framework.[27]

Principles applicable to IWL seek to regulate different aspects of water resources under the law of international watercourses, including the no-harm principle and the equitable and reasonable utilization of resources. This entails striking the balance between the different principles at stake. General IEL principles complete the regulatory IWL framework, with the precautionary principle at the centre of the system. By applying a precautionary approach, the burden of proof is reversed in favour of conservation. Under this principle, any proposed activity with potential impacts on water resources should be scrutinised, and the applicant has to prove that it would not have detrimental environmental impacts. Other IEL principles, such as sustainable development, and common heritage rules, also apply to this sector. These general principles and rules of IWL codified in the various legal instruments are equally applicable to surface waters

25 David Freestone and Salman M.A. Salman, 'Ocean and Freshwater Resources', in Daniel Bodansky, Jutta Brunnée, and Ellen Hey (eds), *The Oxford Handbook of International Environmental Law* (Oxford University Press 2008).

26 Stephen McCaffrey, 'International Water Law for the 21st Century: The Contribution of the U.N. Convention' (2001) 118 *Journal of Contemporary Water Research and Education*, available at https://core.ac.uk/download/pdf/60534697.pdf accessed 1 April 2020.

27 Stefano Burchi, 'Legal Frameworks for the Governance of International Transboundary Aquifers: Pre- and Post-ISARM Experience' (2018) 20 *Journal of Hydrology: Regional Studies*, pp. 15–20.

and groundwater resources. It is worth mentioning that there is no uniform or homogeneous application of the rules as, in some cases, principles such as the common interest principle[28] are not relevant for the regulation of some water resources.[29] Substantive and procedural principles and multilateral conventions set out the framework in which agreements display their effects, adjusting and adopting the content of their provisions in older or subsequent treaties.

Interpretation tools may assist in carrying out compliance tasks through specific treaty bodies instituted under each treaty. In *Gabcikovo-Nagymaros*, the International Court of Justice (ICJ) resorted to the principles of equitable utilisation of natural resources, alluding to 'evolving provisions of environmental law.'[30] In the ruling the ICJ made it clear that IWL encompasses a series of contemporary principles and concepts, such as the precautionary principle, intergenerational equity and prior and continuous environmental impact assessment.[31]

Main compliance issues and the nature of the problems observed in the practice of IWL are related to access to water resources, sustainable use of the resources as well as prevention and control of transboundary water pollution. Water pollution is a growing problem caused by discharges into the aquatic environment and into the rivers and watercourses of one State that straddle national boundaries and can affect another through transport, diffusion or dispersion originating from industrial sources such as pulp mills, iron and steel smelters, and petrochemical industries.[32] Other sources of pollution include chemicals, waste of various origin and organic matter, which are frequently discharged into rivers, lakes and streams that lie beneath common borders.[33] One of the main challenges is indirect pollution, such as the pollution originated by the discharge of hazardous substances into aquifers that straddle two States. Emissions can be transported by surface waters or by the wind, being deposited on a body of water or on the soil filtering into groundwater sources. Clearly, chemical pollution of surface waters is a major environmental problem which can alter the ecological status of water bodies. Under EU law, river basin-specific pollutants are considered part of the ecological status.[34]

28 Wolfgang Benedek, Koen De Feyter, Matthias C. Kettemann, and Christina Voigt, *The Common Interest in International Law* (Intersentia 2014).

29 Jutta Brunnée and Stephen J. Toope, 'Environmental Security and Freshwater Resources: Ecosystem Regime Building' (1997) 91 *American Journal of International Law*, pp. 26–59.

30 E. Hey, 'International Water Law Placed in a Contemporary Environmental Context: The Gabcíkovo-Nagymaros Case' (2000) 25(3) *Physics and Chemistry of the Earth, Part B: Hydrology, Oceans and Atmosphere*, pp. 303–308.

31 Ibid.

32 United Nations Water, *Transboundary Waters* (2020), available at https://www.unwater.org/water-facts/transboundary-waters/ accessed 1 April 2020.

33 UNEP, *Preliminary Assessment of the Water Quality Situation in Rivers in Latin America, Africa and Asia, A Snapshot of the World's Water Quality* (2016), available at https://uneplive.unep.org/media/docs/assessments/unep_wwqa_report_web.pdf accessed 1 April 2020.

34 European Union-Environment, *Strategies against Chemical Pollution of Surface Waters* (2019), available at https://ec.europa.eu/environment/water/water-dangersub/candidate_list_1.htm#:~:-text=%2F11%2FEC.-, Chemical%20pollution%20of%20surface%20waters%20and%20the%20

Strategies to address these problems vary. Under European Union legislation measures against chemical pollution of surface waters have two components. The first consists of the selection and regulation of substances and pollutants that threaten the sustainability of water resources as an EU-wide concern (the priority substances). Member States select the substances of national or local concern (river basin specific pollutants) for control at the relevant level. The second element is the setting of environmental quality standards that are then implemented through different regulatory tools.[35] Disparities across EU Member States concerning implementation of the directive create differentiation in terms of the level of protection.[36]

In IEL, environmental objectives and the principles underpinning the protection of water resources. The solutions articulated therein are of a more a remedial nature in order to control water pollution. Some of the problems refer to the quality and quantity of water, and are dealt with by upper and lower riparian owners along international rivers. Remedial measures, however, are not sufficient to tackle the main problems observed in practice in this area of IEL; the ex post grievance remedial mechanisms should be part of a more comprehensive approach including ex ante measures. This is the specific approach taken in various regional and bilateral international agreements.

3 Multilateral treaties/conventions and international case law on water resources, including trans-boundary waters and watercourses: different types of compliance mechanisms

Different types of water resources are subject to the respective sets of regulations that deal with those resources that show similar characteristics. On a global scale, different normative instruments in the matter take on board international law regulating groundwater and international river/lake/basin governance arrangements.

Water scarcity and water security have become relevant in the face of the world's freshwater crisis, in which access to water resources is not guaranteed, with a significant percentage of the world's population living in river basins under current or future water stress and suffering severe water shortage.[37] As a

Water%20Framework%20Directive, and%20development%20of%20control%20measures accessed 1 April 2020.

35 Nikolaos Voulvoulis, Karl Dominic Arpon, and Theodoros Giakoumis, 'The EU Water Framework Directive: From Great Expectations to Problems with Implementation' (2017) 575 *Science of the Total Environment*, pp. 358, 358–366.

36 Johanna Söderasp and Maria Pettersson, 'Before and After the Weser Case: Legal Application of the Water Framework Directive Environmental Objectives in Sweden' (2019) 31(2) *Journal of Environmental Law*, pp. 265–290.

37 V. Smakhtin, C. Revenga, and P. Doll, 'Taking into Account Environmental Water Requirements in Global-scale Water Resources Assessments' (Comprehensive Assessment Secretariat 2004), available at https://www.researchgate.net/publication/241486821_Taking_into_account_

result, a considerable portion of the world's population will lack access to sufficient freshwater resources, which also hinders sustainable development and the fulfilment of Sustainable Development Goals.[38]

Different legal considerations arise for each 'water body', groundwater and surface water, as discussed in the previous section. Seen from a legal standpoint, water resources are regulated in distinctive sets of norms, which have confronted the issue of compliance with IWL in different ways. The diversity of international legal instruments and compliance models is nothing new to IWL. There is no single compliance mechanism, but there are several legal techniques used in the context of IWL underpinned by common legal principles and obligations: duty to cooperate, principle of equitable utilization, obligation not to cause transboundary harm and the precautionary principle, amongst others.

Traditionally, bilateral agreements between riparian States along rivers flowing between them and sharing water resources have been common in IWL. Multilateral and universal instruments present numerous advantages in terms of governance and compliance; however, the main caveat is how to reach consent and to ensure compliance with IWL provisions. The adoption of multilateral environmental agreements, such as the UNECE Water Convention, represents a further development in IWL. As a multilateral agreement, the UNWC is open to all States, reaching consensus over specific issues and agreeing on general provisions that can be used as a framework for the negotiation of bilateral and regional agreements. A panoply of dispute settlement mechanisms are listed in Article 33, ranging from negotiations to more sophisticated mechanisms, such as arbitration.[39]

The primary purpose of IWL, as an international legal regime, is to establish a coherent framework of enforceable rights and obligations, which ensures predictability and fosters the achievement of common goals. To this aim, soft-law instruments have assisted States in compliance with IWL, such as Geneva Strategy on Compliance.[40] Other instruments have sought to achieve consistency in compliance with IWL, promoting, at the same time, the goal of sustainable development.[41] In terms of compliance, these instruments encompass a set of rights and obligations governing the use of freshwater resources, preserving their

---

environmental_water_requirements_in_global-scale_water_resources_assessments accessed 1 April 2020.

38 United Nations, Sustainable Development Goals, available at https://www.un.org/sustainabledevelopment/?s=Water accessed 1 April 2020.

39 'Article 33. Settlement of disputes 1.In the event of a dispute between two or more parties concerning the interpretation or application of the present Convention, the parties concerned shall, in the absence of an applicable http://www.unwatercoursesconvention.org/the-convention/ accessed 1 April 2020.

40 Geneva Strategy and Framework for Monitoring Compliance with Agreements on Transboundary Waters: Elements of a Proposed Compliance Review Procedure, Expert's Report, UN Doc MP.WAT/2000/5.

41 Dr Patricia K. Wouters and Alistair S. Rieu-Clarke, *The Role of International Water Law in Promoting Sustainable Development*.

availability from an intra- and inter-generational perspective while also prior-itising sustainable development and having regard for the needs of vulnerable groups.[42]

International treaties concerning international aquifers are distinct in nature as they are bilateral or involve States concerned. Interestingly, agreements re-garding aquifers that straddle the international boundary lines of states are a rel-atively recent phenomenon. Some of the regional approaches to management of water resources appear to be more holistic and have generated a number of new stances grounded in principles that apply to a wider spread of pollution sources.

Given the relevance of water resources and the EU's position on the matter, the Water Framework Directive (WFD) comprises under its regulatory framework var-ious water bodies including 'groundwater bodies' which means distinct volumes of groundwater within an aquifer or aquifers.[43] The innovation in compliance consists in the comprehensive approach adopted in EU legislation and national law to address water pollution, achieving specific targets and water quality standards. Member States aim to achieve good qualitative and quantitative status of all water bodies (including marine waters up to one nautical mile from shore).

In Europe, the UNECE Convention on the Protection and Use of Trans-boundary Watercourses and International Lakes (Water Convention) and the Protocol on Water and Health[44] have codified a number of rules and general principles applicable in the European region.[45] Although the Water Convention was initially negotiated as a regional instrument, it was opened up for accession to all UN Member States in 2016.[46] The Water Convention sets up a mechanism to strengthen international cooperation and national measures in the area of ecologically sound management and protection of transboundary surface waters and ground waters.

One compliance-related aspect that is interesting to observe across these ex-amples is whether it might be plausible to extrapolate compliance mechanisms rules regarding watercourses adopted in one region to other regions.

4 International water law (IWL) and the law of trans-boundary aquifers

IWL offers many nuances in terms of compliance, as it encompasses different water bodies considered from a transboundary perspective and regulated under

42 DFID 2001 Water Crisis Strategy, available at https://www.ircwash.org/sites/default/files/DFID-2001-Addressing.pdf accessed 1 April 2020.

43 European Union, 'Introduction to the EU Water Framework Directive', available at https://ec.europa.eu/environment/water/water-framework/info/intro_en.htm accessed 1 April 2020.

44 The Protocol was concluded under the auspices of UNECE and WHO-Europe. Information available at https://www.unece.org/env/water/pwh_text/text_protocol.html 1 April 2020.

45 The Convention on the Protection and Use of Transboundary Watercourses and International Lakes (Water Convention) Was Adopted in Helsinki in 1992 and Entered into Force in 1996, available at https://www.unece.org/env/water/text/text.html accessed 1 April 2020.

46 Chad and Senegal have become the first non-European Parties in 2018.

regimes separately instituted which has led to various systems.[47] IWL principles also apply across these different sub-systems from transboundary water resources management to groundwater resources. Based on customary international law, these principles are incorporated into recent international conventions and treaties.

Despite progress achieved in other areas, the regulation of transboundary aquifers has been overlooked in IEL until recently.[48] Different sets of international legal instruments governing transboundary aquifers are scattered in IEL, comprising provisions in international agreements and one codification attempt: the 2008 Draft Articles on the Law of Transboundary Aquifers (Draft Articles) adopted by the ILC.[49] Equally important are the interactions between the regulation of transboundary aquifers and the UN Watercourses Convention (UNWC), which may also serve as guidance with respect to transboundary water resources. In Europe, the law of transboundary aquifers also includes the UNECE Convention on the Protection and Use of Transboundary Watercourses and International Lakes (UNECE Water Convention)[50] and the UNECE Model Provisions on Transboundary Groundwater.[51] In addition, there are few bilateral and multilateral agreements focussing on specific transboundary aquifers, as discussed below. In relation to implementation and compliance, several initiatives have emerged in the field of transboundary aquifers.[52] To name just one, the Internationally Shared Aquifer Resources Management (ISARM).[53]

Aquifers are a source for groundwater, being defined in legal instruments as 'a permeable water-bearing geological formation underlain by a less permeable layer' (Article 2.a of the Draft Articles on Transboundary Agreements).[54] They are considered transboundary when they are situated in different States, it is estimated that there are approximately 600 transboundary aquifers and groundwater bodies around the world. Transboundary aquifers constitute approximately

---

47 Terje Tvedt and Tadesse Kasse Woldetsadik (eds), *A History of Water*, Series III, Volume 2: Sovereignty and International (Bloomsbury 2015).

48 G. Eckstein and F. Sindico, 'The Law of Transboundary Aquifers' (2014) 23 *Review of European Comparative & International Environmental Law*, pp. 32–42.

49 International Law Commission, Draft articles on the Law of Transboundary Aquifers (2008), ECE/MP.WAT/40, available at https://legal.un.org/ilc/texts/instruments/english/draft_articles/8_5_2008.pdf 1 April 2020.

50 The Convention on the Protection and Use of Transboundary Watercourses and International Lakes (Water Convention) was adopted in 1992 and entered into force in 1996.

51 UNECE, Model Provisions on Transboundary Groundwaters (2014), available at https://www.unece.org/fileadmin/DAM/env/water/publications/WAT_model_provisions/ece_mp.wat_40_eng.pdf 1 April 2020.

52 Raya Marina Stephan,' International Water Law for Transboundary Aquifers – A Global Perspective' (2018) 4(2) *Central Asian Journal of Water Research*, pp. 48–58.

53 This is a joint initiative of UNESCO-IHP, UN/FAO, and the International Association of Hydrogeologists (IAH), which traces its origins back to the Ministerial Declaration of the Hague on Water Security in the 21st Century (March 2000).

54 Christina Leb, *Cooperation in the Law of Transboundary Water Resources* (Cambridge University Press 2013).

97% of the available freshwater on the planet, hence playing a key role in global water security and fulfilling a significant function in terms of the sustainability of ecosystems and water supply.[55]

In an attempt to class international agreements regulating transboundary aquifers, some of them are of a bilateral nature, like the very first contemporary international treaty regulating on transboundary aquifers. This bilateral agreement dates back to 1977 and it was concluded between France and Switzerland.[56] Another more recent example, it is the agreement on the Al-Sag/Al Disi Aquifer, signed in 2015 by Jordan and Saudi Arabia.[57] Some of these agreements function as predecessors to the draft articles, acting as the same time as the main source for the provisions contained therein. Other similar agreements are of a more informal nature, being based on memoranda of understanding or even minutes of meetings, such as the one regulating the Nubian Sandstone Aquifer System (1992 and updated in 2000) signed by Chad, Egypt, Libya and Sudan. Another agreement type of agreements are trilateral agreement or tri-lateral consultative arrangement for the North-Western Sahara Aquifer System, made by Algeria, Libya and Tunisia in the period 2002–2008 which consists, technically, of minutes of meetings and joint ministerial declarations. A good example is the agreement (formally, a Memorandum of Understanding) made in 2009 by Mali, Niger and Nigeria for the establishment of a tri-lateral consultative arrangement for the Iullemeden Aquifer System (IAS).[58] An interesting feature of international treaty practice in this field is that some agreements have been replaced before entering into force that may indicate effectivity issues. In other words, the agreement is not in force yet, however it is due for replacement by a later agreement (also technically, a Memorandum of Understanding). To illustrate, the agreement made in 2014 by Algeria, Benin, Burkina Faso, Mali, Mauritania, Niger and Nigeria for the Iullemeden and Taoudeni/Tanezrouft Aquifer Systems (ITAS) and the establishment of a comparable multi-partite Consultative Mechanism for the ITAS.[59]

---

55 According to the 2019 United Nations World Water Development Report, approximately 2.5 billion people depend solely on groundwater resources to satisfy their basic needs. Groundwater provides drinking water to more than half of the global population and supplies 43% of the water used for irrigation.

56 In chronological order, this is the first agreement on record and it was concluded in 1977 by France and Switzerland on the Genevese Aquifer, which was re-negotiated in 2007. Leaving no one behind (2019), available at https://www.unwater.org/publications/world-water-development-report-2019/ accessed 1 April 2020.

57 Agreement between the Government of the Hashemite Kingdom of Jordan and the Government of the Kingdom of Saudi Arabia for the Management and Utilization of the Ground Waters in the Al-Sag/Al-Disi Layer.

58 Integrated and Sustainable Management of Shared Aquifer Systems and Basins of the Sahel Region, RAF/7/011 Iullemeden Aquifer System (2017), available at https://www.iaea.org/sites/default/files/raf7011_iullemeden_basin.pdf accessed 1 April 2020.

59 Ibid.

Finally, subregional agreements also regulate transboundary aquifers such as the agreement on the Guarani Aquifer, concluded in 2010 by Argentina, Brazil, Paraguay and Uruguay.

Draft articles on the Law of Transboundary Aquifers (2008) put forward a series of provisions reflecting international practice in the sector.[60] The draft articles follow a traditional international law structure based on state sovereignty. To regulate the management of water resources, the articles draw upon pre-existing bilateral, regional and international agreements and arrangements on groundwaters.

It is worth to bear in mind that as the text states

> even if the general obligations are formulated in mandatory language, the modalities for achieving compliance with the main obligations remain recommendatory, in order to facilitate compliance by States. Monitoring would generally be less important when the aquifer or aquifer system is not utilized.[61]

Although not being formally adopted, these articles can be implemented based on reciprocity. They also address areas to be revisited, including sovereignty and recharge zone states.[62] The Draft Articles interact with other relevant IWL instruments, they are interrelated. Nevertheless, criticisms arise as it does not appropriate addresses the circumstances of joint water management.[63] Finally, a normative approach to the UNWC and the law of transboundary aquifers, reveals the necessary interactions between the regimes to ensure an appropriate level of compliance.

Amongst the various regional agreements discussed, the Guarani Aquifer Agreement between four MERCOSUR Member States represents an attempt to regulate the usage of shared water resources, guaranteeing, at the same time, their conservation.[64] Because of the geographical extension, the Guarani Aquifer System as a transboundary aquifer represents an interesting case for the present study.[65] The Guarani Aquifer System (GAS) is one of the largest reservoirs of freshwater worldwide shared by Argentina, Brazil, Paraguay and Uruguay. There

---

60 Text adopted by the International Law Commission at its sixtieth session, in 2008, and submitted to the General Assembly as a part of the Commission's report covering the work of that session (A/63/10).
61 Draft Articles, Article 13.7.
62 David J. Devlaeminck, 'Reassessing the Draft Articles on the Law of Transboundary Aquifers through the Lens of Reciprocity' (2020) *International Journal of Water Resources Development*.
63 Flavia Rocha Loures and Alistair Rieu-Clarke, The UN Watercourses Convention in Force: Strengthening International Law for, at 276.
64 Sindico Francesco, Hirata Ricardo, and Manganelli Alberto, 'The Guarani Aquifer System: From a Beacon of Hope to a Question Mark in the Management/Governance of Transboundary Aquifers' (2018) 20 *Journal of Hydrology Regional Studies*, pp. 49–59, available at https://pure-portal.strath.ac.uk/en/publications/the-guarani-aquifer-system-from-a-beacon-of-hope-to-a-question-ma accessed 1 April 2020.
65 The Guarani aquifer is one of the largest reservoirs of freshwater, it contains enough fresh water to fulfil the needs of world's population.

is an international treaty in place that regulates the management of this transboundary aquifer concluded under the auspices of MERCOSUR: the Guaraní Aquifer Agreement (GAA).[66]

From a regulatory standpoint, the GAA relies on the UN International Law Commission Draft Articles on the Law of Transboundary Aquifers, which is referred to in its preamble. The GAS has led to continued transboundary cooperation between the four countries, not only restricted to the use of shared transboundary water resources but also focussing on conservation and protection of the aquatic ecosystem.

As an innovative initiative that fosters compliance, it is worth mentioning the GAS Project (Project for Environmental Protection and Sustainable Development of the Guaraní Aquifer System) carried out by the four countries sharing the resource, the Global Environment Facility (GEF), the World Bank and the Organization of American States (OAS).[67] This joint collaboration resulted in a Declaration of Basic Principles and Action Guidelines, which acknowledge the nature of the Guaraní Aquifer, as a transboundary shared water resource and the need to protect it from pollution and achieve a sustainable management.[68]

Scholars in the field divide the cooperation articulated around the use and conservation of the resource into main different periods: a first period (2002–2010) of positive cooperation, marked by a better understanding of the aquifer leading to the adoption of the Guarani Aquifer Agreement in August 2010. This period was followed by a second period (2010–2017) with a slowdown in transboundary cooperation, with some cross border projects and initiatives linked to past and existing international projects and a final period in which the ratification by the remaining state and entry into force. In this latter period, Argentina, Brazil and Uruguay ratified the agreement, with the last ratification by Paraguay pending to be submitted for the agreement to enter into force.[69]

Key elements for implementation and compliance are the adoption of good substantive and institutional practices, taking stock of transboundary cooperation that have occurred until now.

66 The signature of the Guarani Aquifer Agreement on 2 August 2010 by Argentina, Brazil, Paraguay and Uruguay represented a significant step due to the few number of treaties dedicated to transboundary aquifer cooperation, the absence of a water conflicts. The official version of the GAA is available (in Spanish) at https://www.internationalwaterlaw.org/documents/regional-docs/Guarani_Aquifer_Agreement-Spanish.pdf accessed 1 April 2020.

67 World Bank, Project for Environmental Protection and Sustainable Development of the Guaraní Aquifer System, available at https://projects.worldbank.org/en/projects-operations/project-detail/P068121 accessed 1 April 2020.

68 Organisation of American States, *Strategic Action Plan* (2009), available at http://www.oas.org/DSD/WaterResources/projects/Guarani/SAP-Guarani.pdf accessed 1 April 2020.

69 Francesco Sindico and Laura Movilla, 'The Interplay between the UN Watercourses Convention and the Law on Transboundary Aquifers (Article 2)', in Laurence Boisson de Chazournes, Makane Moise Mbengue, Mara Tignino, Komlan Sangbana, Jason Rudall (eds), *Convention on the Law of the Non-Navigational Uses of International Watercourses* (Oxford University Press 2018), available at https://pureportal.strath.ac.uk/en/publications/the-interplay-between-the-un-watercourses-convention-and-the-law- accessed 1 April 2020.

5 The UN watercourses convention: a turning point for IWL?

Conservation and management of water resources has been addressed on the international and regional levels and in the works leading to the UNWC.[70] Although hailed as an innovative and comprehensive treaty governing the usage, management and protection of international watercourses, the United Nations Watercourses Convention (UNWC) did not enter into effect for a long period.[71] The process of codification in this area was set in motion at the same time of the law of the sea.[72]

The required number of ratifications and the time elapsed since the adoption, resulted in a lengthy and complex process of ratification, delaying the implementation of the UNWC to different later stages.[73] This is a multilateral and universally accepted treaty codifying law applicable to freshwater resources.[74] In its configuration, the UNWC, as an overarching legal instrument, it lays down the responsibilities and rights of all Member States to ensure cooperation over transboundary watercourses.[75] Evidently, the level of detail and the type of provisions qualify more as a guidance for the successive formulation of other bilateral and regional agreements governing transboundary water cooperation. The UNWC goes beyond to offer as a cooperation forum for states to settled any issues peacefully and agree on the sharing of the benefits of international watercourses.[76]

Some criticism has arisen with regard to the vagueness of the rules set forth in the UNWC as this may hinder compliance amongst Member States. From a purely effectiveness stance, the UNWC provides some elements to foster its role in enforcing provisions. However, without a proper follow-up and compliance mechanism, key provisions of the Convention would be rendered ineffective.

Particular attention deserve the substantive provisions of the UNWC that attempt to regulate the joint use of water resources. Of course, the scope is to regulate 'uses of international watercourses and of their waters for purposes

---

70 Adopted by the General Assembly of the United Nations on 21 May 1997. Entered into force on 17 August 2014. See General Assembly resolution 51/229, annex, Official Records of the General Assembly, Fifty-first Session, Supplement No. 49 (A/51/49), available at https://legal. un.org/ilc/texts/instruments/english/conventions/8_3_1997.pdf accessed 1 April 2020.

71 Bhargav Sriganesh, *Compliance with UN Watercourses Convention: Half Full or Half Empty?* 12 May 2017, available at https://www.e-ir.info/2017/05/12/compliance-with-un-watercourses-convention-half-full-or-half-empty/ accessed 1 April 2020.

72 André Nollkaemper, 'The Contribution of the International Law Commission to International Water Law: Does it Reverse the Flight from Substance?' (1996) 27 *Netherlands Yearbook of International Law*, pp. 39–73.

73 Patricia Wouters, 'The Legal Response to International Water Conflicts: The UN Watercourses Convention and beyond (1999) 42 *German Year Book International Law*, p. 293.

74 The Convention was adopted in May 1997, 106 Member States of the UN supported the Convention. Only few States (China, Turkey and Burundi) voted against the agreement.

75 UNWC, Articles 5 and 7.

76 Loures et al. 2009, 10.

other than navigation and to measures of protection, preservation and management related to the uses of those (international) watercourses and their waters'[77] whereby 'international watercourse' is defined as 'a watercourse, parts of which are situated in different States'.[78]

Principles regulating compliance with IWL, Equitable and reasonable utilization and participation.[79] Equally important is the obligation not to cause significant harm[80] and the obligation to cooperate.[81]

Dispute settlement methods under Art 33 of the UNWC, include the list of traditional dispute settlement compliance mechanisms based on the parties' consent: negotiation, good offices and mediation, conciliation, joint watercourse institutions or submission of the dispute to arbitration or to the International Court of Justice by adjudication. The main innovation in this regard, wherever these methods prove unfruitful consists in the possibility to carry out a compulsory fact-finding procedure conceived as a compulsory conciliation.

The question concerning the shift operated by the UNWC entails looking into implementation and compliance. With regard to compliance, the main contribution of the UNWC has been the codification of customary international law and filling legal gaps in the management of transboundary watercourses.[82] The UNWC is an international legal instrument with significant formal authority and legitimacy to shift the focus in IWL, devoting more attention to compliance. Although the UNWC has its shortcomings, it has the virtue to offer a stable framework for the negotiation, conclusion and development of new international treaties, devising more sophisticated compliance mechanisms.

6 The human right perspective: enforcing the human right to water

Compliance with IWL at international and national law has a clear impact on the enjoyment of human rights. Lack of appropriate management and non-compliance have deep implications for the enjoyment of human rights. Water conflicts between States affect access to water and management of water resources. The interface between a proper management of water resources and access to water is

---

77 UNWC, Article 1.1.
78 UNWC, Article 2.b.
79 Part Ii. General Principles. Article 5.
80 Article 7 1.Watercourse States shall, in utilizing an international watercourse in their territories, take all appropriate measures to prevent the causing of significant harm to other watercourse States.
81 Article 8. General obligation to cooperate. 1. Watercourse States shall cooperate on the basis of sovereign equality, territorial integrity, mutual benefit and good faith in order to attain optimal utilization and adequate protection of an international watercourse.
82 Alistair Rieu-Clarke, Marie-Laure Vercambre, Lesha Witmer, Everything You Need to Know about the UN Watercourses Convention, Flavia Loures, January 2015, available at https://www.gcint.org/wp-content/uploads/2015/09/UNWC.pdf 1 April 2020.

evidenced in various international cases. Some national legislations provide tools for resolving them.

Parallel to these developments, there is an emerging recognition in international human rights law of adequate access to water as a human right. The recognition of access to water as a human right in various international legal instruments offers another layer for the analysis of compliance from a comparative perspective. Notwithstanding this, there are difficulties of ensuring the effective implementation of the right to water. In exploring the different avenues for implementation, new insights on the human right to water provide new perspective on compliance and enforceability; referred to as 'justiciability' of the right. The need for a new approach implies addressing 'the deep inequalities in life chances that divide countries and people within countries on the basis of wealth, gender and other markers for deprivation'.[83]

Taking into account all these circumstances, the justiciability of the right to water or, in other words, the effective access of citizens to safe water and sanitation is crucial. The enforceability of the right to water and, in general, of Economic, Cultural and Social Rights (ECSR) is a transnational issue, which has been raised by prominent scholarship over the past years. In a future scenario of scarcity, the availability of international and national legal mechanisms for redress is critical. In this regard, transnational environmental law is shaping national environmental systems and case law. As a result, the international trend toward the recognition of the right to water is reflected also in national courts.

The evolution of the right to water can be traced back to the resolutions and declarations of the various conferences and forums and other developments of the early 1970s. The evolution of the right to water has occurred under the international legal regime for the protection and promotion of human rights, namely, under the Universal Declaration of Human Rights and the International Covenant on Economic, Social and Cultural Rights. The role of the Committee on Economic, Social and Cultural Rights in fostering the recognition of a specific right to water through the issuance of General Comment No. 15, which identifies the content of the human right to water. Looking at the management of water resources through the lenses of human rights entails the legal recognition and enforcement of the right to water, pointing the attention to some policy aspects that related to the right, such as participatory water management regimes. This approach is bolstered also by the authority that lies with the numerous leading cases from national jurisdiction to harness progress to a fully-fledged recognition of the right to water.

General Comment No. 15 represents a momentum to efforts aimed at translating those soft-law commitments into substantive, precise and legally binding obligations. In this evolution, a number of General Assembly resolutions relating to water and climate change (including the Sustainable Development

---

83 Human Development Report 2006, 'Beyond Scarcity: Power, Poverty and the Global Water Crisis', at 27, available at http://hdr.undp.org/en/media/HDR06-complete.pdf 1 April 2020.

Goals), contributing a significant body of soft-law provisions, which provides further evidence about an incipient (and ever evolving) right to water in public international.[84]

New mechanisms for ensuring compliance with water law have been set up in domestic jurisdictions. One of the tools relied upon by national courts are public hearings. The leading case Matanza-Riachuelo/Mendoza Case is an example of regulatory innovation in water pollution control.[85] The extent to which these mechanisms can be deployed in other jurisdictions. By extrapolating the normative and basis of a human right to water within the fabric of the IWL, new stances to the use of shared resources and water management.

MENDOZA BEATRIZ SILVA ET AL VS. STATE OF ARGENTINA ET AL ON DAMAGES (DAMAGES RESULTING FROM ENVIRONMENTAL POLLUTION OF MATANZA/RIACHUELO RIVER)

Supreme Court of Justice of Argentina – Judgment 8 July 2008

Summary

In July 2004, a group of residents of the Matanza/Riachuelo basin filed a suit before the Supreme Court of Argentina against the national government, the Province of Buenos Aires, the City of Buenos Aires and 44 companies seeking compensation for damages resulting from pollution of the basin, stoppage of contaminating activities and remedy for collective environmental damage. In July 2008, the Court issued a decision in which it required the national government, the Province of Buenos Aires and the City of Buenos Aires to take measures to improve the residents' quality of life, remedy the environmental damage and prevent future damage. The Court established an action plan requiring the government agency responsible for the Matanza/Riachuelo basin, ACUMAR[1], to fulfil specific measures, including: (a) producing and disseminating public information; (b) controlling industrial pollution; (c) cleaning up waste dumps; (d) expanding water supply, sewer and drainage works; (e) developing an emergency sanitation plan; and (f) adopting an international measurement

(Continued)

---

84 Salman M.A. Salman and Siobhán McInerney-Lankford, 2004. The Human Right to Water: Legal and Policy Dimensions. Law, Justice, and Development; Washington, DC: World Bank, available at https://openknowledge.worldbank.org/bitstream/handle/10986/14893/302290PAPER0Human0right0to0H2O.pdf?sequence=1&isAllowed=y 1 April 2020.

85 J.M. Belisle, La causa Mendoza, in B. Olmos Giupponi (ed), *Cambio Climatico, Derechos Humanos y Medio Ambiente* (Dike 2011).

system to assess compliance with the plans goals. In order to ensure adequate enforcement, the Court delegated the enforcement process to a federal court, Juzgado Federal de Primera Instancia de Quilmes, to monitor enforcement of the decision. Furthermore, the Court created a working group formed by the national Ombudsman and the NGOs[2] that had been involved in the case as non-litigant parties, seeking to strengthen and enable citizen participation in monitoring enforcement of the decision.

In its decision, the Court did not expressly adopt a human rights perspective. However, the Court stated that the action plan's objective should be improving the residents' quality of life and required specific sanitation programs to be adopted to meet the needs of the basin's population. The wording of the decision leaves open the possibility of promoting the human rights issue in the execution stage. Furthermore, the NGOs, in their submissions as third parties to the case, held that in this case several economic, social and cultural rights are directly affected. The main affected right is the right to health, which covers basic health factors, including but not limited to access to clean and drinking water, to adequate sanitation conditions and to a healthy environment.

15. (…) effective implementation requires a program (or action plan) that properly addresses the identified behaviour with technical precision, the identification of a subject who is obliged to comply with the decision, setting objective indicators to allow periodical monitoring over the outcomes, and ample participation in the monitoring.

16. The River Basin Authority (…) is obliged to carry out the program, and will assume the responsibility for any non-compliance or delays in carrying out the goals set. The Authority must comprise representatives of the State, the province of Buenos Aires and the Autonomous City of Buenos Aires, who are responsible for the watershed under the obligations set in the Constitution and local and regional laws.

17. The present ruling mandates that the River Basin Authority complete the following program:

Objectives

The program must simultaneously purse three objectives, as follows:

1   Improving the quality of life of the river basin inhabitants;
2   Environmental restoration of all river basin's components (water, air, soil);
3   The prevention of any foreseeable harm.

In order to determine the level of compliance of these objectives, the River Basin Authority must adopt one of the available international measurement systems and notify the relevant tribunal of the compliance with this decision within 90 working days. Failure to comply with this decision within the mandated period will result in the imposition of a daily fine.

Enforcement of the Decision and Outcomes:

The Court ordered the government authorities found responsible to fulfill the objectives and schedules given in the decision. Throughout enforcement of the decision, the court in charge has sought ways to single out concrete actions and expand the said objectives, and ACUMAR, through the Plan de Saneamiento Integral submitted in February 2010, has expanded the objectives even more. In spite of such efforts, throughout this process the enforcement court has requested the Ombudsman to issue an opinion on the adequacy, quality and sufficiency of the measures established by ACUMAR. In the months following the sentence, the working group has stated that, although ACUMAR made efforts in 2010 to work towards fulfilling the terms of the decision, it has not yet wholly met any of the obligations set forth in the decision and in the plan established by ACUMAR. Therefore, there have been several requests for fines against responsible officials. The process has also included the establishment of indicators (http://www.acumar.gov.ar/pagina/204/indicadores-informes, 2011 and 2012), hearings, timetables and the responsibility of specific governmental authorities, in order for the enforcement court to define terms missing in the decision and to understand the stage of progress of certain individual measures.

Beyond enforcement, this decision changed the way politics are done in the basin by establishing that the authority in charge of executing the clean-up plan be ACUMAR, an inter-jurisdictional agency, whose function is to correct the issues of poor coordination among agencies and applicable regulations and to improve the oversight of polluting activities. Furthermore, the decision opened spaces for civil society participation in policymaking and monitoring processes. The working group is involved on a permanent basis in monitoring Supreme Court orders, replying to court requests and organizing meetings with grassroots organizations to promote and expand citizen awareness and to channel the concerns of the basin's residents.

In 2016, the Supreme Court took note of implementation gaps relating to the 2008 decision and ordered the Basin Authority, ACUMAR, to create a detailed plan to comply with that ruling.

In a November 2016 hearing, petitioners had showed that the ACUMAR was not in compliance with the 2008 ruling. In response, the Court ordered ACUMAR to produce a report by March 1, 2017,

(*Continued*)

detailing a compliance plan, including specific timetables for compliance; additionally, the Court obligated ACUMAR to issue periodic progress reports to monitor compliance. The 2016 decision recalled that the earlier ruling had ordered ACUMAR, the State of Argentina, the Buenos Aires Province and the City of Buenos Aires to implement a Comprehensive Plan for Environmental Rehabilitation (PISA). The PISA was to include three objectives: improving the quality of life for the river basin residents, the rehabilitation of the environment and the prevention of foreseeable harms.

The 2016 Court stressed that ACUMAR must comply with all of the PISA objectives and identified seven areas for special attention: (1) A system of effective control and inspection of industrial contamination must be developed; (2) ACUMAR must work with the City of Buenos Aires and the towns within that province to collect trash in the area, particularly around the banks of the river, to prevent open-air dumps; (3) ACUMAR needs to expand the availability to potable water and sewer services and track progress in creating sewer systems; (4) ACUMAR must comply with the Marco Convention regarding the relocation of at-risk towns and settlements, and the City of Buenos Aires should continue construction of the towpath to towns 21–24 and 26 and relocate the residents; (5) Buenos Aires, through ACUMAR, must provide an update on the housing complexes it committed to build for the relocation of residents of towns 21–24 and 26 and give a date when construction will finish; (6) ACUMAR must implement an effective public health plan, including preventative care, emergency care and continuing care to those suffering health problems in areas of the river basing that are vulnerable or experience high poverty. ACUMAR must give information detailing the number and geographic distribution of health problems related to contamination and how they are improving and report on the development progress of health care systems; (7) ACUMAR must develop a system of quality indices that comply with international standards to monitor environmental quality, particularly regarding the condition of surface water. With special attention to these priorities, the Court ordered the federal judges of the lower courts to intensify control over ACUMAR's compliance with the PISA objectives.

Source: SAIJ http://www.saij.gob.ar/corte-suprema-justicia-nacion-federal-ciudad-autonoma-buenos-aires-mendoza-beatriz-silvia-otros-estado-nacional-otros-danos-perjuicios-danos-derivados-contaminacion-ambiental-rio-matanza-riachuelo-fa08000047-2008-07-08/123456789-740-0008-0ots-eupmocsollaf Author's translation

Pulp mills

Pulp Mills on the River Uruguay (Argentina v. Uruguay), ICJ, Judgment of 20 April 2010

(1). The obligation to contribute to the optimum and rational utilization of the river (Article 1) 170–177 (2). The obligation to ensure that the management of the soil and woodland does not impair the regime of the river or the quality of its waters (Article 35) 178–180. (3). The obligation to co-ordinate measures to avoid changes in the ecological balance (Article 36) 181–189. (4). The obligation to prevent pollution and preserve the aquatic environment (Article 41).

175. The Court considers that the attainment of optimum and rational utilization requires a balance between the Parties' rights and needs to use the river for economic and commercial activities, on the one hand, and the obligation to protect it from any damage to the environment that may be caused by such activities, on the other hand. The need for this balance is reflected in various provisions of the 1975 Statute establishing rights and obligations for the Parties, such as Articles 27, 36, and 41. The Court will therefore assess the conduct of Uruguay in authorizing the construction and operation of the Orion (Botnia) mill in the light of those provisions of the 1975 Statute, and the rights and obligations prescribed therein.

176. The Court has already addressed in paragraphs 84 to 93 above the role of CARU with respect to the procedural obligations laid down in the 1975 Statute. In addition to its role in that context, the functions of CARU relate to almost all aspects of the implementation of the substantive provisions of the 1975 Statute. Of particular relevance in the present case are its functions relating to rule-making in respect of conservation and preservation of living resources, the prevention of pollution and its monitoring, and the co-ordination of actions of the Parties. These functions will be examined by the Court in its analysis of the positions of the Parties with respect to the interpretation and application of Articles 36 and 41 of the 1975 Statute.

177. Regarding Article 27, it is the view of the Court that its formulation reflects not only the need to reconcile the varied interests of riparian States in a transboundary context and in particular in the use of a shared natural resource, but also the need to strike a balance between the use of the waters and the protection of the river consistent with the objective of sustainable development. The Court has already dealt with the obligations arising from Articles 7 to 12 of the 1975 Statute which have to be observed, according to Article 27, by any party wishing to exercise its right to use the waters of the river for any of the purposes mentioned therein insofar as such use may be liable to affect the regime of the river or the quality

(Continued)

of its waters. The Court wishes to add that such utilization could not be considered to be equitable and reasonable if the interests of the other riparian State in the shared resource and the environmental protection of the latter were not taken into account. Consequently, it is the opinion of the Court that Article 27 embodies this interconnectedness between equitable and reasonable utilization of a shared resource and the balance between economic development and environmental protection that is the essence of sustainable development.

WATER FRAMEWORK DIRECTIVE

Quality Standards

Article 4

Environmental objectives

1   In making operational the programmes of measures specified in the river basin management plans:

a   for surface waters

    i   Member States shall implement the necessary measures to prevent deterioration of the status of all bodies of surface water, subject to the application of paragraphs 6 and 7 and without prejudice to paragraph 8;

    ii   Member States shall protect, enhance and restore all bodies of surface water, subject to the application of subparagraph (iii) for artificial and heavily modified bodies of water, with the aim of achieving good surface water status at the latest 15 years after the date of entry into force of this Directive, in accordance with the provisions laid down in Annex V, subject to the application of extensions determined in accordance with paragraph 4 and to the application of paragraphs 5, 6 and 7 without prejudice to paragraph 8;

    iii   Member States shall protect and enhance all artificial and heavily modified bodies of water, with the aim of achieving good ecological potential and good surface water chemical status at the latest 15 years from the date of entry into force of this Directive, in accordance with the provisions laid down in Annex V, subject to the application of extensions determined in accordance with paragraph 4 and to the application of paragraphs 5, 6 and 7 without prejudice to paragraph 8;

iv   Member States shall implement the necessary measures in accordance with Article 16(1) and (8), with the aim of progressively reducing pollution from priority substances and ceasing or phasing out emissions, discharges and losses of priority hazardous substances

without prejudice to the relevant international agreements referred to in Article 1 for the parties concerned;

b   for groundwater

i   Member States shall implement the measures necessary to prevent or limit the input of pollutants into groundwater and to prevent the deterioration of the status of all bodies of groundwater, subject to the application of paragraphs 6 and 7 and without prejudice to paragraph 8 of this Article and subject to the application of Article 11(3)(j);

ii   Member States shall protect, enhance and restore all bodies of groundwater, ensure a balance between abstraction and recharge of groundwater, with the aim of achieving good groundwater status at the latest 15 years after the date of entry into force of this Directive, in accordance with the provisions laid down in Annex V, subject to the application of extensions determined in accordance with paragraph 4 and to the application of paragraphs 5, 6 and 7 without prejudice to paragraph 8 of this Article and subject to the application of Article 11(3)(j);

iii   Member States shall implement the measures necessary to reverse any significant and sustained upward trend in the concentration of any pollutant resulting from the impact of human activity in order progressively to reduce pollution of groundwater.

Measures to achieve trend reversal shall be implemented in accordance with paragraphs 2, 4 and 5 of Article 17, taking into account the applicable standards set out in relevant Community legislation, subject to the application of paragraphs 6 and 7 and without prejudice to paragraph 8;
(c) for protected areas

Member States shall achieve compliance with any standards and objectives at the latest 15 years after the date of entry into force of this Directive, unless otherwise specified in the Community legislation under which the individual protected areas have been established.

Source: European Union. https://eur-lex.europa.eu/eli/
dir/2000/60/oj

Judgment of the Court (First Chamber)

3 October 2019

(Reference for a preliminary ruling — Environment — Directive
91/676/EEC — Protection of waters against pollution caused
by nitrates from agricultural sources — Objective of reducing
pollution — Waters affected by pollution — Maximum nitrate level
of 50 mg/1 — Action programmes adopted by the Member States —
Rights of individuals to have such a programme amended — Locus
standi before the national authorities and courts)
Case C-197/18, Wasserleitungsverband Nördliches Burgenland
and Others

Locus standi of individuals

30 According to settled case-law of the Court, it would be incompatible with the binding effect conferred by Article 288 TFEU on a directive to exclude, in principle, the possibility that the obligations which it imposes may be relied on by the persons concerned (judgments of 19 January 1982, Becker, 8/81, EU:C:1982:7, paragraph 22; of 7 September 2004, Waddenvereniging and Vogelbeschermingsvereniging, C 127/02, EU:C:2004:482, paragraph 66; and of 20 December 2017, Protect Natur-, Arten- und Landschaftsschutz Umweltorganisation, C 664/15, EU:C:2017:987, paragraph 34).

31 In particular, where the EU legislature has, by directive, imposed on Member States the obligation to pursue a particular course of action, the effectiveness of such action would be weakened if individuals were prevented from relying on it before their national courts and if the latter were prevented from taking it into consideration as an element of EU law in deciding whether the national legislature, in exercising the choice open to it as to the form and methods for implementation, has kept within the limits of its discretion set out therein (judgments of 24 October 1996, Kraaijeveld and Others, C 72/95, EU:C:1996:404, paragraph 56, and of 26 June 2019, Craeynest and Others, C 723/17, EU:C:2019:533, paragraph 34).

32 It follows, as the Advocate General observed in point 41 of her Opinion, that at least the natural or legal persons directly concerned by an infringement of provisions of a directive must be in a position to require the competent authorities to observe such obligations, if necessary by pursuing their claims by judicial process.

33 In addition, 'where they meet the criteria, if any, laid down in [the] national law, members of the public' have the rights provided for in Article 9(3) of the Aarhus Convention. That provision, read in conjunction with Article 47 of the Charter of Fundamental Rights of the European Union, imposes on Member States an obligation to ensure effective judicial

protection of the rights conferred by EU law, in particular the provisions of environmental law (see, to that effect, judgment of 20 December 2017, Protect Natur-, Arten- und Landschaftsschutz Umweltorganisation, C 664/15, EU:C:2017:987, paragraph 45).

34 The right to bring proceedings set out in Article 9(3) of the Aarhus Convention would be deprived of all useful effect, and even of its very substance, if it had to be conceded that, by imposing those conditions, certain categories of 'members of the public', a fortiori 'the public concerned', such as environmental organisations that satisfy the requirements laid down in Article 2(5) of the Aarhus Convention, were to be denied of any right to bring proceedings (judgment of 20 December 2017, Protect Natur-, Arten- und Landschaftsschutz Umweltorganisation, C 664/15, EU:C:2017:987, paragraph 46).

35 In order to determine whether natural and legal persons such as the applicants in the main proceedings are directly concerned by an infringement of the obligations provided for in Directive 91/676, it is necessary to examine the purpose and the relevant provisions of that directive, the proper application of which is asserted before the referring court.

36 The purpose of Article 1 of Directive 91/676 is to reduce water pollution caused or induced by nitrates from agricultural sources and to prevent further such pollution. To that end, Article 5 of that directive provides that, in accordance with the conditions which it lays down, Member States are to establish action programmes and, if necessary, adopt additional measures or reinforced actions.

37 In accordance with Article 2(j) of that directive, 'pollution' is defined as the discharge, directly or indirectly, of nitrogen compounds from agricultural sources into the aquatic environment, the results of which are such as to cause hazards to human health, harm to living resources and to aquatic ecosystems, damage to amenities or interference with other legitimate uses of water.

38 That concept is given specific expression in Article 3(1) of Directive 91/676 and, in particular, in Annex I A, point 2 to that directive, according to which Member States must at least consider that groundwaters are polluted if they contain more than 50 mg/l nitrates or could be polluted if, in the absence of appropriate measures taken under Article 5 of that directive, those levels could be exceeded.

39 Therefore, it follows from Article 2(j) and Article 3(1) of Directive 91/676 that nitrate levels in groundwater that exceed or could exceed 50 mg/l must be considered to be such as to interfere with the legitimate use of water.

(*Continued*)

40 It follows from the above that a natural or legal person having the option of drawing and using groundwater is directly concerned by that threshold being exceeded or the risk of it being exceeded, which is capable of limiting that person's option by interfering with the legitimate use of that water.

41 In view of the variety of uses referred to in Article 2(j) of Directive 91/676, the fact that values over that threshold do not, as such, involve a danger to the health of the persons wishing to bring an action is not capable of calling into question that conclusion.

42 As regards in particular the situation of the applicants in the main proceedings, it is apparent from the order for reference that, pursuant to Paragraph 10 of the Law on water rights 1959, they are entitled to operate groundwater wells at their disposal for domestic or commercial needs.

43 To the extent that the nitrate levels in the groundwaters in question exceed or could exceed 50 mg/l, the use of that water by the applicants in the main proceedings is interfered with.

44 According to the order for reference, exceeding that threshold is such as to prevent them from being able to make normal use of the water from their wells or, at the very least, to force them to incur costs for its decontamination.

45 Consequently, natural and legal persons such as those in the main proceedings are directly concerned by the failure to attain the main objective of Directive 91/676, laid down in Article 1 thereof, of reducing and preventing water pollution caused or induced by nitrates from agricultural sources as a result of the infringement of certain obligations of the Member States deriving from that directive.

46 It follows that natural and legal persons, such as the applicants in the main proceedings, must be in a position to require national authorities to observe those obligations, if necessary by bringing an action before the competent courts.

On the extent of the obligation to reduce and prevent pollution

47 As regards the obligations deriving from Directive 91/676, the referring court wishes to know, in particular, whether the maximum nitrate level of 50 mg/l in groundwater, provided for in Annex I A, point 2 to that directive, is a deciding factor for obliging the competent national authorities to amend the action programmes they have adopted pursuant to Article 5(1) to (4) of that directive or to adopt additional measures, in accordance with Article 5(5) of that directive.

48 In that regard, it must be recalled that, in accordance with the Court's settled case-law, in interpreting a provision of EU law it is necessary to consider not only its wording but also the context in which it

occurs and the objectives pursued by the rules of which it is part (judgment of 7 February 2018, American Express, C 304/16, EU:C:2018:66, paragraph 54 and the case-law cited).

49 As the Advocate General observed in point 55 of her Opinion, under Article 37 of the Charter of Fundamental Rights of the European Union, Article 3(3) TEU and Article 191(2) TFEU, EU policy on the environment aims at a high level of protection.

50 It follows from paragraphs 36 to 39 of the present judgment that, by attaining its objective of reducing water pollution caused or induced by nitrates from agricultural sources and preventing any further such pollution, Directive 91/676 seeks to allow individuals to make legitimate use of water, which means that the nitrate level must not exceed 50 mg/l.

51 As the Advocate General observed in points 72 and 73 of her Opinion, Directive 91/676 provides for specific instruments to combat water pollution by nitrates from agricultural sources. It applies where the discharge of nitrogen compounds of agricultural origin makes a significant contribution to the pollution (judgment of 29 April 1999, Standley and Others, C 293/97, EU:C:1999:215, paragraph 35). In that connection, it must be noted that the Court has previously held that such a contribution is significant where agriculture contributes, for instance, 17% of the total nitrogen in a specific basin (see, to that effect, judgment of 22 September 2005, Commission v Belgium, C 221/03, EU:C:2005:573, paragraph 86). If that condition for the application of Directive 91/676 is satisfied, it is for the Member States to determine, in accordance with Article 3(1) of that directive, the status of the waters within their territory.

52 Where, pursuant to that latter provision, read in conjunction with Annex I A to Directive 91/676, water must be considered as being affected or capable of being affected, Member States are required to adopt the measures provided for in Article 5 of that directive, namely action programmes and, if necessary, additional measures and reinforced actions (see, to that effect, judgment of 21 June 2018, Commission v Germany, C 543/16, not published, EU:C:2018:481, paragraph 60).

53 As regards action programmes, their implementation is inextricably linked to Article 3(1) of Directive 91/676, since, as long as the water is or could be polluted in the absence of appropriate action programmes adopted pursuant to Article 5(4) of that directive, Member States are obliged to adopt such action programmes. The measures contained therein are, in any event, broadly determined by Directive 91/676 itself, as is apparent from Article 5(4) thereof, read in conjunction with Annex III thereto.

(*Continued*)

54 It is true that Member States have a certain latitude as regards the precise methods of implementing the requirements of Directive 91/676. However, they are, in all circumstances, obliged to ensure that the objectives of that directive, and consequently the objectives of European Union policy in the area of the environment, are achieved, in accordance with the requirements of Article 191(1) and (2) TFEU (judgment of 4 September 2014, Commission v France, C 237/12, EU:C:2014:2152, paragraph 30).

55 It follows from Article 5(5) of that directive that Member States are required to take, in the framework of the action programmes, such additional measures or reinforced actions as they consider necessary if, at the outset or in the light of experience gained in implementing the action programmes, it becomes apparent that the measures referred to in Article 5(4) will not be sufficient to attain the objectives laid down in Article 1 of that directive.

56 According to the case-law of the Court, it follows that the Member States must take such additional measures or reinforced actions at the point at which it first becomes clear they are necessary (see, to that effect, judgment of 21 June 2018, Commission v Germany, C 543/16, not published, EU:C:2018:481, paragraph 53 and the case-law cited).

57 In order to fulfil the aforementioned obligation in particular, Member States are required to monitor the water status closely. Thus, in accordance with the first subparagraph of Article 5(6) of Directive 91/676, they are required to draw up and implement monitoring programmes.

Source: http://curia.europa.eu/juris/document/document. jsf?text=&docid=218620&pageIndex=0&doclang=EN&mode=lst&dir=&occ=first&part=1&cid=1286876

LATIN AMERICAN WATER TRIBUNAL

Decision

La Parota Dam

UN Committee on Economic, Social and Cultural Rights (CESCR), UN Committee on Economic, Social and Cultural Rights: Concluding Observations of the Mexico, 9 June 2006, E/C.12/MEX/CO/4

C. Factors and difficulties impeding the implementation of the Covenant

9. The Committee notes the absence of any major factors or difficulties impeding the effective implementation of the Covenant in the State party.

D. Principal subjects of concern

10. The Committee is concerned about reports that members of indigenous and local communities opposing the construction of the La Parota hydroelectric dam or other projects under the Plan Puebla-Panama are not properly consulted and are sometimes forcefully prevented from participating in local assemblies concerning the implementation of these projects. It is also concerned that the construction of the La Parota dam would cause the flooding of 17,000 hectares of land inhabited or cultivated by indigenous and local farming communities, that it would lead to environmental depletion and reportedly displace 25,000 people. It would also, according to the Latin American Water Tribunal, violate the communal land rights of the affected communities, as well as their economic, social and cultural rights.

Source: https://www.refworld.org/docid/
45377fa20.html [accessed 24 May 2020]

Bibliography

Belisle, JM, 'La proteccion constitucional del medio ambiente en Argentina: Reflexiones a la luz del caso "Cuenca Riachuelo"', in B Olmos Giupponi (ed), *Cambio Clima'tico, Derechos Humanos y Medio Ambiente* (Dike 2011), pp. 57–74.

Benedek, Wolfgang, De Feyter, Koen, Kettemann, Matthias C, and Voigt, Christina, *The Common Interest in International Law* (Intersentia 2014).

Boisson de Chazournes, L, *Freshwater and International Law: The Interplay between Universal, Regional and Basin Perspectives* (UNESCO World Water Assessment Programme 2009).

Brunnée, J and Toope, SJ, 'Environmental Security and Freshwater Resources: Ecosystem Regime Building' (1997) 91 *American Journal of International Law*, pp. 26–59.

Burchi, S, *Domestic Water Laws for Effective Governance and for Compliance with International Commitments* (International Association for Water Law -AIDA- 2016).

Burchi, S, 'Legal Frameworks for the Governance of International Transboundary Aquifers: Pre- and Post-ISARM Experience' (2018) 20 *Journal of Hydrology: Regional Studies*, pp. 15–20.

Carvalho, L et al., 'Protecting and Restoring Europe's Waters: An Analysis of the Future Development Needs of the Water Framework Directive' (2019) 658 *Science of the Total Environment*, pp. 1228–1238.

Court of Justice of the European Union, Water Framework Directive, Cases concerning the infringement of the WFD have proliferated, see, for instance, Commission v Spain (Détérioration de l'espace naturel de Doñana) Case C-559/19.

Cullet, P, *Water Law and Water Sector Reforms* (Oxford University Press 2009).

Delli Priscoli, JA and Wolf, T, *Managing and Transforming Water Conflicts* (Cambridge University Press 2010).

Devlaeminck, DJ, 'Reassessing the Draft Articles on the Law of Transboundary Aquifers through the Lens of Reciprocity' (2020) *International Journal of Water Resources Development*.

Eckstein, G, and Sindico, F, 'The Law of Transboundary Aquifers' (2014) 23 *Review of European Comparative & International Environmental Law*, pp. 32–42.

European Union, 'Introduction to the EU Water Framework Directive', available at https://ec.europa.eu/environment/water/water-framework/info/intro_en.htm, accessed 1 April 2020.

European Union-Environment, Strategies against Chemical Pollution of Surface Waters (2019), available at https://ec.europa.eu/environment/water/water-dangersub/candidate_list_1.htm#:~:text=%2F1%2FEC.,Chemical%20pollution%20of%20surface%20waters%20and%20the%20Water%20Framework%20Directive,and%20development%20of%20control%20measures accessed 1 April 2020.

FAO-Legal Office, Some General Conventions, Declarations, Resolutions and Decisions Adopted by International Organizations, International Non-Governmental Institutions, International and Arbitral Tribunals, on International Water Resources – FAO Legislative Study 65 (Development Law Service 1998), available at https://www.peacepalacelibrary.nl/ebooks/files/w9549e00.pdf accessed 1 April 2020.

FAO Legal Office, *Sources of International Water Law*, FAO Legislative Study 65, (Development Law Service 1998).

Freestone, D, and Salman, MA Salman, 'Ocean and Freshwater Resources', in D Bodansky, J Brunnée, and E Hey (eds), *The Oxford Handbook of International Environmental Law* (Oxford University Press 2008), pp. 337–361.

Hey, E, 'International Water Law Placed in a Contemporary Environmental Context: The Gabcíkovo-Nagymaros Case' (2000) 25(3) *Physics and Chemistry of the Earth, Part B: Hydrology, Oceans and Atmosphere*, pp. 303–308.

Howarth, W, and McGillivray, D, *Water Pollution and Water Quality Law* (Shaw & Sons 2001).

ICJ, Pulp Mills on the River Uruguay (Argentina v. Uruguay), Judgment of 20 April 2010, available at https://www.icj-cij.org/en/case/135/judgments accessed 1 April 2020.

International Law Commission, Draft Articles on the Law of Transboundary Aquifers (2008), ECE/MP.WAT/40, available at https://legal.un.org/ilc/texts/instruments/english/draft_articles/8_5_2008.pdf accessed 1 April 2020.

Leb, C, *Cooperation in the Law of Transboundary Water Resources* (Cambridge University Press 2013).

Mager, U, *International Water Law Global Developments and Regional Examples* (Jedermann-Verlag GmbH 2015).

Marrella, F, 'On the Changing Structure of International Investment Law: The Human Right to Water and ICSID Arbitration' (2010) 12 *International Community Law Review*, p. 335.

McCaffrey, SC, 'Case International Commission of the Oder', in Max Planck Encyclopedia of International Law [MPIL] (Oxford University Press 2007), available at https://opil.ouplaw.com/view/10.1093/law:epil/9780199231690/law-9780199231690-e1298 accessed 1 April 2020.

McCaffrey, S, 'International Water Law for the 21st Century: The Contribution of the U.N. Convention' (2001) 118 *Journal of Contemporary Water Research and Education*, available at https://core.ac.uk/download/pdf/60534697.pdf accessed 1 April 2020.

Nollkaemper, A, 'The Contribution of the International Law Commission to International Water Law: Does it Reverse the Flight from Substance?' (1996) 27 *Netherlands Yearbook of International Law*, pp. 39–73.

Organisation of American States, Strategic Action Plan (2009), available at http://www.oas.org/DSD/WaterResources/projects/Guarani/SAP-Guarani.pdf accessed 1 April 2020.

PCIJ, River Oder Case (1929), File E. b. XX. Docket XVII. 2. Judgment No. 16, 10 September 1929, available at http://www.worldcourts.com/pcij/eng/decisions/1929.09.10_river_oder.htm 1 April 2020 accessed 1 April 2020.

Raya Marina, S, 'International Water Law for Transboundary Aquifers – A Global Perspective' (2018) 4(2) *Central Asian Journal of Water Research*, pp. 48–58.

Rieu-Clarke, A, Vercambre, ML, Witmer, Lesha, Everything You Need to Know about the UN Watercourses Convention, Flavia Loures, January 2015, available at https://www.gcint.org/wp-content/uploads/2015/09/UNWC.pdf accessed 1 April 2020.

Rocha Loures, F, and Rieu-Clarke, A, *The UN Watercourses Convention in Force: Strengthening International Law for Transboundary Water Management* (Routledge 2017).

Salman, Salman MA and McInerney-Lankford, Siobhán. 2004. The Human Right to Water: Legal and Policy Dimensions. Law, Justice, and Development; Washington, DC: World Bank, available at https://openknowledge.worldbank.org/bitstream/handle/10986/14893/302290PAPER0Human0right0to0H20.pdf?sequence=1&isAllowed=y accessed 1 April 2020.

Sindico, F and Movilla, L, 'The Interplay between the UN Watercourses Convention and the Law on Transboundary Aquifers (Article 2)', in Laurence Boisson de Chazournes, Makane Moise Mbengue, Mara Tignino, Komlan Sangbana, Jason Rudall (eds), Convention on the Law of the Non-Navigational Uses of International Watercourses (Oxford University Press 2018), available at https://pureportal.strath.ac.uk/en/publications/the-interplay-between-the-un-watercourses-convention-and-the-law-accessed 1 April 2020.

Sindico, F, Hirata, R, and Manganelli, A, 'The Guarani Aquifer System: From a Beacon of Hope to a Question Mark in the Management/Governance of Transboundary Aquifers' (2018) 20 *Journal of Hydrology Regional Studies*, pp. 49–59, available at https://pureportal.strath.ac.uk/en/publications/the-guarani-aquifer-system-from-a-beacon-of-hope-to-a-question-ma accessed 1 April 2020.

Smakhtin, V, Revenga, C, and Doll, P, 'Taking into Account Environmental Water Requirements in Global-scale Water Resources Assessments' (Comprehensive Assessment Secretariat 2004), available at https://www.researchgate.net/publication/241486821_Taking_into_account_environmental_water_requirements_in_global-scale_water_resources_assessments accessed 1 April 2020.

Söderasp, J, and Pettersson, M, 'Before and After the Weser Case: Legal Application of the Water Framework Directive Environmental Objectives in Sweden' (2019) 31(2) *Journal of Environmental Law*, pp. 265–290.

Stockholm International Water Institute (SIWI), available at https://www.siwi.org/icwc-course-international-water-law/ accessed 1 March 2020.

Tvedt, T, Woldetsadik, T, and McIntyre, O, (eds), *A History of Water*, Series III, Volume 2: Sovereignty and International (Bloomsbury 2015).

United Nations, Convention on the Law of the Non-navigational Uses of International Watercourses 1997, available at https://legal.un.org/ilc/texts/instruments/english/conventions/8_3_1997.pdf accessed 1 April 2020.

United Nations, CSD 2001, World Water Vision 2000, UN CSD 1998, Agenda 21 1992, Dublin Statement 1992.

UNECE, Model Provisions on Transboundary Groundwaters (2014), available at https://www.unece.org/fileadmin/DAM/env/water/publications/WAT_model_provisions/ece_mp.wat_40_eng.pdf accessed 1 April 2020.

UNECE, The Convention on the Protection and Use of Transboundary Watercourses and International Lakes (Water Convention) Was Adopted in Helsinki in 1992 and Entered into Force in 1996, available at https://www.unece.org/env/water/text/text.html accessed 1 April 2020.

UNECE, The Protocol Was Concluded under the Auspices of UNECE and WHO-Europe. Information available at https://www.unece.org/env/water/pwh_text/text_protocol.html accessed 1 April 2020.

UNEP, Preliminary Assessment of the Water Quality Situation in Rivers in Latin America, Africa and Asia, A Snapshot of the World's Water Quality (2016), available at https://uneplive.unep.org/media/docs/assessments/unep_wwqa_report_web.pdf accessed 1 April 2020.

UNESCO, Hydro-diplomacy, Legal and Institutional Aspects of Water Resources Governance: From the International to the Domestic Perspective: Training Manual, Document code:SC-2016/WS/20 (2016), available at https://unesdoc.unesco.org/ark:/48223/pf0000245262 accessed 1 April 2020.

United Nations, Geneva Strategy and Framework for Monitoring Compliance with Agreements on Transboundary Waters: Elements of a Proposed Compliance Review Procedure, Expert's Report, UN Doc MP.WAT/2000/5.

United Nations, Human Development Report 2006, 'Beyond Scarcity: Power, Poverty and the Global Water Crisis', available at http://hdr.undp.org/en/media/HDR06-complete.pdf accessed 1 April 2020.

United Nations, Sustainable Development Goals, available at https://www.un.org/sustainabledevelopment/?s=Water accessed 1 April 2020.

United Nations Water, Transboundary Waters (2020), available at https://www.unwater.org/water-facts/transboundary-waters/ accessed 1 April 2020.

Vinogradov, S, Wouters, P, and Jones, P, *Transforming Potential Conflict into Cooperation Potential: The Role of International Water Law* (UNESCO/IHP/WWAP 2003), available at https://unesdoc.unesco.org/ark:/48223/pf0000133258 accessed 1 April 2020.

Voulvoulis, N, Arpon, KD, and Giakoumis, T, 'The EU Water Framework Directive: From Great Expectations to Problems with Implementation' (2017) 575 *Science of the Total Environment*, pp. 358, 358–366.

World Bank, Project for Environmental Protection and Sustainable Development of the Guaraní Aquifer System, available at https://projects.worldbank.org/en/projects-operations/project-detail/P068121 accessed 1 April 2020.

Wouters, P, 'The Legal Response to International Water Conflicts: The UN Watercourses Convention and Beyond' (1999) 42 *German Yearbook of International law*, pp. 293–336.

Wouters, P and Rieu-Clarke, A, 'The Role of International Water Law in Promoting Sustainable Development' (2001) 12 *Water Law*, pp. 281–283.

Ziganshina, D, 'International Water Law in Central Asia: Commitments, Compliance and beyond' (2009) 20(2/3) *Journal of Water Law*, pp. 96–107, available at http://www.lawtext.com/lawtextweb/default.jsp?PageID=2&PublicationID=8&pubSection=4#15 accessed 1 April 2020.

Conclusions

From the beginning, International Environmental Law (IEL) has offered more reactive than proactive solutions to cases of transboundary environmental harm. These legislative and policy responses have been slowly modified over the years on the basis of various events that have brought about innovation in implementation and compliance with IEL norms. A burgeoning scholarly literature has addressed the question of compliance and implementation. In the body of this book, four different claims are made about compliance and effectiveness in IEL.

First, theories about compliance with IEL can largely be divided into two categories: those which take formal implementation as the decisive factor which determines success and those which look beyond formal processes and mechanisms in search of innovative approaches that foster compliance and prevent non-compliance. Interestingly, the consequences of these new standpoints and techniques are observed in different areas of IEL regulated through Multilateral Environmental Agreements (MEAs). Looking at the various MEAs in force, they have introduced more advanced mechanisms and tools to deal with cases of non-compliance with IEL norms.

As a second point, a number of questions arise when it comes to the implementation of IEL and monitoring compliance with IEL norms. These mainly concern whether there are really success stories to consider as a blueprint that could be used to foster more effective practices. It also relates to the coverage of the examples observed and the extent to which they may convince sceptics about the functions and operation of IEL. In addressing this issue, compliance systems face challenges determined by the de-centralised characteristics of the IEL system and its heterogeneity. A quantum leap in terms of compliance may be represented by a recasting of compliance and non-compliance mechanisms, resulting in a fundamental modification across the various sub-systems of IEL. In this sense, the Montreal Protocol represented a breakthrough, heralding a new era for non-compliance procedures. Rules governing monitoring bodies, such as those on admissibility and those enhancing the participation by different actors, can be considered the primary rules in this system.

Third, in this landscape, it seems crucial to overcome the divide between soft law and hard law, becoming more aware of artificial distinctions by assigning each type of norms a different role in ensuring compliance with IEL.

The interaction between compliance and effectiveness represents a fourth and crucial area. Effectiveness translates into positive behavioural change or, in other words, into a modification of conduct not only in inter-State relations but also internally in the States that are in line with the objectives set out in the respective treaty. The level of effectiveness indicates to what extent the IEL norm has achieved its goal by fostering positive change (emissions reduction, a particular manner of managing water resources, inter-state cooperation, making reparation possible). Building a robust body of evidence about compliance may facilitate the task of determining the degree of effectiveness. Quantitative studies measuring the impact of norms in IEL can facilitate the emergence of new compliance systems or new standpoints to look at the effectiveness of the norms.

We have considered three crucial areas for the development of innovation in IEL. First, the climate change model offers a more centralised, classic model, open now to private sector engagement. In turn, biodiversity presents more innovations in terms of compliance with IEL, postulating a new era for compliance that moves beyond the inter-state system by incorporating the private sector. International water law offers more dispersion within several areas, less codified. Innovation resides in the possibility to tap into this practice to deploy new methods of ensuring compliance with IEL.

Interaction between the various systems through a systemic approach to IEL is crucial for the progress of the normative systems, as it is to develop a dynamic consideration of compliance, moving away from strict enforcement and embracing non-compliance. In terms of the various strands involved in IEL compliance, some considerations are (in order):

- **Where does innovation lie?:** To answer this question it is necessary to master the intricacies of non-compliance, interpreting it as a category separate from compliance. This entails scrutinising the composition and institutional structure of monitoring bodies and compliance procedures. Scholars distinguish between a technical and a political nature of compliance mechanisms and procedures. Although those processes of a more political nature offer more flexibility, they may risk opening up a negotiable process with no clear results.
- **Liability:** Up to now, State responsibility has been the predominant international law regime applicable to deal with non-compliance, but more creative solutions are emerging. Fundamental limitations are observed in the international law system, like the scarce involvement of private parties and the restricted nature of reparation (discussed below), which leads to significant gaps in the system. The transboundary harm prevention duty remains at the heart of the liability system.
- **Involvement of the private sector:** Whilst development is observed in specific sub-areas, such as biodiversity, the private sector (including businesses and non-profit organisations) continues to be marginalised from law-making and mainstream compliance. Increasingly, due diligence approaches are emphasising the obligation of States to ensure that activities within their

jurisdiction and control respect the environment, and that implies the duty to take action to avoid transboundary harm.

- **Reparation:** In IEL reparation has taken the form of returning the environment to the way it was before the breach took place under the international responsibility regime. New regimes follow a preventative approach, aimed at avoiding the occurrence of environmental damages.
- **Dispute settlement:** A fundamental change in managing non-compliance that is observed consists in the adoption of different methods of dispute avoidance, moving towards a new notion of conflict resolution.

New practices are paving the way for the development of novel mechanisms in IEL. Clearly, the future of compliance with IEL will draw on the evolution of non-compliance procedures in light of the increasing practice observed in the various IEL sub-fields. This implies moving beyond the inter-state matrix to incorporate other relevant stakeholders and international actors which hold the key to improving each relevant area for the protection of the environment on a global scale, as discussed in the rest of the book.

Index

Note: **Bold** page numbers refer to tables and page numbers followed by "n" denote endnotes.